MW00630211

Early East Tennessee Taxpayers

Taxpayers

Compiled By:

Pollyanna Creekmore

New Material COPYRIGHTED 1980
  By; The Rev.Silas Emmett Lucas,Jr.

SOUTHERN HISTORICAL PRESS
% The Rev. S. Emmett Lucas, Jr.
P. O. Box 738
Easley, South Carolina   29640

ISBN   0-89308- 145-0
Library of Congress Card Catalog Number: 79-57154

Dedicated

to the Memory of

Marguerite Bartlett Hamer, Ph. D.

1890-1979
Assistant Professor
The University of Tennessee, 1920-1958

and

to the Memory of, and in Honor of
the Other Founders
of the

East Tennessee Historical Society

PREFACE

The material in this volume has been available for the past quarter of a century in the East Tennessee Historical Society's annual **Publications**. Some of the numbers containing the tax lists are now out-of-print. While many libraries do have complete sets of the **Publications**, many others do not. Many persons have suggested and urged that these lists be reprinted in a single volume. The Society has granted permission to the Reverend Silas Emmett Lucas, Jr., Proprietor of the Southern Historical Press, to reprint the lists, and to add to the usefulness of the work, he has included a full name index.

The work in this volume was done in the years that I was on the staff of the McClung Historical Collection of the Lawson McGhee Library. In connection with the duties and responsibilities of the library position, I served, without additional compensation, as Secretary of the East Tennessee Historical Society, 1948-1969. However, my association with the Society began in 1939 while I was a student at the University of Tennessee. While at the University I had such fine professors as Dr. Marguerite B. Hamer, who introduced me to the Society and to local history, and the late Dr. Stanley J. Folmsbee, Professor of History and Editor of the Society's **Publications.**

The Society's Executive Committee voted in 1948 to begin the series, "Early East Tennessee Taxpayers," but it was not until 1952 that the series began to appear. The pressures of a busy library schedule with little assistance left little time during library hours to compile the series.

Those persons to whom I am indebted are given credit in the appropriate places. In addition to those persons mentioned, special thanks should go to Mrs. Edwin M. Johnson for her assistance in preparing the copy for the printer.

Pollyanna Creekmore

September, 1979

INTRODUCTION

During the War of 1812 the original Federal census records of several states were destroyed, it is thought, when the British army burned some of the buildings in Washington. Among those records lost were the population schedules for the state of Tennessee. Later the returns for the East Tennessee counties for the Census of 1820 were lost. The National Archives, in a Reference Service Report, dated January 14, 1955, states: "Before 1830, the census schedules were turned over (by the enumerators) to the United States District Marshals, who were responsible for taking the census, (and in turn) to the Clerk of the Federal District court in each locality. The Clerk was then responsible for keeping them in the local Court House. In 1830, the schedules were ordered sent to Washington, and it is not known whether the Tennessee schedules (except for Rutherford County) were lost while in the custody of the Clerks of the Federal District Courts or whether they were lost or burned subsequently to being sent to Washington."

The absence of these records together with the total or partial destruction at various times of many of the counties' records makes it difficult to obtain a list of the early residents of Tennessee. This series is an attempt to reconstruct a list of the early residents by counties through the use of tax lists.

TABLE OF CONTENTS

PAGE

1. Anderson County - 1801. . . . .   1 - 21

2. Blount County - 1801. . . . .   23 - 54

3. Knox County - 1806. . . . .   57 - 96

4. Grainger County - 1799. . . . .   97 - 119

5. Jefferson County - 1800 . . . . 121 - 139

6. Carter County - 1796. . . . . 141 - 148

7. Sullivan County - 1796. . . . . 149 - 159

8. Hawkins County - 1809-1812. . . . . . 161 - 175

9. Greene County - 1805. . . . . 177 - 185

10. Washington County - 1778. . . . . . . 187 - 201

11. Washington County - 1787. . . . . . . 203 - 214

12. Campbell County - 1818. . . . . 215 - 232

13. Cocke County - 1839 . . . . 233 - 264

14. Greene County - 1783. . . . . 265 - 277

15. 1795 Map of Blount County   27

16. Boundries of Knox County.   55

17. Map of Sullivan County - 1832.   151

18. Bill for the Creation of Washington
     County.   194

19. Map of Campbell County - 1832   219

20. Map of Cocke County - 1832.   241

21. Index 279ff

ANDERSON COUNTY, TENNESSEE—1801

EARLY EAST TENNESSEE TAXPAYERS

Compiled by Pollyanna Creekmore

During the War of 1812 the original Federal census records of several states were destroyed when the British army burned some of the office buildings in Washington. Among those records lost were the census records for the state of Tennessee. Later the records for the East Tennessee counties for the Census of 1820 were lost.

The absence of these records together with the total or partial destruction at various times of many of the counties' records makes it difficult to obtain a list of the early residents of Tennessee. This series is an attempt to reconstruct a list of the early residents by counties through the use of tax lists and petitions.

The first lists to be presented are the first tax lists of Anderson County, 1802.

The compiler wishes to thank Mrs. Augusta B. Fothergill of Richmond, Virginia, from whose admirable book, *Virginia Taxpayers,* she first conceived the idea, and to her many friends who have given encouragement in this project.

I. ANDERSON COUNTY

Anderson County was created by a legislative act of November 6, 1801, from fractions of Knox and Grainger counties.[1] Knox County had been created from fractions of Greene and Hawkins counties in 1792,[2] Greene from Washington in 1783,[3] and Hawkins from Sullivan in 1786.[4] Grainger County had been created from fractions of Hawkins and Knox counties in 1796.[5]

In the act of 1801 the boundaries of Anderson County were described as

> beginning on the Chestnut ridge where the Knox and Grainger line crosses it, thence north forty-five degrees west, to the northern boundary of this state, thence south forty-five degrees west, to a point from whence south, forty-five degrees east, will strike Wallen's [Walden's] ridge one quarter of a mile above the gap of the Indian fork of Poplar creek, thence to the double springs[6] on the east fork of said creek, thence a direct course to Clinch river, opposite the mouth of Hickory creek, thence up the lines of Knox county to the beginning.[7]

The county was named for Joseph Anderson (1757-1837), one of the judges of the Territory South of the Ohio River, 1791-1796, and United States senator from Tennessee, 1797-1815.[8] Anderson had come originally from Delaware, but was the progenitor of a notable East Tennessee family.

Anderson County itself has been partitioned in the formation of other counties. The first major portion was removed when Campbell County was created in 1806.[9] Other portions went into Scott County, created in 1849,[10] and Union County, created in the same year.[11]

---

[1]George Roulstone (comp.), *Laws of the State of Tennessee* (Knoxville, 1803), 274. Hereafter cited as Roulstone, *Laws.*

[2]*Ibid.,* iv.

[3]Edward Scott (comp.), *Laws of the State of Tennessee, Including Those of North Carolina Now in Force in This State From the Year* 1715 *to the Year* 1820, *Inclusive* (Knovxille, 1821), I, 282. Hereafter cited as Scott, *Laws.*

[4]*Ibid.,* 378.

[5]Roulstone, *Laws,* 95.

[6]The present Oliver Springs, named for Douglas Oliver who settled nearby. See note to follow.

[7]Scott, *Laws,* I, 724.

[8]Austin P. Foster, *Counties of Tennessee* (Nashville, 1923), 5; Fay E. McMillan, "A Biographical Sketch of Joseph Anderson (1757-1837)," East Tennessee Historical Society's *Publications* (Knoxville), No. 2 (1930), 93.

[9]Scott, *Laws,* 945.

Before 1791 the land from which the county was formed was claimed by the Cherokee Indians. The claims were extinguished by the Treaty of Holston, 1791, and the Treaties of Tellico of 1798, 1804, and 1805.[12]

The act which created the county provided that a court of pleas and quarter sessions be held "on the second Mondays of March, June, September and December," and that the first court be held "at the house where Joseph Denham, senior, now lives, on the second Monday of December next."[13]

William Lea, Kinza Johnston, William Standefer, William Robertson, Joseph Grayson, Solomon Massingale, and Hugh Montgomery were appointed commissioners to "fix on a place the most convenient as near the river Clinch, on the north side as the nature of the case will admit, between the Island Ford and where Samuel Worthington now lives, for a court house, prison and stocks . . . ." Fifty acres of land were purchased from John Leib, and the town was named Burrville.[14] After Burr's conspiracy the name was changed to Clinton, probably in honor of George Clinton of New York.[15] The county was attached to Hamilton District, and three jurors were to be elected to attend the superior court in Knoxville.[16]

After the county was organized on December 14, 1801, the court ordered the tax rates at a session on March 9, 1802.[16]

> Ordered by the Court that a Tax for the year 1802 be levied on all Taxable property in Anderson County in the following manner (viz)

On each hundred acres of Land	6¼ cents
On each white poll	6¼
On each black poll	12½
On each stud horse kep [*sic*] for mares	25
On each Town Lott [*sic*]	12½

The county courts were authorized to tax property by an act passed October 25, 1797, in which the taxable property was listed and the manner of taking the taxes was prescribed.[17] White polls consisted of "all free males and male servants between age of twenty one and fifty years"; slaves, "all slaves male and female, between the age of twelve and fifty years."[18] The

---

[10]*Acts*, 1849-50 (ch.45, sec. 1), 145.

[11]*Ibid.* (ch. 61, sec. 1), 181.

[12]The texts of these treaties may be found in Charles C. Royce, "The Cherokee Nation of Indians: a Narrative of Their Official Relations with the Colonial and Federal Government," Bureau of Ethnology, *Fifth Annual Report*, 1883-84 (Washington, 1887), 121-378.

[13]Roulstone, *Laws*, 276.

[14]*Ibid.*, 275; Goodspeed Publishing Company, *History of Tennessee, East Tennessee Edition* (Chicago, 1887), 839. Hereafter cited as Goodspeed, *Hist. of Tenn.*

[15]Scott, *Laws*, I, 1146.

[16]Roulstone, *Laws*, 276.

[17]Anderson County, Tennessee, Minutes of the Court of Pleas and Quarter Sessions (MS in compiler's possession), March 9, 1802. Hereafter cited as Minutes.

[18]Roulstone, *Laws*, 114.

justices of the peace were appointed to receive a list of the taxable property in the captains' companies of militia, on March 9, 1802.[19]

The lists which are to follow were returned to the Anderson County court on June 16, 1802.[20] Later they were transcribed into a book kept for the purpose. The first lists are in the handwriting of Stephen Heard, the first clerk.

The following lists give the names of the first residents of Anderson County, together with a few men who owned land, but lived elsewhere. Notes are given on a few individuals, but due to space limitations these are kept to a minimum.

Key to Column Numbers

[1] Number of Acres
[2] "Situation where the land lies"
[3] Free Polls
[4] Black Polls
[5] "Town Lotts"

There is a sixth column in the original, "Stud Horses," but only five individuals were designated as owning any: Richard Luallen of Jeoffrey's Company, James Crain of Haile's Company, William Right of Robbins' Company, Jacob England and Samuel Worthington of McCamey's Company, Jason Cloud and George Moyers of Cloud's Company, and George Whitton of Medlin's Company, each owning one.

A List of the Taxable property and Polls in Captain Linvill's Compy[21] taken by R. Pollock Esquire 1802.

	[1]	[2]	[3]	[4]	[5]
Anderson, Archibald			1		
Alley, James			1		
Arbuckle, James			1	1	
Brooton, John			1		
Burton, Robert[22]	11,208		3		

[19]*Ibid.*, 114-15.
[20]*Ibid.*, 115; Minutes, March 9, 1802.
[21]Almost all of these people's land fell into Campbell County upon its creation in 1806. The first complete extant tax lists of Campbell (1818) are published in George L. Ridenour, *The Land of the Lake: a History of Campbell County, Tennessee* (LaFollette, 1941), 105-08.
[22]For key to column numbers, see end of Introduction.
[23]North Carolinian, who was agent for Henderson and Company. For a discussion of the Company's lands in Powell's Valley, which included part of Anderson County, see Samuel C. Williams, "Henderson and Company's Purchase Within the Limits of Tennessee," *Tennessee Historical Magazine* (Nashville), V (1919), 5-25; see also Archibald Henderson, "The Transylvania Company, Study in Personnel," *The Filson Club History Quarterly* (Louisville), XXI (1947), 3-21, 228-242, 327-349.

	[1]	[2]	[3]	[4]	[5]
Carlock, Abraham[24]			1		
Curnutt, Reuben			1		
Cope, Andrew			1		
Curnutt, David			1		
Curnutt, John			1		
Campbell, Thomas	25		1		
Campbell, Archibald			1		
Carlock, Isaac			1		
Carlock, Job			1		
Carlock, Jacob			1		
Coons, John			1		
Davis, George			1		
Durham, William[25]			1		
Fips, Joshua[26]			1		
Fips, John			1		
Friley, Caleb[27]			1	1	
Grimes, George[28]			1		
Graham, Spencer[29]	156		1	1	
Greenwood, Bailey	623		1		
Halfacre, Michael[30]			1		
Hays, Joseph			1		
Inglish, Joseph	135			2	
Inglish, Joshua	300		1	1	
Jackson, David			1		
Inglish, John[31]	150		1		
Lamb, John	131		1		
Linville, Richard[32]	397		1		
Lewis, James			1		
May, David			1		
Maid, James[33]			1		
May, Reynolds			1		
McGuire, William			1		

[24]Cornet in cavalry regiment, Hamilton District, 1796, while living in Jefferson County. Mrs. John Trotwood Moore (comp.), *Record of Commissions of Officers in the Tennessee Militia*, 1796-1811 (Nashville, 1947), 19. Hereafter cited as *Commissions*.

[25]Probably from Blount County, where he was a lieutenant, 1796. *Ibid.*, 4. *missions*, 4.

[26]Variously Phipps, Phibbs, etc.

[27]Removed to White County where he was a captain, 1807. *Ibid.*, 48.

[28]Lieutenant, Grainger County militia, 1800; early constable. *Ibid.*, 13; Minutes, December 16, 1801.

[29]Captain, Grainger County militia, 1800. Moore, *Commissions*, 13.

[30]Variously Huffacre, Huffaker, etc. First sheriff, Campbell County, 1806-1807; captain, Campbell County militia, 1807; trustee, Franklin Academy, 1806. Goodspeed, *Hist. of Tenn.*, 846; Moore, *Commissions*, 38; Scott, *Laws*, 1, 934.

[31]Commissioner to fix the county seat of Campbell County, 1806. *Ibid.*, 945.

[32]Sheriff of Campbell County, 1810-1816; Campbell County was organized at his house, 1806; commissioner to fix county seat of that county, 1806. Goodspeed, *Hist. of Tenn.*, 846; Scott, *Laws*, 946, 945; Ridenour, *Land of the Lake, passim.*

[33]Probably Moad. Thomas Mead (Moad, Mode) was sheriff of Campbell County, 1807-1810. Goodspeed, *Hist. of Tenn.*, 846.

	[1]	[2]	[3]	[4]	[5]
McNees, George			1		
Morris, Absalom			1		
McCrackin, James	300		1		
Pollock, William³⁴			1		
Pollock, John			1		
Ruckman, Isaiah			1		
Rains, John			1		
Richards, Lewis			1		
Runnels, John³⁵			1		
Sharp, Joseph	130		1		
Stanley, Harris			1		
Sharp, Richard			1		
Sweeton, Robert			1		
Stanley, Reuben			1		
Stanley, Page			1		
Saunders, John			1		
Sweeton, John			1		
Thomas, James			1		
Vaught, Andrew			1		
Whitman, David			1		
Whitman, Jacob			1		
Wilson, Eli			1		
White, Daniel³⁶			1		
Wilson, Abraham			1		
Wilson, Levi			1		
Wilhite, Elijah			1		

A List of the Taxable property & Polls in Captain Jeofferys Compy taken by Joseph Sinclair Esquire 1802.

Armstrong, John	163	Poplar ck	1
Do	111	B. [uffalo?] C. [reek]	
Adair, Thomas	640	B[ol]d Valley	1
Asher, Robertson			1
Arnold, John			1
Armstrong, Robert			1
Austin, William	80	Clinch R.	
Ashlock, William	25	Clinch R.	1
Brazleton, Isaac	450	Poplar Ck	1
Bray, John	200	C. [linch] R. [iver]	1
Bowling, Benjamin			1
Clodfelter, John³⁷	200	Cane Ck	1
Crocket, Alexander			1
Claxson, Constantine³⁸			1

³⁴Interchangeable with Polk.
³⁵Interchangeable with Reynolds.
³⁶First register of Campbell County, 1806-1815. *Ibid.*, 846.
³⁷One of a group of German settlers from Pennsylvania who settled in the section which became known as "Dutch Valley." Raymond Clifford Seeber, A History of Anderson County, Tennessee (Master's thesis, University of Tennessee, Knoxville, 1928), 25.
³⁸*Ibid.*

	[1]	[2]	[3]	[4]	[5]
Crawford, Samuel[39]	640	C. R.	1		
Cole, Alexander			1		
Denham, Joseph[40]				4	
Davis, William	500	Clinch R.			
Dotson, Oliver	320		1		
Farmer, Andrew			1		
Forrest, Richard			1		
Farmer, John			1		
Farmer, Henry	150	Pop. [lar] Ck	1		
Farmer, Fredk			1		
Green, James			1		
Gordon, Geo. & Robert	1920	Pop. Ck			
Howard, John[41]			1		
Hogshead, William[42]	320	Clinch R.	1		
Hoslar, George[43]			1		
Jacobs, Zachariah			1		
Jacobs, Greenberry			1		
Johnson, Craven	163	Pop Ck	1		
Johnson, William			1	1	
Jameson, John			1		
Jeoffery, Jeremiah[44]	150	Clinch R.	1	1	
Jeoffery, Joseph	200	Pop Ck	1		
Johnson, Kinza[45]	640		1		
Kerby, John[46]	300	Big Val.	1		
Luallen, Richard[47]	200	Cane Ck	1	1	
Linard, Jacob[48]	150	Cane Ck	1		
Leib, John[49]	640	Clinch R.	1		
Lea, Joseph[50]	200 P	[owell] R. [iver]	1	1	

[39]First surveyor. Minutes, March 9, 1802.
[40]Anderson County organized at his house. Roulstone, *Laws*, 276.
[41]Early constable. Minutes, March 8, 1802.
[42]Early lawyer and surveyor from Augusta County, Va. Roulstone, *Laws*, 276. Name often appears as Hodsett. Notes in compiler's collection.
[43]Also Hassler, Hostler, etc. Family of German origin from Pennsylvania. Anderson County, Tennessee, Census of 1850 (microfilm in Lawson McGhee Library of original population schedules in National Archives, Washington, D. C.), Family No. 232. Hereafter cited as Census of 1850, by family numbers.
[44]Captain, Knox County militia, 1799. Moore, *Commissions*, 23.
[45]First register; Revolutionary soldier, born in Maryland; commissioner to fix county seat, 1801. Minutes, December 16, 1801; Penelope Johnson Allen, *Tennessee Soldiers in the Revolution* (Bristol, 1935), 23; Roulstone, *Laws*, 275; notes from compiler's collection.
[46]One of the first justices of the peace; represented Anderson and Roane counties in 7th General Assembly, 1807. Minutes, March 9, 1802; Philip M. Hamer (ed.), *Tennessee, A History*, 4 vols. (New York, 1933), II, 1001.
[47]Also Lewallen, Llewellyn, etc. A Revolutionary soldier (1763-1833), born in Prince Edward County, Va., where he served in the militia. Revolutionary War Pension File, National Archives, Washington, D. C. Hereafter cited as Rev. War Pens. File. See also notes in compiler's collection.
[48]Variously Leinart, Lynart, etc. One of a group of German settlers from Pennsylvania. See footnote 37; Census of 1850, Family No. 490.
[49]Also Leab. See footnote 37. Early meetings of court held at his house. Land on which county seat was laid out obtained from him. Minutes, June 15, 1803.
[50]Lieutenant, Knox County militia, 1799. Moore, *Commissions*, 23.

	[1]	[2]	[3]	[4]	[5]
Long, John	700	Clinch R.			
Leech, John			1		
Lea, Jesse	250	Cold Ck	1		
McPeek, Ezekiel			1		
McClung, Charles[51]	1600	Pop Ck			
Do	300	Buffalo			
McPeters, Joseph[52]			1		
McCamey, William[53]	200	Pop Ck	1	2	
Mankin, William			1	2	
McBride, John	200	Cane Ck	1		
McComus, Stephen			1		
Noble, Lewis			1		
Potter, Benjamin[54]			1		
Pankey, Stephen	150	Pop Ck			
Patterson, William	150	Pop Ck	1		
Puckett, James D.[55]	150	Pop Ck	1		
Patterson, Robert			1		
Panken, Stephen			1		
Puckett, Claiborne			1		
Pankey, John			1		
Parker, Benjn C.[56] By Wm.					
Maclin his Agent	3500	Clinch R.			
Roberts, Moses			1		
Revis, Isham			1		
Roberts, Nathan	122	Clinch R.	1		
Revis, Henry	600	Cold Ck	1		
Rhea, John	320	Cane Ck			
Stone, John	1640	Clinch R.			
Sartain, John				2	
Slover, Aaron			1		
Spessard, John[57]	112	Cane Ck	1		
Sadler, Fredk[58]	378	Cane Ck			
Shinliver, Charles [59]	315	Pop Ck	1		
Shears, John				1	

---

[51]Resident of Knox County where he was first clerk, merchant and surveyor. Sketch in Mary U. Rothrock (ed.), *The French Broad-Holston Country: A History of Knox County, Tennessee* (Knoxville, 1946), 446-47. Hereafter cited as *French Broad-Holston*.

[52]Revolutionary soldier born 1757 in North Carolina. Later he was resident of Morgan County where he drew pension for his service in the N. C. militia. Rev. War Pens. File, *loc. cit.;* Zella Armstrong, *Twenty-four Hundred Tennessee Pensioners* (Chattanooga, 1937), 78; notes in compiler's collection.

[53]Variously McAmy, McKamey, etc. One of the first justices of the peace, and formerly an ensign, Knox County militia, 1799. Moore, *Commissions*, 24; Minutes, March 9, 1802.

[54]Later an ensign, 13th regiment, 1809. Moore, *Commissions*, 68.

[55]An early constable. Minutes, March 8, 1802.

[56]Formerly a cornet in cavalry volunteers, Knox County militia, 1800, and trustee, Union Academy, 1806. Moore, *Commissions*, 24; Scott, *Laws*, I, 934.

[57]One of a group of settlers from Pennsylvania. See footnote 37. Census of 1850, Family No. 330.

[58]Leader of the colony of German settlers from Pennsylvania. See footnote 37.

[59]Son-in-law of above; born 1776, in Pennsylvania. See footnote 37; Census of 1850, Family No. 327.

	[1]	[2]	[3]	[4]	[5]
Simpson, Thomas			1		
Sinclair, Robert			1		
Standefer, Israel	100	Cane Ck		1	
Standefer, Samuel[60]			1		
Sinclair, Joseph[61]	300	Clinch R.	1	1	
Stinnett, William			1	2	
Thomas, John			1		
Tunnel, William[62]	270	Pop Ck			
Taylor, James	125	Cane Ck	1		
Terry, Joseph[63]			1		
Terry, Samuel			1		
Vowel, Page	150	Pop Ck	1		
Williams, John			1		
Walker, George			1		
Welden, John			1		
Willingham, John			1		
Williams, Saml			1		

A List of Taxable property and polls in Capt Haile's Compy taken by Gibson Harden Esquire 1802.

	[1]	[2]	[3]	[4]	[5]
Brazil, Richard			1		
Brazil, Valentine[64]			1		
Baid, James			1	3	
Crain, James			1		
Dunnivan, John			1		
Dolton, Bradley			1		
Davidson, William	640				
Fulton, Thomas[65]			1		
Gammel, John			1		
Gammel, William			1		
Gollaher, Joseph	500	Clinch R.	1		
Guthry, George			1		
Gollaher, John			1		
Golston, John	160	R [ocky] Branch			
Hagler, Abraham	192	Clinch R	1		
Hudson, Burrel			1		
Haile, Nathan[66]	160	R Branch	1		
Heard, James			1		
Horn, Thomas			1		
Harden, Gibson[67]			1	1	

[60]Formerly ensign, 1799, and lieutenant, 1801, Knox County militia. Moore, *Commissions*, 25.

[61]One of the first justices of the peace. Minutes, March 9, 1802.

[62]Later (1811) first major, 13th regiment, Anderson County. Moore, *Commissions*, 106.

[63]Formerly ensign, Knox county militia, 1799, *Ibid.*, 25.

[64]From Wilkes County, N. C., and formerly an ensign, Knox County militia, 1800. *Ibid.*, 21.

[65]Commissioned ensign, Knox County militia, 1801. *Ibid.*, 22.

[66]Commissioned ensign, 1799, and captain, 1801, Knox County militia. *Ibid.*, 23.

[67]An early justice of the peace. Minutes, June 15, 1802.

	[1]	[2]	[3]	[4]	[5]
Hendrix, Esquire[68]			1		
Hackworth, Augustin[69]	50	Clinch R	1		
Hackworth, Nicholas			1		
Kinkaid, Thomas	500	C Creek			
Kincaid, John			1		
Meredith, Frederick			1		
Mattocks, Danl			1		
Pate, Anthony			1		
Peters, Henry			1		
Peters, Tobias			1		
Parsons, Thomas[70]			1		
Robertson, David	340	B Creek	1		
Robertson, James				1	
Shannon, Charles			1		
Smith, James			1		
Stross, John			1		
Simmons, James			1		
Scarbrough, James[71]	600	Clinch R	1	1	
Shaddon, Joseph			1		
Scarbrough, David			1		
Terry, John			1		
Walker, Thomas			1		
Young, John	200	B Creek			

A List of the Taxable property and polls in Capt Wilson Compy. Taken by Wm Underwood Esquire 1802.

	[1]	[2]	[3]	[4]	[5]
Byrum, Alden[72]			1		
Bookout, Charles			1		
Brumley, John			1		
Craven, William			1		
Certain, David[73]			1		
Duncan, Rolly	100	B[old] Valley	1		
Edwards, Samuel			1		
Elliott, Amos			1		
Gilbert, Felix			1		

[68]Commissioned captain, 14th regiment, Roane County, 1810. Moore, *Commissions*, 99.

[69]Revolutionary soldier from Bedford County, Va. Reuben Gold Thwaites and Louise Phelps Kellogg (eds.), *Documentary History of Dunmore's War*, 1774 (Madison, 1905), 409.

[70]Revolutionary soldier (1749-1825); drew pension for service in the Virginia line. Armstrong, *Tennessee Pensioners*, 87.

[71]Operated a ferry on Clinch River; early justice of the peace and member of family from whom the village of Scarborough was named (now in Oak Ridge). Minutes, June 14, 1802, *passim.*

[72]Member of pioneer East Tennessee family of whom Ebenezer Byrum was progenitor; settled early in that part of Washington County which was cut off into Greene County upon the creation of the latter in 1783; early settler of Knox County. The name is perpetuated in Byrum's Fork of Hind's Creek. Allen, *Tennessee Soldiers*, 16; J. G. M. Ramsey, *The Annals of Tennessee to the End of the Eighteenth Century* (reprinted, Kingsport, 1926), 341; Minutes, *passim.*

[73]Also Sartain.

	[1]	[2]	[3]	[4]	[5]
Harmon, William			3		
Hill, James			1		
Hancock, Joel			1		
Harmon, Paril			1		
Hoskins, Elias[74]			1		
Kounce, John[75]			1		
Leach, James			1		
Lawler, John			1		
Latham, Samuel			1		
McGriff, Thomas			1		
Philpot, Richard			1		
Philpot, Isaac			1		
Parks, John			1		
Reaves, John			1		
Rich, John			1		
Ridenour, Henry[76]			1		
Ridenour, Martin[77]			1		
Sinclair, John			1		
Sharp, William			1		
Sharp, John	123½	B Valley	1		
Siler, John			1		
Stanley, Garland			1		
Stanley, Rhodes			1		
Thompson, Wm			1		
Underwood, Wm[78]	115	Hinds Ck	1	1	
Wilson, Jesse			1		
Wilson, Benjamin			1		
Williams, David			1		
Williams, Edward			1		
Williams, John			1		

A List of Taxable property & polls in Capt Robbins Compy for 1802 taken by Wm Underwood Esquire.

Blagg, John			1		
Creely, William			1		
Cunningham, James			1	1	
Day, John[79]	175	Clinch R	1	1	
Derick, Jacob			1		
Derick, William			1		
Fry, Philip			1		
Giddens, Randal			1		

---

[74]Revolutionary soldier who served in the North Carolina militia. Allen, *Tennessee Soldiers*, 23.

[75]Variously Coonce, Counce, Counts, etc.

[76]Revolutionary soldier. Ridenour, *Land of the Lake*, 46.

[77]*Ibid.*

[78]One of the first justices of the peace. Minutes, March 9, 1802.

[79]Lived at Day's Ford on Clinch River later in Campbell County. Minutes, *passim.*

	[1]	[2]	[3]	[4]	[5]
Grills, Elliott[80]	100	Clinch R	1	2	
Havens, William[81]			1		
Hinkle, Henry			1		
Hart, Thomas[82]	5000	Hinds Ck			
Do	3230	Pow Val			
Hart, David	2687	Clinch Sur			
Do	1625	Pow Val			
Harness, John			1		
Jackson, Churchwell			1		
Jue, Robert			1		
Lamar, William			1		
McDaniel, Archibald			1	1	
McCamey, Robert			1		
McWhorter, John	400	Clinch R	1	1	
Mayberry, Isaac			1		
McWhorter, Moses	220	Big Val	1	1	
McAdoo, John[83]	152		1	1	
Patton, Matthew			1		
Robbins, William			1		
Robbins, Jonathan			1		
Right, William			1		
Robbins, Isaac			1		
Smith, Joseph			1		
Smith, Samuel			1		
Sevoirs, William			1		
Scruggs, John	200	Big Val	1	3	
Tipton, Shadrach			1		
Wallace, John			1		
Young, Henry			1		

A List of taxable property and polls in Capt McCamey's Compy for 1802. By John McCamey Esquire.

Alred, Solomon[84]			1		
Aldridge, Nathan	50	Brush [y] Fk	1		
Alred, Thomas			1		
Butler, Thomas[85]	1000	Pop Ck			
Bounds, John	140	Brusy Fk	1		
Cook, Joseph			1		
Carpenter, Thomas			1		

---

[80]One of family from Montgomery County, Va.; commissioned captain, Knox County militia, 1799. Lewis Preston Summers, *Annals of Southwest Virginia*, 1769-1800 (Abingdon, 1929), 742, 936. Hereafter cited as Summers, *Annals*. See also Moore, *Commissions*, 23.

[81]An early justice of the peace. Minutes, December 13, 1803.

[82]One of the members of Henderson and Company and related to William Blount, governor of Southwest Territory. Archibald Henderson, "The Transylvania Company, Study in Personnel," *loc. cit.*

[83]Revolutionary soldier who fought at the Battle of King's Mountain; ancestor of William Gibbs McAdoo. Allen, *Tennessee Soldiers*, 26; *French Broad-Holston*, 443-44.

[84]From North Carolina where he was born 1772. Census of 1850, Family No. 265.

[85]One of several brothers from Virginia who settled near Oliver Springs.

	[1]	[2]	[3]	[4]	[5]
Chitwood, Pleasant[86]			1		
Chitwood, Lazarus			1		
Choat, Austin			1		
Choat, Austin			1		
Choat, Christopher			1		
Duncan, John	100	Clinch	1		
England, Jacob			1		
England, Joseph			1		
England, John			1		
Gallaher, Peter			1		
Griffith, William			1		
Griffin, Jessee			1		
Galbreath, Alexander	300	Brush. Fk.			
Galbreath, James	359	Brush. Fk.			
Do	521	Pop Ck	1		
Horton, William	300		1		
Hutson, John			1		
Hastler, Michael[87]	175		1		
Hastler, Michael			1		
Hawkins, Matthew			1		
Hackett, John[88]	560	B Fork			
Jones, Thomas	250	East Fk		2	
Juland, George	125	B Fk			
Jones, Matthew			1		
Juland, John			1		
Key, David			1		
Key, Zachariah[89]			1		
Key, Peter			1		
Long, Tobias			1		
Long, Edward			1		
Long, Robert			1		
Lively, John			1		
Moore, Joseph	50			1	
Mayberry, John			1		
McAmey, John[90]	150	Pop Ck	1	1	
Oliver, Douglas[91]	380	E Fork	1	3	
Porter, James	214	E F & C R	1		
Porter, Robert			1		
Peak, Jacob	100	East Fk	1	2	

---

[86]From Cumberland County, Va., via Rutherford County, N. C.; married Sally Cowan, daughter of David Cowan of Sevier County, Tennessee.

[87]See footnote 8.

[88]Early settler of Knox County who removed to Rhea County. *French Broad-Holston*, 27.

[89]Formerly lieutenant, Knox County militia, 1799. Moore, *Commissions*, 23.

[90]First ranger; formerly ensign, 1797, and lieutenant, 1801, Knox County militia. Minutes, December 16, 1801; Moore, *Commissions*, 23.

[91]Revolutionary soldier born in King and Queen County, Va., in 1752; served in the Revolution while living in Caroline County, Va.; settled on the East Fork of Poplar Creek at the "Double Springs," which is now Oliver Springs. Rev. War Pens. File; Armstrong, *Tennessee Pensioners*, 86.

	[1]	[2]	[3]	[4]	[5]
Pate, Joseph			1		
Penaro, William			1		
Roberson, Stephen	150	Beav [er] Ck	1		
Roberson, William	230	East Fork	1	1	
Rippeto, William			1		
Selvay, William			1		
Stonecipher, Danl			1		
Standefer, William[92]	404	East Fk		3	
Shewmake, Robert			1		
Standefer, James[93]			1		
Selvidge, Michael			1		
Stonecipher, Michael			1		
Tunnell, John			1		
Williams, Reuben			1		
Worthington, Saml	640	Clinch			
Wasson, Elisha			1		
Worthington, Thomas			1		
Wasson, John			1		
Worthington, Samuel	160		1		
Worthington, James			1		

A List of Taxable Property & Polls in Captain George Stelles Compy as returned by R. Pollock Esqr for the year 1802.

	[1]	[2]	[3]	[4]	[5]
Adkins, James[94]			1	1	
Baker, Samuel			1	1	
Baker, John			1	1	
Christmon, Isaac			1	1	
Cunningham, Jacob			1		
Caves, John			1		
Cunningham, Moses			1		
Combs, Job			1		
Cowan, Alexander			1		
Craboight, Charles			1		
Hill, Thomas[95]				6	
Hobbs, James			1		
Haynes, Richard			1		
Layne, John			1		
Long, James			1		
Lea, Luke	300			2	
Lea, Zachariah	120		1		

[92]One of the first justices of the peace and commissioner to fix county seat; formerly a lieutenant, Hawkins County militia, 1790 (which then included Knox), and lieutenant, Knox County militia, 1792. Minutes, March 9, 1802; Roulstone, *Laws*, 275; Clarence E. Carter (ed.), *The Territorial Papers of the United States, IV, The Southwest Territory* (Washington, 1936), 437, 449. Hereafter cited as *Territorial Papers*.

[93]Later United States congressman serving six terms until his death in 1837. *Biographical Directory of the American Congress*, 1776-1949 (Washington, 1950), 1853.

[94]An early constable. Minutes, December 16, 1801.

[95]First trustee, 1801-1806. Goodspeed, *Hist. of Tenn.*, 840.

	[1]	[2]	[3]	[4]	[5]
Lea, David			1		
Lamar, John			1		
Lea, William	1040		1		
Montgomery, Hugh[96]			1	8	
McKehen, George			1		
Murrah, William			1		
Murrah, Keaton			1		
McDonald, Redmond			1		
Marcum, Josiah			1	1	
Marcum, Arthur			1		
Morris, Shadrach	1000		1		
Morris, Benjamin			1		
Martin, Danl			1		
McBride, William			1		
McKinney, Henry			1		
Mowry, Valentine			1		
Newman, John			1		
Nobels, William			1		
Pollock, Robert Junr			1		
Pollock, Robert[97]			1		
Ray, John Esqr	1000				
Scallions, Peter			1		
Sweeton, Dutton			1		
Steele, George			1		
Tolbert, Fredk			1		
Vanoy, Jonathan			1		
Vanoy, Jesse			1		
Wilhight, Conright	100		1	1	
Wallen, Evan			1		
White, Joel			1		
Williams, Benjamin			1		

A List of Taxable Property and Polls in Jason Clouds Company. Taken by James Grant Esquire for 1802.

Abbot, James	200	P River	1	
Archer, Richmond			1	
Adair, John	15	Buffalo	1	
Adair, Alexander	200	No Clinch	1	
Bowling, Joel	100	P River	1	
Burrus, Elijah			1	
Brock, Sherrard Junr			1	
Baker, Abednego			1	
Brock, Sherrard Senr	50	No Clinch		
Brown, John			1	
Bowman, Henry			1	

[96]One of the first justices of the peace and later one of first for Campbell County; trustee, Franklin Academy, 1806. Minutes, March 8, 1802; Scott, *Laws*, I, 934; Ridenour, *Land of the Lake, passim.*
[97]Interchangeable with Polk. One of the first justices of the peace. Minutes, March 9, 1802.

	[1]	[2]	[3]	[4]	[5]
Ball, Capt. James V.					2
Bird, Charles Lee					4
Cloud, Jason			1	1	
Cooper, William			1		
Carson, John			1		
Chandler, Shadrach			1		
Cunningham, Jonathan	280	P. River			
Carr, Walter			1		
Campbell, Patk[98] and Terence					1
Chandler, Richd assignee					2
of Campbell, George W					1
Denton, Jonah	150	No P. River			
Dobbs, William			1		
Evans, Walter	100				1
Ferrel, Charles	200		1		
Griffith, Thomas	200	So P. River			
Gess, John[99]			1		
Grant, James[100]	300				3
Hancock, John			1		1
Hatfield, Richard			1		
Hancock, William	120		2		1
Hogg, James[101]	7751				
Inglish, William			1		
Jones, Levi			1		
Johnson, William			1		
Lewis, Major Thomas					1
McNutt, James	193	So Clinch	1		
McCoy, Samuel			1		
Moyers, George	100		1		
McCaffery, Terence[102]					1
Norris, Samuel			1		
Owens, Willis			1		

[98]Merchants of Knoxville.

[99]Variously Gist, Guess, Guist, etc. Revolutionary soldier. Allen, *Tennessee Soldiers*, 20.

[100]Revolutionary soldier from Connecticut where he served under Return J. Meigs, and a reputed friend of George Washington; first chairman of county court; clerk of Campbell County court, 1806-1810; founder of the town of Grantsboro (1798) at the junction of Powell and Clinch Rivers (now inundated); trustee, Franklin Academy, 1806; lieutenant colonel commandant 33rd regiment, 1808; died January 31, 1824, aged 71. Minutes, *passim;* Moore, *Commissions*, 52; Ridenour, *Land of the Lake, passim.*

[101]A member of Henderson and Company, born in Scotland, 1729. His son, Walter Hogg Alves, surveyed much of the company's land in Powell's Valley and his note-books are preserved in the Tennessee Papers of the Draper Collections in the State Historical Society of Wisconsin (Photostatic copies in McClung Collection, Lawson McGhee Library, Knoxville). Archibald Henderson, "The Transylvania Company," *loc. cit.*

[102]Also McAffry. Commissioned lieutenant, Knox County militia, 1801; became one of the earliest cabinet makers of Knoxville. He and his wife Martha (Patsy) Clopton McAffry are buried in the First Presbyterian Church Cemetery, Knoxville. Moore, *Commissions*, 23; notes in compiler's collection.

	[1]	[2]	[3]	[4]	[5]
Ryan, John			1		
Ryan, Harris	200	P. River	1		
Ross, Angus	50	No P. River	1		
Rains, Jonathan			1		
Ridenour, John Junr			1		
Ridenour, Joseph			1		
Ryan, William				1	
Reedy, Shadrack				1	
Snodderly, John	200		1		
Smith, Richard			1		
Smith, Thomas	100	No P. River			
Smith, Ephraim	640	Indian Ck			
Strader, Jacob	125½	Ford P R	1		
Salter, John	1625	H & S Co S [urvey]			
Shulbred, Jas & Eliza Deas	2154½				
Scott, Edward				1	
Smith, Genl Benjn	7345				
Terry, John			1		
Umstead, John[103]	7334			1	
Whitton, William			1		
Whiteside, Jenkin				5	
Wilson, George				1	

A List of Taxable Property and Polls in Captn Medlins Co for 1802. Taken by Fredk Miller Esquire.

	[1]	[2]	[3]	[4]	[5]
Bradberry, John	200	dry Buff	1		
Brummit, Thomas			1		
Brummit, Wm[104]			1		
Cobel, Daniel			1		
Cull, William			1		
Duncan, Thomas			1		
Golstein, Stephen			1		
Harlas, David			1		
Harlas, George			1		
Harlas, Henry Senr		d Buff	1		
Harlas, Henry Junr			1		
Harlas, Philip			1		
Holt, Michael			1		
Holt, William			1		
Helms, Jonathan			1		
Hudson, Thomas	330	BBCR	1		
Kean, John	320	Hinds Ck			

[103]A member of Henderson and Company. After the death of John Luttrell, one of the original members, he married the widow, Susannah Hart Luttrell, daughter of Thomas Hart, another charter member.

[104]Revolutionary soldier who drew a pension for his service in the Virginia militia. Armstrong, *Tennessee Pensioners*, 21.

	[1]	[2]	[3]	[4]	[5]
Kitchen, John[105]			1		
Love, S. A. for Sam Love of Virginia	6650	W[alnut] Cove			
Lewis, John			1		
Lay, Joel			1		
Lewis, William			1		
Lewis, Stephen			1		
Lay, William			1		
Massingale, Solomon[106]	200	dry Buff	1	1	
Medlin, Harden			1		
Medlin, Richard	220	dry Buff	1		
Medlin, Robert	100	dry Buff	1		
Medlin, William	100		1		
Medlin, Wm Owen	75	dry Buff			
Miller, Fredk[107]	200	Clinch R	1		
Miller, Michael			1		
Pore, Peter			1		
Ricket, Stephen			1		
Ragsdale, Britain			1		
Robertson, Cornelius			1		
Robertson, Charles			1		
Robertson, Townsend			1		
Russell, Henry	300	Dry B	1		
Sharp, Conrad	790	Big Val			
Do	400	So C River			
Do	390	Lost Ck			
Sharp, Henry	197	Big Val			
Shetters, George	640	Hinds Ck	1		
Stout, Samuel	1000				
Tilman, Tobias[108]	227	So of Clinch			
Do	350	No of Clinch			
Travis, George			1	1	
Widner, Lewis	600				
Whitton, George	150	Big Buf			
Whitton, Robert			1		
Worrick, John[109]			1		
Worrick, Wiley			1		

A List of Taxable Property & Polls in Capt Davis's Company for the year 1802. Taken by James Butler Esquire.

Aldridge, Nathan	440	Clinch			
Aldridge, William	200	Clinch	1		
Asher, William			1		
Brazle, William	100	Wolf Val	1		

---

[105]Revolutionary soldier who drew a pension for his service in the Virginia militia. *Ibid.*, 66; Moore, *Commissions*, 13.

[106]One of the first justices of the peace and commissioner to fix the county seat. Minutes, March 8, 1802; Roulstone, *Laws*, 275.

[107]One of the first justices of the peace. Minutes, March 9, 1802.

[108]From Montgomery County, Va. Summers, *Annals*, 927.

[109]Warrick, which name is perpetuated in Warrick's Cross Roads, Union County.

	[1]	[2]	[3]	[4]	[5]
Brazle, George	100	Clinch			
Brazle, Robert[110]	89	Rac[coon] Val	1		
Bickerstaff, Henry			1		
Bowman, John	200	Big Val	1		
Benson, Thomas	100	Wolf Val	1		
Butler, James[111]	200	Clinch	1		
Bray, James	84	Rac Val	1		
Chainey, Jacob	150	Clinch	1		
Caton, James			1		
Davis, Nathaniel	200	Bull Run	1		
Dever, John	147	B Run			
Frost, Joseph	100	Wolf V			
Frost, Samuel[112]	400	Wolf V	1		
Frost, John	400				
Frost, Thomas Junr	300	Rac V	1	1	
Frost, Thomas Senr[113]	190	Rac V			
Farmer, Henry	550	Clinch			
Frost, Edward	160	Big V	1		
Frost, Micajah	225	Rac V	1	1	
Grayson, Joseph[114]	300	Wolf V	1		
Garner, John[115]	1000	Clinch	1		
Guthry, Boyce			1		
Gastin, Alexander	114	B[ull] Run	1		
Ginnins, Danl	200	Rac V	1		
Gibson, John			1		
Ginkins, Aaron			1		
Goard, Ayers			1		
Hobbs, Joel[116]	240	Big V	1		
Hobbs, James	103	Big V	1		
Hall, David[117]			1		
Hanna, John	200	B Run	2		

---

[110]An early constable. Minutes, March 8, 1802.

[111]One of the first justices of the peace and formerly captain, Knox County militia, 1799; probably the James Butler who died 1803, with administration granted to "Elizabeth Butler widow and relict." Minutes, March 9, 1802, September 12, 1803; Moore, *Commissions*, 21.

[112]One of the trustees of Union Academy, 1806. Scott, *Laws*, I, 934.

[113]From Washington County, Va.; died 1807. Summers, *Annals*, 1184; Minutes, December 15, 1807.

[114]First coroner and commissioner to fix county seat. Minutes, December 16, 1801; Roulstone, *Laws*, 275.

[115]Born Chatham (later Randolph) County, N. C., 1776; removed with father to Sevier, and then to Blount County, Tenn. Notes in compiler's collection.

[116]Formerly a captain, Knox County militia, 1797, and a son-in-law of No. 117. Moore, *Commissions*, 23.

[117]Revolutionary soldier born in Pittsylvania (later Henry) County, Va.; removed to Wilkes County, N. C., where he served in the militia, and from there moved to Greenville County, S. C.; progenitor of the Hall family of Anderson County and not to be confused with Thomas Hall of Knox County, for whom Hall's Cross Roads in that county is named. Rev. War Pens. File; notes in compiler's collection.

	[1]	[2]	[3]	[4]	[5]
Heard, Stephen[118]			1		
Houston, Robert	1500	H&C Sur			
Do	200	Pilot Knob			
Jacobs, Edward			2		
Kirkpatrick, Alexr[119]	150	Clinch	1		
Lindar, Jacob	180	Big V	1		
Macey, Robert			1		
Meloney, John			1		
Menefee, John[120]	408	B Run			
Norman, Isaac	200	B Run	1		
Norman, Henry	69	Rac V	1		
Norman, Aaron			1		
Nelson, William			1		
Owen, Jesse	63	Chesn R[idge]			
Pearson, William			1		
Pratt, Thomas			1		
Portwood, Page[121]	92	Big V	1		
Philips, Thomas			1		
Roysden, Jesse[122]			1		
Ragland, Reuben	100	Big V	1		
Ragland, William	100	Big V	1		
Roberson, Joseph	100	Clinch	1		
Shelton, Palatiah[123]	640				
Shelton, Gabriel			1		
Stephenson, Edward	150	Clinch	1	1	
Stinnett, Isham	150	Clinch	1	1	
Smith, Laton[124]	200	Rac V	1		
Tenan, Robert by Charles McClung	370	No of Clinch			
Ussery, William[125]	70	B Run	1		
Ussery, Saml	100	Wolf V	1		
Whitnal, William			1		
Wood, Obadiah[126]	100	Clinch			

[118]First clerk of the court who transcribed the original records from which this copy is made and later lieutenant colonel commandant, 13th regiment, 1808. Minutes, *passim;* Moore, *Commissions,* 50.

[119]Progenitor of Kirkpatrick family of Anderson County. Notes in compiler's collection.

[120]Justice of the peace, 1791, Hawkins County, and of Knox County, 1792; captain, Hawkins County militia, 1790; speaker, house of representatives, State of Franklin. *Territorial Papers,* 437, 443, 449; sketch in Samuel C. Williams, *History of the Lost State of Franklin* (Johnson City, 1927), 308.

[121]Revolutionary soldier who served under George Rogers Clark in the Northwest Campaign. Rev. War Pens. File; notes in compiler's collection.

[122]Roysdon; also Risden. Early surveyor and schoolteacher; trustee, Union Academy, 1806. Roulstone, *Laws,* 276; Scott, *Laws,* I, 934.

[123]Removed to Rhea County.

[124]A Revolutionary soldier born in Maryland; served in militia while living in Washington County, Va.; later removed to Bledsoe County, where he died, 1840. Rev. War. Pens. File.

[125]Commissioned lieutenant, Knox County militia, 1800. Moore, *Commissions,* 25.

[126]Revolutionary soldier who drew a pension for his service in the North Carolina line. Armstrong, *Tennessee Pensioners,* 119.

	[1]	[2]	[3]	[4]	[5]
Wilson, Thomas	200	B Run	1	2	
Young, John			1		

List of Lands & Polls returned at September Term 1802 and since.

	No. of Acres	Place where Land Lies	Polls
William Reed	200		
William Farmer	1000	No of Clinch	1
By John Kerby Esquire		opposite the Mouth B Run	

The following were made by
  James Grant Esquire:

James Hogg	8847	
John Umstead	4032	
Genl Benjamin Smith	1343	
Walter Alves[127] 2 Lotts	10750	

Hugh Montgomery Esqr made
  the following viz:

The Heirs of L. H. Bullock[128]	5375	
For Richard Bullock	3250	
Charles I. Love	1500	W. Cove
Robert Tives for David Hart	4262	

---

[127]Son of James Hogg, No. 101. He married Amelia, daughter of William Johnston, one of the original members of Henderson and Company. Archibald Henderson, "The Transylvania Company," *loc. cit.*

[128]One of the members of Henderson and Company. *Ibid.*

(To be continued with II, Blount County, in *Publications* No. 24)

EARLY EAST TENNESSEE TAXPAYERS

Compiled by Pollyanna Creekmore

II. Blount County, 1801[1]

Blount County was created out of Knox County by an act passed at the second session of the territorial assembly at Knoxville, on July 11, 1795, and named in honor of William Blount, the first and only territorial governor.[2] Knox County had been created from fractions of Greene and Hawkins counties in 1792.[3] Greene was created from Washington in 1783,[4] and Washington was established in 1777, the oldest county in the state.[5] Since the creation of Blount County in 1795, the territorial limits have been added to by the Treaty of Tellico, 1798, and Calhoun's Treaty of 1819. A portion was taken into Loudon County upon its creation in 1870.[6]

Although Blount County was not established until 1795, the first settlement by white people took place more than a decade before, around 1782 or 1783.[7]

In order to understand the history of the settlement of the section which became Blount County, it is first necessary to know something of the geographical position of the county. A glance at the map will show that it is bounded on the east by Sevier County (which has as its northern boundary the French Broad River) and the Great Smoky Mountains; on the

---

[1]For the introduction to series see *Publications*, No. 23, pp. 115-16. In preparation of No. II, the compiler wishes to thank Mr. J. W. Marshall and Mr. Runa White, county court clerk and register, of Blount County, respectively, Mrs. B. W. Gandrud of Tuscaloosa, Alabama, and to many others who have contributed in some way.

[2]George Roulstone (comp.), *Laws of the State of Tennessee* (Knoxville, 1803), 60-61. Hereafter cited as Roulstone, *Laws;* William H. Masterson, "William Blount and the Establishment of the Southwest Territory, 1790-1791," East Tennessee Historical Society's *Publications* (Knoxville), No. 23 (1951), 3-31. The new county was made a part of Hamilton District.

[3]Roulstone, *Laws,* iv.

[4]Walter Clark (ed.), *The State Records of North Carolina,* 14 vols, continuing earlier series of *Colonial Records* (Goldsboro, 1905), XXIV, 539-40. Hereafter cited as *N.C.S.R.*

[5]*Ibid.,* 141-42. The first tax lists of Washington County (1778) will be printed in this series.

[6]*Acts of Tennessee,* 1870, pp. 4-9 (Ch. 2). The original name of Loudon County was Christiana.

[7]*Memorial of Tennessee Legislature to United States Congress* (Nashville, 1806), copy in Legislative Papers, Tennessee Archives, Nashville. "That the settlements made on lands within the limits of this state, south of French Broad and Holston [Tennessee] and West of Big Pigeon rivers, commenced some time in the year, 1782 or 1783 . . . ." Until 1874 the present Tennessee River from the junction of the French Broad and the Holston, near Knoxville, to the mouth of the Little Tennessee, at Lenoir City, was known as the Holston, and the present Little Tennessee as the Tennessee. This is often confusing, especially in locating early sites, as the land in the calls of the early grants and deeds is usually located by water courses.

south by the Little Tennessee River; on the west by Loudon County; while the Tennessee River forms almost all of its northern boundary, dividing it from Knox County. Thus all of the region comprising the present counties of Blount and Sevier is south of the French Broad River, a region which has had "a singular and remarkable history."[8]

At the time that the first settlement of this region by white people took place, all of what is now Tennessee was a part of the state of North Carolina. The Revolutionary War was drawing to a close, and only two years before, in 1780, a great many of the men from the upper settlements in Washington, Sullivan, and Greene counties had taken part in the Battle of King's Mountain, and only two months after that some of the same men took part in the Battle of Boyd's Creek,[9] located in present Sevier County.

The route followed by Colonels Arthur Campbell and John Sevier in the Boyd's Creek campaign was over the Great Indian Warpath which led through the entire length of Blount County to the Cherokee Indian towns on the Little Tennessee River. It was the same route which had been followed by Colonel William Christian in the campaign of 1776 against the Cherokees,[10] and again used by Sevier in the later Indian campaigns.

After the Revolutionary War ended there followed a period of difficulty between the United States and several states over the matter of the state's western lands, which the United States wanted the states to cede to Congress. In 1783 North Carolina passed a law which opened its western lands and established a land office for their entry and purchase. By this act the land below the French Board River was reserved to the Cherokee Indians as hunting grounds. The act also prescribed a penalty for anyone who made entries or surveys on the lands south of French Broad; however, North Carolina did make some grants in the reservation and received money from the grantees.[11]

As early as 1782 there were complaints by the Indians about the settlers on their lands south of French Broad. In a letter to Colonel John Sevier, dated February 11, 1782, the governor of North Carolina wrote: "I am distressed with the repeated complaints of the Indians respecting the daily intrusions of our people on their lands beyond the French Broad River."[12] The Governor instructed Sevier to warn the intruders and if they did not remove to drive them off by force.

---

[8]Samuel Cole Williams, *History of the Lost State of Franklin* (New York, 1933), 218. Hereafter cited as Williams, *Lost State*.

[9]For accounts of these campaigns see Lyman C. Draper, *King's Mountain and its Heroes. . .* (Cincinnati, 1881); J. G. M. Ramsey, *The Annals of Tennessee to the End of the Eighteenth Century* (reprinted, Kingsport, 1926). Hereafter cited as Ramsey, *Annals;* Samuel Cole Williams, *Tennessee During the Revolutionary War* (Nashville, 1944).

[10]*Ibid*, 48-60; Ramsey, *Annals, passim.*

[11]*N.C.S.R.*, XXIV, 478-82.

[12]*Ibid.*, XVII, 14-15.

On June 2, 1784, the North Carolina legislature passed an act for the cession of its western lands subject to the conditions that North Carolina should satisfy her soldiers' claims, and that all entries to land she had authorized should be recognized, and that a state or states should be formed from the territory.[13] The United States Congress was given one year to accept the cession.

When North Carolina closed the land office set up under the act of 1783,[14] as a result of the act of 1784, a furor went up in the western country. Leaders from the various counties took steps to form a government which resulted in the State of Franklin.[15]

At the first session of the legislature of Franklin, which ended on March 31, 1785, among the several acts which were passed was one called "An Act to divide Greene County into three separate and distinct counties, and to erect two new counties by the name of Caswell and Sevier."[16] The historian Ramsey thought that Caswell "occupied the section of country which is now Jefferson, and extended probably west . . . extended down the French Broad and Holston to their confluence, and perhaps further west. . . . The other new county embraced what is still known as Sevier County, south of French Broad, and also that part of Blount east of the ridge dividing the waters of Little River from those of [Little] Tennessee."[17]

There is good reason to believe that a Blount County of the State of Franklin came into existence at this time, for in the *Pennsylvania Packet* of January 5, 1786, under the heading of "State of Frankland, August Session, 1785," a call was made for the inhabitants to elect members to a convention to consider the cession act of 1784, "in the following numbers for each county, viz. Washington, 15; Sullivan, 12; Green [*sic*], 12; Caswell, 8; Severn [Sevier], 6; Spencer, 5; Wayne, 4; Blurt [probably Blunt, for Blount], two. . . ."

Meanwhile, John Sevier and other officials of Franklin had negotiated the first of two treaties with the Cherokee Indians. This first one was held at the mouth of Dumplin Creek, on the north bank of French Broad River (in present Sevier County) on May 31, 1785. The treaty fixed the ridge dividing the waters of Little River from those of the (Little) Tennessee as the dividing line between the possessions of the whites and the Indians. The Indians ceded *all claim to lands south of the French Broad and Holston* (Tennessee), lying east of that ridge. [Italics mine.]

---

[13]*Ibid.*, 561-63.
[14]*Ibid.*, 563-64.
[15]For a full, authoritative account see Williams, *Lost State;* also Ramsey, *Annals.*
[16]*Ibid.*, 294.
[17]*Ibid.*, 295.

The other treaty or conference was held at Chota Ford and Coyatee, on the Little Tennessee River, from July 31 to August 3, 1786. The boundary between the whites and the Indians was fixed at the Little Tennessee.[18]

In November of 1785 the United States had negotiated the Treaty of Hopewell with the Cherokees. Article Five of this treaty provided:

> If any citizen of the United States, or other persons, not being an Indian, shall attempt to settle on any of the lands westward or Southward of the said boundary [French Broad River] which are hereby alloted to the Indians for their hunting grounds, or having settled will not remove from the same within six months after the ratification of this treaty, such persons shall forfeit the protection of the United States, and the Indians may punish him or not as they please, provided that this article shall not extend to the people settled between the fork of French Broad and Holston Rivers, whose particular situation shall be transmitted to the United States in Congress assembled, for their decision thereon, which the Indians agree to abide by.[19]

Under the Treaty of Dumplin most of the earliest settlement of Blount County took place, the settlers following the route of the Great Indian Warpath and establishing their homes along the many streams which drain the county. By 1786 there were enough settlers to form two Presbyterian congregations, New Providence,[20] at Craig's Station, the site of the present city of Maryville, and Eusebia, located near the head of Boyd's Creek, in what became known as the "Bogle Settlement."[21]

By March, 1787, it is known that the State of Franklin had opened a land office for the purchase of lands in the tract south of French Broad, but there are no surviving records to show who purchased lands; however, it is known that the land was sold at forty shillings per hundred acres in furs, ten shillings "in hand," and two years' credit for the other thirty shillings.[22] There are a few scattered records in the public records of Greene County which contain names of individuals known to be living in Blount County at the time.[23]

The State of Franklin was never recognized and died out in 1788; therefore, the treaties of Dumplin and Coyatee were not valid, and the settlers on the lands south of French Broad River were considered en-

---

[18]The texts of these treaties may be found in *N.C.S.R.*, XXII, 649-50, 655-59.

[19]Charles C. Royce, "The Cherokee Nation of Indians: a Narrative of Their Official Relations with the Colonial and Federal Government," in Bureau of American Ethnology, *Fifth Annual Report*, 1883-84 (Washington, 1887), 133-34, 153-58.

[20]Will A. McTeer, *History of New Providence Presbyterian Church, Maryville, Tennessee, 1786-1921* (Maryville, 1921). Hereafter cited as McTeer, *New Providence Church.*

[21]Will A. McTeer, *Eusebia Church History, Homecoming, August 31,1924* ([Knoxville, 1924]).

[22]*N.C.S.R.*, XXII, 678.

[23]See footnote 41, below.

A PORTION OF A MAP PRINTED IN 1795 SHOWING BLOUNT COUNTY AND EAST TENNESSEE.

croachers on the Indian lands. Since they were outside the limits of any government, they set about to organize some system of governing themselves. Representatives of the inhabitants met on January 12, 1789, and framed the "Articles of Association," by which they were presumably governed until the Southwest Territory was established.[24]

Beginning in 1787, when by another proclamation the settlers were ordered off these lands, there began a series of Indian attacks. For their protection the settlers built small fortifications known as stations to which the outlying settlers might flee for protection in time of attack. Those within the present limits of Blount County were Gamble's, Houston's, Henry's, Ish's, Kelly's, Bird's, Craig's Black's Calvin's, Well's, and Gillespie's.[25]

In 1789 North Carolina did cede her western lands to the United States. One section of this act provided:

> That this act shall not prevent the people now residing south of French Broad, between the rivers [Little] Tennessee and Big Pigeon, from entering their pre-emptions on that tract, should an office for that purpose be opened. . . .[26]

The Territory South of the River Ohio was established in 1790 by the United States Congress, with William Blount as governor. One of the earliest official acts which Blount undertook was to negotiate the Treaty of Holston with the Cherokee Indians, which he did at Knoxville, on July 2, 1791. By the provisions of the treaty "a line was established, to the south of which the Indians were to withdraw and beyond which the settlers were not to encroach." This line became known as the Indian Boundary. "That section of the line crossing East Tennessee was described in the treaty as beginning on the North Carolina boundary at a 'point from which a line extended to the river Clinch shall pass the Holston [Tennessee] at the ridge which divides the waters running into the Little River from those running into the Tennessee [Little Tennessee]'."[27] The location of the line was uncertain, and it was not surveyed until 1797. Meanwhile settlement advanced and pushed the location southward.

In 1792, when Knox County was established, it included all of the territory which became Blount County in 1795. Many of the early Knox County officials appointed by Blount were men living in what was later

[24]These "Articles" are printed in Ramsey, *Annals*, 435-36; also in Williams, *Lost State*, 226-28.

[25]Ramsey, *Annals, passim*.

[26]Clarence E. Carter (ed.), *The Territorial Papers of the United States*, IV, *The Territory South of the River Ohio, 1790-1796* (Washington, 1936), 6. Hereafter cited as Carter, *Territorial Papers*, IV.

[27]Mary U. Rothrock (ed.), *The French Broad-Holston Country: A History of Knox County, Tennessee* (Knoxville, 1946), 43. Hereafter cited as *French Broad-Holston Country*. The text is in Carter, *Territorial Papers*, IV, 60-67.

Blount County, and most of them were appointed to the same office by Blount when the new county was organized.[28]

The act which created Blount County described its bounds as:

Beginning upon the south side of the river Holston [Tennessee], at the mouth of Little River, then up the meanders of Stock Creek upon the south side to the head of Nicholas Bartlet's mill pond at high waters, thence to a direct line to the top of Bay's Mountain leaving the house of James Willis to the right, within forty rods of the said line, thence along Bay's Mountain, to the line of the county of Sevier, thence with that line to the eastern boundary of the Territory, thence southwardly to the line of the Indians according to the treaty of Holston, and with that line to the river Holston [Tennessee], and up the meanders of the river Holston [Tennessee], upon the south side, to the beginning. . . .[29]

The act also provided that a court of pleas and quarter sessions be established and that the first meeting take place at the home of Abraham Wear.

William Wallace, Joseph Black, Samuel Glass, David Craig, John Tremble (Trimble), Alexander Kelly, and Samuel Henry were appointed commissioners to fix the county seat by obtaining fifty acres of land and laying it out into a town "to be known by the name of Maryville," no doubt, in honor of Mary Grainger, wife of Governor William Blount. The commissioners selected the site of Craig's Station, and obtained fifty acres of land from John Craig.[30]

The first court for the county met at the home of Abraham Wear on September 14, 1795, "Present William Wallas, William Lowry, Oliver Alexander and James Scott who produced Commissions of the peace from his Excellency, Governor Blount. . . ."[31] Other justices who appeared were David Craig and George Ewing. William Wallace was appointed chairman of the Court; John McKee, clerk; William Wallace, register; Littlepage Sims, sheriff; Robert Rhea, coroner; John McKee, trustee.[32]

After the county was organized and for several years, the tax rates were fixed and the lists of taxables were ordered to be taken by the county court. The county courts were authorized to tax property by a legislative act passed October 25, 1797, in which the types of taxable property were listed and the method of taking the taxes was prescribed. White polls consisted of "all free males and male servants between the age of twenty one and fifty years"; slaves, "all slaves male and female, between the age of

---

[28]*Ibid.*, 449-50, 469-71.
[29]Roulstone, *Laws*, 60.
[30]Blount County Deeds (Courthouse, Maryville), Book I, 186, Book II, 29. Hereafter cited as Deeds.
[31]Blount County Minutes of Court of Pleas and Quarter Sessions (Courthouse, Maryville; typewritten copy, McClung Collection, Lawson McGhee Library). Hereafter cited as Minutes.
[32]*Ibid.*

twelve and fifty years."[83] The amount of tax to be levied was also specified. In order to provide for the poor the county courts were also empowered to levy a poor tax upon property.[84]

On February 25, 1801, the Blount county court ordered the list of taxable property to be taken.[85] The tax rate for the year was the same as the preceding year, all that the law would allow.[86] Meanwhile, the poor tax had been fixed at six cents on every hundred acres of land, six cents on each black poll, and three cents on each white poll.[87]

By the provisions of the state law regarding the taxing of property the clerk of the county court was required to return "the bond given by the said sheriff for the collection of public taxes, and shall without delay transmit the same, together with a copy of the tax list of his county, to the treasurer of the district, and also a like copy to the next meeting of the general assembly."[88]

The following lists are transcribed from a microfilm copy of an original certified copy returned by James Houston, Blount County court clerk, to the Tennessee general assembly, now on file in the Tennessee Archives. They are not of record in Blount County. In the Archives there is a similar list for 1800;   also a supposedly complete list for 1805. All of these lists have been microfilmed by the compiler, through the courtesy of Robert T. Quarles, Tennessee Archives, Nashville, and are available in the McClung Collection, Lawson McGhee Library.

While these tax lists are for 1801, it should be pointed out that a great majority of the men listed as owning land did not obtain a clear title to their land until after 1806, when the compact of that year was entered into between the state of Tennessee, the United States, and North Carolina. By the provisions of Tennessee law the settlers south of French Broad River were given the opportunity of purchasing the lands which they claimed by right of pre-emption and occupancy which had been recognized in the Cession Act of 1789 and Article XI, section 31 of the Constitution of 1796. They were to be charged only $1.00 an acre instead of the minimum price of $2.00 an acre established for other unappropriated lands by the compact of 1806. These Tennessee grants are on file in the Land Office at Nashville, and very few of them are of record in the Blount County Courthouse at Maryville.

There is a total of 680 names on these lists, which is of interest in contrast of the total population of Blount County according to the territorial

---

[83]Roulstone, *Laws*, 114-20.
[84]*Ibid.*, 121-23.
[85]Minutes, February 25, 1801.
[86]*Ibid.*, February 28, 1801.
[87]*Ibid.*, November 29, 1800.
[88]Roulstone, *Laws*, 118.

census of 1795 of 2,816 (of whom 183 were slaves), and of 5,516 according
to the "Schedule of the whole number of Persons in the District of Tennessee," 1801. In the latter year the population of Maryville was 71.[39]

All of the names on these lists cannot be identified due to lack of space;
therefore,the compiler has included notes only on a few representative ones.
Of great assistance in the compiling of these notes have been the Papers
of Will E. Parham in the McClung Collection.

The late Will E. Parham, of Maryville, spent the greater part of his
later life in searching for information on Blount County families. He had
collected notes and planned to write a county history which never material-
ized.

The public records of the county on file in the Courthouse have suffered
some destruction, principally in a fire in 1879. The early marriage bonds
and licenses had never been recorded in books, neither had the wills until
after the Civil War. The Minutes of the Court of Pleas and Quarter Sessions from 1812 to 1813, and 1818 to 1834, were destroyed, along with the
majority of the loose papers of that court. All of the records of the circuit
court were lost.

In cooperation with the Mary Blount Chapter, Daughters of the American Revolution, Maryville, Mr. Parham copied many of the early records,
including all of the old marriage licenses and bonds. He also abstracted
many other records, among them early deeds. In connection with his searches
he visited many cemeteries in Blount and adjacent counties where he copied
tombstone inscriptions.

Upon Mr. Parham's death in 1946, his papers were bequeathed to the
McClung Historical Collection, Lawson McGhee Library, Knoxville, where
they may be consulted. The most useful part of these papers consists of
correspondence to and from individuals seeking information about their
ancestors; however, it should be emphasized that these notes do not include
all Blount County families, only those for which Mr. Parham had been engaged to make a search, or those in which he was interested personally. These
searches frequently involved the investigation of records of other East Tennessee counties.

The compiler of these lists of taxpayers has had access not only to the
Parham Papers, but also to many historical and genealogical materials which
Mr. Parham did not use.

---

[39] Carter, *Territorial Papers*, IV, 404; *Second Census: Return of the Whole Number of Persons within the Several Districts of the United States. . .* (reprinted [Wash-
ington], 1802; photostatic copy in University of Tennessee Library ,Knoxville), p. 2R.

Key to Column Numbers

[1] Land
[2] Free Poles [*sic*]
[3] Black Poles [*sic*]
[4] Town Lots

There are two additional columns in the original entitled "Billiard Tables" and "Stud Horses." No individuals were listed as owning any of the former, and only six individuals were designated as owning any of the latter: William Boyd and Michal Nyman of Bogle's Company, William Dav_idson and Meshech Tipton of Montgomery's Company, John Lowry, attorney, and John Sharp of Alexander's Company, each owning one.

CAPTAIN BOGLE'S COMPANY FOR THE YEAR 1801.[40]

	[1]	[2]	[3]	[4]
Bogle, Samuel[41]	150	1		
Bell, John	150	1		
Bogle, Joseph[42]	150	1	1	
Boyd, Robert[43]	100	1		
Boyd, William	200	1		
Bowerman, John	30	1		
Bogle, Hugh[44]		1		
Bogle, Andrew[45]	200	2		
Carson, David	200	1		
Cusack [Cusick], John B.[46]		1		
Cunningham, John	100	1		
Cup [Cupp], David[47]		1		

[40]For key to column numbers, see end of Introduction.

[41]Son of Joseph and Jean McAntyre Bogle; born in Cumberland County, Pa., May 24, 1765; married September 14, 1797, in Blount County, Eleanor Williams; buried Eusebia Cemetery. For a full account of this family see Leila Mason Eldridge, *Bogle Family Records* (Atlanta, 1937).

[42]Brother of Samuel Bogle *(supra);* born July 5, 1759, died April 10, 1811; married January 3, 1786, in Greene County, Tenn., Margaret Houston. Samuel Rutherford Houston, *Brief Biographical Accounts of Many Members of the Houston Family* . . . (Cincinnati, 1882), 231-32. Hereafter referred to as *Houston Family.*

[43]Commissioned captain in cavalry volunteers, Blount County, 1796. Mrs. John Trotwood Moore (comp.), *Record of Commissions of Officers in the Tennessee Militia, 1796-1811* (Nashville, 1947), 4. Hereafter cited as Moore, *Commissions.*

[44]Son of Andrew Bogle *(infra),* born January 31, 1780.

[45]Revolutionary soldier born April 26, 1753, in Fermanaugh Township, Cumberland County, Pa.; removed to Rockingham County, Va., where he served in the militia; about 1786 removed to what became Blount County near Eusebia Church, where he died November 29, 1813. He and his wife Elizabeth (Campbell) Bogle are buried in Eusebia Cemetery. Eldridge, *Bogle Records.*

[46]Member of family which lived in the Boyd's Creek Valley of Blount and Sevier counties.

[47]One of a group of German families who settled on Crooked Creek. Among others were Halfley, Kunse, Nyman, and Thomas, most of whom came from southwest Virginia. Lambert Reed *(q.v.)* married Margaret Coontz, January 10, 1799, in Washington County, Virginia. An Evangelical Lutheran Church was in existence as early as 1812, with Reverend C. D. H. Schmidt as pastor; however, a deed was not

	[1]	[2]	[3]	[4]
Coats, John		1		
Cup, Jacob[48]	80	1		
Caldwell, Carson		1		
Durham, William[49]	200	1	8	
Davis, Samuel[50]	150	1		
Dunlap, James	100	1		
Dunlap, John	100	1		
Davidson, James		1		
Davis, James	100	1		
Dunlap, Adam	100	1		
Davis, Elijah	500	1		
Finley, Robert	800			
Graves, Stephen	50	1		
Garnor [Garner], John F.[51]	400		2	
Garnor, James[52]		1		
Houston, William	100	1		
Halfley, Conrod	800			
Kunse [Cuns, Coontz, Kuns, Kuntz], Adam	400	1		
Kirkpatrick, Charles	800	1		
Kirkpatrick, Thomas		1		
Kennedy, John	100	1		
Kunse, John	100			
Kunse, Henery	100	1		
King, Johnston	50	1		
Kirkpatrick, James		1		
Legg, Jonathan		1		
[Leg]g, Matthew		1		
[Ki]ng, Robert	100	1		

---

made until 1838, when Henry Long *(q.v.)* deeded to Christian Long and Jacob Long, trustees of St. John's Evangelical Lutheran Church, one acre of land "for and in Consideration of the love of the gosble [*sic*] and for divers other causes and considerations." The church was first called Thomas, and in the deed Henry Long made it is stated that the acre was "a part of tract of land 400 1/4 Acres granted to Jacob Thomas." Jacob Thomas, Sr. died in 1804. *Deeds*, S, 26.

[48]Probably the father of David Cup *(supra)*; lived on Nails Creek where he purchased land in 1800. Deeds.

[49]Commissioned lieutenant, Blount County militia, 1801. Moore, *Commissions*, 4.

[50]Revolutionary soldier born December 24, 1755, in that part of Augusta County, Va., which became Rockbridge; served in various campaigns, 1776-80; removed to Washington County, Va., where he remained until 1797, when he removed to Blount County, and in 1808 to that part of the Mississippi Territory which became Madison County, Ala., where he died August 31, 1842. His Revolutionary War pension file is most interesting. Revolutionary War Pension File (National Archives, Washington, D. C.) S 16 756; obituary in *Huntsville* (Ala.) *Democrat*, April 30, 1843; notes in compiler's collection, and information supplied by Mrs. B. W. Gandrud Tuscaloosa, Ala. (No notes in Parham Papers.)

[51]Revolutionary soldier born in Prince William County, Va., December 25, 1749; removed to Chatham (later Randolph) County, N. C., where he served in the militia as a private soldier and a pilot; removed to Sevier, and then to Blount County, Tenn.; died and buried at the Headrick Cemetery, on Little River. Progenitor of the Garner family of Blount County; his daughter, Elizabeth, married Samuel Henry "of Little River," and his son John married Rachel Henry. Rev. War Pens. File; Parham Papers; and notes in compiler's collection.

[52]Son of above.

	[1]	[2]	[3]	[4]
[Ma]rtin, Warner[53]	500	1	2	
McMurry, Samuel[54]	150			
Malcom, Alexander	100			
McTeer, Robert Senr[55]	600	1		
McTeer, Robert Junr	50	1		
McKain, Nancy	100			
Murrin, Robert	100	1		
McCammon, Samuel	150	1		
McCammon, Thomas		1		
McMurry, James	100			
McCauly [McCallie], John[56]	200	1	1	
Martin, Luke	100	1		
Nyman [Neiman, Niman], Margaret	100			
Nyman, Michal	80	1		
Pickens, John[57]	200	1		
Palmer, Samuel		1		
Richardson, John	200	1		
Rhea [Ray], John[58]	100	1		
Reed, Lambert Senr	50			
Reed, Lambert Junr	50	1		
Simms [Sims], James[59]	100	1		
Skean [Skeen], James	100	1		
Trimble, John		1		
Thomas, Adam	100	2		
Thompson, John	50	1		
Tipton, Benjamin	250	1		
Tipton, Joseph	122	1		
Upton, James	100	1		

[53]Removed to Alabama, where his son, Joshua Lanier Martin (1799-1856) was twelfth governor of the state. Thomas McAdory Owen (ed.), *History of Alabama and Dictionary of Alabama Biography*, 4 vols. (Chicago, 1912), IV, 1166.

[54]Along with William McMurray received North Carolina land grant No. 1120, dated January 12, 1793, for land "in our county of Green [*sic*], on Crooked Creek," registered in Knox County, 1794; in Blount County, 1802. Deeds, I, 35.

[55]Revolutionary soldier (1740-1824), from Cumberland County, Pa.; received North Carolina grant No. 952, dated December 26, 1791, for 800 acres of land "in Green [*sic*] County, on Ellijoy Creek"; joins Benjamin Tipton, J. McKamie, Samuel Bogle, Williams. A descendant, the late Major Will A. McTeer of Maryville, was especially interested in local history and genealogy, and upon his death in 1925, his papers were given to the McClung Collection, Lawson McGhee Library, by his son, Wilson McTeer, now professor of psychology, Wayne University.

[56]Born in Scotland in 1754; came to America at the age of 18, and served in the Revolutionary War; died March 21, 1831; ancestor of the prominent McCallie family of Chattanooga, Tennessee. Another descendant was the late W. O. Whittle of Knoxville, whose collection of genealogical papers is now in the McClung Collection. Obituary in *Knoxville Register*, March 30, 1831.

[57]Progenitor of the Pickens family of Blount and Sevier counties; he and his wife, Lettitia Hannah Pickens, are buried in Eusebia Cemetery. For an account of their descendants see Nellie Pickens Anderson, *The John Pickens Family* (Rockford, Tenn., 1952).

[58]Perhaps the John Rhea who received North Carolina grant No. 1502, dated July 12, 1794, for 940 acres of land "in Green [*sic*] county, on both sides of Little River, in Murphy's Cove," registered in Knox County, 1795; in Blount County, 1807. Deeds, I, 142.

[59]Revolutionary War soldier born 1750; drew a pension for his service in the

	[1]	[2]	[3]	[4]
Upton, Isaac[60]		1		
Vickers, James	300	1		
Vance, David[61]	100	1	1	
Williams, John Junr	50	1		
Wallace, George		1		
Williams, Richard	50	1		1
Williams, John, Stiller	100	1		

CAPTAIN MONTGOMERY'S COMPANY

	[1]	[2]	[3]	[4]
Bromley, James		1		
Beard, George		1		
Blair, John		1		
Blair, William		1		
Brown, John		1		
Blizard, Thomas		1		
Black, Gavin[62]	200	1		
Bradley, John[63]		1		
Beard, Henry		1		
Beaty, Samel		1		
Conway, Thomas		1		
Conway, Joseph		1		
Conway, Jessey		1		
Camron, Samuel		1		
Campbel, John		1		
Davis, James		1		
Davis, Thomas	50	1		
Davidson, William[64]				
Finley, John		1		
Finn, Jesse		1		
Frier, John		1		
Goforth, Zacharia[65]		1		
Goodman, Stephen		1		
Herse [Hess], John[66]		1		

Virginia militia; an early constable. Zella Armstrong, *Twenty-four Hundred Tennessee Pensioners* (Chattanooga, 1937), 106. Hereafter referred to as *Tennessee Pensioners*. See also Minutes, December 15, 1795.

[60]Removed to Marion County, Ala. Census of 1840, original population schedules, Marion County, Ala. (National Archives, Washington, D. C.; microfilm in Alabama Department of Archives and History, Montgomery, Ala.).

[61]Gave land for the Cedar Grove Baptist Church and Cemetery located on Nail's Creek; deed dated August 24, 1833. Deeds, M, 417.

[62]Lived on Crooked Creek near Black's Blockhouse; active in the Indian campaigns of the territorial period; commissioned lieutenant, Blount County militia, 1796; removed to Alabama. Moore, *Commissions*, 4; notes in compiler's collection.

[63]Commissioned second major, Blount County militia, 1796. *Ibid.*

[64]An early justice of the peace. Minutes, March 14, 1796.

[65]A Revolutionary War soldier born in 1758; received a pension for his service in the North Carolina militia while a resident of Wayne County, Tennessee; early Blount County constable. *Tennessee Pensioners*, 47; Minutes, June 12, 1796.

[66]Commissioned lieutenant, Blount County militia, 1796; at a meeting of the county court on September 13, 1796, it was "ordered that John Huse [*sic*] have leave to build a mill on a place called Murphy's Creek"; name is perpetuated in Hesse Creek. Moore, *Commissions*, 5,

	[1]	[2]	[3]	[4]
Little, Thomas		1		
Wm Lowry for Jas				
W. Lackey	1500			
Morrison, Thomas[67]		1		
Montgomery, Alexander[68]		1		
McClanahan [McClannahan], James		1		
Millar [Miller], Alexander	200	1		
Montgomery, Robert		1		
McClanahan, Matthew[69]		1		
More [Moore], James		1	1	
More, Alexander		1		
Millar, Andrew	300			
McClanahan, David		1		
Manuel, Cudbert		1		
Manuel, Valentine		1		
McMurry, Robert		1		
McClung, Charles[70]	500			
[N]elson, John		1		
Rhea, Jessee		1		
Rhea, John		1		
Richardson, Obadiah		1		
Ramsey, Richard		1		
Smith, John[71]		1		
Stafford, Stephan		1		
Snider [Snyder], Peter[72]		1		
Smith, Samuel		1		
Tate, Isaac		1		
Tipton, Meshech		1		
Tarwater, Jacob		1		
Tarwater, Lewis		1		
Walker, Joseph		1		
Walker, Isaiah		1		
Wise, John		1		

CAPTAIN ALEXANDER'S COMPANY[73]

	[1]	[2]	[3]	[4]
Alexander, Oliver[74]	300		1	
Alexander, Benjamin		1		
Alexander, John[75]	150	1	2	

[67]Commissioned lieutenant, Blount County militia, 1799. *Ibid.*
[68]Commissioned captain, Blount County militia, 1799. *Ibid.*
[69]Commissioned ensign, Blount County militia, 1799; lieutenant, 1801. *Ibid.*
[70]Resident of Knox County, where he was the first clerk, a merchant, and surveyor; engaged in much land speculation. Sketch in *French Broad-Holston Country*, 446-47; Deeds, *passim.*
[71]Commissioned ensign, Blount County militia, 1796. Moore, *Commissions*, 5.
[72]Commissioned ensign, Blount County militia, 1801. *Ibid.*
[73]Almost all of the company lived in the town of Maryville.
[74]One of the first justices of the peace, 1795; wood ranger, 1796; stray master, of Blount County. Minutes, September 14, 1795, June 12, 1796, September 12, 1797.
[75]Commissioned lieutenant in cavalry regiment, Hamilton District, 1796; captain, 1796, Blount County. Moore, *Commissions*, 4.

	[1]	[2]	[8]	[4]
Alexander, John	100	1		
Burk, William[76]	233½	1	1	1
Berry, Thomas	200	1		1
Bolu [Bellew, Billieu, Billue], James	100	1		
Brown, Isaiah		1		
Blackburn, Gidion[77]	505	1		
Cunningham, David		1	½	
Cunningham, Miles		1	½	
Culton, Robert	190	1		
Drew, John	640	1		1
Danforth, Josiah[78]	7640	1	8	
Donahoe [Donohoo], Charles[79]		1		
Denning, Matthew		1		
Donaldson, Robert[80]	200	1		
Fitzgerald, Patrick		1		
Garrison, John		1		
Glass, William	800	2		
Gardener, John[81]		1		1
Hart, Joseph[82]		1		
Hargas [Hargis], William		1		
Hart, Alexander	200	1		
Hooks [Hooke], Robert	150	1		
Lowry, John atty[83]	500	1	1	2

[76]Sheriff of Blount County, 1800-02; early tavern keeper. Goodspeed Publishing Co., *History of Tennessee*, East Tennessee edition (Nashville, 1887), 833; Minutes, June 14, 16, 1796.

[77]Early Presbyterian preacher, teacher, and missionary; pastor of New Providence Church, Maryville. For a full account of his varied career see Verton M. Queener, "Gideon Blackburn," East Tennessee Historical Society's *Publications*, No. 6 (1934), 12-28; McTeer, *New Providence Church.*

[78]A native of Massachusetts; married September 2, 1790, in Washington County, Va., Sarah Roane, reputedly a sister of Archibald Roane, second governor of Tennessee; contractor for one of the first Blount County courthouses; owned much property in Maryville where he kept a tavern; engaged in considerable land speculation and was involved with Richard G. Waterhouse in the famous suit over a 19,000 acre tract in Rhea County, Tenn. Lewis Preston Summers, *Annals of Southwest Virginia, 1769-1800* (Abingdon, 1929), 1259. Hereafter cited as Summers, *Annals.* See also Minutes, June 14, 1796, September 15, 1797, August 26, 1800; Penelope Johnson Allen, "Leaves From the Family Tree," *Chattanooga Times*, January 20, 1935.

[79]Member of family originally from Augusta County, Va., who first settled in Sevier County, about 1788; sheriff of Blount County, 1816-1820; married Margaret Weir, daughter of Joseph Weir of Blount County; removed to Monroe County. Allen, "Leaves from the Family Tree," *loc. cit.*, February 4, 1934; Goodspeed, *History of Tennessee*, 833.

[80]Commissioned ensign, Blount County militia, 1800. Moore, *Commissions*, 4.

[81]Merchant of Maryville; trustee, Maryville Female Academy. *Wilson's Knoxville Gazette*, July 20, 1812.

[82]Revolutionary war soldier; born in Loudoun County, Va., June 1761; early elder and clerk of session of New Providence Church; removed to Indiana where he died June 20, 1841. McTeer, *New Providence Church*, 53-55.

[83]Probably one of those who received North Carolina grant, dated June 8, 1797, for 200 acres of land "in our county of Green [sic] now called Blount," on Crooked Creek, south side of Holston (Tennessee) and French Broad rivers, registered 1799. Deeds, I, 132.

	[1]	[2]	[3]	[4]
Lowry, John mercht[84]		1	1	2
Logan, Alexander	400	1		
Montgomery, John[85]		1		2
Montgomery, James S		1		
McClanahan, James		1		
Minnis, John[86]	640			
McBath, William	200	1		
McFaddian [McFadden], Joseph	80	1		
McNeely, Samuel		1		
McNutt, Alexander	130	1		
Ogleby, David	100	1		
Paxton, Samuel[87]	200	1		
Panther, Alexander		1		
Pedigrew [Pettigrew], Matthew		1		
Russel, John		1		
Russam, John	33½	1		
Rhea, John atto	900			
Stone, Edward		1		
Sharp, John	400	1	3	1
Thairman [Thurman], Joseph		1		
Taylor, John		2		1
Woods, John[88]	123	1	5	5
Wilkinson, John[89]		1		8
Wilson, James		1		
Wallace, William[90]	400	1	1	
Whiteaker [Whittaker], John	200	1		
Wier, Joseph Junr		1		
Wier, Joseph Senr[91]	300	1		

---

[84]Early merchant of Maryville; trustee, Porter Academy, 1806. Edward Scott (comp.), *Laws of the State of Tennessee* (Knoxville, 1821), I, 934.

[85]Trustee, Porter Academy, 1806. *Ibid.*

[86]Progenitor of the Minnis family of Blount County. For an account of some members see Anderson, *Pickens Family, passim.*

[87]Born about 1754 in that part of Augusta County, Va., which became Rockbridge; from Blount County he removed to Adair County, Ky., in 1802, and then to Giles County, Tenn. W. M. Paxton, *The Paxtons* . . . (Platte City, Mo., 1903), 232-34. Samuel Paxton's church letter signed by Gideon Blackburn is printed in this volume.

[88]Revolutionary soldier born in Orange County, N. C., April 6, 1766; served in the Battle of King's Mountain; represented Blount County in general assembly; kept tavern at Maryville; commissioned ensign, Blount County militia, 1799; earlier he had served under Sevier in the Indian campaigns of the 1790's; died June 8, 1838. Rev. War Pens. File; Minutes, December 16, 1796; Moore, *Commissions,* 6; obituary in *Knoxville Register,* June 20, 1838.

[89]Early lawyer; name is perpetuated in Wilkinson Pike; compiler of *A Collection of the Laws, or Legislative Acts in Force in the State of Tennessee* . . . (Knoxville, 1811), and *A Biblical Nomenclature* . . . (Knoxville, 1820); represented Blount County in general assembly.

[90]One of the first justices of the peace; commissioner to fix the county seat. Minutes, *passim.*

[91]Revolutionary War soldier who took part in the Battles of King's Mountain and Guilford Courthouse, while living in Washington County, Virginia; married in Augusta County, Virginia, on February 19, 1783, Margaret Sharp, who was born December 22, 1763; died March 11, 1820. Rev. War Pens. File.

	[1]	[2]	[8]	[4]
Weir, James Senr[92]	800	1	1	
Wier, James Junr	100	1		
Wier, John	800	1	1	1

CAPTAIN McGINLEY'S COMPANY

	[1]	[2]	[8]	[4]
Alexander, Ebenezar[93]	1			
Alexander, Joseph[94]	1			
Bowers, Daniel	1			
Buchanan, Edward	1			
Culton, James	1			
Crawford, James	1			
Duncan, John[95]	1	1		
Forguson [Ferguson], Robert	1			
Forguson, John	1			
Forguson, Hugh	1			
Finley, Joseph	1			
Gilbreath, Wm	1			
Gilmore, John	1			
Gold, John	1			
Houston, Samuel[96]	1	1		
Harris, John	1			
Harris, Wm	1			
Harris, Jonathan	1	1		
Houston, John[97]	1			
James, John	1			
Ingland [England], Thomas	1			
Long, Henery	1	1		
McGinley, James[98]	1	1		

---

[92]Original member New Providence congregation; died March 11, 1821. McTeer, *New Providence Church*, 29.

[98]One of the witnesses to the Treaty of Dumplin Creek, 1785.

[94]Commissioned ensign, Blount County militia, 1800. Moore, *Commissions*, 4.

[95]Revolutionary War soldier (1752-1836), born in Rockbridge County, Va., where he served in the militia; came early to Blount County, where he married at Craig's Station on July 17, 1788, Margaret Alexander; an original member of New Providence Church, he and his wife are buried in the church cemetery. Rev. War Pens. File.

[96]Son of Matthew and Martha Lyle Houston, and a second cousin of Sam Houston of Texas fame who came with his widowed mother Elizabeth Paxton Houston to Blount County in the spring of 1807. Elizabeth Paxton Houston died September 8, 1831, and is buried in the Baker's Creek Presbyterian Cemetery. *Paxton Family*, 238-39; 25-34; *Houston Family, passim;* Marquis James, *The Raven* (Indianapolis, 1929), 1-30; *Knoxville Register*, September 14, 1831.

[97]Revolutionary War soldier (1761-March 30, 1835), who drew a pension for his service in the Virginia militia. Rev. War Pens. File; *Houston Family.*

[98]Revolutionary soldier born in Pennsylvania in 1763; served in Battle of King's Mountain; reputed to be a teacher in the first school at Craig's Station; commissioned captain, Blount County militia, 1800; died March 26, 1834. Moore, *Commissions*, 5.

	[1]	[2]	[3]	[4]
McCanles, Robert		1		
McRanels [McReynolds], John⁹⁹		1		
McRanels, Joseph		1	1	
Posey, Daniel		1		
Rorax, Martin		1		
Rowan, Samuel		1		
Sloss, Joseph		1		
Simons, Wm		1	1	
Thomas, Jacob		1		
Timberman		1		
Thompson, James		1		
Thomas, John		1		
Timberman, Jonathan		1		
Timberman, Matthew		1		
Timberman, Jacob		1		
Timberman, George		1		
Trippet, Jonathan		1		
Thomas, George		1		
Thomas, Henry		1		
Tedford, Joseph¹⁰⁰		1		
Wallace, Joel¹⁰¹		1	1	
Wallace, Adam		1		
Wallace, Benj		1		
Wallace, Wm		1		
Wallace, David		1		
Weir, Abraham¹⁰²		1		
Wier, Hugh¹⁰³		1		
Weir, Jonathan	640	1		
Wallace, John		1		
Wallace, Andrew		1		

CAPTAIN COWAN'S COMPANY

	[1]	[2]	[3]	[4]
Arehart [Airhart, Earhart, Hairhart], Henery	300	1	3	
Alexander, Wm		1		
Alexander, Thomas		1		
Armstrong, Wm		1		
Alexander, Jeremiah		1		
Besley [Beasley], Wm	200		2	
Bigham [Bingham], Wm	225	2		

⁹⁹Commissioned ensign, Blount County militia, 1800. *Ibid.*

¹⁰⁰A Revolutionary War soldier; his widow, Mary Tedford, applied for a pension on his service. Commissioned captain, Knox County militia, 1792. Carter, *Territorial Papers*, IV, 449; Minutes, December 2, 1844.

¹⁰¹As an ensign was in command of Black's Station, on Crooked Creek, in 1792; commissioned ensign, 1795, lieutenant, 1796, Blount County militia; married Esther Houston; removed to Morgan County, Ala. Ramsey, *Annals*, 565; Carter, *Territorial Papers*, IV, 469; Moore, *Commissions*, 5; *Houston Family*, 205-08.

¹⁰²First court of Blount County held at his house. Minutes, September 14, 1795.

¹⁰³Received North Carolina grant No. 956, dated December 26, 1791, for 140 acres "in our county of Green [*sic*] on head of Pistol Creek," registered 1806. Deeds, I, 128.

	[1]	[2]	[3]	[4]
Bigham, Samuel		1		
Boyd, James	300	1		
Boyd, George		1		
Bigham, Natth	100	1		
Cowan, Robert		1		
Carr [Kerr], James		1		
Cowan, James	100	1		
Carr, Samuel	300	1		
Cowan, John Senr	150	1		
Carr, David	200	1		
Coope, Baracias		1		
Dickson, Thomas		1		
Dickson, John		1		
Edmondson [Edmiston, Edmundson], John	100	1		
Gilbreath, Hugh	100	1		
Gilbreath, Thomas	100	1		
Hanna [Hannah], Joseph		1		
Hanley, Saml[104]	400	1		
Hanley, Saml for				
J. Cowan	100			
Kelsoe, Hugh[105]	400	1	1	
Logan, Wm	125	1		
Licans, John	100	1		
Lassiter, Burrel[106]	300	1	1	
Montgomery, John	100	1		
Martin, James	250	1	1	
Montgomery, Hugh	300	1		
Millar, David[107]				4
McCord, David	75	1		
Montgomery, George		1		
Montgomery, David		1		
Montgomery, James		1		
Null, John Junr		1		
Nicles [Nichols], George	50	1		
Norwood, Samuel		1		

---

[104]Revolutionary soldier born 1752; served in the Battle of Point Pleasant, and at Battles of King's Mountain and Boyd's Creek; also served as a captain under John Sevier in the Indian campaigns; a member of the Tennessee Constitutional Convention of 1796, from Washington County; a member of the general assembly; removed to Franklin County in 1809; died November 24, 1840. See sketch in Williams, *Lost State*, 319-20.

[105]Owned land where the town of Morganton (originally Portville) was established (now in Loudon County); established a mill early on Baker's Creek which runs through the town. Minutes, May 31, 1799. Morganton was established in 1813. The commissioners were William Lowery, James I. Green, John Eakin, Richard Dearmon, Matthew Wallace, James Wyley, John Lambert, Sr., and Joseph Duncan.

[106]Removed to Wilcox County, Alabama. Census of 1820 (microfilm in Department of Archives and History, Montgomery, Ala.).

[107]Lived at the Militia Springs; at a meeting of the court on May 30, 1800, "Ordered that David Miller have liberty to sell liquors at his own house at the Militia Springs at Tavern rates."

	[1]	[2]	[8]	[4]
Null, John Senr[106]		1		
Orr, Joseph		1		
Rogers, Joseph		1		
Richey, James	75	1		
Robenson, Daniel		1		
Russle, Vance		1		
Sheets, Jacob		1		
Skiles, Wm		1		
Skiles, George		1		
Stuart, Wm		1		
Townsley, George		1		
Thompson, John	150	1		
Utter, Abraham[109]	150	1		
Wallace, John		1		
Wallace, Wm	200	1		
Wiley, Alex	200	1	1	
Wallace, David	100	1		
Woolf, Jacob	100	1		
Wallace, Matthew[110]		1	2	

CAPTAIN SCOTT'S COMPANY

	[1]	[2]	[8]	[4]
Airhart, Nicolus	150	1		
Adams, Wm	200	1		
Boyd, John	100	1		
Blackburn, Benj		1		
Cooper, John	500	1		
Cooper, George		1		
Craig, John[111]		1	8	1
Craig, David[112]	500	1	2	
Chaffin, Robert		1		
Craig, James Junr		1		
Cook, Michael	100	1		
Craig, James Senr		1	1	
Craig, Wm		1		

---

[106]Revolutionary War pensioner. *Tennessee Pensioners*, 85.

[109]Revolutionary soldier born May 9, 1765, in Massachusetts; lived in Cumberland County, Pa., during the Revolution, and in 1784 or 1785 removed to "Nolichucky," Tenn.; a member of Baker's Creek Presbyterian Church; in 1831 removed to Boone County, Ind., presumably where he died January 14, 1851. Rev. War Pens. File S 32 563; Baker's Creek Presbyterian Church, Minutes of Session (photostatic copy in McClung Collection, Lawson McGhee Library); *Pennsylvania Archives* (Harrisburg, 1898), Series III, v. 3, p. 447.

[110]One of the first justices of the peace; at a meeting of the court on December 15, 1795, it was "ordered of Court that Mathew Wallas have liberty to build a public mill on his own land on Bakers Creek." Minutes, March 13, 1796, December 15, 1795.

[111]Presumably the John Craig who founded Craig's Station, which became the city of Maryville. He removed to Mississippi Territory before 1809.

[112]Justice of the peace, Knox County, 1792, and of Blount County, 1795; a member of the Tennessee Constitutional Convention of 1796, representing Blount County; commissioned lieutenant colonel commandant, Blount County militia, 1796. Carter, *Territorial Papers*, IV, 449, 469; Minutes, September 14, 1795; Moore, *Commissions*, 4.

	[1]	[2]	[3]	[4]
Copland [Copeland], David		1		
Dickson, Samuel	200	1		
Dunlap, George		1		
Dilzill [Dalzell, Delzell], John	100	1		
Dothero, Michel		1		
Ewing, John	200			
Edwards, Mark	100	1		
Edwards, John		1		
Evans, Edward	200		1	
Edmondson, James		1		
Fisher, John		1		
Gauld [Gault, Gould, Gold], Samuel	50	1		
Hanna, John Jun	200	1		
Henery [Henry], Charles		1		
Hanna, Wm Senr		1		
Hamontree, James		1		
Hack, Andw		1		
Hamontree, Jeremiah	100	1		
Holaway, John	60	1		
Hanna, Wm Junr		1		
Henery, Samuel[113]	300	1	1	
Hogg, Saml		1		
Houston, James[114]		1	2	
Hutton, Josiah	500	1		
Hammantree, John		1		
Holten, Daniel		1		
Jackson, John	100			
Jackson, Andw	200	1		
Kenedy, John		1		
Logan, James	600	1		
Logan, Henery		1		
McGhee, Barcley[115]	2300	1	9	3
McNab [McNabb], Wm		1		
Montgomery, Alexander	150			
McCartney, John	200	1		
Millar, Saml		1		
Mowrey, John		1		

---

[113]Revolutionary soldier (1762-July 13, 1824) from Hanover County, Va.; settled early on Nine Mile Creek where Henry's Station was established. James Henry (1755-1791), reputedly a brother, settled on Ellijoy Creek near Little River, and had a son, Samuel Henry *(q. v.)*, who is often confused with his uncle. Parham Papers.

[114]Son of Samuel and Elizabeth McCroskey Houston, born November 12, 1757, in that part of Augusta County, Virginia, which became Rockbridge; member Constitutional Convention of 1796; member general assembly; clerk of circuit court for forty years; married first in 1780, Esther Houston, daughter of Matthew; second, Pollie Gillespie, daughter of James Gillespie, Sr. For account of his ancestry and descendants see *Houston Family*, 209-20.

[115]Early merchant and land speculator from Lancaster County, Pa.; progenitor of the McGhee family of Knox, Blount, and Monroe counties; died August 17, 1819, aged 59 years, 11 months and 2 days. C. M. McClung Papers (McClung Collection, Lawson McGhee Library), VII, *passim.*

	[1]	[2]	[3]	[4]
McTeer, James Senr		1		
McKemy [McCamey, McKamey], James		1		
McCampbell, Sollomon[116]	400	1		
McGill, Robert	300	1		
McConald [McConnell], James		1		
McKee, John Junr		1		
McGhee, John	167	1	2	
Means, Wm	400		1	
Maxwell, Thomas		1		
McMeans, John		1		
McCurkin, Thomas	100			
McTeer, James Senr	100	1		
Mayben by James W. Lackey	500			
Posey, Joseph	200	1		
Parks, John		1		
Ross, John	50	1		
Ritchey, David		1		
Sloan, Robert		1		
Sloan, William[117]		1		
Simons [Simmons], John		1		
Sloan, James	200	1		
Sloan, John	200	1		
Sloan, Alexander		1		
Scott, James[118]	640	1		
Shields, Robert		1		
Tedford [Telford], George[119]		1		
Tedford, Robert[120]		1		
Tedford, Thomas		1		
Tedford, Alexander		1		

[116]Commissioned ensign, 1796, lieutenant, 1800, Blount County militia. Moore, *Commissions*, 5.

[117]Commissioned cornet in cavalry regiment, Hamilton District, 1796. *Archibald Sloan* received North Carolina grant No. 1072, dated November 27, 1793, for 200 acres of land "lying and being in our County of Washington on the North fork of Nine Mile Creek the Waters of [Little] Tennessee River including the Big flag Spring on the War path . . .corner of *Alexander Sloans* Land . . . a corner of *William Sloans* land . . . on *John Sloans* land," surveyed August 10, 1782, by Micheal Rawlin, deputy surveyor, Washington County; *John Sloan* and *William Sloan* were chain carriers. Moore, *Commissions*, 5; Deeds, I, 136.

[118]Born in Ireland, 1760; came to America about the time of the Revolution; one of the first justices of the peace; commissioned lieutenant, Knox County militia, 1792; captain, Blount County militia, 1795, 1796; active in the Indian campaigns under Sevier; at a meeting of the county court it was "ordered that James Scott have liberty to build a public grist mill on his own land on Bakers Creek"; removed to Knoxville, where he died August 30, 1823. Not to be confused with another James Scott of Knox County who was a native of Orange County, N. C., and a Revolutionary War pensioner. Carter, *Territorial Papers*, IV, 449, 469; Moore, *Commissions*, 5; obituary in *Knoxville Register*, 1823.

[119]Commissioned ensign, 1795; lieutenant, 1796, Blount County militia; brother of Robert and John Tedford *(q. v.)*. Carter, *Territorial Papers*, IV, 469; Moore, *Commissions*, 5.

[120]Revolutionary soldier born in 1760; drew a pension for his service as a sergeant in the Virginia line; took part in the Battle of King's Mountain; a brother of John Tedford *(q. v.)*. Rev. War Pens. File.

	[1]	[2]	[3]	[4]
Tedford, John[121]		1		
Wilson, Robert		2	1	
White, James		1		
Wilcox, Issac	200	1		
Waren, Michael		1		
Williams, Samuel		1		
Yarien [Yearin], Michael	146	1		
Yarien, Frederick		1		
Young, John		1		

CAPTAIN GILLASPIE'S COMPANY. BLOUNT COUNTY 1801

	[1]	[2]	[3]	[4]
Able [Abel], Cain		1		
Bowerman, Peter		1		
Broils [Broyles], George[122]		1		
Adams, Thomas[123]	100	1		
Bice, Wm	100	1		
Barnes, Wm	100	1		
Boterite [Boatright], Daniel		1		
Bourden [Borden], Adon		1		
Conner, Terrance[123]	300	1		
Castalor, Martin	100	1		
Casteel, Joseph		1		
Craig, Alexander	100	1		
Chamberlan, Hanna[124]	500			
Fouster [Foster], Robert		1		
Gaut, Wm		1	1	
Gaut, John		1		
Gillespie, John		1		
Gillaspie, Robert		1		
Gillaspie, Wm[125]			2	
Gillaspie, James[126]		1	2	

---

[121]Revolutionary soldier born 1750 in Ireland; came to America in 1753 with his parents who settled in Rockbridge County, Va.; served in the militia; commissioned captain, 1781; in battle of Guilford Court House where his brother, Capt. Alexander Tedford, was killed; came to Blount County in 1786 or 1787, where he died July 14, 1832. Rev. War Pens. File, S3776; *The Paxton Family*, 225; *Letter From John Paxton to His Children* (Columbus City, Iowa, 1901).

[122]Commissioned lieutenant, Blount County militia, 1799. *Ibid.*

[123]Received North Carolina grant No. 979, dated December 26, 1791, for 300 acres in "our county of Green [sic] on the South Side of Holston [Tennessee] River"; surveyed by James Lackey, and registered in Greene County, November 17, 1792. Deeds, I, 121.

[124]Received North Carolina grant, dated January 1, 1795, for 1,000 acres of land on south side of Holston (Tennessee) River "on Chamberlain Branch and Henderson Branch." Deeds, I, 9.

[125]Perhaps the William Gillaspie who was an original member of New Providence Church; died December 1, 1833. McTeer, *New Providence Church*, 29.

[126]Received North Carolina grant No. 1326, dated February 4, 1795, for 640 acres "in our County of Green [sic] on south side of Little River"; Gillespie's or "Burnt" Station located on Little River was attacked by Indians in 1788. (For an account see Ramsey, *Annals*, 518-19); commissioned captain, Blount County militia, 1797, 1800. Deeds, II, 332; Moore, *Commissions*, 4.

	[1]	[2]	[3]	[4]
Henderson, Joseph	175	1		
Henderson, John	50	1		
Hichland, John	640	1	1	
Henderson, Wm		1	2	
Hampton, Joshua		1		
Hail [Hale], Wm		1		
Hucheson [Hutchison, Hutchinson], Samuel		1		
Laurence [Lawrence], Martin		1		
Lackey, Arch[127]	640	1		
Miser, George		1		
Maxwell, Robert		1		
McCulley, John	100	1		
Meriot, John	100	1		
Maxwell, John		1		
O'Conner, Thomas		1		
Ruhl [Rule], Wm		1		
Rogers, Thomas		1		
Sullavan, John		1		
Stewart [Stuart], Alexander	100	1		
Sherrel, John[128]	323	1	1	
Taylor, David[129]		1		
Taylor, James[130]	175	1		
Teel, John		1		
Vaught, Andrew		1		
Walker, James	100	1		
Whitenbarger, Henery[131]	250	1		
Young, Wm	200	1		

CAPTAIN KELLEY'S COMPANY FOR THE YEAR 1801.

	[1]	[2]	[3]	[4]
Anderson, James	470	1		
Bond, Henery	460	1		
Benham [Bonham], Daniel	150	1		
Bibles, John	200	1		
Bailey, Robert		1		

---

[127]Received North Carolina grant No. 970, dated December 26, 1791, for 200 acres of land "in our County of Green [*sic*] on waters of [Little] Tennessee"; commissioned captain, Blount County militia, 1796. Deeds, I, 119; Moore, *Commissions,* 5.

[128]Commissioned lieutenant in cavalry regiment, 1796; lieutenant, 1799; in 1799 he sold a landing and road in Blount County leading to Stoney Point Ferry, to George Farragut, of Knox County, the father of Admiral David Farragut. *Ibid.*; Deeds, I, 15.

[129]Early tavern keeper. Minutes, December 16, 1796.

[130]Revolutionary soldier born in Culpeper County, Va., January 30, 1760; removed to Surry County, N. C., where he served in the militia as a substitute for Joseph Myers; later he served as a captain and an ensign. Rev. War Pens. File.

[131]Lived on Lackey's Creek near Louisville; the land on which Middlesettlements Methodist Episcopal Church and Campground were built was bought from him. The deed to this property was made February 22, 1820, and the trustees were Samuel Saffell, Charles Warren, John Norwood, Henry Whittenbarger, Jr., Ambrose Cox, Benjamin Bonham, and Henry Whittenbarger, Sr. Deeds, II, 303.

	[1]	[2]	[3]	[4]
Casteel, Edward[182]	50	1		
Cook, George	50	1		
Casteel, John	150	1		
Caldwell, David[183]	400	1	3	
Cartrite [Cartwright], Thomas		1		
Cart, Richd	300	1		
Essery, Thomas	150	1		
Franks, John	150	1		
Folkner [Faulkner], James	160	1		
Folkner, Joseph	150	1		
Forguson, Henery	300	1		
Greenaway, James[184]	950	1	3	
Griffith, Wm	100	1		
Hughs [Hughes], Robert	200	1		
Hughs, Moses[185]	229	1	1	
Hail, Isom	50	1		
James, Bennet	150	1	1	
Jones, Ebenezar	200	1		
Kelly, Alexander[186]	600		2	
Kelley, John[187]	300	1		
King, John		1		
King, Samuel	200	1		
McKinley, James		1		
Mayo, Valantine	250	1	1	
Michel [Mitchell], Mordecai		1		
Millar, Andw[188]	400	1	4	
Millar, John	100	1		
Maxwell, James		1		
McComes, John	200		2	
McKinzey [McKenzie], Daniel	150			

[182]Commissioned ensign, Blount County militia, 1799. Moore, *Commissions*, 4.

[183]Commissioned justice of the peace, Knox County, 1794; captain, Blount County militia, 1799; trustee, Maryville Female Academy, 1813. Carter, *Territorial Papers*, IV, 461; Moore, *Commissions*, 4.

[184]One of the first justices of the peace; member Constitutional Convention of 1796. Minutes, September 15, 1795.

[185]Commissioned lieutenant, Blount County militia, 1800. Moore, *Commissions*, 5.

[186]Served as second major, Greene County militia, and as justice of the peace for same county under the State of Franklin; commissioned lieutenant colonel, Knox County militia, 1792; lieutenant colonel commandant, Blount County militia, 1795; represented Knox County in the territorial assembly; one of the commissioners to lay out Maryville; along with Stockley Donelson and Archibald Lackey received North Carolina grant No. 213, dated October 4, 1794, for 1,000 acres of land on the north side of (Little) Tennessee on Nine Mile Creek, including "Col. James White's camp." *N.C.S.R.*, XXII, 702; Carter, *Territorial Papers*, IV, 329, 449, 469; Roulstone, *Laws*, 60; Deeds, I, 132.

[187]Commissioned ensign, 1796; captain, 1800, Blount County militia. Moore, *Commissions*, 5.

[188]Received North Carolina grant No. 978, dated December 26, 1791, for 300 acres of land "on Nine Mile Creek in our County of Green [*sic*]." Martha Miller, the widow of one Andrew Miller, applied to the court for a certificate to draw a pension for his Revolutionary service. According to W. E. Parham he lived about three miles below Morganton, later at Clover Hill.

	[1]	[2]	[3]	[4]
Nave, George		1		
Parkhill, David	100	1		
Pride, Burtin[139]	250	1		
Robenet [Robbinett], Moses		1		
Richey [Ritchey], Andrew		1		
Richey, Thomas	275	1	1	
Stephenson, Nicolas	480	1		
Saterthite [Saterwhite], David	100	1		
Simpson, Thomas		1		
Taylor, Thomas		1	1	
Trimble, Arch	100	1		
Trimble, John[140]	250	1	1	
Washam, Jeremiah	100			
Whitenbarger, Abrah	100	1		
Washam, Alexsan	200	1		
Winters, Samuel	1060	1		
Washburn, Sherord		1		
Washam, John	100	1		

CAPTAIN COLVILLE'S COMPANY FOR THE YEAR 1801.

	[1]	[2]	[3]	[4]
Beard, Arch		1		
Barnet, Joseph		1		
Breeze, Thomas		1		
Beard, James		1		
Beaty, John		1		
Campble [Campbell], Robert	100	1		
Colville, George		1		
Campble, James	100	1		
Caldwell, George[141]		1	1	
Coulter, Richd Junr		1		
Coulter, Charles		1		
Caldwell, John	400	1		
Colville, Joseph[142]	430	1		
Caldwell, David		1	1	
Davidson, Andrew		1		
Ewing, John	120	1		

---

[139]Revolutionary War soldier born in Pennsylvania, 1758; at an early age removed to Orange County, and then Caswell County, N. C., where he served in the militia; removed from Blount County to Morgan County, Ala. Rev. War Pens. File, W 10 930.

[140]One of the first justices of the peace; commissioner to fix the county seat 1795; operated a ferry on Holston (Tennessee) River; Minutes, September 14, 1795; Roulstone, *Laws*, 60.

[141]Revolutionary soldier from Virginia, where he was born in 1759. *Tennessee Pensioners*, 23.

[142]Received North Carolina grant No. 829, dated April 15, 1790, for 400 acres of land "lying and being in our County of Green [*sic*] on Crooked Creek Including the plantation Whereon the Said Colville now liveth"; sheriff of Blount County, 1796-1800; 1802-1804; commissioned captain, Blount County militia, 1796; operated a mill on Crooked Creek. Deeds, I, 135; Goodspeed, *History of Tennessee*, 833; Moore, *Commissions*, 4.

	[1]	[2]	[3]	[4]
Ewing, George[143]	300	1	1	
Ewing, James		1		
Ewing, Wm		1		
Gamble, Andw[144]		1		
Gillaspie, James		1	1	
Gamble, John		1		
Gamble, Josiah[145]	1380	1	2	
Greer, Arthur		1		
Henery, Wm		1		
Henery, Samuel[146]		1		
Holton, John		1		
Kenedy [Kennedy], Andrew[147]	200	1	3	1
Keeble, Wm[148]		1		
McMurry, Wm	290	1		
McCulloch, John		1		
Moor, Thomas		1		
McCanles, John		1		
McCulloch, Saml		1	1	
Nicolson [Nicholson], John		1		
Partin, Samuel		1		
Phillips, Abraham	180	1		
Walker, Samuel		1		
Regan [Ragan], Ahimas[149]		1		
Regan, John[150]		1		
Regan, Charles			2	
Rider, John		1	1	
Rhea, Hugh		1	1	

[143]Revolutionary soldier born in 1758; drew a pension for his service in the Virginia militia; an original member of New Providence Church; one of the first justices of the peace; died July 4, 1840; his widow, Margaret Ewing, died March 4, 1849. Minutes, V. (February, 1840), VI, (November, 1843, November, 1844, April 2, 1849); McTeer, *New Providence Church*, 29; *Tennessee Pensioners*, 41; Minutes, March 14, 1796.

[144]Son of Josias Gamble, *infra*; commissioned ensign, Blount County militia, 1796. Moore, *Commissions*, 4.

[145]Progenitor of the prominent Gamble family of Blount County; a native of Chester County, Pa.; married Ann Gamwell. For an account of their descendants see A. Marion Gamble, *The Gamble Ancestry* ([Maryville?], 1909). The family settled at Gamble's Station, on Little River.

[146]Son of James Henry, Revolutionary soldier (1755-1791), and Jean McNabb, born October 12, 1777; lived on Little River near the mouth of Ellejoy Creek, and not to be confused with Samuel Henry of Bakers Creek; married Elizabeth Garner, daughter of John F. Garner *(q. v.);* died June 13, 1867. Henry Family Bible Record in Parham Papers; notes in compiler's collection.

[147]Revolutionary soldier born 1751; died May 5, 1834; received a pension for his service in the North Carolina line; he and his wife, Rachel Penny Kennedy, are buried at Baker's Creek Cemetery; trustee, Maryville Female Academy; operated early grist and saw mill on Little River. Minutes, V, 44 (October 5, 1834, December 12, 1796); Rev. War Pens. File.

[148]Revolutionary soldier born 1755, presumably in Fauquier County, Va.; died December 30, 1834. Rev. War Pens. File, W 1 880; Minutes, V, 56 (March 26, 1833).

[149]Commissioned ensign, Blount County militia, 1801. Moore, *Commissions*, 5.

[150]Commissioned ensign, Blount County militia, 1795. Carter, *Territorial Papers*, IV, 469.

	[1]	[2]	[3]	[4]
Rhea, James		1		
Ragin, Benj	1			
Snider, John	1			
Snider, George[151]	1			
Smith, Andrew	1	1		
Taylor, James	1			
White, David		1		
Wier, Samuel	532			
Weir, John	300	1		
Walker, John[152]		1		
Wilson, Isaac		1	1	

CAPTAIN—JAMES—ALESON'S COMPANY FOR THE YEAR 1801.

	[1]	[2]	[3]	[4]
Allan [Allen], James[153]	50			
Akin [Aiken, Eaken], Saml		1		
Alensan, Robert		1		
Alkenson [Allison], John[154]	200	1	1	
Brown, David	100	1		
Bowerman, Michel	300	1		
Boen [Bowen], Wm	100			
Baker, Wm	50	1		
Blankinship, Isom	100			
Baker, Charles	220			
Brown, Elija		1		
Boyd, Alexander		1		
Cowan, Arch[155]	300	1		
Canedy [Kennedy], Walter	60	1		
Clemans, John		1		
Cochain [Cochran], James[156]		1		
Ford, Alex	200	1		
Gillaspie, Alex		1		
Gillaspie, Zacharia		1		
Ghormley, Joseph	100	1		
Gamble, Andw	350	1		

---

[151]Born in Shenandoah County, Va., January 1, 1769; commissioned cornet in cavalry volunteers, Blount County militia, 1796; became a prominent Baptist preacher in Blount, and in 1821 moved to Monroe County, where he died August 31, 1846. Moore, *Commissions*, 5; sketch in J. J. Burnett, *Sketches of Tennessee's Pioneer Baptist Preachers* (Nashville, 1919), 486-88.

[152]Commissioned lieutenant, Blount County militia, 1796. Moore, *Commissions*, 5.

[153]One of a colony of Quakers who settled in the section around present Friendsville; died December 10, 1815. The Newberry Monthly Meeting (now Friendsville) was established May 14, 1808; however, Lost Creek Monthly Meeting (in Jefferson County) on January 24, 1801, "granted Friends of Lower Settlement the privilege of holding meetings every First Day excepting the one following monthly meetings." The records of Newberry Monthly Meeting are published in William Wade Hinshaw (ed.), *Encyclopedia of American Quaker Genealogy*, 6 vols. (Ann Arbor, 1936), I, 1137-63. Hereafter referred to as Hinshaw.

[154]Commissioned captain, Blount County militia, 1800. Moore, *Commissions*, 4.

[155]Deputy clerk, 1796. Minutes, June 13, 1796.

[156]Commissioned ensign, Blount County militia, 1800. Moore, *Commissions*, 4.

	[1]	[2]	[3]	[4]
Gray, Wm	300	1		
Gibson, John	300	1		
Gailey, James[157]		1	1	
Gibson, Andw		1		
Gibson, Thomas[158]		1		
Hussey, Christopher	250	1		
Hall, Andw		1		
Hackney, Hugh[159]		1		
Husse [Hussey], Elija	200	1		
Ish, Elizabeth[160]	640			
Jones, Johnston[161]	100	1		
Jones, Thomas[162]	100	2		
Jones, Samuel[163]		1		
James, Samuel		1		
Jones, Francis	100	1		
Johnston, John Junr		1		
Jones, Ann	200			
Jones, Pistimas		1		
Knox, Joseph		1		
Lackey, Andw		1		
McCalister [McAllister, McCallister], John	600	1		
Montgomery, Humphrey	300	1		
Matthes [Matthews], James[164]	640			
Matthes, Jonathan		1		
Mardick [Murdock], Wm	90	1		
McCulley, Solloman	300	1		
McCulley, Robert		1		
Oatts, David		1	1	
Osburn [Osborne], Alexander	100	1		
Rogers, James	100	1		
Russle, James		1		

---

[157]Commissioned ensign, Blount County militia, 1800. *Ibid.*, 4.

[158]Operated "a public grist mill on his own land on Galaher [*sic*] Creek." Minutes, September 14, 1795.

[159]One of a colony of Quakers who settled near Friendsville; born October 21, 1779, and died November 11, 1814. Hinshaw, I, 1141.

[160]Widow of John Ish, who was killed by Indians in 1794 at Ish's Station on the Holston (Tennessee) River at which place John Sevier made his headquarters during the Indian campaigns of 1793. John Ish was reputed to have been a native of Holland; came to America from England and settled in Cumberland County, Pa.; served as a private in Second Company, Seventh Batallion, Cumberland County militia; married Elizabeth Kepener on May 5, 1782, in Greenwood Township; received North Carolina grants Nos. 973 and 974, dated December 26, 1791, for a total of 840 acres of land "in Green [*sic*] County on South Side of Holston [Tennessee] River." Elizabeth Ish died July 22, 1821. Ramsey, *Annals*, 370, 422, 564-65, 579, 581, 583-84, 587; Deeds, I, 121, 134.

[161]A Quaker, died June 14, 1831. Hinshaw, I, 1143.

[162]A Quaker who was born July 9, 1734, and died January 19, 1823. His wife, Jane, was born March 30, 1748, and died July 16, 1825. *Ibid.*

[163]A Quaker who was born September 12, 1775, and died September 14, 1859; his wife, Joanne, was born June 22, 1780. *Ibid.*

[164]Revolutionary soldier born December 10, 1750, in North Carolina where he served in the militia; married Susannah Laughlin; died January 25, 1802, and is buried in the Friends Cemetery at Friendsville. Rev. War Pens. File.

	[1]	[2]	[3]	[4]
Rhodes, George	200	1		
Reid, Samuel	600	1		
Small, William		1		
Shaw, Samuel		1	1	
Smart, Francis	200	1	3	
Wilson, David		1		
Watson, James	300	1		
Woody, John	100	1		
Walker, John	150	1		

CAPTAIN DeARMAND'S COMPANY FOR THE YEAR 1801.

	[1]	[2]	[3]	[4]
Baugher [Boyer], Jacob	150	1		
Brumley, Barnet	100			
Barelet [Bartlett], Joseph[165]		1		
Brim, Edmond		1		
Boghard [Bogart], Cornelius		1		
Carter, Mcaja [Micajah]		1		
Chanler [Chandler], Richd	80	1		
Caldwell, Thomas	50	1	1	
Charles, Isaac		1		
Cawood, Moses		1	1	
Cochain, John[166]		1	1	
Doherty [Dougherty], John	100	1		
DeArmand, David[167]	100	1		
DeArmand, Richd[168]	150	1		
DeArmand, Saml[169]		1		
Edington, John	100	1		
Frew, Archd		1		
Glass, Samuel[170]	350	1	1	
Gillaspie, Alex		1		
Gillaspie, Wm		1		
George, Samuel		1	1	
Houston, James	300	1	1	

---

[165]Lived near the Knox County line at Bartlett's Mill, named for Nicholas Bartlett, who established a mill early on Stock Creek; commissioned ensign, Knox County militia, 1796. Roulstone, *Laws,* 60; Moore, *Commissions,* 21.

[166]Commissioned ensign, Blount County militia, 1795. Carter, *Territorial Papers,* IV, 469.

[167]Son of Thomas and Mary Flenniken DeArmond of Mecklenburg County, N. C.; removed to Mississippi, and then to Feliciana Parish, La. Information from R. C. d'Armand, Knoxville.

[168]Brother of David DeArmond *(supra)* and Samuel DeArmond *(infra);* in 1792, as a corporal he was in command of Ish's Station; commissioned ensign, 1797, lieutenant, 1799, captain, 1799, Blount County militia; removed to Lawrence County, Ala., where he died in 1819. Ramsey, *Annals,* 565; Moore, *Commissions,* 4; information from R. C. d'Armand.

[169]Removed to Mississippi, then to Feliciana Parish, La. *Ibid.*

[170]One of the commissioners to lay out Maryville; commissioned first major, Blount County militia, 1795; member of Constitutional Convention of 1796, representing Blount County; senator from Blount and Sevier counties in Third General Assembly, 1799. Roulstone, *Laws,* 60; Carter, *Territorial Papers,* IV, 469; Ramsey, *Annals,* 650; Hamer, *Tennessee: A History,* 4 vols. (New York, 1933), II, 999.

	[1]	[2]	[3]	[4]
Hudson, Richd	100	1		
Hanna, Andw	150			
Hanna, Robert Junr		1		
Hanna, Robert Senr		1		
Harris, Samuel		1		
Jones, Lewis	228	1		
Irvin, Robert		1		
Irvin, James		1		
Kirbey, Richd	100		3	
Kirbey, Joseph		1	2	
Loveless, David		1		
Liddy, John		1		
Lackey, Jas. W. for Maj. Lackey	800	2	2	
McClure, Charles	150	1		
Moor, Mary			1	
McCulloch, Thomas[171]			3	1
McCullock, James		1		
Maxwell, Mary			1	
Pearce, Robert	200	1		
Pearce, James	200	1		
Pearce, John		1		
Rogers, John	100	1		
Rogers, Isaac		1		
Rogers, Reuben[172]		1		
Rankin, John	300	1		
Stockton, Marshall		1		
Singleton, John[173]	500	1	2	
Thornhill, Armsted	100	1		
Wheller [Wheeler], Wm	200	1		
Woods, Patrick		1		
Woods, Joseph Junr		1		
Woods, John		1		
Willis, James	100			

State of Tennessee
Blount County   The within is the amount of the tax and taxable property returned to my office for the year 1801.

Attest   J. Houston C. B. C.

[Endorsed]
House Representatives Octr 10th 1801
Referd to the Committee on Finance
Ed Scott Clerk
In Senate 0th Octr 1801
Read and refered as above
G Roulstone Clk

[171]Commissioned justice of the peace, Knox County, 1792; also of Blount County upon its creation in 1795; operated a mill on Little River near present Rockford. Carter, *Territorial Papers*, IV, 449, 469; Minutes, September 15, 1795.
[172]Commissioned ensign, 1799, lieutenant, 1800, Blount County militia. Moore, *Commissions*, 5.
[173]Commissioned captain, Knox County militia, 1792; ensign, 1795, and first major, 1796, Blount County militia; name is perpetuated in Singleton's Station. Carter, *Territorial Papers*, IV, 449, 469; Moore, *Commissions*, 5.

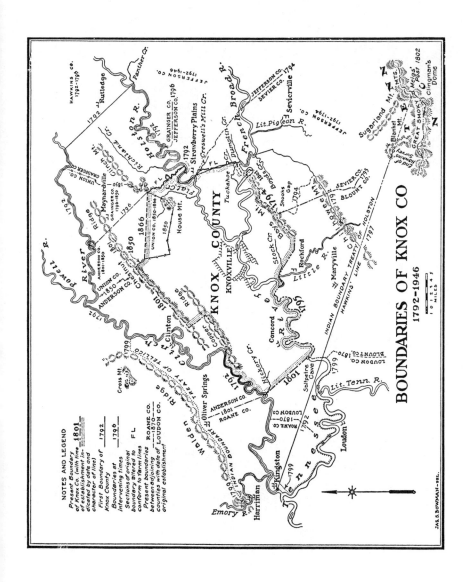

BOUNDARIES OF KNOX CO
1792–1946

NOTES AND LEGEND

Present Boundary
of Knox Co. (with time 1801
of establishment in-
dicated by date and
character of line)

First Boundary of 1792
Knox County

Boundaries at 1796
intervening times

Sections of original
boundary altered to FL
conform to war lines

Present boundaries
between adjoining ROANE CO.
counties with date of —1870—
original establishment LOUDON CO.

JAS. S. BOWMAN—DEL.

EARLY EAST TENNESSEE TAXPAYERS

Compiled by Pollyanna Creekmore

III, Knox County, 1806[1]

Knox County was one of the first two counties created by the territorial government at Knoxville, on June 11, 1792.[2] The land was taken from Hawkins[3] and Greene Counties.[4] In 1795 Blount County was taken from Knox;[5] and in 1796 Grainger County[6] was taken from Knox and Hawkins; in 1801 Roane County was cut off,[7] and in the same year Anderson County was created from Knox and Grainger counties.[8] Not until 1850 was any other territory removed. In that year Union County was created from portions of Knox, Grainger, Anderson, Claiborne, and Campbell counties.[9] Upon its creation Knox County was a part of Washington District, but on March 12, 1793, along with Jefferson County,[10] it was made a part of the newly-created Hamilton District.[11]

For the settlement and early history the reader is referred to the East Tennessee Historical Society's *The French Broad-Holston Country: A History of Knox County, Tennessee,* edited by Mary U. Rothrock (Knoxville, 1946).

The following tax lists for 1806 are the earliest extant lists for Knox County. The original book in which these lists are recorded is in the McClung Historical Collection, Lawson McGhee Library, Knoxville.

No attempt has been made to make extensive identification of the names on these lists, for the sources both printed and manuscript available for historical, biographical, and genealogical information on these early residents and landholders are extensive. The records of Knox County, with the exception of some loose papers, have been preserved and are available in the courthouse at Knoxville. Many of the marriage bonds and licenses

---

[1]For the introduction to this series see East Tennessee Historical Society's Publications (Knoxville), No. 23 (1951), 115-16. Hereafter cited E. T. H. S. *Publications.* In preparation of No. III, the compiler wishes to thank Mrs. Penelope Johnson Allen, Chattanooga; Laura E. Luttrell, Knoxville; and Prentiss Price, Rogersville, Tennessee.

[2]George Roulstone (comp.), *Laws of the State of Tennessee* (Knoxville, 1803), iv-v. Hereafter cited Roulstone, *Laws.*

[3]Edward Scott (comp.), *Laws of the State of Tennessee Including Those of North Carolina Now in Force From the Year 1715 to the Year 1820, Inclusive* (Knoxville, 1821), I, 378. Hereafter cited as Scott, *Laws.*

[4]*Ibid.*, 282.

[5]*Ibid.*, 60-61. See Blount County tax lists for 1801 in *Publications*, No. 24 (1952), 125-54.

[6]Scott, *Laws,* 95-97.

[7]*Ibid.*, 274

[8]*Ibid.* See Anderson County tax lists for 1802, in *Publications*, No. 23, 115-35.

[9]*Acts*, 1849-50 (ch. 61, sec. 1), 181.

[10]Jefferson County was created June 11, 1792, mostly from Greene County and a bit of Hawkins County. Roulstone, *Laws,* iv-v.

[11]*Ibid.*, vi.

were lost before they were recorded. The records in the county court clerk's office, including the minutes, wills, estate records, and marriages, are intact. The conveyances of property are kept in the office of register of deeds. The early conveyances, both warranty and trust deeds, are recorded in the same books, and are very well indexed. The records of the circuit and chancery courts are intact. The records of the supreme court excepting the last fifteen years have been moved to the new building of the Tennessee State Library and Archives at Nashville.

Typewritten copies of some of the early county records were made by the Tennessee Historical Records Survey. This project was initiated by the Work Projects Administration. The Tennessee State Library was the sponsoring agent with the University of Tennessee Library and the Daughters of the American Revolution Library as subscribers. At the end of the project the State Library was the only one with a complete set of the transcriptions, the other two libraries not having subscribed to certain items. The Survey also copied many church records and a few records in private ownership, some of them from Knox County.

The McClung Historical Collection has typewritten, photostatic, and microfilm copies of various records including microfilm copies of the population schedules of the federal decennial census records, 1830-1860, 1880. The census of 1850 has been published by Miss Laura E. Luttrell of Knoxville (Knoxville, 1951).

Very few Knox County records have been published. Some records were included in Mrs. Jeanette Tillotson Acklen's *Tennessee Records,* Vol. 1 (Nashville, 1933).

The county courts in Tennessee were authorized to levy a tax on property by a legislative act passed October 25, 1797,[12] in which the types of taxable property were listed and the method of taking the taxes was prescribed. Other acts were passed[13] amending minor provisions of this act, but it remained substantially the same until civil districts were established.

By the provisions of the act of 1797 white polls consisted of "all free males and male servants between the age of twenty one and fifty years"; slaves, "all slaves male and female, between the age of twelve and fifty years."

The general assembly on November 13, 1801, passed "An Act to authorize the court of Knox County to lay a tax for the building of a prison and stocks in Knoxville."[14]

---

[12]*Ibid.,* 114-20.
[13]*Ibid.,* 250; Scott, *Laws,* I, 829.
[14]Roulstone, *Laws,* 293.

On Saturday, October 10, 1805, the court "proceeded to lay a Court and Jail tax Year 1806 which is laid as follows to Wit—[15]

	County Tax	Jail Tax
On each hundred acre of land	.25	.12½
On each Taxable Free poll	.25	.12½
On each Taxable Slave	.50	.12½
On each Stud kept for covering Mares	.50	1.
On each Merchant, Hawker Or Pedlar	5.00	

There is a total of 1245 names on these lists, which is of interest in contrast to the total population of Knox County according to the "Schedule of the whole number of Persons in the District of Tennessee," 1801.[16]

Key to Column Numbers

[1] Number of acres
[2] Free polls
[3] Slaves
[4] Lots
[5] Studs

TAX LIST 1806.

1. CAPTN BOOTH'S COMPANY

Names	[1]	[2]	[3]	[4]	[5]
Allen and McCauley		1			
Anthony, John		1			
Allstot, Robert by N. Kearnes		1			
Adair, William		1			
Bright, John	200	1			1½
Bearden, Richard[17]		1	5	1	
Bickham, Gittig by James Park				½	
Booth, Edwin E.[18]		1		½	
Blount College Trustees by Samuel Carrick	2				
Brown, William		1			
Bartholomew, Joseph[19]		1			
Burk, Isham		1			
Crozier, John[20]		1	3		

[15]Knox County Minutes of Court of Pleas and Quarter Sessions (Courthouse, Knoxville). There are indexed, typewritten copies in Old Records Department, Courthouse, and University of Tennessee Library, Knoxville.
[16]See illustration, f. 106.
[17](1771-June 16, 1845); a native of Granville County, N.C.; removed to Tennessee in 1802; a Methodist; kept a tavern in Knoxville located on the site of the present Andrew Johnson Hotel. *Knoxville Register*, June 18, 1845.
[18]Married October 16, 1808, Mrs. Alice Murphy, widow of Dennis Murphy; died November 17, 1824. Wilson's *Knoxville Gazette*, Oct. 19, 1808; *Knoxville Register*, Nov. 19, 1824.
[19](1764-May 11, 1831); a saddler; Revolutionary soldier. *Knoxville Register*, May 18, 1831.
[20]See biography in Mary U. Rothrock (ed.), *The French Broad-Holston Country*, (Knoxville, 1946), 403-04; obituary in *Knoxville Register*, Sept. 19, 1838.

	[1]	[2]	[3]	[4]	[5]
Craighead, Robert[21]	500		1	1	
Cox, Lewis[22]		1	2		
Carter, William		1	1		
Charter, James	5	1			
Campbell, George W.[23]	2700	1	3	3½	
Campbell, Patrick[24]	3559¼	2	2	4⅞	
Campbell, James[25]		1			
Cowan, Nathaniel[26]	612	1	1	3	
Carter, Landon heirs[27] by James Charter				1	
Cormack, Edward		1			
Carrick, Samuel[28]	300	1	1		
Cash, Benjamin		1			
Dowler, Francis[29]		1		½	
Dardis, James[30]		1	2	½	
Deddle, John		1			
Davis, Amos		1			
Dardis, Thomas[31]		1			

[21](June 27, 1751-May 7, 1821); captain in the Revolutionary War in Mecklenburg County, N.C.; removed to Tennessee, 1789; justice of the peace; elder in the First Presbyterian Church, Knoxville, in whose cemetery he is buried; married, 1773, Hannah Clark. James Geddes Craighead, *The Craighead Family: a Genealogical Memoir of the Descendants of Rev. Thomas and Margaret Craighead, 1658-1876* (Philadelphia, 1876), 74-75; *Knoxville Register*, May 15, 1821.

[22](Nov. 21, 1768-Nov. 18, 1833); a native of North Carolina; removed to Tennessee, 1796; married Nov. 9, 1809, Emily Holt, daughter of Robert Holt *(q.v.);* lived on Kingston Pike at present Ten Mile Creek. *Knoxville Register*, Nov. 20, 1833.

[23](Feb. 9, 1769-Feb. 17, 1848); a native of the parish of Tongue, Scotland; emigrated with his parents to North Carolina in 1772; graduated from Princeton College, 1794; admitted to bar in North Carolina, and began practice in Knoxville; removed to Nashville where he had a long and distinguished career as a congressman, statesman, diplomat. *Dictionary of American Biography*, 21 vols. and index (New York, 1928-1944), III, 452; also articles and edited documents by Weymouth T. Jordan in E.T.H.S. *Publications*, Nos. 10 (1938), 13 (1941), 15 (1943), 19 (1947).

[24]A merchant; married July 3, 1800, Rhoda Ingles, daughter of Thomas and Eleanor (Grills) Ingles. George F. Mellen, "Thomas Ingles Again," *Knoxville* (Tenn.)*Sentinel*, Feb. 8, 1916.

[25](1772-Oct., 1837); merchant; in 1802 he advertised goods "from Baltimore . . . at his Store adjoining the Printing Office"; cashier, Branch Bank of Tennessee; elder, First Presbyterian Church. *Knoxville Gazette*, Aug. 4, 1802; *Knoxville Register*, Nov. 8, 1837.

[26](1763-Aug. 2, 1830); one of first two merchants of Knoxville; native of Ireland; died at Salem, Franklin County, Tenn. *Knoxville Register*, Aug. 11, 1830.

[27](1760-June 5, 1800); Revolutionary soldier; North Carolina entry taker; treasurer of Washington and Hamilton districts; resident of Carter County, Tenn., which was named in his honor; the county seat, Elizabethton named for his wife Elizabeth Maclin (1765-Feb. 27, 1842). For accounts of the Carter, Maclin, and related families see Octavia Zollicoffer Bond, *The Family Chronicle and Kinship Book* . . . (Nashville, 1928); Revolutionary War Pension File (National Archives, Washington, D. C.), W 900; Zella Armstrong, *Notable Southern Families*, 5 vols. (Chattanooga, 1918-1928), II, 61-74.

[28](July 17, 1760-Aug. 17, 1809); pastor, Lebanon Presbyterian Church; president, Blount College. *French Broad-Holston Country*, 392-93.

[29]Merchant; in 1803 the firm of Dowler and Shall was located "opposite Mr. Hayne's [*sic*] tavern." *Knoxville Gazette*, Oct. 31, 1803.

[30](July 26, 1766-Dec. 25, 1846). *French Broad-Holston Country*, 407-09.

[31]Lawyer; brother of James Dardis *(q.v.)* French *Broad-Holston Country*, 407-08; *Wilson's Knoxville Gazette*, March 17, 23, April 29, 1810.

	[1]	[2]	[3]	[4]	[5]
Dade, Townsend[82] by James Trimble			1		
Echel, Charles		1			
Fournier, N.H.S.[83] estate by James Charter				½	
Formwalt, Jacob		1		1	
Ferquhason, Robert		1			
Fleshart, Francis[84]		1		½	
Greer, Joseph by James Charter	410	2	9	4	
Grant [Rosicrans], Richard Rosey		1			
Glade, August		1			
Gamble, John N.[85]		1		2	
Haynes, Stephen[86]			5	1	
Hart, Robert		1			
Henley, David[87] by Hugh Stewart	970			15	
Hindman, James				1	
Hood, John B.[88]		1	1		
Hewitt, Nathaniel[89]		1			
Humes, Thomas[40]	770	1	2	2½	
Hillsman, John[41]	1576	1	1	5	
Harralson, William		1			
Hunt, Willson by James Charter	1½				
Johnston, Noble		1			
Johnston, Christopher		1	2		

[82]An attorney from King George County, Va., who practised a few years in East Tennessee and returned to Virginia.

[83]A native of France; physician; during the last illness of William Blount, Dr. Fournier lived in Blount's home; however, he preceded Blount in death.

[84]From Botetourt County, Va., where he married May 6, 1794, Elizabeth Wysong; died before 1812; his daughter, Elizabeth, married Henry Watterson of Hawkins County. Lewis Preston Summers, *Annals of Southwest Virginia, 1769-1800* (Abingdon, 1929), 509.

[85]A native of Pennsylvania; brought to Tennessee by Francis Alexander Ramsey as a tutor in his family; deputy county court clerk; lived on lot No. 32 in Knoxville; later removed to Fourth Creek at site of the present Bearden; died Nov. 14, 1818; his widow married John Hooke of Roane County, Tenn. James Gettys McGready Ramsey, Autobiography (MSS., typed copy, McClung Collection, Lawson McGhee Library, Knoxville), 14; *Knoxville Register*, Nov. 17, 1818.

[86]Tavern keeper, at the "Sign of General Washington on Cumberland Street." *Knoxville Gazette*, Aug. 4, 1802.

[87]Agent of U. S. War Department. *French Broad-Holston Country*, 426-28; Samuel C. Williams, "Colonel David Henley," E.T.H.S. *Publications*, No. 18 (1946), 3-24.

[88]Printer; first printed the *Camden* (S. C.) *Intelligencer* in 1803; he came to Tennessee from Lincoln County, N. C., and in 1805 he published at Greeneville, the *Tennessee Express and Greeneville Monitor;* in 1806 he was printing *The Knoxville Gazette;* later he published at Rogersville, *The East Tennessee Gazette*, and the *Western Pilot;* in 1816 he removed to Huntsville, Ala., where he printed the *Huntsville Gazette.*

[89]A saddler.

[40]Early merchant; his son, Thomas W. Humes, became president of the University of Tennessee. *French Broad-Holston Country*, 431-32.

[41](Nov. 17, 1764-Dec. 8, 1850); a native of Amelia County, Va., where though a youth he served in the Revolutionary War; came to Tennessee and taught school at the Cumberland Settlement (present Nashville); returned to East Tennessee about 1793 and opened a store; about 1809 he removed to a farm on Third Creek in Knox County. *Knoxville Register*, Dec., 12, 19, 1850; J. J. Burnett, *Sketches of Tennessee's Pioneer Baptist Preachers* (Nashville, 1919), 231-33.

	[1]	[2]	[3]	[4]	[5]
King, William by John Crozier	200				
King and Crozier				4	
King, William and Co.		1			
Kearnes [Karns, Carnes], Nicholas		1	1	1¼	
Kimbull, John		1			
Lavender, John[42]	518	1	1	1¾	
Lareau [Larew], George		1			
Laton [Leighton], Patrick		1			
Long, William		1			
McCorrey, Thomas[43]		1	1	1	
Maclin, William[44] by Thomas McCorry				1	
May, Francis[45] by Thomas McCorry				1½	
McGhee, James		1			
McAffry, Terrence[46]		1		1½	
Morrow, William[47]	201	1		1	
McGuire, Patrick[48]		1			
McCay, Spruce[49] by James Charter	4280				
Miller, Pleasant M.[50]	5600	1	7	2	
Nickoll, Josiah[51]		1	1	1½	
Parker, Benjamin C.				1	
Park, James and William[52]	400	4	3	4	

[42](1773-April 1, 1826); married Feb. 11, 1796, Polly Gilliam, daughter of Devereaux Gilliam; removed to Philadelphia, Roane (now Loudon) County, Tenn. *Knoxville Register*, April 10, 1826.

[43]Owned the "Eagle Bend" Farm, in Anderson County; removed to Davidson, later Madison County, Tenn.

[44]Secretary of state of Tennessee, 1796-1810; died at his farm in Blount County, Tenn., Sept. 24, 1810. Bond, *Family Chronicle and Kinship Book, passim;* Wilson's *Knoxville Gazette*, Sept. 29, 1810.

[45]A physician; resident of Nashville; married Mary McConnell, daughter of General James and Mary (Lawson) White; died at Nashville, Nov. 28, 1817; his widow married Judge John Overton, July 28, 1820. *Knoxville Register*, Dec. 9, 1817; Aug. 1, 1820.

[46](1770-April 8, 1830); a cabinet maker; he and his wife Martha (Patsy) Clopton McAffry are buried in the First Presbyterian Church Cemetery, Knoxville. *Knoxville Register*, April 14, 1830.

[47]Born Derry County, Ireland, Jan. 3, 1759; died March 24, 1830; buried First Presbyterian Church Cemetery; his wife was Isabelle Mebane, born Guilford Court House, N. C., March 7, 1781; died Sept. 17, 1854. *Knoxville Register*, March 31, 1830; tombstone inscriptions.

[48]Died Nov. 8, 1831, in Jefferson County, Tenn.; married a sister of Joseph Prigmore. *Knoxville Register*, Nov. 23, 1831.

[49]Resident of Salisbury, N. C.; son-in-law of Judge Richard Henderson and preceptor of Andrew Jackson.

[50]Lawyer, judge; a native of Campbell County, Va.; of Quaker parentage; married Mary Louisa Blount, daughter of Governor William and Mary Grainger Blount; after the death of Gov. Blount, he became guardian of Barbara Blount; removed to "Holly Hill," Madison County, Tenn., 1825; died in Gibson County, Apr. 26, 1849. *French Broad-Holston Country.* 456-57.

[51]A merchant of Knoxville; removed to Nashville where he was president of the Nashville Branch of the Bank of the United States; died May 31, 1833. *Impartial Observer* (Knoxville), Sept. 10, 1800; *Knoxville Register*, June 12, 1833.

[52]Brothers who were natives of County Donegal, Ireland; came to Knoxville in 1796, where they were life-long merchants; their firm's account books, 1803-46, are in the McClung Collection, Lawson McGhee Library; William Park died Aug. 31, 1846; James Park, Sept. 19, 1853. James Park, *The Family Record of James Park, Deceased, From His Marriage in 1804 down to March, 1907* (Knoxville, 1907); Armstrong, *Notable Southern Families*, III, 87-108.

	[1]	[2]	[3]	[4]	[5]
Pritchett, Ephraim[53]		1			
Purris, John[54]		1			
Rawlings, Moses[55]		1			
Rhea, John[56]	520			2	
Reynolds, John		1			
Roulstone, George[57] estate by John Lavender	553		2	1½	
Roe, Walter ass.				1	
Reed, Henry		1			
Scott, Edward[58]		1	2	½	
Strong, Joseph C.[59]		1	1	½	
Strong, David		1			
Saunders, John		1		1	
Sharp, Jesse	100	1	1	1	
Steel, Samuel		1			
Sharpless, Jesse by James Park	200				
Sharky, Thomas	40	1			
Shawl, George		1			
Thatcher [Ellen] Widow by N. Kearnes				½	
Tinley, John		1		1	
Trimble, James[60]		1		½	
Webb, John[61]		1	2	2	
Wetzell, John H.[62]		1		1	
Wolf, George		1			
Whiteside, Jenkin[63]	40			1	
Wilson, George[64]		1	3	1	
Woods, Eathen by James Charter	38¼				

---

[53]A captain; merchant of Nashville, died Sept. 15, 1822. *Knoxville Register,* Sept. 24, 1822.

[54]A prominent resident of Kingston; died September, 1829; ruling elder and first clerk of session, Bethel Presbyterian Church.

[55]Tavern keeper at the "Sign of the Indian King." *Knoxville Gazette,* Oct. 31, 1803.

[56]Congressman (1753-May 27, 1832); of Sullivan County, Tenn. See Marguerite B. Hamer, "John Rhea of Tennessee," E.T.H.S. *Publications,* No. 4 (1932), 35-44; also in her *Cameos of the South* (Philadelphia, 1940), 63-75.

[57]Publisher and editor of the *Knoxville Gazette,* the first printer in the territory now the state of Tennessee; first postmaster of Knoxville. Samuel C. Williams, "George Roulstone: Father of the Tennessee Press," E.T.H.S. *Publications,* No. 17 (1945), 51-60; *Knoxville Gazette,* Aug. 15, 1804; *French Broad-Holston Country,* 476-78.

[58](1772-Aug. 8, 1852); lawyer, jurist; compiler of *Laws of the State of Tennessee* (Scott's Revisal) (Knoxville, 1821); removed to Mississippi. *French Broad-Holston Country,* 481-82.

[59](Oct. 3, 1775-Nov. 3, 1844); physician and prominent citizen of Knoxville. *French Broad-Holston Country,* 492-93; *Knoxville Register,* Nov. 13, 1844.

[60]Attorney; married Nov. 10, 1808, Letitia Clark, daughter of Thomas Norris Clark of Southwest Point (Kingston, Tenn.). Wilson's *Knoxville Gazette,* Nov. 16, 1808.

[61]Born Sept. 19, 1776, in Cumberland County, Pa.; died Knoxville, Oct. 28, 1848, and buried in cemetery of First Presbyterian Church; married first, Rebecca, daughter of George McNutt *(q.v.),* owned and operated an early brickyard and tannery; built a home which is still standing (1954) at the southwest corner of State Street and Hill Avenue. Tombstone instriptions; *Knoxville Register,* Nov. 1, 8, 1848.

[62]Hatter of Knoxville. *Impartial Observer,* May 28, 1800.

	[1]	[2]	[3]	[4]	[5]
White, Moses[65]	800½	1	2		

2. CAPTAIN BISHOP'S COMPANY

Names	[1]	[2]	[3]	[4]	[5]
Allbright, John	60				
Byram, Ebenezer, Senior[66]	213		1		
Byram, Ebenezer, Junior		1			
Bishop, Jacob		1			
Bayless, Hezekiah[67]	1022	1			
Bowman, John	140				
Braden, James[68]		1			
Braden, James Junior		1			
Bayles, John[69]	255	1			
Bishop, Matthew	400				
Bishop, Joseph		1			
Bishop, Stephen	300	1	1		
Bradshaw, Joseph		1			
Bayles, Daniel	196	1			
Bayles, George	100	1			
Carmichael, John	92	1			
Caldwell, Alexander[70]	400	1			
Caldwell, Benjamin		1			
Copeland, William	350				
Cartwright, William		1			
Cartwright, John		1			
Crippen, John	30	1			
Carmichael, Hugh	367				
Carmichael, Hugh Junior	75	1			
Copeland, Douglass		1	1		
Copeland, David			1		
Elliot, Thomas	171	1			
Elliot, Jacob	2	1			

---

[63]Lawyer; moved to Nashville; became U. S. senator; died Sept. 24, 1822, in Russel's Valley, Ala. *Knoxville Intelligencer*, Oct. 8, 1822. At the time of his death he held large holdings of real estate in Tennessee, including the tavern at Bean's Station in Grainger County.

[64]Printer; publisher of *Wilson's Knoxville Gazette;* state senator; married in Knoxville, Dec. 31, 1799, Mrs. Margery (Greer) Johnson; removed to Nashville, where he printed the *Nashville Gazette;* a prominent Mason; died Nov. 10, 1848.

[65](April 22, 1775-May 30, 1830); son of James and Mary Lawson White; married Isabella McNutt, daughter of George McNutt *(q.v.)*. *Knoxville Register*, June 2, 1830;*Knoxville Chronicle*, June 2, 1830.

[66]Progenitor of a family which settled first in Greene County, while still a part of Washington County; one of the first settlers on Beaver Creek.

[67]A Revolutionary soldier who drew a pension; removed to Alabama.

[68]A Revolutionary soldier who served in North Carolina.

[69]Revolutionary War soldier who drew pension for service in Virginia militia. Rev. War Pension File.

[70](1755-May 24, 1830); Revolutionary War soldier. *Knoxville Register*, June 9, 1830.

	[1]	[2]	[3]	[4]	[5]
Elliot, Israel	383½				
Ellis, Francis	291	1			
Frazier, Julian[71]	25	1	1		
Frazier, Thomas		1			
Frazier, Samuel[72]	471				
Frazier, Beriah[73]	143	1	2		
Frake, Michael	200				
Gammon, Harris[74]	250	1			
Gilliam, Spencer[75]	100	1			
Garen, John		1			
Geron, Joseph	380	1			
Gammon, John	50	1			
Gammon, Lewis		1			
Gault, Thomas	300	1	1		
Gray, Leven	125	1			
Hall, Thomas[76]	150	1	1		
Hall, Thomas Junior		1			
Hinds, Levi	250		1		
Hamilton, James		1			
Hunter, James	1¼	1			
Hinds, Levi Junior	150	1	1		
Henderson, Peter		1			
Havenridge, John		1			
Hamilton, Francis	283				
Human, Bazel	100	1			
Jackson, Jeremiah		1			
Jones, Jesse	100	1			
Julian, Stephen	129	1			
Julian, Benjamin		1			
Kirkpatrick, John		1			
Lumpkins, Robert	340		2		
Lay, James		1			
McCloud, Andrew		1			
McClain, Andrew		1			
McCloud, Robert		1			
Maxwell, Hugh	582	1			
McCloud, James	200	1			
Majors, Smith	297	1	2		

[71]Son of Samuel Frazier, *infra;* removed to Paris, Henry County, Tenn.

[72]A Revolutionary soldier who served in Battle of King's Mountain, married Rebecca Julian; removed to Greene County where he was a member of New Hope Monthly Meeting, Society of Friends; died at present Bearden, Knox County; his remains have been reinterred in the Highland Memorial Cemetery nearby.

[73]Son of Samuel Frazier, *supra;* married first, Ann Rees; second, Barbara Gibbs, daughter of Nicholas Gibbs *(q.v.);* removed to Rhea County, Tenn.

[74](1757-Dec. 28, 1843); Revolutionary soldier. *Knoxville Register,* Jan. 10, 17, 1844.

[75]Son of Thomas Gilliam, who was killed by Indians near Raccoon Valley Station, May 25, 1793.

[76]Revolutionary soldier born Mar. 1, 1758, in Orange County, N. C., where he served as private in militia; married Sept. 25, 1783, Nancy Hays; died July 21, 1833; name is perpetuated in Hall's Cross Roads, Knox County. Rev. War Pension File; *Knoxville Republican,* Aug. 7, 1833.

	[1]	[2]	[3]	[4]	[5]
Owens, John	116				
Parker, Jesse	200				
Parker, Jonathan	300	1			1
Peery, George	884	1	4		
Ricketts, William		1			
Ricketts, Reuben		1			
Sidens, James	100	1			
Shell, Christian	300	1			
Sumpter, Thomas[77]		1			
Shoemaker, Evan	96	1			
Smith, Robert	100	1			
Smith, Henry		1			
Smith, Alexander	50				
Stephenson, Robert	25	1			
Tindell, William		1			
Tyler, Thomas		1			
Williams, Benjamin[78]	150				
Weatherly, Joseph		1			
Willson, Thomas		1			

3. CAPTAIN BOND'S COMPANY

Names	[1]	[2]	[3]	[4]	[5]
Able, John		1			
Able, Cain		1			
Andrew, Samuel		1			
Barger, Jacob	150	1			
Bond, Stephen	300	1			
Bond, William		1			
Brooks, Samuel		1			
Brooks, Joseph[79]	150	1			
Boyd, Thomas	180				
Cowan, Joseph	100				
Cannon, John	100		2		
Cannon, Zachariah	122	1			
Cannon, Robert		1			
Cannon, Bartlett[80]	84	1	1		
Campbell, David[81]	161	1	1		

[77]Revolutionary War soldier who drew pension for service in North Carolina militia.

[78]Revolutionary War soldier who drew pension for service in Virginia militia.

[79]Son of John and Ann (Irwin) Brooks; married in Knox County, Mary Gamble, daughter of Robert and Mary (McElroy) Gamble; moved to Rhea County in 1806; became a member of the first court and captain of the militia district; died in 1810. Penelope Johnson Allen, "Leaves from the Family Tree," *Chattanooga Times*, Dec. 3, 1933.

[80]Hatter living in Grassy Valley. *Knoxville Gazette*, Jan. 26, 1803.

[81]For identification of the various Campbells on these lists see Laura E. Luttrell, "Some Founders of Campbell's Station, Tennessee: A Genealogy of Alexander, David and James Campbell," *E.T.H.S. Publications*, No. 25 (1953), 89-110, No. 26 (1954), 107-31.

	[1]	[2]	[3]	[4]	[5]
Campbell, David	868		4		
Campbell, David Junior		1	2		
Campbell, William		1			
Campbell, James	478	1	1		
Campbell, James		1			
Cowan, James		1			
Douglass, William	320	1			
Gillespie, Jacob[82]	100				
Gillespie, Thomas	93	1			
Gamble, Robert[83]	245	3			
Gamble, John	195	1			
Gilbreath, John[84]	1200	2	3		1
Gour, Thomas	180				
Gour, William		1			
Givens, Samuel	510		3		
Hall, Hilard by Wm. Lackey		1			
Johnston and McClure	200	2		½	
Kerr, William	200	1			
Kerr, Andrew		1			
Lackey, William	100				
Love, Robert[85]	300				
Low, David	190	1			
Means, Robert		1			
Mims, Daniel	93	1			
McGill, David	622	1			
Martin, James		1			
Martin, George[86]	440				
McCollum, John		1			
Montgomery, James, estate	360	2			
Moor, Tenan		1			
McNeill, John[87]	1327	1	6	1	
McAllister, Charles		1			
McClellan, John	700	1	2		
McCaleb, Archibald[88]	350	1			
Nugent, James		1			
Pelham, John estate by Wm. Lackey	100				
Phibbs, Richard		1			
Priggmore, Joseph[89]	100		2		
Russell, Matthew	350	1	1		

[82]Revolutionary War soldier who drew pension for service in Virginia militia.
[83]Revolutionary soldier born in Ireland in 1732 and came with his parents to Bucks County, Pa., then to Augusta County, Va.; an early settler of Knox County. See Allen, "Leaves from the Family Tree," *loc. cit.*, Dec. 3, 1933.
[84]Lived on Turkey Creek; buried in Pleasant Forest Cemetery.
[85]Died in 1825. *Knoxville Register*, July 3, 1844.
[86](1747-Dec. 16, 1823); one of the first settlers in Grassy Valley. *Knoxville Register*, Jan. 9, 1824.
[87](c1743-July 23, 1833). *Knoxville Register*, July 31, 1833.
[88]Native of South Carolina; one of the founders of Campbell's Station; Revolutionary soldier; died Sept. 16, 1813. *Wilson's Knoxville Gazette*, Sept. 27, 1813.
[89]From Pennsylvania where he married *circa* 1780, Keziah Moore; died in Roane County, c1818.

	[1]	[2]	[3]	[4]	[5]
Rogers, Joseph	300	1	1		
Roane, Archibald[90]	414	1	4		
Russell, Andrew	466	1			
Smith, John	200	1			
Smith, Joshua		1	1		
Swan, George	150	1			
Sheerer, Peter by George Swan	242				
Sterns, George	118½	1	2		
Townsend, Taylor[91]	207	1	1		
Vickers, James	150	1			
Wells, Rosegill		1			
Whiteman, John		1			
Wallace, David B.		1			

4. CAPTAIN BOYD'S COMPANY

Names	[1]	[2]	[3]	[4]	[5]
Adamson, Simeon	115				
Bales, John	157¼	1			
Bales, Jacob	93¾	1			
Boyd, William	100		1		
Boyd, John[92]		1			
Bean, Jacob		1			
Blackley, Charles	146				
Brown, Felix[93]	200	1			
Brown, William	200		4		
Brown, John		1			
Blue, Douglass	69	1			
Bales, Purnell	70	1			
Bowman, Samuel	400	1	1		
Clift, James	75	1			
Callen, Charles	200				
Callen, John		1			
Camron, Agness	150				
Cook, John		1			
Douglass, Edward	200	1			
Dodd, Josiah[94]	185		1		
Evans, Joseph	200	1			
Fulton, Hugh	100	1			

[90]Second governor of Tennessee (1801-1802); name is perpetuated in Roane County, Tenn. *Knoxville Register*, Jan. 22, 1819; *Western Monitor* (Knoxville), Jan. 12, 1819; *Dictionary of American Biography*, XV, 640-41; for genealogy, William Henry Egle, *Pennsylvania Genealogies; Scotch-Irish and German* (Harrisburg, 1886), 539-44.

[91]From Augusta County, Va.; operated a ferry on Holston (Tennessee) River; died 1832.

[92](1776-Sept. 15, 1846); a captain of militia. *Knoxville Standard*, Sept. 22, 1846.

[93]Married daughter of Gawen Leeper of Hawkins County; lived in McPheeters Bend, Hawkins County, 1787; son of William Brown *(infra)*.

[94]Married Mary Luttrell, daughter of Richard Luttrell of Amherst County, Va.

	[1]	[2]	[3]	[4]	[5]
George, James		1			
Grant, Thomas	100	1			
Huntsman, Jacob			2		
Hadley, William	50				
Howell, David W.	900	1			
Harralson, James	255	1			
Hippingstall, Joseph	190				
Hackney, Benjamin	441	1	1		
Lavis, John		1			
Longwith, Reuben	289	1			
Leaky, William	331½				
Leaky, John		1			
Luttrell, William	150	1			
Leaky, Levy	565	1			
Mulvany, William		1			
Mulvany, Clary	100				
Manifold, Benjamin[95]	1250				
McMillin, John	200	1			
Mason, James	50				
Manifold, George		1			
McMahon, John	130	1			
Mowry, Peter	300	1			
McClure, Robert	146	1			
McMillan, Alexander[96]	2420½		2		
Moon, Jonah	400	1			
Newman, Edmond	147	1			
Pursley, William	450	1	3		
Patton, Thomas	150	1			
Roberts, Jacob	302¼	1			
Roberts, Moses	100	1			
Raper, Jacob		1			
Ruth, Edward	256	1			
Ransbarger, John	100	1			
Scott, Wilson	250	1			
Stanley, Joseph	100	1			
Smith, John		1			
Steel, Peter	170				
Sample, Samuel[97]	183				
Taylor, Andrew		1			
Todd, Samuel	120	1	1		
Underwood, John	128¾	1			
Underwood, George	100	1			

---

[95]A native of York County, Pa.; came to Knox County about 1797 settling on the French Broad River where a station was established; operated a mill in which he was fatally injured, Sept. 23, 1820; a brother-in-law of Abraham McCleary *(q.v.)*. J. B. Manifold, *The Story of Benjamin and Annabel Manifold and Their Environments and Descendants* (Greenacres, Wash., 1953).

[96](1750-Aug. 23, 1837); Revolutionary soldier. *Knoxville Register*, Aug. 30, 1837; for account of family see Armstrong, *Notable Southern Families*, I, 152-66; also Luttrell, "Some Founders of Campbell Station," *loc. cit.*

[97]Revolutionary soldier who drew a pension for his service in Virginia militia.

	[1]	[2]	[3]	[4]	[5]
White, James	100				
White, John		1			1
White, James, Junior	130	1			
Walker, George[98]	100	1			
Walker, Prudence	400				
Witt, John, Senior[99]	150		2		
Witt, Jesse	166	1			
Watt, Joseph	300				

5. CAPTAIN CHILES COMPANY

Names	[1]	[2]	[3]	[4]	[5]
Ayres, David	640	1			
Ayres, Chastity	516				
Armstrong, Joseph		1			
Chiles, Roland[100]	609	1	3		
Chiles, John[101]	50	1			
Childress, John	130	1			
Crain, Benjamin		1			
Council, Hodges	200	1	1		
Council, Jesse[102]	230				
Council, John	210	1			
Council, Matthew	100	1			
Council, Isaac		1			
Davis, George	100	1			
Farmer, David	100	1			
Frost, Joseph	98	1			1
Fuson, Thomas	250	1			
Goad, Thomas		1			
Goad, William		1			
Grason, Jesse		1			
Hendrex, Garret	300				
Hendrex, Luke	200	1			
Hendrex, Morgan		1			
Haston, David	111	1			
Hall, Samuel	100	1			
Hackworth, Augustine[103]	50				
Johnston, Isaac		1			
Johnston, Francis	150				
Killion, Henry		1			
Litel, Andrew		1			

[98]Died Sept. 11, 1822. *Knoxville Register*, Sept. 24, 1822.
[99](1740-1825); Revolutionary soldier from Amherst County, Va.
[100]Died 1825 in Anderson Co., Tenn. *Knoxville Register*, Aug. 7, 1844.
[101]Captain in War of 1812. "Died recently in Anderson County." *Knoxville Register*, Dec. 30, 1846.
[102]Will probated Jan. 1831, Knox County, Tenn., Estate Book, V, 34.
[103]Revolutionary War soldier who previously had served with Virginia troops at Battle of Point Pleasant in Dunmore's War.

	[1]	[2]	[3]	[4]	[5]
Lea, Samuel	108	1			
Low, Aquilla Senior[104]	400		5		
Low, Aquilla Junior					
Low, Richard	293	1	1		
Low, Caleb	640	1			
Matheny, Luke	100				
Matheny, Robert		1			
Matheny, John		1			
Maybury, George[105]	460	1			
Nothren, William					
Pruitt, Isaac	390	1			
Read, Thomas	210	1	3		
Roane, William	600	1			
Roach, James	100	1			
Scott, James[106]	350	1			
Scott, Laurence	200	1			
Scott, Garrett		1			
Terry, Micaijah [sic]		1			
Willson, Richard	100				
Woolton, Richard		1			
Woolton, John		1			
Woolton, Benjamin		1			
Woolton, William	325				
Yarnell, Joseph[107]	150				
Yokeham, Jacob	240	1			

6. CAPTAIN CONWAY'S COMPANY

Names	[1]	[2]	[3]	[4]	[5]
Alldridge, Nathan	100				
Alldridge, William	97	1			
Bell, William[108]	500	1	2		
Bruar, William	200				
Bruar, John		1			
Branham, Edward		1			
Byram, Levi	86½	1			

[104]Will proved July, 1819; Caleb Low and John Callaway, executors. Estate Book, III, 99; *Knoxville Register*, July 6, 1819.

[105]Revolutionary soldier, born Oct. 1760, in New Jersey; died 1836 in Perry County, Ala. Rev. War Pension File.

[106]Revolutionary soldier who drew pension in Knox County for his service in Orange County, N. C.

[107](1764-Aug. 20, 1826); son of Daniel Yarnell, Sr., of Knox County; lived on Beaver Creek. *Knoxville Register*, Sept. 6, 1826. Allen, "Leaves from the Family Tree, *loc. cit.*, Sept. 29, 1935.

[108]Will proved Oct. 1813; member of family for whom Bell's Campground was named. On April 7, 1810, John Menifee made a deed to two acres of land lying north of Beaver Creek to John Childress *(q.v.)*, Soloman McCampbell, Jeremiah Tindall, Daniel Yarnell, Michael Yarnell, George Lucas, and Thomas Wilson, trustees, for the purpose of building a meeting house and campground to be free to all religious denominations. Knox County, Tenn., Estate Book, III, 67.

	[1]	[2]	[3]	[4]	[5]
Conner, William	91	1			
Conway, Charles		1			
Childress, Robert	340	1			
Childress, John¹⁰⁹	3870	1			
Childress, Mitchell¹¹⁰	264				
Childress, William		1			
Conner, William	120	1	1		
Cotterel, John		1			
Campbell, Lewis		1			
Cox, Curd¹¹¹		1	1		
Dever, James		1			
Duffell, William		1			
Elliott, James		1			
Edmonson, Samuel		1			
Foster, Michael		1			
Ferguson, James		1			1
Hanson, Jonathan		1			
Husbans, Harmon		1			
Hill, Henry					
Ingram, Purnell	474	1			
Julien, Rene	100	1			
Julien, John		1			
Jentry, Aaron		1			
Low, Robert		1			
Lucas, George	800	1			
Lucas, George for Peter B. Stuart	470				
Lucas, George for Betsy Sapping	470				
Lucas, George for Abigail Lucas	340				
Lucas, Robert	600				
Lewis, James		1			
Lawson, William		1			
Lawson, Robert		1			
Menefee, John¹¹²	1718	2	6		
McLane, Joseph	400	1			
Millican, James		1			
Millican, John	117	1			
McClean, Stephen		1			
McClean, William		1			
Narramore, John		1			
Ogg, Daniel		1			
Pate, Anthony		1			
Renshaw, John		1			

¹⁰⁹Revolutionary War soldier who drew a pension for service in the Virginia militia; in 1813 John Childress, Sr., lived on Bull Run about three miles above Thos. Manifee's Mill. *Wilson's Knoxville Gazette*, Oct. 25, 1813; Rev. War Pension File.

¹¹⁰Revolutionary War soldier who drew pension for service in North Carolina militia. Rev. War Pension File, S 426.

¹¹¹Revolutionary War pensioner, born 1762, in Charlotte County, Va. Rev. War Pension File, S 3169.

¹¹²See sketch in Samuel C. Williams, *History of the Lost State of Franklin* (Johnson City, 1927), 308.

	[1]	[2]	[3]	[4]	[5]
Renshaw, William		1			
Roysdon, Robert[112]		1			
Renshaw, Moses		1			
Roads, John		1			
Stowell, George	150				
Tindall, Jeremiah	150		1		
Tindall, Samuel	180	1			
Tivis, Robert for T. Hart	3000				
Woods, Ephraim	200	1			
Woods, Joseph	150	1			
Woods, Zebulan		1			
Williams, Jonathan		1			
Yarnell, Mordicai	67	1			

7. CAPTAIN COX'S COMPANY

Names	[1]	[2]	[3]	[4]	[5]
Buckner, Ricey		1			
Buckner, John		1			
Buckner, Presley[114]	200	1			
Bletcher, William	100				
Brannam, Edward		1			
Cox, Samuel	700	1	3		
Clayton, Jesse		1	1		
Campbell, Andrew		1			
Davis, Chesley		1			
Doyle, Stephen	100				
Davis, George		1			
Easly, Samuel	400	1			
Ellis, Robert	100	1			
George, Samuel		1			
George, Traverse	150	1			
Hankins, Abraham[115]	320	1			
Hambleton, Isaiah		1			
Hankins, David	250	1			
Hubbs, John	250	1			
Higgins, John	100	1			
Hankins, John		1			
Heath, William	123	1			
Isom, John		1			
Johnson, George	200	1			
Jones, Isaac		1			
Kizer, Peter		1			
Love, Joseph[116]		1			

[112]Also Risden; an early surveyor.
[114]Removed from Sullivan to Knox County, then to Indiana where he died.
[115]Revolutionary soldier who drew pension for service in Virginia militia.
[116](1779-June 3, 1831); died at his residence in the Southern Liberties of Washington, Rhea County. *Knoxville Register*, June 8, 1831.

	[1]	[2]	[3]	[4]	[5]
Mitchell, John		1	3		
Miller, John[117]	1076		3		
McBride, Pleasant	100	1			
Mitchell, William		1			
McPherson, Samuel		1			
Nation, Abraham		1			
Nation, Thomas	150				
Nation, Edward		1			
Newport, Richard	100				
Pate, Anthony		1			
Reames, Bartlett		1			
Smith, Robert		1			
Smith, Joseph		1			
Smith, Joel		1			
Skaggs, Charles Junior	50	1			
Skaggs, Charles Senior	100				
Skaggs, Eli	620	1			
Skaggs, James	170	1			
Vaughn, William		1			
Vaughn, Reuben		1			
Willson, Jeremiah	75	1			

8. CAPTAIN DUNLAP'S COMPANY

Names	[1]	[2]	[3]	[4]	[5]
Alt, Jacob	50	1			
Alt, Michael[118]	204	1			
Alvis, Walter	7974				
Alvis, Walter for George T. Cooper	896				
Alt, George	117	1			
Adair, John[119]	1190		3		
Anderson, William[120]	997½	3	2		
Anderson, William Ex. of Andrew McCampbell	379				
Berry, Josiah[121]		1			
Bowen, William	309	1			
Bounds, Francis	50	1			

[117](1747-Aug. 25, 1832); Revolutionary soldier known as "Racoon" John; married Eve, daughter of Lewis Widner. *Knoxville Register*, Sept. 12, 1832.

[118]Will made March 28, 1816, proved April, 1827, names sons, George, Jacob, Conrad, Frederick, John; wife, Mary, and daughter, Charity, who married Henry Baker and had six children. Estate Book, IV, 299.

[119](1731-Feb. 24, 1827); North Carolina entry taker of Sullivan County. *Knoxville Register*, March 28, 1827; *The Enquirer* (Knoxville), March 28, 1828. Estate Book, IV, 288 (April 5, 1824).

[120]Revolutionary War soldier; served in Rockbridge County, Va.; died Dec. 17, 1830, aged about 71 years. *Knoxville Register*, Dec. 22, 1830; Estate Book, V, 42.

[121]Died October 26, 1806; his widow, Nancy, married Michael Davis of Knox County, Dec. 17, 1808. Michael Davis' homemade arithmetic books containing a family record is in the McClung Historical Collection, Lawson McGhee Library.

	[1]	[2]	[3]	[4]	[5]
Bounds, Francis agent for Jesse					
Bounds estate	250		3	1	
Brooks, Moses[122]	250	1			
Brooks, Moses agent for Alexander McNutt	140				
Bennett, Daniel		1			
Breeze, James	150	1			
Crawford, Moses	290				
Chapman, Thomas[123]	700	1			
Chapman, Miles	680	1			
Chapman, Asahel	320	1			
Carrithers, Andrew	200	1			
Crawford, Samuel	200	1	1		
Crowder, Greenham	107	1	3		
Clark, Thomas N. by J. Love	1160				
Dodd, James		1			
Davis, James estate by Robert Houston	150	1	1		
Dunlap, Hugh[124]	160	1	4		
Dunn, Francis by Jesse Sharp	200				
Emerson [Emmerson], Thomas[125]	220	1	6		
Edmonson, John	150	1			
Emmerson, Littleton T.		1			
French, Henry		1			
Green, James		1			
George, Soloman[126]		1			
Grills, Elliott[127]	353	1	3		
Garner, John		1			
Gibbs, George		1			
Hobson, George	450	1			
Hankins, Margaret			2		
Houston, Robert[128]	1509	1	4	1½	
Jones, Esther	200				
Kimbrel, Charles		1			
Kimbrel, Peterson		1			
Kearnes, Charles	200	2			

[122]Son of John and Ann (Irwin) Brooks, born April 1, 1760, in Augusta County, Va., Jan. 25, 1830; fought in the Battles of King's Mountain and Guilford Court House; removed to Greene County, N. C., and in 1787 to what is Knox County; married in 1787 or 1788 Agnes (Gamble) Fowler (June 9, 1765-Aug. 2, 1826), widow of Robert Fowler, Jr., who died in Washington County, Tenn., in 1784, and daughter of Robert and Mary (McElroy) Gamble. By her first husband she had one daughter, Esther Ann Fowler, who married Samuel Fleming, of Knox County. Allen, "Leaves from the Family Tree," *loc. cit.*, Dec. 24, 1933.

[123]First register of Knox County; a native of Pennsylvania, he and his family were originally Quakers, but were disowned because of their participation in civil and military affairs.

[124]Early merchant; married June 12, 1794, Susannah, daughter of Capt. Devereaux Gilliam *(q.v.);* removed to Paris, Henry County, Tenn. See biography of a son, Richard G., in *French Broad-Holston Country*, 412-13.

[125]First mayor of Knoxville; died at Jonesboro. *Knoxville Register*, Aug. 2, 1837; *French Broad-Holston Country*, 413-15.

[126](1758-Oct. 30, 1830). *Knoxville Register*, Dec. 15, 1830.

[127]Son of John Grills of Hawkins County.

[128](1765-April 2, 1834); first sheriff of Knox County. *Knoxville Register*, April 9, 1834; *French Broad-Holston Country*, 430-31.

	[1]	[2]	[3]	[4]	[5]
Love, Samuel	500	1	2		
Lareau, George	220				
Lareau, Abraham	180	1			
Love, Joseph	321	1	1		
Lister, Reuben		1			
Massingale, Michael[129] by R. Houston	400				
Mooris, William		1			
Murphy, Robert	165				
Marshall, Thomas	251½	1			
Morton, Jesse		1			
McCampbell, Andrew	584				
McCampbell, William	200	1			
Moor, John	110				
Massey, Peter		1			
Masterson, Aron		1			
Monkey, Henry	100	1			
McKinley, Samuel[130]	150	1			
McNutt, George[131]	320		4		
Massey, Thos.		1			
McSpadden, Archibald by John Love	200				
Morris, Nimrod		1			
Moor, Jacob		1			
Martin, John	150				
Ozburn, Isaac		1			
Russell, John by Thomas Emmerson	200				
Stout, Abraham		1			
Shedderly, Michael[132]	100	1			
Schrader, Jacob	200	1			
Sheets, Daniel by E. Grills		1			
Teel, Edward	181¾		2		
Terry, John	130				
Vernon, Solomen		1			
Vernon, Isaac		1			
Wheel, Benjamin	836	1	4		
White, Henry	280	1			
Waggoner, John[133]	250	1			

[129]Born March 1, 1756, Presumably in Northampton County, N. C.; came to Watauga in 1770; Revolutionary soldier; moved to Buffalo Creek, Grainger County, 1789. S. E. Massengill, *The Massengills, Massengales and Variants* (Bristol, 1931), 202-06.

[130]Born 1755 in Chester County, Pa., removed to Sullivan County, Tenn., 1781, and to Knox County, in 1800; married 1790 Prudence Campbell: died Jan. 16, 1845. *Knoxville Register*, Jan. 29, 1845; *French Broad-Holston Country*, 449.

[131]Born 1751 in Ireland; lived in Rockbridge County, Va., where he served in the Revolution, taking part in the Battle of King's Mountain; removed shortly after Revolution to what is now Jefferson County, Tenn., then to Knox County; died Jan. 5, 1823. *Knoxville Register*, Jan 7, 1823; *French Broad-Holston Country*, 451-52.

[132]Born 1778 in Pennsylvania; died Sept. 21, 1846. *Knoxville Standard*, Sept. 22, 1846.

[133](1744-Oct. 13, 1824); one of the founders of Macedonia Methodist Church, the oldest Methodist Church in Knox County. *Knoxville Register*, Oct. 15, 1824; *Knoxville Enquirer*, Oct. 20, 1824.

	[1]	[2]	[3]	[4]	[5]
Whitechurch, William		1			
Wells, Stephen		1			
Welker, Jacob[184]	188				
White, James[185]	1471			4	4
Williams, John[136]		1		1	
White, Hugh L.[187]	395	1	4	3	
White, Andrew	35	1	6	1	

9. CAPTAIN HARDIN'S COMPANY

Names	[1]	[2]	[3]	[4]	[5]
Ashworth, Joseph	445	1			
Blan, John		1			
Brown, Sylvanus		1			
Catchem, Joseph	1631/3	1			
Catchem, Edward	365	1			
Courtney, John		1			
Catchem, Hugh	100	1			
Courtney, Jonathan	198	1			
Davis, Walter		1			
England, Ezekiel	250	1	1		
England, John	200	1			
England, Joseph		1			
Fulsher, Carson	228				
Grayson, John	200	1			
Gallagher, George	600	1			
Grayson, Benjamin		1			
Hardin, James	550	1	2		
Hambright, John[188]	200	1			
Hambright, Benjamin		1	1		
Hellums, John	237		2		

[184]Progenitor of the Welcker family of Tennessee; the Welcker family papers are in the McClung Collection, Lawson McGhee Library.
[185]Founder of Knoxville; son of Moses White of Rowan County, N. C., where he was born in 1747; married Mary, daughter of Hugh Lawson. *French Broad-Holston Country*, 503-05. Calvin Morgan McClung of Knoxville was a descendant and collected many notes on the family, now in the McClung Historical Collection, Lawson McGhee Library, which also has the family Bible of James and Mary Lawson White.
[136]Son of Joseph and Rebeckah Williams, born in Surry County, N. C., Jan 29, 1778; married Melinda, daughter of James and Mary Lawson White; became U. S. senator; died at Knoxville, Aug. 10, 1837. *French Broad-Holston Country*, 505-06.
[187]Son of James and Mary Lawson White, born Oct. 30, 1773, in Rowan, now Iredell County, N. C.; U. S. senator and presidential candidate; died at Knoxville, April 10, 1840. *French Broad-Holston Country*, 501-02; also articles by L. P. Gresham in E.T.H.S. *Publications*, Nos. 18 (1946), 19 (1947).
[188]John H. Hambright, son of Col. Frederick and Sarah (Hardin); born in North Carolina March 17, 1762; died in McMinn County, Feb. 6, 1830; married Oct. 28, 1784, Nancy Black of North Carolina; Revolutionary soldier; in Battle of King's Mountain; Sarah Hardin was a sister of Colonel Joseph Hardin *(q.v.)*. John Morgan Wooten, "Leaves from the Family Tree," *Chattanooga Times*, December 30, 1934.

	[1]	[2]	[3]	[4]	[5]
Hellums, William		1			
Hellums, William	229	1			1
Hightower, Joshua		1			
Hardin, Gibson	300	1	1		1
Hardin, Amos[139]	800	1			
Howard, Reason	200	1			
Holt, Joel	125	1			
Hellums, John	140	1			
Hardin, Benjamin	200	1			
Howard, Thomas		1			
Halmark, Thomas[140]		1			
Howard, Samuel		1			
Johnston, Ambrose		1			
Lee, Permit Senior	100				
Lee, Permit Junior		1			
Lee, Abraham		1			
Love, John		1			
Lewis, Henry		1			
Lewis, Samuel	100				
Low, Andrew R.		1			
McCart, Robert		1			
Maxwell, David	930	1	5		
Maxwell, John	164	1			
Meloney, John		1			
Phipps, John	80				
Pate, Stephen	100	1			
Pruitt, Jacob	300	1	3		
Pepper, James		1			
Rogers, Thomas	275	1			
Rucker, Austin		1			
Rucker, Tiner		1			
Rutherford, Samuel		1			
Steel, William		1			1
Steel, Ninian	396	1			
Steel, John	200	1			
Shelton, Cuthbert	200	1			
Scarborough, James	100	1			
Shannon, Charles		1			
Smith, James		1			
Scroggins, Henry		1			
Scarborough, Robert	100	1			
Tiner, Lewis[141]		1			
Tirpin, Martin		1			
Walker, Buckner	50	1			
Walker, Jesse	55	1			
Walker, George	225				
Willson, Joseph		1			

[139](1780-Aug. 25, 1840). *Knoxville Register*, Sept. 16, 1840.
[140]A constituent member of the Mouth of Richland Baptist Church in present Grainger County, Tenn.
[141]Removed to Hamilton County, Tenn., where he was living in 1830.

10. CAPTAIN HAISLET'S COMPANY

Names	[1]	[2]	[3]	[4]	[5]
Anderson, William	150	1			
Burnett, Joseph	100				
Burnett, Benjamin	300	1			
Bowman, John	50	1			
Bowman, Samuel	60	1			
Bodkin, Hugh	150	1			
Brown, John		1	1		
Cruize, James[142]	200	1	1		
Chesnut, Robert	25				
Colker, Charles	100	1			
Cruse, Walter	100	1			
Cruise, Allison		1			
Cunningham, William	183	1			
Carpenter, Thomas		1			
Cruise, Gideon[143]	100	1			
Crank, Thomas		1			
Cozby, James[144]	640		1		
Cozby, John[145]		1			
Dunlap, Samuel	100	1			
Dunlap, George	100	1			
Dozier, Peter	150	1			
Dunn, William[146]	100				
Evans, William	100				
Finley, John	50				
Green, Jesse	400				
Gorton, Elijah	250	2			
Gillespie, James	70				
Hill, John		1	1		
Houston, Robert	150	1			
Haislet, George W.		1			
Hensley, George W.		1			
Huffacre, George[147]	400	2			
Hinds, William	200				
Johnston, James	100				
Jones, Jeremiah[148]	50	1			

[142]Revolutionary soldier who drew pension in Knox County.
[143]Revolutionary soldier from Amherst County, Va.; died Aug. 12, 1834. Rev. War Pension File, S 39371.
[144]Physician; Revolutionary soldier, rescuer and friend of John Sevier; died in Hamilton County, Feb. 13, 1831. *Knoxville Register*, Feb. 23, 1831.
[145]Son of Dr. James Cozby; married Aug. 1808, Abigale McBee; removed to Rhea County, Tenn.
[146]Revolutionary soldier who drew a pension for service in the Virginia militia; died at Knoxville, Dec. 19, 1837. *Knoxville Register*, Dec. 27, 1837.
[147]Born in Pennsylvania, Aug. 7, 1757; Revolutionary War soldier; took part in Battle of Long Island Flats, 1776, for which he received a pension; died Nov. 8, 1838, in Knox Co. *Knoxville Register*, Nov. 28, 1838; for an account of the family see Hugh D. Huffaker, *History and Genealogy of Michael Huffaker and His Descendants in America* (Chattanooga, 1927).
[148]Removed to Hamilton County, where he was first register. 1819.

	[1]	[2]	[3]	[4]	[5]
Kerr, Samuel	80	1			
Keener, Woolrick		1			
Kennedy, James	274	1			
Keener, Peter[149]	100				
Long, Robert	150	1			
Legg, Matthew	50	1			
Montgomery, Samuel	100	1			
Monday, William	100		2		
Monday, Joshua		1			
Monday, William Junior		1			
McCammon, John[150]	200	1			
McCall, John	150				
McKeehan, James	50	1			
McBath, Robert	150	1			
Murphy, Dennis[151]	200		8		1
Moor, James	50				
Maxey, Shaderick	125	1			
Pain, Chesley	25	1			
Prior, Harris		1			
Rhea, Archibald	300	1	1		
Reed, Jerimiah	450	1			
Reed, Solomon	100	1			
Reid, Jacob	50	1			
Shook, William[152]	150				
Shook, William	100	1			
Shook, Abraham	100	1			
Shook, Isaac	50	1			
Shook, Jacob		1			
Shook, Harman		1			
Swisher, Michael		1			
Slatery, Patrick	100				
Wrinkle, George	150				
Wrinkle, George Junior	30	1			
Willson, Isaac	100	1			
Wrinkle, Jacob		1			
Waterhouse, Richard G.[153]		1			

---

[149]For an account of the family see R. C. d'Armand, *The Dearmond Families of America* (Knoxville, 1954).

[150]Died April 23, 1838, in the 92nd year; member of Associate Reformed or "Seceder" Presbyterian Church, located on present Sevierville Pike, now extinct. *Knoxville Register*, May 2, 1838.

[151]Died before Oct. 1808, when his widow married Major Edwin E. Booth. Wilson's Knoxville Gazette, Oct. 19, 1808.

[152]Member of family which came from Hampshire County, Va., now West Va.; name is perpetuated in Shook's Gap.

[153]Born in Hunterdon County, New Jersey; removed to Knox, then to Rhea County, Tenn., where he was a large landowner and prominent promoter of Tennessee Valley; died March 7, 1827. Allen, "Leaves from the Family Tree," *loc. cit.*, Jan. 20-27, 1935; *Knoxville Register*, March 21, 1827.

11. CAPTAIN JACK'S COMPANY

Names	[1]	[2]	[3]	[4]	[5]
Armstrong, Robert[154]	170	1	2		
Armstrong, John	500	1	1		
Amonet, John	250	1			
Brock, Lewis		1			
Baldwin, William		1			
Barclay, Felix	94	1			
Brock, Pearson		1			
Brownen, James		1			
Brock, George	200		1		
Bayles, Caleb	100	1			
Campbell, Alexander	300	1	1		
Craighead, Thomas[155]		1			
Carpenter, John	126	1			
Davenport, William			2		
Dunlap, James		1			
Dodd, William	30	1			
Faris, Richard		2	1		
Fisher, William	100	1			
Fisher, Daniel		1			
Gillespie, Thomas	440	2	2		
Gilliam, Deverix[156]	220	1	4		
Gibson, Samuel	235				
Gibson, John	235	1			
Jack, Jeremiah[157]	296¾	1	1		
Jack, George		1			
Jones, George J.		1			
Luttrell, James[158]	157		1		
Luttrell, John[159]	124	1			
Luttrell, William		1			
McNutt, John	500	2			
McNutt, Robert		1			
Merryman, Francis[160]	200	1			
Newman, Jacob[161]	250	1			
Newman, John		1			

[154]For account of members of the Armstrong family see Armstrong, *Notable Southern Families*, I, 5-24.

[155](Mar. 6, 1781-Sept. 16, 1839); son of Capt. Robert Craighead; married Dec. 23, 1803, Mary Gillespie; died in Hamilton County. *Craighead Family*, 99.

[156]Usually Devereaux. Revolutionary soldier; settled Gilliam's Station at the fork of the French Broad and Holston rivers. J. G. M. Ramsey, *The Annals of Tennessee* (reprinted, Kingsport, 1926), *passim*.

[157]Born Nov. 13, 1750, in Washington County, Maryland; moved to Nolichucky, 1778, and then to present Knox County; died June 23, 1833. *Knoxville Register*, June 26, 1833.

[158]Revolutionary soldier; ancestor of James C., James C., Jr., and Samuel B. Luttrell, all mayors of Knoxville. *French Broad-Holston Country*, 440-42.

[159]Married Annis Jackson, daughter of Peter Jackson; ancestor of John King Luttrell, congressman from California.

[160]Revolutionary soldier who drew pension for his service in the Virginia militia; died July 31, 1826. *Knoxville Register*, Aug. 2, 1826.

[161]Revolutionary soldier who drew pension for service in Pennsylvania militia.

	[1]	[2]	[3]	[4]	[5]
Null, Henry	131	1			
Patterson, Robert[162]	249	1	1		
Pickle, Christian[163]	320				
Pickle, Christian Junior		1			
Pickle, John		1			
Pickle, Henry		1			
Robertson, Willoughby	106	1			
Tenor, Jacob		1			
Witt, George	300	3			
Wolf, George[164]	200				

12. CAPTAIN LONAS' COMPANY

Names	[1]	[2]	[3]	[4]	[5]
Brown, Thomas	210	1	2		
Bogan, William	550	1			
Bell, Samuel	160	1			
Childress, James		1			
Carruth, Rachael[165]	125		1		
Carter, Joseph	650				
Cox, James		1			
Coker, Demsy		1			
Carruth, William	96				
Craig, James W.[166]	200	1	1		
Carmichael, George	507	1			
Durham, Thomas		1			
England, Aron		1			
Fouts, David		1			
Fouts, George		1			
Greer, Thomas	335	1	4		
Gentry, Jesse	100	1			
Gray, Peter		1			
Gilbreath, David		1			
Gilbreath, Thomas		1			
Gentry, William		1			

---

[162]Born in Mecklenburg County, N. C., Dec. 17, 1768; served in Battle of King's Mountain; after close of Revolutionary War moved to Knox County while it was still a part of Hawkins; married *circa* 1787 or 1788, Rhoda Witt (born Dec. 11, 1776), daughter of Abner Witt *(q.v.)*. Allen, "Leaves from the Family Tree," *loc. cit.*, Dec. 17, 1933.

[163]Will proved July, 1814. Estate Book, II, 112.

[164]Revolutionary soldier who served in Pennsylvania.

[165]Born 1738 in Pennsylvania; prisoner of Indians for seven years; married three times; came to Knoxville from North Carolina; died May 13, 1823. *Knoxville Register*, May 16, 1823.

[166]Son of Robert Craig; born Dec. 3, 1768, in Lancaster County, Pa.; removed to Washington County, Va., then to Knox County, Tenn., where he died Dec. 1, 1846. *Knoxville Register*, Dec. 9, 1846.

	[1]	[2]	[3]	[4]	[5]
Hudiburgh, Thomas[167]	449	1			
Henderson, Daniel[168]	280				
Horn, Jacob	400	1			
Hickey, Cornelius[169]	90	1			
Harmon, Jacob		1			
Hoke, Michael	100	1			
Houston, Peter		1			
Haney, Spencer		1			
Haney, Samuel		1			
Knave [Nave], Jacobs estate by Jacob Lonas	133				
Kearnes, Henry	213	1			
Keeth, John		1			
Kenny, Jacob	90				
Kearnes, Michael		1			
Kearnes, Valentine	545	1			
Lonas, Henry[170]	734	1	2		
Lonas, Jacob	250	1	1		
Looney, Moses[171]	320		3		
Luttrell, James C.[172]	180	1	1		
Looney, Peter	115	1			
Murray, Robert[173]	237	1		½	
Monday, John		1	1		
Miser, George	150	1			
McKiddy, James		1	2		
Miller, James	3630	2	14	1	
McCullough, James	20	1			
Miller, Robert	600	1	2		
Nooris [Norris], Samuel		1			
Pruitt, Martin	211				
Pruitt, Isaac		1			
Pruitt, Jacob		1			
Pyran, Joshua		1			
Porter, James	140	1			
Porter, Robert		1			
Rawlings, Michael[174]	150	1	1		
Roach, John		1			

---

[167]A resident of Carter County, Tenn.; before coming to Knox County shortly before 1800; prominent member of the Baptist church at Beaver Ridge (now Ball Camp); removed to Morgan County, Indiana.

[168]Son-in-law of Dr. James Cozby *(q.v.)*, removed to Rhea, later Hamilton County; one of Cherokee enumerators for census of 1830; died 1835.

[169]Son of John Hickey, whose will was proved in Henry County, Va., Dec. 25, 1784.

[170]Born in Bucks County, Pa., Sept. 4, 1765; removed to Knox County, 1795; died July 27, 1848. *Knoxville Tribune*, August 9, 1848.

[171]A captain; died July 12, 1824. *Knoxville Register*, July 16, 1824.

[172](1776-Oct. 21, 1824); justice and deputy marshall of East Tennessee; post-master of Knoxville. *Knoxville Register*, Oct. 22, 1824.

[173]Died Jan. 14, 1829, "an old inhabitant of this place." *Knoxville Register*, Jan. 21, 1829.

[174]Removed to Bledsoe County, Tenn.

	[1]	[2]	[3]	[4]	[5]
Rentfro, Stephens estate by Moses Looney			2		
Stickly, Leva	150				
Sample, William		1			
Snow, Morgan		1			
Thompson, William		1			
Thompson, James	200				
Tillery, John	262	1			
Tillery, Samuel		1			
Whiteman, William	200	1			
White, Caleb			2		
Witt, Abner[175]	151				
Witt, Charles		1			
White, Benjamin[176]	1	2	1		
Young, John	100	1			

13. CAPTAIN PRICE'S COMPANY

Names	[1]	[2]	[3]	[4]	[5]
Armstrong, James[177]	2480		3		
Allen, John	116				
Cobb, Sally[178]	376		7		
Cobb, William P. by Sally Cobb	608		5		
Cobb, Sarah by Pharaoh Cobb	608		5		
Carter, William	185	1			
Clap, Laudewick	200	1			
Carter, Peter		1			
Davis, Thomas	116	1	3		
Douglass, Thomas	200	1			
Douglass, Jonathan[179]	200				
Douglass, Johnathan for Joseph Young	320				
Elliot, Matthew	130	1			
Epps, Edward[180]		1			

---

[175]Descendant of a French Huguenot who emigrated to the colony of Virginia and settled at Mannikentown; moved to Knox County and lived there until 1806, when he moved to Jackson County, Tenn.; returned to Knox County for a year or two; then moved to Rhea County and settled on Sale Creek, where several of his sons and sons-in-law had preceded him. Allen, "Leaves from the Family Tree," *loc. cit.*, Dec. 17, 1933.

[176]Revolutionary soldier; died Aug. 24, 1827, at Decatur, Ala. *Knoxville Register*, Sept. 5, 1827.

[177](1736-Sept. 28, 1813); known as "Trooper" because of his military service in Ireland; *Wilson's Knoxville Gazette*, Oct. 4, 1813; Armstrong, *Notable Southern Families*, I, 1-18; *French Broad-Holston Country*, 370-71.

[178]Widow of William Cobb, whose home near Bluff City was the first seat of government of the Southwest Territory.

[179](April 25, 1752-Nov. 9, 1840); Revolutionary soldier; lost an eye in the Indian foray, 1777; lived in Carter's Valley (present Hawkins County) in 1777; died in Alabama.

[180]Born in Sussex County, Va., c1776; died in Knox County, 1840. For an account of his descendants see Mary Lou Johnson and Mae L. Treadwell, *Family of Edward Eppes of Knox County, Tennessee* (Knoxville, 1951).

	[1]	[2]	[3]	[4]	[5]
Fristoe, Robert[181]	200				
Fristoe, Robert Junior[182]		1			
Finley, John		1			
Graves, William	200		2		
Groves, Stephen		1			
Grantum, John		1			
Hankins, Able	200	1			
Huffer [Hoffar], Daniel[183]		1			
Harralson, Major		1	2		
Irwin, Francis	260	1			
Jones, Hester	200				
Jones, John		1			
John, Zephaniah	295				
Kearnes, John	100				
Kearnes, James		1			
Kein [Kain], John[184]	1450	1	16		
Large, Joseph		1			
Lion [Lyon], Thomas	350	1			
Little, Adam		1	1		
Lion, John	100	1	1		
Legg, James		1			1
Lisby, Moses		1			
Legg, Edward	177½				
Legg, Edward for Wm. Black	130				
Legg, John	250	1			
Morrow, Alexander	500		8		
Morrow, Richard	150	1			
McMunn, William	200	1			
McCauley [McCallie], Edward		1			
Mattox, Valentine	270				
Mitchell, Charles		1			
Medley, Richard		1			
Markland, Nathan B.	200	1	8		
McBee, William	505		7		
McBee, Lemuel		1			
McAnally, John	208				
Markland, Nathan B. for John Colland	500				
Maybury, Francis	120				
Moore, Nancy		1			
Maggot, William		1			

---

[181]Early Baptist preacher; removed to Missouri, where he died. Burnett, *Pioneer Baptist Preachers*, 160-61.

[182]Married Nov. 14, 1811, Susan Groves, daughter of William Groves, *(q.v.)*. *Wilson's Knoxville Gazette*, Dec. 2, 1811.

[183](1773-Sept. 12, 1827); lived at McBee's Ferry on Holston River; his obituary calls him "one of the greatest mechanical geniuses in East Tennessee." *Knoxville Enquirer*, Sept. 26, 1827; *Knoxville Register*, Sept. 19, 1827 (the two notices differ as to his age).

[184]Captain in militia; died July 6, 1831; father of Jennie, Mattie, and Kittie Kain; the latter two were among the first women students at Blount College, now University of Tennessee. *Knoxville Register*, July 13, 1831.

	[1]	[2]	[3]	[4]	[5]
Osburn, Daniel	147				
Price, Edward	500	1			
Pearson, Jacob	100	1			
Pearson, Abel		1			
Right [Wright], Enock		1			
Roach, John		1			
Reardy, Joseph	100	1	2		
Robertson, Isaac		1			
Sharp, John		1			
Standfield, Soloman		1			
Stewart, James	200				
Stewart, James Junior		1			1
Shipe, Adam		1			
Stewart, Robert		1			
Tomlin, John	100	1			
Underhill, William	100	1			
White, Martha	700		3		
Williams, George	200		1		
Williams, William		1			
Walters, Claiborne		1			

14. CAPTAIN JAMES REYNOLDS COMPANY

Names	[1]	[2]	[3]	[4]	[5]
Bletcher, William		1			
Bradley, William		1			
Burk, Isaac	125	1			
Crawford, English	110	1			
Clap, David[185]	230	1			
Chamberlain, Jeremiah[186]	732				
Damewood, Malachi	230	2			
Damewood, Henry	90	1			
Foust, John	135	1			
Ferguson, William	190	1			
Graham, Nathanial	350	2			
Grave, John	183	1			
Grave, Daniel	225	1			
Hill, John		1			
Halbert, Joel	270		1		
Halbert, John		1			
Harbison, James	315	1			1
Hailey, Claiborne		1	1		
Hailey, John	162	1			
Holland, Peter	150	1			

---

[185]Born in Orange (now Alamance) County, N. C.; married April 22, 1793, in Montgomery County, Va., Betsy Graves, daughter of Boston *(q.v.)* and Sarah (Ephland) Graves.

[186]Resident of Grainger County, where he died in 1824.

	[1]	[2]	[3]	[4]	[5]
Johnston, Robert[187]		1			
Johnston, John	150	2			
Kelley, Joseph	130	1			
Kirk, Elijah		1			
Kearnes, Sarah			1		
Kearnes, James	275	1	1		
Kelly, Thomas		1			
Kelly, Michael	250		1		
Lower, Henry	375	1			
McDonald, Reuben	535		1		
Mynatt, George Estate	235				
McHaffy, John	284	1			
Mynatt, William[188]	200	3	2		
Mynatt, John[189]	150	1			
Nosler, Bostian[190]		1			
O'Donald, Michael	150	1			
Price, Reuben	200	1			
Peterson, William	235	1	2		
Peters, Nathanial	337	1			
Rutherford, John[191]	283	1			
Rutherford, Loyd		1			
Rutherford, Ezekiel		1			
Rutherford, Absalom[192]	500	1			
Roberts, Henry	315	1	1		
Roberts, William	200	1			
Reynolds, James		1			
Reynolds, Thomas		1			
Sharp, Samuel[193]	150				
Smith, John		1			
Sharp, Moses	50	1			
Sawyers, John[194]	1000		1		
Taylor, Henry		1			
Tablor, Michael	100	1			
Wood, Samuel	75	1			
Williams, Alexander		1			
Zachariah, Gilbert		1			

---

[187]Perhaps the man of that name who drew a pension in Knox County for his Revolutionary service in the Virginia militia.

[188](1756-Jan. 13, 1831); member of Baptist Church. *Knoxville Register*, Jan. 19, 1831.

[189](1773-Jan. 2, 1827). *Ibid.*, Jan. 17, 1827.

[190]Earlier a resident of Montgomery County, Va. Summers, *Annals of Southwest Virginia, passim.*

[191]Will proved April, 1817. Knox County, Tenn., Estate Book, II, 336.

[192]Revolutionary War soldier who drew a pension for his service in Virginia militia; came from Wythe County, Va. Rev. War Pension File.

[193]Revolutionary soldier who drew pension for service in Virginia militia.

[194](1746-Nov. 20, 1831). For an account of him and his descendants see Madison Monroe Harris, *Family History of Col. John Sawyers and Simon Harris and Their Descendants* (Knoxville, 1913).

15. CAPTAIN JOHN REYNOLDS COMPANY

Names	[1]	[2]	[3]	[4]	[5]
Adair, David	300	2			
Anderson, Jacob	170	1	1		
Averett, Jesse	200	1			
Bayles, William	90	1			
Brassfield, Thomas	458	1	1		
Baker, Tilman	100	1			
Baker, Henry estate by Tilman Baker	284½				
Dunning, Samuel	137	1			
Dunlap, John	201½	1			
Davis, Charles		1			
Davis, Samuel		1			
Foust, Christian	250	1			
Foust, John	50	1			
Forgy, Andrew	321	1			
Forgy, Hugh	250	1			
Forgy, Alexander	321	1			
Gibbs, John	150	1			
Gibbs, Nicholas Junr	160	1			
Graves, Bostian[195]	537				
Graves, Peter		1			
Gibbs, Nicholas	285				
Ditto for John Bonds estate	180				
Gibbs, David	170	1			
Gibbs, Jacob	150	1			1
Hankins, Absalom	273	1			
Hinds, John	793	1			
Hinds, Sylvanus		1			
Hinds, John Junior		1			
Hinds, Samuel	100	1			
Heavins, James	300	1			
Hains, Israel	150	1			
Halmark, George		1			
Halbert, Stephen	200	1			
Howarton, Jackson		1			
Johnston, William	200	1			
Jackson, William	150	1			
McCampbell, Isaac[196]	115	1			
Miltabarger, William		1			
Ozburn, Charles	150	1			
Peirce, George		1			

[195]Revolutionary War soldier born in Pennsylvania; served in Revolution while living in Orange County, N. C.; moved to Montgomery County, Va., then Knox County, Tenn.; married Sarah Ephland, whose sister Mary married Nicholas Gibbs, *infra.* Rev. War Pension File, R 4213; Genevieve E. Peters, *Know Your Relatives: The Sharps, Gibbs, Graves, Elfland, Albright, Loy, Miller, Snodderly, Tillman, and Other Related Families* (Washington, D. C., 1953).

[196]For an account of the McCampbell family see Samuel T. Wilson, *Isaac Anderson: Founder and First President of Maryville College* (Maryville, Tenn., 1932), 138-54.

	[1]	[2]	[3]	[4]	[5]
Pierce, Robert	300	1			
Pugh, Jacob	100	1			
Reynolds, John	500	1			
Roberts, William	290				
Spence, James	600				
Smith, Joseph	120				
Thompson, Richard	200		2		
Thompson, John	371½	1	3		
Trout, George	50	1			
Trout, William	64	1			
Taylor, Isaac		1	2		
Vall [Devault], Michael D.	200				
Wood, Enos	104				
Wood, Joseph	201½	1			
Woodward, Thomas	145				
Wilson, Augustine	350	1			
Wear, John	100	1			

16. CAPTAIN TAYLOR'S COMPANY

Names	[1]	[2]	[3]	[4]	[5]
Aikman, William by Adms.	124				
Brannum, Plesant		1			
Brothers, Thomas		1			
Brannum, Daniel		1			
Blackburn, Benjamin		1			
Birdwell, Joseph Estate by Lewis Hill	200				
Barton, Roger[197]	763		1		
Barton, Gilbreath		1	1		
Bennett, Peter[198]	550		5		
Bond, Isaac	230	1			
Currier, James		1	1		
Clift, Henry		1			
Currier, James A.		1			
Campbell, John	178	1	3		
Cavett, Agnes[199] Excts.	640				
Dougan, John	145	1			
Donald, John by Matthew Donald	165				
Fleming, David by S. G. Ramsey	157				

[197](July 9, 1747-June 4, 1822); a native of Augusta County, Va.; Revolutionary soldier; removed from Knox to Anderson County; father-in-law of John Crozier (*q.v.*).

[198](1752-Apr. 9, 1822); Revolutionary War soldier; born in Virginia; served in Revolution while a resident of Granville County, N. C.; married c1773 in King William County, Va., Elizabeth Pomfret, born Jan. 1, 1753, in Virginia, and died in Knox County, July 7, 1845. Rev. War Pension File, R 754.

[199]Widow of Moses Cavett; a Richard Cavett, probably his son or brother, who removed to Madison County, Ala., drew a pension for his Revolutionary War service. In the application he gives an unusual account of life on the frontier in Sullivan County at the time of the Revolution.

	[1]	[2]	[3]	[4]	[5]
Fleming, Betsy by S. G. Ramsey	159				
French, Joseph		1			
Fryar, John	155				
Fleming, Samuel	157	1			
Fleming, Polly	277				
Farragut, George[200]	300				
Griffis, William	150				
Hill, Edward		1			
Holt, Robert	250	1	4		
Holt, Irby		1			
Hackett, John	1375		2		
Knox, William	200	1			
Love, John	350	1			
Low, John	640				
Low, Abraham	100	1			
McAllister, Joseph	117	1			
McCown, James	100	1			
McWhinney, Thomas	100				
McCullock, James		1			
Martin, John	200				
McClung, Charles[201]	4980	2	9		
Pickens, Robert by J. Dougan	50				
Pride, Benjamin	333 1/3	1	2		
Paul, John		1			
Parker, William E.	150				
Russell, Brice	248	1			
Ramsey, Samuel G.[202]	380	1	4		
Russell, James	225	1	1		
Swan, Isaac	200	1			
Swan, James	581		1		
Swan, James Adm. of Harvey Swan	155				
Swan, Samuel	200	1	1		
Swan, John estate by Samuel Swan	195				
And John Love Administrators					
Scott, Willie	143	1			
Scott, Abraham		1			
Spilman, Thomas		1			
Sterling, Hannah	298		1		
Sterling, Samuel		1			
Sterling, Henry	173	1			
Thompson, Samuel	150				
Thompson, Robert		1			
Thompson, William		1			
Thompson, David		1			

[200](Sept. 29, 1755-June 4, 1817); father of Admiral David Glasgow Farragut. *French Broad-Holston Country*, 416-17; also Samuel C. Williams, "George Farragut," *E.T.H.S. Publications*, No. 1 (1929), 77-94.

[201]Surveyor of Knoxville. *French Broad-Holston Country*, 446-47.

[202](Oct. 20, 1771-July 5, 1817); Presbyterian minister; lived at Ebenezer about ten miles south of Knoxville, where he conducted the Ebenezer Academy. *Knoxville Register*, July 31, 1817; *French Broad-Holston Country*, 472-73.

Thompson, Samuel Junior		1			
Taylor, Cawfield	214	1			
Vance, Elizabeth Exct.	140				
Walker, John	275	1			
Walker, Matthew	275	1			
White, James		1			
Walton, Henry		1			
Walton, James		1			
Wilson, Mary by Thomas Brothers			1		

17. CAPTAIN TIPTON'S COMPANY

Names	[1]	[2]	[3]	[4]	[5]
Anderson, Thomas	100	1			
Anderson, Daniel[203]	100				
Anderson, Daniel	150	1			
Anderson, Samuel		1			
Brewer, Oliver		1	1		1
Baker, Charles	100				
Bartlett, Nicholas[204]	150				
Barnett, William	138	1			
Colker, William	300				
Casteel, Francis	440				1
Casteel, Abednigo, Junior	100	1			
Casteel, Abednigo	150				
Casteel, Mesheck	50	1			
Casteel, Shadrack	150	1			
Colker, Jude	50				
Cunningham, Rosannah	118				
Carson, Alexander	150	1			
Depus, Asher		1			
Davis, Richards	80	1			
Dearmond, Richard J.		1			
Dearmond, William	13	1			
Davis, James	100	1			
Dullwitt, John	50				
Dearmond, John Junior	376	1			
Dearmond, John[205]	400				
Edington, William		1			
Estes, Micaijah		1			
Evans, Mary	100				
Flenniken, Samuel[206]	875	1	1		
Flenniken, James W.	150	1			
Greenlee, Francis	50	1			

[203]Died July 11, 1818, aged 111 years. *Knoxville Register,* July 21, 1818.
[204]A Quaker from Greenbrier County, Va. (now West Va.); prior to 1787, operated a mill on Stock Creek at the Knox-Blount line; will proved April, 1814. Estate Book, II, 97.
[205]See R. C. d'Armand, *The Dearmond Families of America.*
[206]*Ibid.*

	[1]	[2]	[3]	[4]	[5]
Givins, William	50	1			
Hood, Andrew		1			
Haislett, William	300				
Haislett, Benjamin C.	50	1			
Husong, Jacob	150	1			
Hood, Aron	200	1			
Hood, Soloman	200	1			
Hood, Thomas		1			
Hicks, Abraham	100	1			
Hicks, Charles	30	1			
Hoan, Jacob	200	1			
Haislett, William		1			
Henderson, Samuel	127	1	1		
Johnston, William	100				
Johnston, Calvin	250	1	1		
Johnston, Joseph	200	1			
Johnston, Isaac		1			
Jones, Mary	100				
Johnston, Robert	300	1			
Kirby, Joseph	200	1	3		1
Kirby, Francis		1			
Keehill, Richards	70				
Lowe, John		1			
Mason, Edward	100				
McCarrel, James	162				
McCammon, Thomas	150	1			
McCandlys, John	300				
McEldry, John	640				
Moor, James	245	1			
Moor, Reuben	640	1			
McWilliams, Andrew	100				
McClellan, William[207]	350				
McClellan, Samuel		1			
McCoy, John	184	1			
Mash, John	100	1			
Nelson, William	100				
Overstreet, William	450		4		
Price, James[208]	100	1			
Porter, James L.	200	1			
Reagan, James	300		3		
Rodgers, Jeremiah	100	1			
Reed, Abraham	244				
Ray, James	60		1		
Smith, Elijah	50	1			
Smith, Aaron	40	1			
Smith, A	100				

---

[207]Revolutionary soldier; died Feb. 24, 1827, aged 84. *Knoxville Register*, Feb. 28, 1827.
[208]Revolutionary soldier who drew pension for service in Virginia militia.

	[1]	[2]	[3]	[4]	[5]
Tipton, William[209]	500	1	2		
Tipton, Reuben	150	1			
Tipton, Abraham		1			
Tarwater, Frederick	100	1			
Tarwater, Jacob	150				
Wheeler, Peter		1	1		
Wheeler, Thomas	100	1			
Hicks, John		1			
Johnston, James		1			

TAXES 1806   RETURNED TO COURT

BOOTH'S COMPANY

Names	[1]	[2]	[3]	[4]	[5]
Salter, John by James Trimble	1343½				
Lewis, Wm. T. by Wm. Maclin	1250				

BISHOP'S COMPANY

	[1]	[2]	[3]	[4]	[5]
Upton, David		1			
Renfrow, John		1			
Moses, Poor by Geo. Bayles	300	1			

BONDS COMPANY

Gibson, John	100
White, Isaac by Sam Givens	400
Pelham's, John estate by Wm. Lackey	100

BOYDS COMPANY

McCleary, Abraham[210]	204
Beard, Hugh by Abraham McClary	386

CHILES COMPANY

Stringfield, Rebecca	50

COX'S COMPANY

Vaughn, William

---

[209]Revolutionary soldier known as "Fighting Billy"; born Feb. 13, 1761, in Shenandoah County, Va.; removed to Greene County, shortly after Revolution where he married Phoebe Moore; father of Reuben and Abraham Tipton *(infra)*; died in Blount County, Nov. 3, 1849. Rev. War Pension File; *Knoxville Register*, Nov. 17, 1849.

[210]A resident of Sevier County, Tenn.; a native of York County, Pa. where he married Rachel Payne; dead by 1819.

DUNLAP'S COMPANY

Youst, Francis	418	1
Medley, John		1
Meek, Adam by R. Houston	401	
Douglass, Sarah by Adam Meek	150	
Scott, William	200	1

COX'S COMPANY

Joel Epperson by Tho. Brassfield		1
Presley Buckner	124	
John Bull		1

HARDIN'S COMPANY

West Walker[211]	200	1

HAISLET'S COMPANY

John Jack	50	1	
Jeremiah Burnett	50	1	
Jacob Moyers		1	
John Doyl[212]	200		
William Montgomery		1	2
William Palmer	50	1	
William Barclay		1	
Thomas Nethery	150		
Margaret Rhea			2
Joseph Bartlett		1	

JACK'S COMPANY

William McCree [McRee]		1
William Craighead		1
John Witt	150	1
Jeremiah Compton by Jno. Witt	100	
Stephen Newberry	30	1
Jesse Sullivan		1
Frederick Nail		1
Jacob Patton	225	1
Kimberly by John Newman	200	

LONAS'S COMPANY

James McCullough	90		
William Nichol	90	1	
William Bell		2	2
Margaret Porter[213] by John Singleton	320		

---

[211]An early Baptist minister.

[212]Revolutionary soldier who drew pension for service in Maryland militia; married Eve Formwalt, widow of John Formwalt.

[213]A resident of Blount County, Tenn.

PRICES COMPANY

	[1]	[2]	[3]	[4]	[5]
Robert Smith		1			
John Steel		1			

JAS. REYNOLD'S COMPANY

James Ailor		1			

JNO. REYNOLD'S COMPANY

John Glass by John Rutherford	225	1			
George Foust	400				
John Meek	400		1		
Jeremiah Pate		1			

TAYLOR'S COMPANY

John Fryar		2			
Elisha Journeygan [Jarnigan]		1			
Jacob Miles		1			
Nicholas Bond	360	1			
William Fryar	150				
John Tooles heirs by John Hackett	666 2/3				

TIPTON'S COMPANY

John McDowell	45				
Joseph McCleary	179½				
Jesse Smith	250				
James C. Luttrell	100				
George Doherty heirs by Geo. W. Campbell	1000				
George Doherty heirs and Martin Armstrong by George W. Campbell	1000				
Thomas Kelland by David Henley	20,000				
William McBee	9				
Joseph Hinds son of Levi	200				
David Low	100				
Paul Cunningham estate by his admr.	300				
	32,716 2/3	36	8		
[Totals	255,858 7/12	967	475	101⅚	15]

REPORTED BY THE SHERIFF OF DOUBLE TAXES

Dry Heirs representatives	5375
do do do	4575
Joseph Williams	200
	10,150

A LIST OF STUDS LICENSED IN 1806

Owner's Names	Horses Names	State Tax	Co. Tax	Jail Tax
John Bowman	Young Twig	$4.00	$ .50	$1.00
Henry Roberts	Chickasaw	3.00	.50	1.00
Edward Routh	Nero	2.00	.50	1.00
Richard Cobb	Young Wildear	3.00	.50	1.00
William Minatt	Young Celo	3.00	.50	1.00
Pumery Carmichael	Lion	2.00	.50	1.00
Account rendered for state tax		$17.00	$3.00	$6.00

EARLY EAST TENNESSEE TAXPAYERS

Compiled by Pollyanna Creekmore

IV, Grainger County, 1799[1]

Grainger County, named for Mary Grainger, wife of William Blount, was one of the counties created in the year Tennessee became a state. On April 22, 1796, the general assembly passed an "Act for erecting part of the county of Hawkins and part of the county of Knox into a separate and distinct county." By section 1 of this act the bounds of the county were laid out.

That the said counties of Hawkins and Knox be divided by the following lines: Beginning on the main road leading from Bull's Gap to Haines's iron works on Mossy creek, at the house of Felps Read, leaving said house in the new county, running a direct course to the Kentucky road, on the north side of Holston river, a quarter of a mile above the house of Thomas Henderson; thence north fifty degrees west to the line that divides this state from the state of Virginia; thence west with said line to a point, north west of the end of Clinch mountain; thence a direct course to the end of Clinch mountain; thence with the ridge that divides the waters of Richland and Flat creeks to Holston river, at the upper end of the first bluff above Boyle's old place; thence up the meanders of said river to the mouth of Panther creek; thence up said creek to the head spring thereof, near the house of John Evans; thence along the main waggon road to the beginning.[2]

The county was attached to Hamilton District.[3]

By acts of the general assembly the lines of Grainger, Hawkins, Knox, and Jefferson counties were altered many times in the nineteenth century, and since 1801 Grainger County has been partitioned in the formation of many other counties. In 1801 parts of Grainger County were erected into the new counties of Anderson and Claiborne.[4] In 1806 parts of Anderson and Claiborne were created into Campbell County,[5] and in 1844 Hancock County was created out of Hawkins and Claiborne.[6] In 1850 Union County

---

[1]For introduction to this series see East Tennessee Historical Society's *Publications* (Knoxville), No. 23 (1951), 115-16. Hereafter cited E. T. H. S. *Publications*. For their assistance in preparation of No. IV, the compiler wishes to thank Mrs. Penelope Johnson Allen, Chattanooga; Mrs. Charles F. Wayland, Sr., Knoxville; and Prentiss Price, Rogersville, Tennessee.

[2]George Roulstone (comp.), *Laws of the State of Tennessee* (Knoxville, 1803), 95-96. Hereafter cited as Roulstone, *Laws*.

[3]*Ibid.*, Sec. 7.

[4]*Ibid.*, 274, 279-81.

[5]Edward Scott (comp.), *Laws of the State of Tennessee, Including Those of North Carolina Now in Force in This State From the Year 1715 to the Year 1820, Inclusive*, 2 vols. (Knoxville, 1821), I, 945.

[6]Henry D. Whitney (comp. and ed.), *The Land Laws of Tennessee* . . . (Chattanooga, 1891), 785. Hereafter cited as Whitney, *Land Laws*.

was created out of portions of Grainger, Knox, Anderson, Campbell, and Claiborne counties.[7] Twenty years passed before any more territory was removed; in that year Hamblen County was erected out of Grainger, Jefferson, and Hawkins counties.[8]

When Grainger County was organized at the house of Benjamin McCarty on June 13, 1796, the following justices, appointed by Governor John Sevier, were present: Thomas Henderson, Elijah Chisum, James Blair, John Estes, Felps Reed, Benjamin McCarty, James Moore, John Bowen, John Kidwell, John Simms, William Thompson, and Major Lea.[9] Ambrose Yancey was elected sheriff; Felps Reed, register; John Estes, ranger; James Moore, coroner. Jesse James, Reuben White, William Smith, Elias Davis, John Rhea, John Hibbert (or Hibberd), Samuel Cox, and James Russell were elected constables.

The first deed probated was a conveyance from Sarah Blair and James Blair, Jr., administrators of the estate of James Blair, to Richard Thompson.[10]

Rutledge, the county seat, was not selected until 1799 although commissioners had been appointed in the act establishing the county.[11] The commissioners appointed for that purpose, Michael Massingale, Henry Howell, Jacob Vanhooser, William Milligan, and John Bristo, selected a site on the plantation of Martin Ashburn. During the intervening time the court met at the house of Captain John Bunch on Richland Creek, doubtless not far from the present site of Rutledge.

The justices each year were ordered to "take in" a list of the taxable property in the county. In the act creating the county the limit of the tax was prescribed. The county courts in Tennessee were authorized to levy a tax on property by a legislative act passed October 25, 1797,[12] in which types of taxable property were listed and the method of taking the taxes was prescribed. Other acts were passed amending minor provisions of this act, but it remained substantially the same until civil districts were established by the Constitution of 1834.

---

[7]*Acts*, 1849-50 (Ch. 61, sec. 1), 181.
[8]Whitney, *Land Laws*, 870.
[9]Grainger County Minutes of Court of Pleas and Quarter Sessions (Courthouse, Rutledge; typewritten copy, University of Tennessee Library). Hereafter cited as Minutes.
[10]*Ibid.*, June 13, 1796.
[11]The commissioners were: David Hailey, Major Lea, Benjamin McCarty, Bartley (or Bartlett) Marshall, and James Blair, Jr.
[12]Roulstone, *Laws*, 114-20.

By the provisions of the act of 1797 white polls consisted of "all free males and male servants between the age of twenty one and fifty years"; slaves, "all slaves male and female, between the age of twelve and fifty years."

The justices of Grainger County were ordered to take in lists of taxable property for year 1799 on February 21. On August 23 the following tax rates[13] were set:

For each white poll	.12½
For each 100 acres of land	.12½
For each Black poll	.25
For each stud horse Kept for covering mares	.25
For each town lott	.12½

The following lists are transcribed from a microfilm copy of an original certified copy returned by Ambrose Yancey, Grainger County court clerk, to the Tennessee general assembly, now on file in the Tennessee State Library and Archives, Nashville. They are not of record in Grainger County. These lists have been microfilmed by the compiler, and are available in the McClung Collection, Lawson McGhee Library. The Library also has original tax lists for Grainger County for other years.

No attempt has been made to make extensive identification of the names on these lists. The sources for information on these names are extensive. The records of Grainger County, with a few exceptions, have been preserved and are available in the courthouse at Rutledge. Typewritten copies of some of the early county records were made by the Tennessee Historical Records Survey. A complete set of the transcriptions is available in the Tennessee State Library and Archives, and some books at the University of Tennessee Library, Knoxville. The McClung Historical Collection has typewritten, photostatic, and microfilm copies of various records.

Key to Column Numbers
[1] Land
[2] White polls
[3] Black polls
[4] Stud Horses
[5] Town Lots

[13]*Minutes*, August 23, 1799.

Tax List in the bounds of Capt. Coxes Company Takin in by William Hankins Esquire. [1799]

Names	[1]	[2]	[3]	[4]	[5]
Acuff, Christopher		1			
Ady, Loyd		1			
Alsop, John		1			
Alsop, John		1			
Black, John	120	1			
Boyd, Robert	400	1			
Beaty, John	200	1			
Brock, Allen	200	1			
Bready, John	100	1			
Brock, George		1			
Cobb, William[14]	1170	1	16	1	
Churchman, Edward		1	1	1	
Churchman, Thomas	200		1		
Cornelius, John		1			
Cox, Thomas	361	1	2		
Coats, Charles	161	1			
Dent, John		1			
Campbell, James	680	1	1		
Dyer, James		1			
Forguson, James	88				
Feers, Jacob		1			
Garner, Obediah		1			
Goen, Thomas		1			
Gibson, Jacob		1			
Garnagan [Jarnagin], Chesley[15]	750	1			
Gibbs, John	498				
Gaines, Robert		1			
Garnagan, Thomas[16]	1475				
Hawkins, John	150	1			
Hawkins, Henry	400	1			
Hawkins, Thomas		1			
Hailey, David			1		

---

[14]Much misinformation has appeared in print about the Cobbs. The Cobbs came from Northampton County, North Carolina, to Watauga in the 1770's. This William Cobb was the son of Benjamin Cobb as is proved by a power of attorney in Washington County, Tennessee, dated September 20, 1793. It was at William Cobb's home in Washington County that Governor William Blount made his home 1790-92. By 1797 William Cobb had moved to Grainger County, and in 1799 he sold his Washington County land. A change of county lines in 1801 placed him in Knox County where he died late in 1802. His widow Sally and his brother Pharoah Cobb of Hawkins County were his administrators. He seems to have been twice married. By his first wife Isabella he had a daughter Sally who married Marston Mead by 1807 and moved to Blount County, Alabama. By his second wife Sally, he had a son William Pharoah Cobb (1798-1827) who married Martha Todd. Their descendants live at Mascot, Tennessee. William Cobb's widow Sally, a wealthy woman, married the Reverend Thomas Wilkerson in August, 1807.

[15](1753-1830), married Mary Witt, daughter of Charles Witt.

[16](Nov. 25, 1774-April 17, 1826); married Martha Barton Mar. 9, 1793, in Jefferson County, Tenn.

Hailey, David	1000	1	
Hodges, James		1	
Hogg, Obediah		1	
Howard, William	1040	1	
Hankins, Edward		1	
Hankins, William	400	1	
Hankins, Abel	250	1	
Hall, James	200	1	
Hamilton, Peter	150	1	
Humberd, William	1000		
Henson, Pall		1	
Hamilton, James	185	1	
Hughs, Robert		1	
Hogg, Reubin		1	
Jones, Harwood	500	1	2
Isaac, Elijah		1	
Inman, Joseph	133	1	
Inman, William		1	
Johnston, Daniel		1	
Kitchen, Jessee		1	
King, William		1	1
Lea, Major[17]	375	1	1
Mitchell, William	172	1	
McDonald, Jane	400		
Mayberry, Francis	1780		
Melicoat, James		1	
Martin, George	180	1	
Mullins, John		1	
Newgin, Thomas		1	
Patterson, John	369		
Perrin, Joel		1	
Perrin, Joseph	200		4
Robertson, James	127	1	
Richards, John		1	
Stone, Robert	400	1	3
Sharp, John	200	1	
Sotherland, Daniel		1	
Sotherland, George		1	
Steward, Alexander	350		
Vances, James	300	1	
Vinyard, John	171	1	
Ware, William		1	
Waddle, Daniel		1	

[17]A Baptist minister (May 21, 1771-July 16, 1822); married, Nov. 17, 1793, Lavinia Jarnagin.

List of Taxable property in part of the Bounds of Captain [Isaac] Lane's Company[18] taken by John Bristo, Esqr. 1799.

Names	[1]	[2]	[3]	[4]	[5]
Arnwin, James	200	1			
Arnwin, John	180			1	
Acuff, John		1			
Acuff, Cain		1			
Blackwood, William		1			
Beelor, Daniel	320	1			
Beelor, John	240		1		
Beelor, Peter	640	1			
Bean, Stephen	400	1			
Bean, John[19]	1000				
Bean, John H.		1			
Bull, George		1			
Bunch, David		1			
Bunch, Martin		1			
Bodle, James	70	1			
Bristo, John	200	1			
Casey, John	220	1			
Casey, Samuel		1			
Casey, James		1			
Cearle, George	320	1			
Clark, Samuel	300	1			
Clark, Edward	360		1		
Capish [Cabbage], Adam		1			
Capish, John	1	1			
Claunch, Barnet		1			
Claunch, John	50	1			
Colen, Joshua		1			
Cheek, Dauson	100	1			
Dunn, Thomas	200	1			
Dodson, Samuel		1			
Frye, Gabriel		1			
Grifith, John		1			
Ginnings, [Jennings], Hezekiah		1			
Ginnings, Royal[20]	200	1			
Harriss, Richard	90	1			
Howeth, William		1			
Holt, Edward		1			
Holt, David		1			
Holt, David, Snr	200	1			

---

[18]These people lived north of Clinch Mountain to Clinch River.

[19]Revolutionary soldier; commissioned captain, Tennessee militia, Oct. 10, 1796. Mrs. John Trotwood Moore (comp.), *Record of Commissions of Officers in the Tennessee Militia, 1796-1811* (Nashville, 1947), 13. Hereafter cited as Moore, *Commissions.*

[20]Revolutionary War pensioner.

Gilington [Gillentine], Nicholas[21]		1
Heziah, Richard	75	1
Forgeson, Benjn		1
Morris, John	1	1
Moore, Abner	1	1
Windham, Rachel[22]	200		4
McFarren, Sam'l		1
Miller, Harmon		1
Terry, Richard		1
Petre, George	200	1
Petre, Adam		1
Petre, John		1
Petre, Daniel	1	1
Piercefield, Sam'l		1
Rambsy, Sam'l		1
Shockley, Richard		1
Shaw, Benjamin	600	1
Smith, Josiah	150	1
Stafford, Stephen		1

List of Taxes and Taxable property in the Bounds of Capt. Horner's Company taken in by William Arnold, Esq. 1799.

Names	[1]	[2]	[3]	[4]	[5]
Ashburn, Martin[23]	600	1	2		1
Arnet, Jacob[24]	600	1			
Alsop, James	235	1			
Arnold, William	400	1	1		
Baker, John	250	1			
Bird, John	100				
Boatman, George		1			
Boatman, Henry	203	1			
Combe, Philip	300	1			
Cotton, Jacob	200	1			
Cox, Richard		1			
Clay, William[25]	110	4			
Coffey, Meredith	200	1			
Christian, Allen	50	1			
Churchman, John		1			
Chamberlin, Jere[26]	670		5		
Conley, John	100	1	1		
Colleson, James	300	1			
Churchman, Edw	550				
Dumvell, Robert	240				

[21]Ancestor of the Sequatchie Valley family.
[22]Widow of Reuben Windham who died 1795 in Hawkins County.
[23]First sheriff of Grainger County.
[24]Left will in Grainger County, dated April 28, 1825.
[25]Revolutionary War pensioner.
[26]Revolutionary soldier.

Duncan, William		1	
Elliot, Jacob		1	
Elliot, Benj		1	
Eaton, Joseph[27]	172		
Guinn [Gwinn], Wm	200	1	
Garrot [Garrett, Jarrett], Absalom		1	
Ginnings [Jennings], Thomas		1	
Ginnings, Wm		1	
Gilmore, John[28]	200	1	
Gipson [Gibson], Garrot		1	
Gipson, Archeles	100	1	
Gilmore, John	350		
Harris, Even	400	1	
Harris, Robert		1	
Hinshaw, John	300	1	
Humphrys, John[29]		1	
Hickman, James	100		
Horner, John	300	1	
Horner, James	100	1	
Hall, John		1	
Howard, Richard	300		
Jones, Thomas	140	1	
Jarnagan [Jarnigan], Noe[30]	500	1	
Long, Joseph	67	1	
Moore, James	405	1	
Murphey, Wm		1	
Mitchell, Benjn		1	
Medlock, John	300	1	2
Morgan, Valentine		1	
Miller, George	57	1	
Morrow, Alexd	244		3
Miller, Martin	150	1	
McFarson [McPherson], Henry		1	
Moore, Sam'l	300		
Moore, James, Esqr	380	1	
Martin, John	86	1	
Maxfield, Seth		1	
Nation, Joseph	320		
Owen, John	274	1	
ODonald, Michel		1	
Ore, Joseph	300	1	1
Pressgrove, George		1	
Perry, Samuel	238	1	
Richardson, James	490	1	

---

[27]Left will in Grainger County, dated June 18, 1808.
[28]Left will in Grainger County, dated July 16, 1804.
[29]Came to Grainger County from Surry County, N. C.
[30]Born July 9, 1768; married Mary Russell, daughter of George Russell; active in public life, he was the enumerator of the federal census of 1810.

Rice, Henry[31]	620	1			
Ray, Joseph		1			
Short, James		1			
Smith, Aron	400	1			
Scrogins, Barton		1			
Smith, Thomas	250	1	1		
Tracker, Edward		1			
Trogdon, Ezecheal	122	1			
Thompson, James	330				
Thompson, Temple	400				
Underhill Wm		1			
Winds, Enoch		1			
Whitehead, Robt.		1			
Williams, Wm		1			
Whitlock, James	385	1			
Williams, Jonathan		1			
Williams, John	200	1			

List of Taxes and Taxable property in the Bounds of Capt. Bowman's Co. taken by John Vanbibber, Esqr. for the year 1799.[32]

Names	[1]	[2]	[3]	[4]	[5]
Ausemus, Peter	1				
Adkins, Thomas	1				
Bowman, Wm	1				
Banneth, John	1				
Berry, John	1				
Boydstone, Thomas	1				
Birdsong, John	1				
Canterberry, Zecheriah	1	1			
Canterberry, John	1				
Coffelt, Daniel	1				
Cain, David	1				
Camron [Cameron], Ezra	1				
Dowtherd, Evan	1				
Devees [Dwees], James	1	1			
Derry luney, Michel	1				
Dunkin, Samuel	1				
Davis, Moses	1				
Fenley, James		1			
Grifith, George	1				
Garrot, Isaac	1				
Hunter, Henry	1				
Hafaker [Halfacre, Huffaker], Michael[33]	1				
Howard, Robert	1				

---

[31]Died about 1818 in Campbell (now Union) County, Tenn.; a Revolutionary soldier, he settled at New Canton, in present Hawkins County, by 1775; settlement known as Rice's Mill.

[32]These people's land fell into Claiborne County upon its creation in 1801.

[33]First sheriff of Campbell County, Tenn.

Hamblin, John	1	
Hart, Hardy	1	
Keywood, Stephen	1	
Keywood, Benjn	1	
King, William	1	
Kirklin, Moses	1	
Kincaid, James	1	
Lewis, Abner	1	
Linch [Lynch], Jeremiah	1	
Munkas, John	1	
Marele, Laurence	1	
Marele, Peter	1	
Newport, Carana [Cavanaugh?]	1	
Powers, Jessee	1	
Pock [?], Thomas	1	
Reed, Solomon	1	
Rul [Ruhl, Rule], George	1	
Shaw, John	1	
Starr, James	1	
Skidmore, Henrix	1	1
Vanbibber, James	1	
Vanbiber, John	1	1
Vanbibber, Peter	1	
Weaver, Saml' Jun	1	
Weaver, Joseph	1	
Weaver, Sam'l Snr	1	
Weaver, John	1	
Whitestton [Whitecotton], Isaac	1	
Yoakum, George[34]	2	1

List of Taxes and Taxable property in the Bounds of Capt. Halfacre's Company as returned by M. Simes, Esqr. 1799.[35]

Names	[1]	[2]	[3]	[4]	[5]
Adams, George		1			
Arthur, Elias		1			
Adams, John		1			
Auston, William, Junr.		1			
Benson, Chirchester		2			
Berry, James	1440				
Baker, Joseph		2			
Bennett, Thomas		1			
Cowan, Alexander		1			
Collums, George		1			
Cleek, John		1			
Cox, Josiah		1			

[34]Along with other settlers principally from Hampshire County, Va. (now West Va.), established Yoakum's Station, in present Claiborne County.

[35]See footnote 31, *supra*.

Cowan, Samuel		1	1		
Chilton, Wm		1			
Cline, Peter		1			
Doherty, Wm. Senr.		1	2		
Harbert, David		1			
Halfacre, Peter		1			
Haskins, Thomas		1			
Hoskins, Elias		1			
James, Wm		1			
Jordan, Ezekiah	640	2			
Lusk, Samuel		1	1		
Lane, William		1	1		
Lee, John	88	1			
Lee, James	600				
Martin, Daniel		1			
McFarland, Duncan		1			
Owen, John, Senr		2			
Owen, William		1			
Peveehous, Abraham	500				
Rains, Henry		1	2		
Ritchee, Alexd[36]	100				
Rector, George		1			
Renfro, James		1	2		
Smith, Gedion		1	1	1	
Stinnett, Isom		1	1		
Stinnett, Benjamin			2		
Stevenson, Edward		1	1		
Stinson, George		1			
Stinson, Robert		1			
Sholley, Michael	200				
Tate, John		1			
Tate, Samuel	600	1	1		
Wallen, Elisha, Junr.		1			
Walker, John		1			
Willson, George		1			
Wallen, Elisha, Senr.	2570	8			

List of Taxes and Taxable property in the Bounds of Captn David Shelton's Company Returned by Isaiah Midkiff, Esqr. for the year 1799.

Names	[1]	[2]	[3]	[4]	[5]
Butcher, Barney	135	1			
Brown, John		1			
Burton, John		1			
Buzby, John	150	1			
Brown, Wm		1			
Coulter, John	1400		1		
Curkham [Kirkham], Wm	200	1			

---

[36]Revolutionary War pensioner.

Carmichael, James	400	1		
Donathan, Elijah	200	1		1
Dodson, James	640	1		
Denson, William		1		
Evans, David		1		
Evans, Joel		1		
Evens, Davis	196	1		
Green, John	200	1		
Grisham, James		1		
Garvis [Jarvis], Suks Luke [?]		1		
Guffee [Guffey], Ephim	100	1		
Hudgings, Robert	50	1	1	
Hudgings, Ambrose		1		
Jackson, Reubin	50	1		
Kimra [?], George		1		
McMane, Dominy		1		
Midkiff, Isaih[87]	95	1		
McDonald, Isaac	300			
Morgan, Henry	150	1		
McEnelly [McAnally], Charles		1		
McGee, John		1		
Norton, Nathan		1		1
Noe, Joseph Snr	310			
Noe, Joseph Junr		1		
Norton, William	100	1		
Piles, Conrod		1		1
Rich, Thomas		1		
Rail [Rayl], Sam'l		1		
Phillips, Hezekiah	75	1		
Reddis, James		1		
Runnels [Reynolds], James		1		
Rains, John		1		
Shelton, David	5301	1	2	
Shelton, Richard		1		
Suirlock [?], Samuel		1		
Shote, Gabriel		1		
Shelton, William	100	1		
Shelton, Ralph	250	1		
Smith, Charles	400	1	1	
Shelton, David		1		
Willson, John		1	1	
Williams, Wm. Junr.		1		
Williams, Wm. Senr.	140	1		

List of Taxes and Taxable property in the bounds of Capt. [George] Bean's Company, returned by William Stone Esquire 1799.

Names	[1]	[2]	[3]	[4]	[5]
Auston, Nathaniel		1			

---

[87]Revolutionary War pensioner.

Arno, Peter		1		
Bean, Jessee[38]		1	2	
Bean, George	50	1	1	
Bean, Elizabeth	200			
Bowen, John	190	1		
Bowen, James		1		
Bowen, Henry Senr[39]	200		1	
Bowen, Henry, Junr.	414	1		
Bunch, Thomas		1		
Blair, William		1		
Briant [Bryant], Joseph	150	1		
Beelor, Joseph		1		
Bliar [Blair], James Junr	200	1		
Bliar, Robert		1		
Bliar, Alexd		1	2	
Buzby, Thomas	20			
Blair, James, Snr	450		2	
Blair, William	200	1		
Counts, Nicholas[40]	327	1	1	
Carnes [Carns, Karns, etc.], Michael	300			
Carnes, Michael Jr		1		
Cooper, Isaac		1		
Campbell, David		1		
Combs, George	425	1		
Crabb, Francis		1		
Crabb, John		1		
Counts, John	200			
Cocke, William[41]	2250			
Crabb, Joseph, Dec'd	640			
Cobb, Joseph[42]	1798	1	1	
Cuningham, Joshua		1		
Henderson, William	286	1		1
Haygood, Tapley		1		
Hipsheers, Mathias		1		
Henderson, Thomas[43]	650	1		

---

[38]Revolutionary War soldier; for an account of him and the Bean family see Mrs. Penelope John Allen, "Leaves from the Family Tree," *Chattanooga Times*, July 8, 1934.

[39]Revolutionary War soldier; left will in Grainger County, dated Mar. 26, 1806.

[40]Member of family of German origin; Revolutionary War pensioner.

[41](1748-Aug. 22, 1828); served in the legislatures of seven states and territories and the United States Senate. For a sketch of this remarkable man see *Dictionary of American Biography*, 21 vols. and index (New York, 1928-1944), IV, 255-56.

[42]Born in Virginia, probably Southampton County in 1769, the son of William. He was early in Grainger County where he married in December, 1797, Mrs. Sarah Smith Blair, widow of Lieutenant Colonel John Blair. There were six children. Joseph Cobb lived at Bean's Station and was a prominent surveyor, and served in the Indian wars. In his old age he moved to Madison County, Tenn., where he died in 1857. His oldest son was Dr. Pharoah Boone Cobb (1798-1889), of Henderson County, Tenn., and Hernando, Miss.

[43]Captain in the Revolutionary War; chairman of first county court of Grainger County; lived at Rocky Spring; removed to Sequatchie Valley.

Hill, William		1		
Hipsheer, Henry		1		
Inglish, Wm dec'd[44]	300			
Jones, William		1		
Jones, Aqualla		1	1	
King, Robert	300			
King, Robert & Thomas	2780			
King, Thomas	1280			
Leabo, Henry	200	1		
Leabo, John	200	1	2	
Leabo, Jacob				
McDonald, Alexd				
Midkiff, John	50	1		
McElkeny [McIlhaney], John		1		
McElkeny, Robt		1		
Moses		1		
Mumpouer, John	100	1		
Mcbroom, Thomas[45]	250	1	2	
Masangale [Massengill], Mikel[46]	200	1	5	
Massey, Jonathan		1		
Mitchell, Richard[47]	1875			
Noe, John		1		
Noe, Peter		1		
Ore, James[48]	3215	1	10	
Patterson, Robert	100	1	1	1
Pannel, Thomas	50	1		
Robertson, Daniel, Jnr	184	1		
Robertson, Hughes	184	1		
Rusel [Russell], Elizabeth[49]	300			
Runnolds, John		1		
Radle, John		1		
Rule, Peter		1		
Sharp, George		1		
Shelton, Nelson		1		

---

[44]Massacred by the Indians, December, 1787; his son Matthew English returned to Grainger County after being ransomed from captivity among the Indians; recovered the Bean Station property through a lawsuit and then sold out to Jenkin Whiteside and removed to Rhea County, Tenn., where he lived on White's Creek. Goodspeed Publishing Company, History of Tennessee, East Tennessee edition (Chicago, 1887), 875.

[45]Removed to Madison County, Ala.

[46]Revolutionary War pensioner.

[47]Resident of Hawkins County, Tenn.

[48]Born in Cecil County, Maryland, Nov. 28, 1762; died June 24, 1812, at Nickojack, Cherokee Nation; a Revolutionary soldier, he moved from Virginia to Tennessee in 1791; commissioned lieutenant colonel, Grainger County, 1796; commanded successful Nickojack Expedition against Lower Towns of the Cherokees, Sept. 13, 1794, as second major of Hawkins County; Indian trader and business partner of John Sommerville with stores at Knoxville and Bean Station; established a grist mill and tavern at Nickojack, where he died.

[49]Widow of George Russell, Revolutionary company commander at Battle of King's Mountain.

Smith, Bartholomeu[50]	520	1	1		
Smith, Harbert		1			
Short, James	250				
Senter, Willis		1			
Smith, John		1			
Wood, John		1			
Williams, Lewis		1			
Windham, Wm Junr		1	1		
Windham, Wm Senr		1			
Ward, John	200	1			
Yancy, Robert	200	1		1	
Yancy, Ambrose[51]		1			

Lists of Taxes and Taxable Property in the bounds of Capt. Hamilton's Co. returned by Andrew Evans Esquire 1799.

Names	[1]	[2]	[3]	[4]	[5]
Arwin, John		1			
Archer, Cornelius		1			
Asher, Daniel		1			
Asher, Robertson		1			
Brown, James	300	1			
Braden, Edward	200	1			
Braden, John		1			
Black, John	500	1			
Buckner, Presley		1			
Brown, James		1			
Brown, Thomas		1			
Brokis, William	100	1			
Bruston, James		1			
Berry, James	640				
Blunt [Blount], Willie[52]	2220				
Caps, Jacob		1			
Craft, Ezechiel		1			
Cook, William	500	1			
Clark, Henry		1			
Clifton, Hardy		1			
Clifton, William	300				
Coats, Jessee	400	1			
Condrey, Benjamin	850	1			
Condrey, Dennis	100	1			
Cood, William		1			
Carwiles, John		1			
Cook, Aron		1			
Davis, Elnathan		1			
Dale, Alexander		1			

---

[50]Removed to Dickson County, Tenn.
[51]Revolutionary War pensioner and first clerk of Grainger County.
[52]Later governor of Tennessee (1809-1815).

Davis, Isaac		1		
Dennis, Joseph	300	1		
Dale, Abel	400	1		
Dennis, Thomas		1		
Green, Joseph[53]	1100			
Green, James	400			
Gambell, Thomas		1		
Hudson, John		1		
Harelson, John		1		
Hamilton, Wm	2029	1		1
Harelson, Wm	333			1
Hudelton, John		1		
Hopper, Archeble	400	1		
Harris, John	100	1		
Hutcherson, Charles[54]	100	1		
Hutcherson, Paul	100	1		
Hudson, Ezekiel		1		
Hudson, Obediah				1
Hudson, James		1		
Hudson, Benjn	200	1		
Harmon, Wm		1		
Hughs, Hardy		1		
Hughs, John		1		
Hord, William	1200			
Jackson, Nathan		1		
James, Jessee		1		
James, Thomas		1		
James, Wm			2	
James, William		1		
Kirkpatrick, James		1		
Kirkpatrick, John	300	1		
Lewis, Fielding		1	1	
Lower, Peter	200		1	
Lanes, James		1		
Lenor, Young	226	1		
McBee, Sam'l		1		
McBee, Isaac	400	1		
Munrow, Robert	400	1		
Mulkey, John		1		
Moswell, Nimrod	73			
McCarver, Archd	400			
Mosgrove, John	150			
Moore, Robert	100	1		
McFeetrage, Matth	500	1		
McFeeter [McPheeters], And[55]	200	1		
Marlow, Thomas		1		

---

[53]Resided in North Carolina.

[54]Removed to Bledsoe County, Tenn.

[55]Revolutionary War soldier who drew a pension for his service in Pennsylvania and North Carolina; removed to Indiana, then to Missouri, where he died 1847.

Nash, John		1	
Norris, George		1	
Noll, William[56]	800		4
Noll, John	200	1	2
ODonal, John	5000		
Peeters, Nathaniel	400		
Peeters, William	400	1	
Parks, Phillip		1	
Selvage, Jeremiah	333	1	
Sions, Nimrod		1	
Sally, John	200	1	
Stanly, Isaac		1	
Savage, Michael	333	1	
Stafford, Stephen	550	1	
Simes, Matthew		1	
Turner, Robert		1	
Tuttle, Peter		1	
Tuttle, James		1	
Tredway, Isom		1	
Tucker, John		1	
Vangriff, Garret		1	
Wamble, Joshua		1	
Waters, Obediah	400	1	
Widner, Henry		1	
Widner, Lewis[57]	400		
Whitefield, Neadom[58]	400		
Williams, John		1	
Williamson, Hugh	3000		
York, Jabaz		1	1
York, Semore		1	

List of Taxes and Taxable property in the bounds of Capt. McKees Company as returned by Benjamin McCarty, Esqr for the year 1799.

Names	[1]	[2]	[3]	[4]	[5]
Bradford, Benja		1			
Bridges, William		1			
Bridges, Thomas		1			
Barton, Henry		1			
Buzby, Thomas	25				
Buzby, John	150	1			
Cocke, John[59]	740	1	6	1	

---

[56]Revolutionary soldier.
[57]Left will in Grainger County dated Dec. 18, 1806.
[58]Resided in Johnston County, N. C.
[59]Probably Grainger County's most distinguished citizen; son of William and Sarah (Macklin) Cocke, born Dec., 1772, in Brunswick County, Va.; died Feb. 16, 1854, Rutledge, Tenn., where he is buried in Methodist Church Cemetery; major general, Tennessee militia in Creek War; congressman; state senator to the Tennessee legislature from Grainger, Jefferson, and Claiborne counties where he introduced the bill for creating a state school for the deaf, December, 1844.

Connor, Abner		1	
Cooper, Cornelius		1	
Cook, Marcuriovs		1	
Cooper, Wm	50		
Cooper, William		1	
Cox, Richard	60		
Collison, Jonathan Sr	600		
Collison, Jonathan	150	1	
Clark, Henry		1	
Daniel, John	175	1	3
Daniel, Francis	150	1	
Davis, William	200	1	
Dorah, John		1	
Davis, David	140	1	
Duke, Pleasent	280	1	1
Evans, John	119		3
Evans, William	350	1	
Formault [Formwalt], John, Sr.	350	2	
Goen, James		1	
Goen, John	90	1	
Grant, Isaac		1	
Howel, Henry	830	1	2 1
Hill, James		1	
Hill, Joab[60]	500	1	
Hodges, Moses		1	
Hays, William		1	
Hodges, Ambrose		1	
Howel, Calip		1	
Howel, John		1	
Howel, William	150	1	
Howel, Melchiah	100	1	
Howel, Benjamin[61]		1	
Jarnagan, John Snr.	200	1	
Jarnagan, Drury		1	
Jarnagan, John		1	
Ivey, Henry	100	1	
Jackson, William		1	
Ivey, Vandimon		1	
Ivey, Backster		1	
Loyd, Owen		1	
Mays, Henry	100	1	1 1
McCarty, James		1	
McKee, Matthew	70	1	
Mason, Reubin		1	
Mays, Sherod	100	1	
Mays, Thomas		1	
Mays, William		1	

[60]Revolutionary War soldier.
[61]Revolutionary War soldier.

McCarty, John		1			
Mitchell, Isaac		1			
Miligan, William	150	1			
McKiver, John for Hudson & Hall	12000				
McCarty, Benjn[62]	300	1	1		
Russel, James	200	1			
Russell, John Sr.		1			
Russel, James		1			
Stiffee, John	640	1	1		
Smith, William	200	1			
Street, Asa		1			
Stone, William	150		2		
Tye, John		1			
Weston, Casper		1			
White, Joseph	482	1			
Campbell, Arthur	640				
Calkahoon, James alias Robert King	640				
Anderson, John	400				
Anderson, Wm	400				
McCarty, James Sr.	950				

List of Taxes and Taxable property in the Bounds of Capt. English Company returned by John Vanbibber, Esqr. 1799.[63]

Names	[1]	[2]	[3]	[4]	[5]
Alley, James	1				
Baker, Samuel	1				
Bruton, James	1	2			
Bruton, Samuel	2				
Bruton, Jacob	1				
Carelock, John	1				
Carelock, Joseph	1				
Caismon [Crismon], Isaac	1	1			
Crowly, John	1				
Crowley, William	1	1			
Durham, William	1				
Devees [Dwees?], Charles	1	1			
Davis, James		1			
Foster, Martin	1				
Gipson, James	2				
Inglish, William	1				
Inglish, John	1				
Inglish, Joseph		1			
McDonald, Redmon	1				
McDonal, Michael	1				

---

[62]Revolutionary War soldier.

[63]Most of these people's land fell into Claiborne County upon its creation in 1801, and later into Campbell County, 1806. See George L. Ridenour, *The Land of the Lake; a History of Campbell County, Tennessee* (LaFollette, 1941), 105-08.

McCracken, James	1
Mosier, Absolum	1
Sweeton, Dutton	1
Sweeton, John	1
Smith, Andrew	1
Murrah, Christopher	1
Sharp, Joseph	1
Toten, Benjamin	1
Tacket, Lewis	1
Vaught, Andrew	1
Wilhite, Bonard	1
Williams, Joseph	1
Womack, Johnston	1
Womack David	1

List of Taxes and Taxable property in the Bounds of Capt. Daniel Taylor's Company as returned by John Estes, Esqr. for the year 1799.

Names	[1]	[2]	[3]	[4]	[5]
Allen, Barnet		1			
August, John		1			
Adams, Roberts Junr		1			
Booker, Barnabas		1			
Bliar, Jossiah					
Cunningham, Thos	100				
Cunningham, James		1			
Cox, Jeremiah		1			
Cox, Harmon	150	1			
Cox, Samuel	100	1			
Cook, William		1			
Corrithers, James		1			
Cooper, John		1			
Cain, Hugh[64]	170	1			
Cannon, John		1			
Davidson, Samuel		1			
Dunkin, John	100	1			
Dunkin, Peter	100	1			
Dodson, Thomas Sr	150		3		
Estes, John [65]	163	1	1		
Estes, Robert	100	1			
Estes, John C.		1			
Estes, Barnet		1			
Estes, Thomas	100	1			
Estes, Ezekiel	774	1			
Hawkins, Samuel B.	200	1			
Estes, Micajah	100	1			

---

[64](1756-Aug. 21, 1851); a native of County Derry, Ireland; died in Hawkins County.
[65]Revolutionary War pensioner.

Hibbard, Lemuel	240		
Harris, Peter	300	1	2
Harris, Samuel		1	
Kidwell, Josiah	200	1	
Long, Robert	225	1	
Laremore, Hugh[66]	100	1	1
Moffet, William	500	2	
Martin, Thomas	75	1	
McMore, Magnes		1	
Marshel, Bartlett[67]	380	1	3
Murphey, William[68]	359		1
Neal, William		1	
Nichols, David		1	
Frank (Negro)	200		
Peter (Negro)	125		1
Johnston, Stephen		1	
Reed, Felps		1	
Riggs, Jessee[69]	400	1	2
Riggs, Reubin	200		
Runnolds, Richard		1	
Smith, William	1005	2	1
Sanders, Phillip		1	
Shepley, Edward	150	1	
Taylor, Daniel[70]	100	1	
Thompson, Richard	200	1	2
Taylor, James[71]	200		2
Witt, Joel		1	
Webster, Abbigal[72]	200		
Blount, John G	7 0000		
Churchman, Edwd	550		
Donelson, Stockley & King, James	1 0000		
Soree, Samuel	8000		

List of Taxes and Taxable property in the bounds of Capt. ·[Isaac] Lane's
Co. North of Clinch River as returned by Elijah Chisum, Esqr. 1799.[73]

Names	[1]	[2]	[3]	[4]	[5]
Auston, **Nathiel**	1040	1			

---

[66]Revolutionary War soldier; married a Miss Rowland, sister of ·Mrs. Daniel Taylor; born in 1759, moved from Grainger County to McMinn County, Tenn., and in 1840 was living in Cooper County, Missouri.

[67]Revolutionary War soldier.

[68]Revolutionary War soldier; a Baptist minister; married first, Martha Hodges, second, Sarah Barton (1748-1817), sister of the Reverend Isaac Barton.

[69]Came from Surry County, N. C.

[70](Aug. 13, 1761-Nov. 25, 1834); Revolutionary War pensioner from Henry County, Va.; married Jane Rowland.

[71](Feb. 28, 1731-April 4, 1815); Revolutionary War soldier; married Ann Owen; graves removed to Bethesda Cemetery at Cheeks X Roads.

[72]Widow of Reuben Webster, who died Dec. 19, 1790, in Hawkins County.

[73]Most of these people's land fell into Claiborne and Anderson counties.

Acklin, Samuel		1	
Beelar, John		1	2
Clark, Thomas		1	
Caps, William		1		1
Collins, Elisha		1	
Chisum, James	340	1	
Cogdale, Joseph		1	
Cunningham, John		1	
Crabb, Joseph		1	
Chisum, Elisha Jr.		1	
Clark, Isham		1	
Cobb, Joseph	780		
Chisum, Elisha	97	1	
Dodson, Nimrod	250	1	
Davis, John	100	1	
Devaul, Abraham			1
Dodson, Jessee Junr	320	1	
Dodson, Jessee Senr.	520	2	1	1
Donelson, Stockley	1 0000		
Gilbert, John		1	
Green, Funny		1	
Grose, John	320	1	
Groves, John		1	
Hurst, John[74]	500	1	
Henderson, Richard		1	
Hailey, Barnebas		1	
Henderson, Thomas		1	
Hunt, John	700	1	
Finley, Samuel		1	
Hill, John		1	
Henderson, Thomas		1	
Harris, Peter		1	
Henderson, Richd & Co.	10 0000		
Johnston, John		1	
Jones, William		1	
Jones, Isaac		1	
Jinings, Wm	300	3	
Jeffers, Thomas	200	1	
Kenney, James	100		
Lockwood, John		1	
Lane, Isaac[75]	320	1	1
Lewallin, Richd[76]		1	
Langham [Lanham], Abel[77]	650	1	
Langham & Lathim	1000		

---

[74]Revolutionary soldier.

[75]Revolutionary War pensioner; removed to McMinn County, Tenn. For an account of the Lane family see Allen, "Leaves from the Family Tree," *loc. cit.*, May 13, 20, 27, 1934.

[76]Revolutionary War pensioner born in Prince Edward County, Va.; died in Anderson County, Tenn.

[77]Revolutionary War pensioner.

Wm Lackey Rowan

Miller, Frederick	340		
Morgan, John		1	
Markham, Beverly		1	
Magers, John		1	
Mower, Nathaniel	200		
Miller, John	400	2	
Mayberry, Francis	640		
Mendingall, Abraham	640		
Neal, Peter	640	1	
Nation, Joseph	320		
Powel, Joseph	320		
Runnolds, William		1	
Roddy, Jessee[78]		1	
Rowan, Henry[79]	1240		
Sharp, Henry[80]	1100	1	1
Sharp, Jacob		1	1
Sharp, Conrod	200	1	2
Sweeton, William		1	
Smith, John		1	
Smith, Ezekiel		1	
Smith, Richard	320		
Smith, Samuel		1	
Savage, William		1	
Shults, Jacob		1	
Simes, James	100	1	
Stroud, William	300	1	1
Suthon, Robert		1	
Shults, Jacob	220	1	
Stubblefield, Lock[81]	300		
Templeton, James		1	
Whittle, Robert		1	
Wright, James		1	
Ward, William	500	1	
Daniel, James	300		2
York, Jeremiah		1	
Evans, Andrew	200	1	

[78]Son of Colonel John Roddye. See Allen, "Leaves from the Family Tree," *loc. cit.*, April 14, 1935.
[79]Married Elizabeth Lathim; in 1815, resident of Overton County, Tenn.
[80]See Mrs. Genevieve E. Peters, *Know Your Relatives* . . . (Washington, D. C., 1953), 10-20.
[81]Robert Loxley Stubblefield of Hawkins County; died 1817.

EARLY EAST TENNESSEE TAXPAYERS

Compiled by Pollyanna Creekmore

V. Jefferson County, 1800[1]

Jefferson County was created by an ordinance of the Territory South of the River Ohio, on June 11, 1792, and named in honor of Thomas Jefferson, then secretary of state.[2] The land was taken from Greene and Hawkins counties. Jefferson County has been partitioned in the creation of Sevier County in 1794,[3] and 1797 when Cocke County was created out of Jefferson and Greene.[4] The territorial limits remained virtually the same from 1797 to 1870, when Hamblen County was created out of Jefferson and Grainger counties.[5]

Upon its creation Jefferson County was a part of Washington District, but on March 12, 1793, along with Knox County, it was made a part of the newly-created Hamilton District.[6]

The first court was held at the home of Jeremiah Matthews on July 23, 1792. The following justices, appointed by Governor William Blount, were present: Alexander Outlaw, James Roddye, John Blackburn, James Lea, Joseph Wilson, Josiah Wilson, Andrew Henderson, Amos Balch and William Cox.[7] The first county officials, also appointed by Governor Blount, who qualified for office were: Joseph Hamilton, clerk; Robert McFarland, sheriff; James Roddye, register, and Robert McCamon, William Job, Robert Pollock (Polk), Josiah Rogers, John Renno (Reneau), Stephen Wolsey and Barsdill Riddle, constables. The lawyers who qualified to practice were: Luke

---

[1]For the introduction to this series see East Tennessee Historical Society's *Publications* (Knoxville), No. 23 (1951), 115-16. Previous installments have been: I, Anderson County, 1802, in No. 23; II, Blount County, 1801, in No. 24; III, Knox County, 1806, in No. 25; IV, Grainger County, 1799, in No. 27.

[2]George Roulstone (comp.), *Laws of the State of Tennessee* (Knoxville, 1803), iv-v.

[3]*Ibid.*, 38-39.

[4]*Ibid.*, 124-26.

[5]Henry D. Whitney (comp. and ed.), *The Land Laws of Tennessee* . . . (Chattanooga, 1891), 870-71. The Grainger County tax lists were published in ETHS *Publications* No. 27 (1955), 97-119.

[6]Roulstone, *Laws*, vi.

[7]Jefferson County Minutes of Court of Pleas and Quarter Sessions (Courthouse, Dandridge). There are indexed, typewritten copies in the Tennessee State Library and Archives, Nashville, and University of Tennessee Library, Knoxville; for record of official appointments by Governor Blount, see Clarence E. Carter (ed.), *The Territorial Papers of the United States*, IV, *The Territory South of the River Ohio*, 1790-1796 (Washington, 1936), *passim*, also *The Blount Journal*, 1790-1796 . . . (Nashville, 1955).

Bowyer, William Cocke, John Rhea, Alexander Outlaw, James Reese, Archibald Roane and Hopkins Lacy.

Dandridge, the county seat, was not laid out until the next year, when at the January term, 1793, the court appointed Alexander Outlaw, George Doherty, Garrett Fitzgerald, Andrew Henderson, and Hugh Kelso to locate the site.[8] The commissioners selected the site near Robert Henderson's meeting house (Hopewell Presbyterian Church) on the French Broad River. Fifty acres of land were donated by Francis Dean; the town was laid off by Samuel Jack and named in honor of Martha Dandridge, wife of President George Washington.

While Jefferson County was established in 1792, the earliest extant tax lists are those of 1800. After Tennessee became a state in 1796, a new act was passed October 25, 1797,[9] authorizing the counties to tax property and specifying types of property taxable and the method of taking them. White polls consisted of "all free males and male servants between the age of twenty-one and fifty years"; slaves, "all slaves male and female between the age of twelve and fifty years." The justices were ordered to take the lists in the militia captains' companies and return them to court. The clerk usually transcribed them into a book kept for that purpose.

The Jefferson County minutes for 1800 appear fragmentary; in all probability pages were misplaced before the book was rebound. No orders for taking the tax lists of 1800 can be located; neither can the record of their return nor the order setting the rates for that year.

The following lists were copied from the original manuscript lists many years ago, and the latter cannot today be located. The copy was published by Mrs. Penelope Johnson Allen, in her "Leaves from the Family Tree," in the *Chattanooga Times*, February 7, 14, 21, 1937. This reprinting is made possible through the permission of Mrs. Allen and the *Chattanooga Times*.

The next available tax lists for Jefferson County, covering the years 1822-1830, are available in the County Court Clerk's Office, Dandridge, and typewritten copies are among those records transcribed by the Tennessee Historical Records Survey, available in the Tennessee State Library and Archives, Nashville, and the University of Tennessee Library, Knoxville. Besides transcribing the county records, the His-

---

8Minutes, Jan. 31, 1793.
9Roulstone, *Laws*, 114-20.

torical Records Survey copied many Bible and tombstone inscriptions in Jefferson County.

Except for the tax lists and a few other loose papers, there is no known destruction of Jefferson County records by fire or otherwise. The deeds were reindexed by the Tennessee Valley Authority when land was acquired for the basins of Douglas and Cherokee Dams.

Key to column numbers

[1] Acres
[2] White polls
[3] Black polls
[4] Town lots

TAXABLE PROPERTY IN CAPT. CARSON'S COMPANY

	[1]	[2]	[3]	[4]
Ashmore, Hezekiah		1		
Ashley, Noah		1		
Bradford, Henry		1		1
Braner, Michael	450	1	1	
Blackburn, John	760	3		
Blackburn, William		1		
Balch, John	115	1		
Barnes, James		1		
Berry, John		1		
Berry, Robert	400	1		
Bogas, Bennett				1
Baker, Joseph				1
Bryan, William				1
Conner, Joseph		1		1
Cresswell, Henry	100	1		
Cofman, Isaac	60	1		1
Campbell, James	100	1		
Carson, Robert	360	1		
Clark, Samuel		1		
Coons, Michael, Senr.	288			
Coons, Michael, Junr.	192	1		
Carson, Samuel	100	1		
Carson, John, Senr.	80			
Carson, David		1		
Carson, John, Junr.		1		
Cotter, Stephen	100	1		
Cowan, James				1
Collinsworth, Coventon				4
Cavander, Alexander				1
Carter, Samuel		1		
Corbett, Elizabeth	200			
Coffee, James	90			
Doherty, James	200	1		2

	[1]	[2]	[3]	[4]
Davis, Nicholas	150	1	1	
Davis, James		1	1	
Duncan, Craven		1		
Doherty, George	300	1	4	1
Dean, John				6
Dean, Benjamin		1		
Ellis, John	50	1		
Adgar, Andrew	125	1		
Elliott, William	150	1		
Forbis, Thomas		1		
Frazer, Hugh	250	1		
Ferrill, James		1		
Gentry, Martin		1		
Grisham, Richard	150			
Gibbons, Patrick	300			
Greene, John		1		1
Guess, Samuel	100	1		
Grisham, Ezekial		1		
Gentry, Robert	220		2	
Gist, William		1		
Grisham, Thompson		1		
Galbreith, Thomas	200	1		
George, Edward	300	1	1	4
Gentry, Bartlett	100	1		
Graham, George	160	1	2	
Grier, John				1
Henderson, John	100	1		
Hallaway, John, Senator	100			
Hallaway, John, Jr.		1		
Hays, John		1	2	
Henry, William	137	1		
Haggard, Henry		1		
Henderson, Andrew	475	1	2	
Henderson, Robert	250	1	2	
Hoskins, William	200	1		
Hickman, Francis	400	1		1
Hibbert, Jedidiah		1		
Humes, Thomas				2
Hickman, Benjamin		1		
Jones, Jones, Jr.		1		
Johnson, Samuel	400			
Johnson, William		1		
Inman, Abednego	457		4	3
Kelso, Hugh	1045	1		1
Kelso, Alexander	266	1	2	1
Kerr, Andrew	200			
Kerr, David	200			
Kimbro, Jesse	100	1	1	
Lewis, Andrew, by John Hays	640			
Lyle, Samuel	245			
Lyle, David	320	1		

	[1]	[2]	[3]	[4]
Martin, Hugh		1		1
McFarlin, John		1		
McFarland, Benjamin	1167		5	1
McGuire, Patrick	450			
McGirt, John	215			1
Morrow, William	335		3	
McAdoo, Andrew	100			
McCuistian, Joseph		1		
McCuistian, James, Sen.	200			
McCuistian, James, Jr.	200	1		
McCuistian, Andrew	150	1		
McSpadden, Esther	300		1	
Neilson, Andrew	150	1		
Nicholson, Jeremiah		1		
Rinehart, Michael	300	1		
Odle, Jonathan		1		
Outlaw, Alexander				1
Price, Ralph		1		
Prigmore, Joseph	600			
Piles, Jesse				1
Randolph, Sarah	400		2	
Rankin, Thomas, Jr.	200	1		
Rankin, Thomas, Senator	250			
Rankin, Richard	610	1		
Russell, James	361	1		
Sterling, John, Senator	180			
Sterling, James		1		
Shadden, Thomas		1		
Shadden, Alexander	210	1		
Sterling, William	100	1		
Sterling, Daniel		1		
Shields, William		1		
Scott, James	300			
Shadden, James, Jr.		1		
Shadden, William		1		
Sample, Moses	400			
Sample, Mathew		1		
Stringer, Edward		1		
Taylor, James		1	1	1
Thomas, William		1		
Talbot, Parry		1		1
Thompson, John		1		
Witt, Joseph	160	1		
Willson, Adam	400	1	2	1
Willson, John		1		
Whitman, David		1		
Willson, William		1		
Willcockson, George				1
Vandyke, Freeman		1		
Total amount	19,663	97	39	44

TAXABLE PROPERTY IN CAPT. HARMON'S COMPANY

	[1]	[2]	[3]	[4]
Alley, Edward		1		
Baker, John		1		
Brown, David		1		
Bradshaw, Samuel	630			
Bratcher, Charles	100	1	1	
Bran, John		1		
Bowman, Jacob	125	1	1	
Bradshaw, William	245	1		
Bradshaw, James	400	1		
Buzby, Thomas	800			
Churchman, John	125	1		
Conner, Richard		1		
Churchman, William	130	2		
Cuckey, Zacariah		1		
Canady, John, Sr.	400	2		
Canady, Charles	200	1		
Canady, John, Jr.		1		
Canady, Porter		1		
Cluck, John		1		
Cluck, Peter		1		
Campbell, George W.	640			
Dennison, John		1		
Edwards, Laben	88	1		
Edwards, Henry		1		
Elmore, David		1		
Greenley, John		1		
Greer, Thomas		1	1	
Grace, Richard	200	1		
Helton, William		1		
Harmon, Lewis	270	1	1	
Harmon, Christopher	185			
Harmon, Jacob	60	1	1	
Hayworth, Stephen		1		
Hornback, John, Sr.	500		3	
Hanes, Christopher	8,000	1	6	
Hanes, John	600			
Hinkle, George	130	1		
Longacre, John	427	1		
Longacre, Benjamin	397	1		
Medley, James		1		
McDonald, David		1		
Mason, Reuben	105			
Mendinghall, Jos'h	200	1		
Mendinghall, Mordica, Jr.		1		
Mendinghall, Mordica		1		
Mendinghall, Mordica, Sr.	400			
Newman, Jonathan		1		
Owens, Joseph		1		
Pope, Jahue	400	1		
Rankins, James		1		

	[1]	[2]	[3]	[4]
Ricketts, Able		1		
Reese, James	670		7	
Rankins, Samuel	250	1		
Rhea, John		1		
Riley, John		1		
Redwell, Charles		1		
Sutherand, David	570			
Smith, John	200			
Snuffer, John		1		
Thompson, William	250	1		
William, Littleton		1		
West, Samuel	147	1		
Woodard, Aron	320	1		
Woodard, Joseph	320	1		
Williams, Arthur			1	
Williams, Joseph		1		
Jackson, Samuel	5,000			
Johnson, Enus	100	1		
Total	23,584	57	23	

TAXABLE PROPERTY IN CAPT. HODGES COMPANY

	[1]	[2]	[3]	[4]
Adamson, Simon	75			
Adamson, John	132	1		
Adamson, Jonathan	63	1		
Beeson, Amariah	200	1		
Baker, James	312	1	1	
Beeson, Thomas	110	1		
Bawldin, Henry			1	
Bullard, Martha	500		2	
Bailey, Richard			1	
Balinger, Lydia	63			
Campbell, John	15			
Clift, James		1		
Cambel, Duncan	150	1		
Davis, John	66	1		
Duncan, John		1		
Dean, Francis	312			
Dean, William	116			
Dick, Henry		1		
Davidson, James	150	1		
Dickerson, Francis		1		
Davis, Robert	164	1		
Evans, James		1		
Ellis, Nehemiah	100	1		
Ellis, Jehu		1		
Frazer, Moses	150	1		
Frazer, William		1		
Goodson, Joseph		1		
Gibson, Garret	110	1		
Green, Joseph	60	1		

	[1]	[2]	[3]	[4]
Glass, John		1		
Hasket, John		1		
Hodges, Charles	800	1	3	
Hammuck, Isaac	400	1		
Hickman, James		1		
Hincha, William	300	1		
Jackson, Nathan		1		
Johnston, William		1		
King, John		1		
Kenady, Rebecah	200			
Kenady, Henry	250	1		
Lewis, Evan	295	1		
Lake, William	200	1		
Line, William	300	1		
Lamor, James		1		
Murrel, Banjamin	300	1		
Mendinghall, Stephen		1		
Mendinghall, Martin	66	1		
Mills, William	316	1		
Myers, John		1		
Mills, Richard	125	1		
Mills, Jacob		1		
McGee, Richard	100	1		
Mills, John, Sr.	200	1		
McGee, John	100	1		
Mills, Samuel	160	1		
Mills, John, Sr.	200	1		
McCullah, Joseph	600		1	
Mills, William		1		
Mills, Asa		1		
Morgan, William		1		
Menley, David		1		
Phillips, Edmond	43	1		
Poage, Robert		1		
Roach, Jordan	500	1	2	
Roberts, John		1		
Rearden, Thomas	320		1	
Ruth, Samuel	110	1		
Ruth, William	200	1		
Ritchey, William	90	1		
Summers, William	140			
Shields, John, Sr.	400			
Shields, John, Jr.		1		
Shields, William		1		
Smith, Thomas		1		
Swain, Elisha	150	1		
Thornbery, Thomas	100	1		
Thornbury, Joseph	175			
Thornbury, Henry, Sr.	270			
Thornbury, Henry, Jr.		1		
Thornbery, Richard	100	1		

	[1]	[2]	[3]	[4]
Turner, Robert	140			
Turner, John	125	1		
Turner, Walter	287	1		
Thornbery, Joel		1		
Vance, James	100	1		
Vance, John	100	1		
Walker, Richard	50	1		
Williams, Allen	117	1		
Wright, Nathan	300	1		
Yell, Moses	568		3	
Meek, Adam	850	1	4	
Goodson, William	1,000	1		
Total	14,269	80	17	

TAXABLE PROPERTY IN CAPT. LANE'S COMPANY

	[1]	[2]	[3]	[4]
Boyles, David		1		
Britton, Benjamin	100	1		
Britton, James	50	1		
Barton, Isaac	285			
Cude, John	155	1		
Cofman, David	450	1	1	
Cofman, Lovel		1		
Carmichel, James	600		3	
Dyer, William		1		
Day, Jesse	340	1		
Day, Levi		1		
Filpot, Timothy		1		
Forrice, James	100	1		
Gregg, Isaac		1		
Green, Francis	200			
Horner, George	80	1		
Horner, William	437			
Howard, John, Sr.	203			
Hoskins, Jesse	340			
Haile, Jonathan		1		
Howard, John, Jr.		1		
Haile, William	200		1	
Irwin, George	320	2		
Kerkpatrick, Hugh	160	1		
Kerkpatrick, David		1		
Kerkpatrick, James		1		
Kerkpatrick, Jacob	370	1		
Lane, Tidence, Sr.	350		1	
Lane, Richard		1		
Lane, Tidence, Jr.	200	1		
Lane, Aquila	321	1	1	
Lathan, John		1		
Lea, Major		1		
Latham, Samuel		1		
McDonald, Alexander, Jr.		1		

	[1]	[2]	[3]	[4]
McDonald, Alexander, Sr.	350			
Nanney, Patrick, Ex.	375	3		
Pangle, Frederick	300	1		
Pangle, John	100	1		
Parkes, Joseph		1		
Parkes, William	330			
Porter, Charles T.	600	1	6	
Rue, Lewis		1		
Roddy, James	1,017		4	
Riddle, Zacariah		1		
Tosh, Martin		1		
White, Samuel	521	1		
White, Thomas		1		
Lea, James	800	1	3	
Total	9,654	40	21	

TAXABLE PROPERTY IN CAPT. TURNER'S COMPANY

	[1]	[2]	[3]	[4]
Brigs, John	250	1		
Brian, Thomas	150	1		
Cales, James	100	1		
Denton, John		1		
Ellice, Lewis	100	1		
Hunter, Samuel	100			
Hunter, George		1		
Hill, William		1		
Hill, Joseph	150			
Jones, David	200	1		
Inman, William H.	100			
Layman, Joseph	100	1		
Lively, Jacob	250			
Layman, Daniel		1		
Leeth, Ebenezer, Esquire	400	1	2	
Leaman, David	100			
McGuire, Cornelius	500			
McGuire, George		1		
McGuire, Isaac		1		
Melcom, George	200	1		
Montgomery, William		1		
McMeans, Isaac	100	1		
Nave, John	200	1	1	
Oneal, Benjamin	100	2		
Parkey, Jacob	250	1		
Russell, David	125	1	3	
Roan, John	200	1		
Renau, George		1		
Slover, Abraham	300			
Slover, Aron		1		
Slover, Abraham, Jr.		1		
Terrel, Benjamin		1		
Turner, James	60	1		

	[1]	[2]	[3]	[4]
Taff, Peter	100	1		
Taff, George	100	1		
Thomas, Griffith	100	1		
Vanhook, Aron	150			
Webb, Jesse	150	1		
Wilson, Daniel		1		
Walters, John	100	1		
Wilson, James	150		1	
Wiley, Alexander		1	1	
Total	5,045	36	8	

TAXABLE PROPERTY IN CAPT. McSPADDEN'S COMPANY

	[1]	[2]	[3]	[4]
Brown, William		1		
Bernet, Michael	302	1		
Brewer, Oliver		1		
Callahan, William	100	1		
Carter, Nathaniel	100			
Cowan, James		1		
Cannon, Joseph		1		
Cannon, Caleb		1		
Cannon, John	100			
Callahan, Charles	300			
Cate, Charles		1		
Cate, Charles, Sr.	350			
Cate, John, Jr.	100	1		
Cate, John	277	1		
Cate, William	250	1		
Edmond, John		1		
Gaut, John	200	1		
George, Silas	740			
Harvey, John		1		
Hopper, Charles	125	1		
Holaway, William	250	1		
Leath, Joseph		1		
Leeth, George		1		
Lawrence, James		1		
Laudermilk, George		1		
Morgan, Richard	400			
Moor, James		1		
Land, Newman	950			
McLand, Joseph		1		
McDonald, Walter	212	1	1	
Manerd, James	200	1		
McSpadden, Samuel	300	1	3	
Molder, John	100	1		
Molder, Polly	70	1		
Morgan, Silas		1		
Mickle, Banser	100	1		
Moon, Joseph	200			
Moon, Nathaniel		1		

	[1]	[2]	[3]	[4]
Mitchel, John		1	1	
McCulle, John		1		
Molder, Henry		1		
McClester, William		1		
Moon, Daniel	100	1		
Mathews, Jeremiah	780	1	1	
Newman, Isaac	400	1	1	
Penn, Richard	100	1		
Potterfield, Richard	30	1		
Patton, Robert	110	1		
Patton, Thomas	150	1		
Patton, John		1		
Rodgers, George		1		
Reno, Thomas		1		
Sellers, John	350	1		
Smith, Thomas	278	1		
Thorp, John	196	1		
Stephenson, Robert		1		
Shenall, Isaac	291	1		
Seeburn, John	174	1		
Seeburn, Edward	350			
Stephenson, Edward	150	1		
Thompson, James	100	1		
Vanhuser, Falts	190	1		
Vanhuser, John	300			
Whitthell, Adam	160			
Total	9,934	45	9	

TAXABLE PROPERTY IN CAPT. McDONALD'S COMPANY

	[1]	[2]	[3]	[4]
Anderson, Joseph	475			
Austin, Archibald		1		
Allen, Benjamin		1		
Anderson, James		1		
Bates, Mathew	75	1		
Black, John		1		
Cooper, Jacob	100			
Campbell, William	423			
Currey, Isaac	143	1		
Cox, William	100	1		
Chamberlain, Jeremiah	400			
Cofman, James		1		
Davis, Benjamin	273		5	
Dallace, Joshua	50	1		
Doggett, Miller	200			
Davis, David		1	1	
Davis, William		1		
Driskill, Mahal		1		
Earls, Frederick		1		
Ford, John	100	1		
Goin, Daniel	100	1		

	[1]	[2]	[3]	[4]
Guthry, Alexander	300	1		
Evans, Jacob	40	1		
Goen, Daniel		1		
Goen, William		1		
Goen, Ezekial	100	1		
Gentry, Ayrs		1		
Howard, Alex'r		1		
Hamilton, Joseph	4,650	1	4	
Harrison, James	200			
Harrison, Benjamin	316		4	
Harrison, William		1		
Hargrave, Benj.		1		
Hargrave, Eli		1		
House, William	100			
Hargrove, Joseph		1		
Harper, Thomas		1		
Jackson, Josiah	315	1	4	
Johnson, William	150			
Irwin, Samuel		1		
Inman, Shedrick	300		3	
Kelly, Isaac		1		
Kelly, Jacob		1	2	
Keith, James		1		
Keith, Nicholas		1		
Keith, James		1		
Lyon, James		1		
McFarland, Robert	400	1	3	
Morris, Jean	675		1	
Morris, John		1	1	
McDonald, John	300	1		
McDonald, James	150	1		
Majors, Abner	100	1		
McClister, James	200	1		
Melona, John	75	1		
Outlaw, Alexander	1,040		8	
Pope, John	75	1		
Riggs, Clisby	250	1		
Riggs, Edward	100			
Rorax, William		1		
Reams, John		1		
Shanks, Nicholas		1		
Sutton, John		1		
Thomas, Peter	100	1		
Webb, George		1		
Willson, Jacob	150			
Willson, Abner		1		
Willson, Isaac		1		
Totals for the company	12,488	51	36	

TAXABLE PROPERTY IN CAPTAIN COPELAND'S COMPANY

	[1]	[2]	[3]	[4]
Adams, James		1		
Carter, Vincent		1		
Cunningham, James	100	1		
Combs, Job	150	1		
Copeland, Soloman	300	1		
Copeland, Rickets	340	1		
Cowan, Jane	300			
Cowan, John	100	1		
Copeland, Stephen	700			
Copeland, Zacheus	250	1		
Collins, John	200			
Collins, Edward	200	1		
Cannon, Abner		1		
Dobbins, Reuben	150	1	1	
Denton, Jacob, Senr.	75			
Denton, Jacob, Junr.	100	1		
Denton, Joseph		1		
Denton, Jacob	200	1		
Evans, John B. by John H.	6,480			
Fout, Jacob	300	1		
Fitzsimmons, Thos. by G. D.				
Griffin, William	150	1		
Graham, George	200			
Gore, Ambrose	100	1		
Giger, George	250			
Geiger, John		1		
Holman, Peter by G. S.	640			
Hughes, Aaron	320			
Hughes, John	300	1		
Hill, John		1	2	
Jones, Thomas	12			
Kenny, John	67			
Lewis, Amos, Jr.		1		
Lowry, Samuel, Sr.	100	1		
Lowry, Samuel Jr.,		1		
Loury, Adam	100			
Loury, James	100	1		
Lough, Jacobs		1		
Loury, Robert	100	1		
Lewis, Jacob	50	1		
Lewis, George	300			
Lewis, William		1		
Lewis, Amos, Sr.	300			
Long, Moses		1		
Moore, William		1		
Moore, John	227		1	
McClamahan, William	238			
McClanahan, Alexander	237	1		
McRoberts, Samuel		1		
Maples, William		1		

	[1]	[2]	[3]	[4]
Osburn, Soloman	50	1		
Pewit, Joel		1		
Roberts, George		1		
Runyon, Freeman		1		
Roberts, Phillips	100			
Roulstone, Mathew	350			
Roulstone, Moses		1		
Roulstone, William		1		
Seehorn, Gabriel		1		
Sweney, James C.		1		
Sweney, Joseph Mc.		1		
Swan, Samuel	125	1	1	
Swingle, George	2,500	1		
Seehorn, John	550			
Swaney, John		1		
Sexton, William		1		
Swingle, John	200			
Taylor, Parmenas	390	1	1	
Turnley, George	75	1		
Thomas, John	100	1		
Turnley, John	75			
Vincent, Thomas		1		
Winton, William	100	1		
Wright, Isaac		1	1	
Wright, Robert		1		
Total for the district	17,901	53	7	

TAXABLE PROPERTY IN CAPT. DAMERON'S COMPANY

	[1]	[2]	[3]	[4]
Burns, Isaac	250			
Beavers, William	200			
Burns, James		1		
Bryan, John		1		
Butcher, Samuel		1		
Brittain, William	150	1		
Cheek, William	200			
Cheek, Willson	100	1		
Cheek, Jesse	360			
Day, Nathaniel	400			
Day, John	100			
Dameron, Joseph	575	3	2	
Donaldson, William	200	1		
Donaldson, Andrew	100	1		
Dameron, Christopher		1		
Evans, George, Esq.	700	2	4	
Fillpot, Joseph		1		
George, Reuben		1		
Huffman, John		1		
Holdaway, Timothy	300			
Hodges, Edmond	200	1		
Howard, James		1		

	[1]	[2]	[3]	[4]
Hatter, Michael	200	1		
Hatter, Phillip	200	1		
Hogget, Soloman		1		
Laymon, Jacob		1		
McFarland, James	250	1		
McGhee, James	150	1		
Majors, Absolom		1		
Majors, Peter		1		
Murphy, David	100	1		
Petty, William		1		
Ryon, Henry		1		
Reddish, William		1		
Shelly, Nathan		1		
Stanbough, Jacob	70	1		
Trotter, James		1	1	
Weaver, Adam	100			
Weaver, George	200	1		
Total for the district	4,745	37	8	

TAXABLE PROPERTY IN CAPT. JAMES FANSHER'S COMPANY

	[1]	[2]	[3]	[4]
Bradford, Benjamin		1	1	
Brown, George	100	1		
Brown, Claiborne	200	1		
Boyd, William	200	1		
Brumit, Owen		1		
Bane, Robert		1		
Chamberlain, Ninian	808		1	
Carson, Mary	200			
Carson, John		1		
Carson, James		1		
Cox, John	87	1		
Cox, Solomon	450	1		
Cox, Henry	60		1	
Cox, William	145	1		
Cannon, Thomas	100	1	1	
Cluck, Henry	100			
Dickin, Thomas	100	1		
Ellis, James	230	1		
Edgar, George	700			
Edgar, Alexander		1		
Edwards, John		1		
Fansher, James		1		
Ford, John	100			
Gordon, George	1,500			
Gray, Jacob		1		
Grissom, Robert		1		
Hunter, James	150	1		
Hill, Robert	200	1		
Hill, Daniel,	190	1	1	
Hill, Samuel, Sr.	289		2	

	[1]	[2]	[3]	[4]
Hill, Samuel, Jr.	108	1		
Hill, Abraham	75	1		
Hill, Hill			2	
Howard, Henry	60	1		
Henderson, David	140	1		
Havens, James	100	1		
Havens, John	200	1		
Harrison, John	200		2	
Jarman, John	100	1		
Jarnigan, Thomas	785		7	
Jenings, William		1		
Knabb, Jacob	850			
Love, William	100	1		
Lerue, Abraham	200	1		
Langdon, Joseph	200	1		
Mays, William	500			
McMullen, Thomas		1		
McClanahan, David	200	1		
McClanahan, Robert		1		
Morrow, John	150			
Moyers, Christopher	200			
Moyers, David	200	1		
Moyers, James	200	1		
Moyers, Joshua		1		
Maxwell, John	100			
Neely, John	300			
Neely, Andrew	200	1		
Neely, James		1		
Patton, Samuel	275	1		
Randolph, Henry		1		
Ritchey, Robert	115			
Ritchey, Joseph		1		
Snoddy, Thomas Esq.	200	1	1	
Skeen, John	200	1		
Snodgrass, William	250			
Snodgrass, Robert		1		
Snodgrass, David		1		
Shelton, Thomas	150		2	
Witt, Elijah	400		3	
Witt, Joseph		1		
Witt, Noah		1		
Witt, Ayers		1		
White, Westley	110			
Total for the district	12,777	52	24	

TAXABLE PROPERTY IN CAPT. WILLIAM BRAZELTON'S COMPANY

	[1]	[2]	[3]	[4]
Brevert, John		1		
Boyd, James		1		
Brazelton, John		1		

	[1]	[2]	[3]	[4]
Bennet, Jessy	100	2		
Ballenger, Moses	150	1		
Beard, Patrick	400	1		
Brazelton, Samuel		1		
Brazelton, Will	370	1	1	
Brazelton, William, Sr.	448			
Caldwell, Alexander		1		
Cox, Dudley		1		
Clerk, George	136	1		
Campbell, James	380	1	1	
Combs, John	500		2	
Coppock, James	237	1		
Coppock, Isaha	111	2		
Coppock, Thomas	210	1		
Caldwell, William	672	1	1	
Cox, William	450		3	
Caldwell, Anthony	280	1		
Duncan, Jere		1		
Doherty, Joseph	200			
Doherty, Joseph, Jr.		1		
Doherty, William		1		
Elmore, Joel	188	1		
Ellis, William		1		
Edward, Joshua		1		
Frazor, Abner		1		
Greer, John	70	1		
Garden, Parish		1		
Hunicut, Joseph		1		
Haworth, James		1		
Haworth, Richard	622	1		
Haworth, Willi		1		
Johnston, John	300			
Jones, Thomas	263	1		
Jackson, Samuel	5,000			
Lacey, William	150	1		
Meire, James		1		
Miles, John	200	1		
Maples, James		1		
Margraves, John		1		
Maulsby, William	300	1		
Murphy, William		1		
Montgomery, Michael	200	1		
McClung, Charles	10,000			
Newman, Aaron	180	1		
Neal, Benjamin	630		3	
Noradyke, Isariel	150	1		
Newman, James	310	1		
Noradyke, Micaja	200	1		
Newman, James		1		
Peek, Adam	2,230	1	2	
Rees, William	250	1	2	

	[1]	[2]	[3]	[4]
Rector, Maximilien		1		
Ruelle, Samuel	252	1		
Rees, Thomas		1		
Smith, Deborah	100			
Shelly, Jeremiah	119	1		
Sellardt, Nathan	139	1		
Sellardt, Samuel		1		
Thornburg, Benjamin	190	1		
Tucker, James	200	1		
Tucker, John		1		
Woodward, Abraham	170	1		
Williams, David		1		
Wright, Edward	170	1		
Wright, Isaac	185	2		
Williams, John	150	1		
Woodward, William	131	1		
Wright, Joshua	100	1		
Williams, Benjamin		1		
Totals for the district	28,633	65	14	

ADDITIONAL LIST OF HODGES COMPANY

	[1]	[2]	[3]	[4]
Gardner, Obediah		1		
Hankins, Richard	500	1		
Hankins, Edward		1		
Hankins, Thomas		1		
King, Mary			3	
Rains, John		1		
Vance, John	100			
Willson, Abraham	63	1		

ADDITIONAL LIST RETURNED JULY TERM

	[1]	[2]	[3]	[4]
Witt, Caleb	400	1		
Majors, Thomas	128			
McBroom, William	250			
McPeetur, Joseph		1		

EARLY EAST TENNESSEE TAXPAYERS

Compiled by Pollyanna Creekmore

VI. Carter County, 1796[1]

Carter County was created on April 9, 1796, by the First General Assembly of Tennessee.[2] The territory was removed from Washington County, the oldest county in the state, which had been created in 1777. The new county was named for Landon Carter, Revolutionary soldier and son of John Carter, prominent Wataugan leader.

Carter County was created out of the eastern part of Washington County. At the time of its creation its eastern boundary was the North Carolina line, its northwestern boundary was Sullivan County, Tennessee, and its northern boundary, Washington County, Virginia. No territory was removed from Carter County until 1836, when Johnson County was created.[3] In 1875 Unicoi County was created out of parts of Carter and Johnson counties.[4]

The earliest settlement by white people in what is now Carter County was in 1769-1770. By 1772 when the Watauga Association had been formed, there were about "seventy plantations."[5]

The first justices of the peace were Andrew Greer, Landon Carter, Nathaniel Taylor, David McNabb, Zachariah Campbell, Guttredge Garland, John Vaught, Joseph Lands, and Reuben Thorn. The first court was held at the house of Samuel Tipton.[6]

---

[1] For introduction to this series see *Publications*, No. 23, pp. 115-16. Previous installments have been: I, Anderson County, 1802, in No. 23; II, Blount County, 1801, in No. 24; III, Knox County, 1806, in No. 25; IV, Grainger County, 1799, in No. 27; V, Jefferson County, 1800, in No. 28.

[2] George Roulstone (comp.), *Laws of the State of Tennessee* (Knoxville, 1803), 100-102.

[3] Henry D. Whitney (comp. and ed.), *The Land Laws of Tennessee* . . . (Chattanooga, 1891), 757-58.

[4] *Ibid.*, 907-08.

[5] Samuel Cole Williams, *Dawn of Tennessee Valley and Tennessee History* (Johnson City, 1937), 364, 377. This volume is extremely useful for information relating to the earliest settlers among the Carter County taxpayers of 1796. See also Frank Merritt, *Early History of Carter County, 1760-1861* (Knoxville, 1950).

[6] Goodspeed Publishing Company, *History of Tennessee, East Tennessee Edition* (Chicago, 1887), 908. Hereafter cited as Goodspeed, *Hist. of Tenn.*

The first officers for the county were: sheriff, Nathaniel Taylor; clerk, George Williams; register of deeds, Godfrey Carriger, Jr.; trustee, Joseph McLin; ranger, Joseph Lands.[7]

Five commissioners were appointed to lay out a place for a county seat. The site chosen was a place known as the Watauga Old Fields, on the east side of Doe River, a short distance above where the river empties into the Watauga. The town was named Elizabethton, in honor of Elizabeth Maclin, wife of Landon Carter.[8]

The town was laid off by Samuel Tipton upon his own land.[9] Of the seventy-seven lots laid off, nine were reserved for public buildings. The remaining lots were disposed of by a lottery.[10]

The system of assessing and collecting public taxes in Tennessee was established by an act passed by the territorial assembly on September 30, 1794.[11] This act prescribed the manner for taking the taxes and designated what property was taxable: "All lands held by deed or entry . . . or by lease, or right of dower, all free males and male servants, between the age of twenty-one and fifty years, all slaves, male and female, between the age of ten and fifty years, all stud horses, and all town lots within this territory."

The territorial law followed the statutes of North Carolina. Under the territorial act and North Carolina acts, the valuation of lands by the hundred acres was fixed arbitrarily, and this would seem to imply a result which was made express in the constitution of 1796, that no one hundred acres of land should be taxed higher than another.

The constitution of 1796 declared that, "All laws and ordinances now in force and use in this Territory, not inconsistent with this Constitution, shall continue to be in force and use in this State until they shall expire, be altered or repealed, by the Legislature. . . ."

The constitution also fixed the rates which could be charged for taxation: "No one hundred acres shall be taxed higher than another, except town lots, which shall not be taxed higher than two hundred acres of land each; no free man shall be taxed higher than one hundred acres, and no slave higher than two hundred acres, on each pole."

---

[7] *Ibid.*
[8] Roulstone, *Laws*, 184.
[9] Goodspeed, *Hist. of Tenn.*, 909.
[10] *Ibid.*
[11] Roulstone, *Laws*, 54-56.

Under the territorial law the sheriff of each county was to summon the justices of the peace for his county to assemble at the courthouse and appoint one justice of the peace for every captain's district in each county and in town one for each town, to receive lists of taxable property in each district. Justices were to fix the time and place in each district for receiving lists of taxable property. The justices were required to advertise at three of the most public places in his district at least fifteen days prior to the time of taking such taxable property. The justices were required to make their returns to the county court and the clerk was supposed to record in alphabetical order the annual returns made by the justices in his county:

> Sec. 10.   And be it enacted, That at the first court in every county, to be held next after the fifth day of January, one thousand seven hundred and ninety five, in every year after the present. Such court shall appoint a justice of the peace for every district in the county, to receive lists of available property for the then present year; and the clerk of each county court shall furnish each justice within twenty days after his appointment, with a fair alphabetical copy at large of the taxable property within this district the preceding year, under the penalty of twenty five dollars for each neglect, to be recovered by action of debt, in the governor's name, in any court having cognizance thereof, and to be applied to the use of the county.

The following list was transcribed from a microfilm copy of the original certified copy returned by George Williams, Carter County, court clerk, to the Tennessee general assembly, now on file in the Tennessee Archives. It is not of record in Carter County. Also in the Archives are lists for 1797, 1798, and 1799. All of these lists were microfilmed by the compiler in 1949, through the courtesy of Mrs. John Trotwood Moore, then Tennessee state librarian and archivist. The films are available in the McClung Collection, Lawson McGhee Library, Knoxville.

The public records of Carter County on file in the courthouse at Elizabethton have suffered some destruction. The early marriage bonds and licenses are not all recorded in books; neither are the wills and estate records, but are kept in metal file boxes in the county court clerk's office.[12] The minutes of the Court of Pleas and Quarter Sessions before 1819, with the exception of the years 1804-05, are missing. The deeds

---

[12] A copy of the original marriage bonds and licenses, 1796-1850, has been transcribed by Robert T. Nave, and is published as Volume 1 of *Tennessee Marriage Records,* edited by Pollyanna Creekmore (Knoxville, 1958).

are all preserved and are available in the register's office. Current instruments are recorded by photostat.

The tax rate for 1796 is unknown due to the loss of the early county court minutes.

CARTER COUNTY, TENNESSEE
TAX LISTS
1796

Key to Column Numbers[13]
[1] Acres of land
[2] White polls
[3] Black polls

"A list of Taxable property in Carter County for the year 1796"

Names	[1]	[2]	[3]	Names	[1]	[2]	[3]
Archer, William		1		Burk, Elihew		1	
Archer, John	200			Burk, Arter		1	
Ashe, Thomas	100	1		Bullinger, Peter	250	1	
Alexander, George	75	1		Ballard, John		1	
Abner, Elisha	205	1		Baker, John	155	1	
Anderson, Thomas, Junr.	155	1		Buckner, William		1	
Anderson, Thomas, Senr.		1		Burk, Abraham		1	
Anderson, Joshua		1		Branstetter, Peter	200	1	
Asher, John	100	1		Barkehouse, John	300		
Ashbrooks, George		1		Boon, Soloman	200	1	
Adams, Jesse		1		Baker, William		1	
Boyd, William	400	1	2	Colyer, Charles	400	1	
Bogart, Samuel	608			Cooper, Nathan		1	
Bailey, Cottril	269½			Curtis, Bolen		1	
Bailey, Charles	240	1		Cooper, Edward		1	
Bogart, Cornelius	194¾	1		Cooper, Joel	177		
Bradford, Benjamin		1		Cobb, Dred	50	1	
Bass, Jeremiah	240	1	9	Cooper, Patience	300		
Bowers, Leonard	50	1		Cooper, John		1	
Bird, James		1		Cooper, Jobe	150	1	
Bishop, Samuel		1		Cunningham, Aaron		1	
Bell, Richard		1		Cunningham, Mary	590		
Brimer, Joseph	300	1		Cumpton, John		1	
Beames, James		1		Cooper, Abraham	100	1	
				Conner, Julius	400	1	3
				Crosson, Samuel		1	

[13] There are two additional columns in the original, "Stud horses" and "Town lots." No individuals were listed as owning any town lots, but thirteen were designated as owners of stud horses with one owning two: Peter Bullinger, Pharoah Cobb, Godfrey Carriger, Sr., Alexander Greer, James Jones, Robert Lusk, Isaac Lincoln, Gidian Metlock, Teter Nave, Edward Smith, Joseph Tipton (2), Nathaniel Taylor, and Samuel Tipton.

Names	[1]	[2]	[3]	Names	[1]	[2]	[3]
Cobb, Pharoah	640	1	8	Estridge, Richard		1	
Carriger, Godfrey, Junr.	322	1		Farmer, John		1	
Carriger, Godfrey, Senr.	1694	1	3	Farmer, Thomas		1	
Cox, John	140	1		Franks, Richard		1	
Carriger, Nicholas	450	1		Folsom, Nathaniel		1	
Carriger, Michael	756	1		Frasher, Alexander		1	1
Cox, Abraham	300	1		Flanary, William	200	1	
Cox, Richard		1		Ford, Joseph	500	1	
Campbell, Solomon	200	1		Fisher, William		1	
Colboth, Jacob		1		Fisher, Anthoney	300		
Carven, Thomas	210	1					
Campbell, Jeremiah	94	1		Grindstaff, Henry		1	
Campbell, Zachariah, Junr.		1		Grindstaff, Michael	80	1	
Campbell, Isaac	150	1		Garland, Guttradge	150	1	
Campbell, Zachariah, Senr.	100			Garland, Joseph	375	1	
Cutberth, Benjamin, Junr.		1		Garland, Samuel		1	
Cutberth, Benjamin, Senr.			1	Gourley, Thomas	50	1	
Cain, Peter		1		Garretson, John		1	
Cain, John	115	1		Gillam, John		1	
Cunningham, William	70	1		Greer, Andrew	1800		3
Carter, Landon	10676	1	7	Garland, Samuel	425		
Carter, John	415	1	2	Garland, Harper	125	1	
Cutberth, Daniel	100	1		Garland, Ambrous	100	1	
Crosswhite, George	100	1		Garland, John	200	1	
				Greer, Alexander		1	3
Davis, William	200		1	Garland, Harper	100	1	
Davis, Nathan	260			Gentry, Joseph	100	1	
Dyer, John	125	1		Griffin, William	200		2
Daniel, Woodson		1		Graves, James		1	
Dunlap, Samuel		1					
Drake, Benjamin	339½			Hail, John		1	
Drake, Abraham		1		Hill, John		1	
Dunkin, Laurance	140	1		Hendricks, Solomon	110	1	
Dunkin, Jesse		1		Humphreys, Jesse	245	1	
Duggard, Julias	183	1		Hanes, George	500	1	
Duggard, William	250	1		Hufman, Daniel	100	1	
				Hudeburk, Thomas	140	1	
English, Henry		1		Haun, Abraham	100	1	
Evans, Archer	160	1		Hendricks, John	600	1	
Eden, James	400	1	1	Hider, John	150	1	
English, Robert	100			Henry, Abraham		1	
Edwards, Solomon		1		Hail, John	349	1	
Emmert, George	279	1		Hider, Michael	150	1	
Evans, Samuel		1		Hider, Elizabeth	150	1	
Elkins, Abraham		1		Hider, Adam		1	
Engle, George		1		Haun, Mathias	100	1	
				Haun, Christopher	100	1	
				Haun, Sebaustein	200		
				Heatherick, Jacob		1	
				Hooser, John		1	
				Helton, Peter		1	

Names	[1]	[2]	[3]
Harden, William		1	
Henderson, John		1	1
Henderson, Peter		1	
Henderson, John, Junr.		1	
Houser, John		1	
Helton, Peter		1	
Heatherly, John		1	
Howard, John	107	1	
Heaton, John	104	1	
Hooker, William		1	
Ivey, James	50		
Ingle, Peter	100	1	
Jones, James	200	1	
Jones, Thomas	100	1	
Jones, Wells		1	
Justice, Jacob		1	
Jenkins, Roland	248	1	
Jenkins, Hugh	100	1	
Jackson, William	300		
James, Rawlings	575	1	
Jones, Lewis	40		
Johnston, John	5000		
King, William		1	
Kite, Richard	150		
Kite, Isaac		1	
Kimmons, Joseph		1	
Lockhart, William		1	
Lackey, Thomas	200	1	
Lusk, Robert	244		
Lusk, Samuel		1	
Lockhart, Robert		1	
Lincoln, Isaac	725	2	4
Lacy, John		1	
Lacy, Philimon		1	
Lacy, James		1	
Large, Joseph		1	
Larew, Samuel		1	
Lay, Jesse		1	
Lay, John	200	1	2
Logan, George	175	1	
Loyd, Levy	100	1	
Loyd, James	50	1	
Loyd, John	100	1	
McInturf, Christopher	400		
McInturf, John, Junr.	218	1	
McInturf, John, Senr.	200	1	
Miller, Jacob		1	
McInturf, Caspar	100		
McNabb, Baptist		1	
McNabb, David, Junr.		1	
Moor, Absolem	50	1	
McGeehen, Brewer		1	
Maxfield, Thomas	180¼	1	
Moor, Daniel	100	1	
McCormack, Robert	60	1	
McCay, John	300	1	
Miers, Peter	40		
McInturf, Israel	60		
McNabb, William	300		
McNabb, David, Senr.	258	1	
Musgrave, Robert	320	1	
Mason, Michael		1	
Morris, Levin	100	1	
Moor, John Parker	120	1	
Metlock, Gidian		1	
Musgrave, Samuel	320	1	1
Metlock, William		1	
Metlock, George	444	1	
Mullins, John		1	
Miller, John		1	
Moreland, Charles		1	
Miller, George	60	1	
Moreland, William	500	1	
Mulkey, Philip	100	1	
Mulkey, Ann	60		
Miller, Chrisley	100	1	
Miller, Daniel	50	1	
Miller, John, Senr.	200	1	
Miller, John, Junr.		1	
Miller, Jacob	50		
Miller, Henry	340		
McQueen, Hannah	370		
McQueen, John		1	
McWilliams, Thomas		1	
Newel, Joseph		1	
Nicholas, Daniel	100	1	
Nave, Teter	200	1	
Nave, John	100	1	
Nave, Abraham	50	1	
Nowland, William		1	
Nowland, John		1	
Nicholson, John	36000		
Peoples, Nathan		1	
Price, John		1	
Poland, John	200	1	
Payton, Joseph	128½		
Price, Thomas	100		

Names	[1]	[2]	[3]
Price, Solomon		1	
Patten, John	430		
Pattrick, Jesse	213		
Pattrick, John		1	
Peoples, William	100		
Peticord, Thomas		1	
Pearson, Abel		1	
Price, James		1	
Peters, John		1	
Peters, Samuel		1	
Payne, Thomas		1	
Parker, James		1	1
Perkins, George	100	1	
Prophit, John	200	1	
Perkins, Jacob	200	1	
Petree, Daniel	50	1	
Petree, Adam	100	1	
Parsons, Robert	50	1	
Peters [Smithpeters] John M. S.	596	1	
Primmer, Mary	100		
Pugh, David	249	1	
Pugh, William	275	1	
Peoples, John	166		1
Range, James	270	1	
Rockhold, Dorson		1	
Rodgers, Robert		1	
Reasoner, Garret	208		2
Right, Thomas	144¾	1	
Right, Robert		1	
Redman, Stephen		1	
Robertson, John	50	1	
Ray, William	25	1	
Rainbolt, Adam	112	1	
Rainbolt, Susannah	100		
Roberts, William	50	1	
Russell, Thomas		1	
Reynold , Moses	100	1	
Robertson, John	100	1	
Reser, John	100	1	
Right, James		1	
Sharp, William	540		
Simmerly, Adam		1	
Simpson, Crisford		1	
Smith, John	100	1	
Smith, Brooks		1	
Smallin, Samuel	29	1	
Scot, Absalom		1	
Skippeth, Needham		1	
Sevier, John, Junr.	139	1	1

Names	[1]	[2]	[3]
Stover, Christian		1	
Stover, John		1	
Sevier, Joseph		1	1
Stover, Daniel		1	
Sevier, Abraham	120	1	
Sevier, Valentine	310		1
Schuyler, Joseph		1	
Simmerly, John	150	1	
Smith, William	100	1	
Smith, Samuel		1	
Swanger, John		1	
Strewel, William		1	
Smith, Nicholas	150	1	
Sewel, Abraham		1	
Smith, Edward	450		
Slymp, Michael		1	
Storm, Peter	300	1	
Storm, Coonrod	100	1	
Smith, Jacob	300	1	
Storm, John	50	1	
Storm, Cornelius	100	1	
Snider, Peter	133	1	
Shown, Leonard	100	1	
Smith, Humphrey	260	1	
Suel, Dorson		1	
Stour, Daniel	300	1	
Suel, Joseph	100	1	
Sands, Joseph	100	1	
Terry, Sarah, widow			1
Terry, Moses		1	
Terry, Jesper		1	
Taylor, James	100	1	
Taylor, Andrew	238	1	
Taylor, Matthew	350	1	
Tipton, Joseph	500		1
Thompson, Joshua	50	1	
Tyre, William	50	1	
Taylor, Isaac	600	1	
Tipton, John		1	
Tipton, Jonathan	187	1	
Taylor, Nathaniel	1500	1	4
Tipton, Isaac	663	1	
Tipton, Samuel	888½	1	2
Tipton, Jonathan, Senr.		1	
Tipton, Thomas	515	1	
Tullis, Samuel	400	1	
Thompkins, Joseph		1	
Terford, William		1	
Thomson, Garsham		1	

Names	[1]	[2]	[3]	Names	[1]	[2]	[3]
Thornton, Reuben	850	1		Windham, William		1	
Vaught, John	600			Worley, John	100	1	
Vintreas, John	325	1		Windham, Aaron		1	
Vandegriff, Gilbert		1		Wilson, Samuel	100	1	
Vandegriff, Jacob		1		White, Richard	480		4
Venoy, William	200	1		Wilson, John		1	
Vest, William		1		Wells, Lewis	164	1	
Vance, John	50	1		Wyman, Henry	400	1	
				Waggonner, Mathias	765	1	2
Wyatt, William		1		Widbey, William	100	1	
Whitson, Jeremiah	145	1		White, James	1300		
Whitson, Charles		1		Wilson, Joseph		1	
Williams, Samuel		1		Western, William		1	
Williams, Archibald	236	1		Western, Joseph			
Williams, Lucreatia	778		5	Wilson, John, Senr.	63		1
Williams, George	317	1		Wilson, Garland		1	
Whitson, Jesse	137	1	4	Waggoner, David	572	1	3
Wiles, John		1		Wilson, William	200	1	
Williams, Francis		1		Walters, Robert		1	
Whitson, Abraham		1		Wilson, John, Junr.	75	1	
Whitson, John		1		Walters, John		1	
Whitson, William		1		Whitson, Thomas	350		
Wyatt, Thomas	100	1		Yeates, Samuel		1	

"A true return Errors excepted—Geo. Williams, C. D."

CORRECTIONS
Carter County, 1796
Contributed by
Edward G. Speer,

Buck, Abraham 1 wp	should be	Buck, Abraham
Conner, Julius 400 a, 1 wp, 3 bp	should be	Conner, Julias
Cutberth, Benjamin, Senr.	should be	Cutberth, Benjamin, Junr.
Davis, Natham 260 a	should be	Davis, Nathan
Estridge, Richard 1 wp	should be	Estrige. Richard.
Hider, Elizabeth 150 a, 1 wp	should be	Hider, Elezebeth
Lay, John 200 a, 1 wp, 2 bp	should be	Linch, John
McInturf, Caspar 100 a	should be	McInturf, Casper
Moor, Absolem 50 a, 1 wp	should be	Moor, Absalom
McGeehen, Brewer 1 wp	should be	McGeeken, Brewer
Metlock, Gidian 1 wp	should be	Metlock, Giddian
Moreland, Charles 1 wp	should be	Morland, Charles
Nave, Teter 200 a, 1 wp	should be	Nave, Peter
Perkins, George 100 a, 1 wp	should be	Pirkins, George
Perkins, Jacob 200 a, 1 wp	should be	Pirkins, Jacob
Parsons, Robert 50 a, 1 wp	should be	Passons, Robert
Reynolds, Moses 100 a, 1 wp	should be	Reynold, Moses
Simpson, Crisford 1 wp	should be	Simpson, Crsford
Smith, Edward 4500 a	should be	Smith, Edward 450 a
Stour, Daniel 300 a, 1 wp	should be	Stout, Daniel
Western, Joseph	should be	Western, Joseph 1 wp
Waggoner, David 572 a, 1 wp, 3 bp	should be	Waggonner, David

In footnote 13, two names were misspelled. The correct
spellings are: Giddian Metlock and Peter Nave.

EARLY EAST TENNESSEE TAXPAYERS

Compiled by Pollyanna Creekmore

VII.   Sullivan County, 1796[1]

Sullivan County, the second oldest county in the state of Tennessee, was created out of the northern part of Washington County by the North Carolina legislature in October, 1779. It also included the portion of North Carolina's western claim, lying north and west of the Holston River, which had been considered to be a part of Virginia since 1771. In that year, when the Indian boundary according to the Treaty of Lochaber was being surveyed, it was decided to use the Holston River instead of the 36° 30' parallel. Since that parallel was also the dividing line between North Carolina and Virginia, the Indian boundary—the Holston River—was accepted also as the boundary between these colonies (later states) until the 36° 30' line was surveyed in 1779. The new county was named in honor of General John Sullivan (1740-1795), an officer in the Continental army. It was reduced in size by the creation of Hawkins County in 1786. Several attempts to create a Powel County out of Sullivan failed.[2]

Most of the original records of Sullivan County were destroyed on the afternoon of September 22, 1863, when a shell from a Federal battery hit the Sullivan County Courthouse at Blountville, setting it afire and destroying all of its contents. Included were the county court minutes and the records of wills and marriages from 1780. The deed books were kept at the home of the register, Frederick Sturm, and escaped destruction. Fortunately, some information concerning the organization of the county was copied from the early minute book before it was destroyed. In 1844 Lyman C. Draper, on a southern trip collecting material on the settlement of the West, stopped at Blount-

---

[1] For introduction to this series see *Publications*, No. 23 (1951), 115-16. Previous installments have been: I. Anderson County, 1802, in No. 23; II. Blount County, 1801, in No. 24; III. Knox County, 1806, in No. 25; IV. Grainger County, 1799, in No. 27; V. Jefferson County, 1800, in No. 28; VI. Carter County, 1796, in No. 30.

[2] Walter Clark (ed.), *The State Records of North Carolina*, XXIV (Goldsboro, 1905), 300; Tennessee Historical Records Survey, *Inventory of the County Archives of Tennessee. No. 82, Sullivan County* (Nashville, 1942), 1-4. See also "Introduction," in Prentiss Price (ed.), "Two petitions to Virginia of the North of the Holston Men, 1776, 1777," East Tennessee Historical Society's *Publications*, No. 21 (1949), 95-99.

ville and took some notes. In the early 1850's Dr. J. G. M. Ramsey, while writing his *Annals of Tennessee,* obtained from a correspondent similar information.[3]

According to these sources, the county court of Sullivan County first met on Monday, February 7, 1780, at the home of Moses Looney. Commissions as justices of the peace were presented by Isaac Shelby, David Looney, Gilbert Christian, John Duncan, William Wallace, and Samuel Smith. The other justices named in the act creating the county, Henry Clark, Anthony Bledsoe, George Maxwell, John Anderson, and Joseph Martin, apparently were absent. John Rhea was appointed clerk and Nathaniel Clark sheriff "till court in course." Isaac Shelby exhibited a commission dated November 19, 1779, signed by Governor Richard Caswell, appointing him colonel commandant of the county. Commissions of the same date appointed David Looney as first major and John Shelby, second major. John Adair was appointed entry taker and Ephraim Dunlap, state attorney. Although not mentioned by either Draper or Ramsey, William Wallace was appointed register of deeds and David Shelby county surveyor, according to land records. The court adjourned to meet again at the house of James Hollis.

For six years the county seat was in the neighborhood of Eaton's Station, now known as Eden's Ridge. When Hawkins County was created out of Sullivan in 1786, a more central location of the county seat was needed. A commission compoed of James Martin, James McNeil, John Duncan, Evan Shelby, Samuel Smith, William King, and John Scott fixed the location at the present site of Blountville. The first court held there met at the home of Joseph Cole. In 1795 Blountville was made the permanent seat of government. Four years earlier provision had been made for the building of a courthouse, jail, and stocks at that place, since thirty acres of land had been conveyed by James Brigham to the courthouse commissioners, John Anderson, George Maxwell, and Richard Gammon, for the purpose. The first courthouse, a massive log structure with a jail in the rear, was replaced

---

[3] The compiler is indebted to Prentiss Price of Rogersville, Tennessee, for this information. See also Draper MSS. 3S138-139 (State Historical Society, Madison, Wisconsin; microfilm in the University of Tennessee Library), and J. G. M. Ramsey, *The Annals of Tennessee to the End of the Eighteenth Century* (reprinted, Kingsport, 1926), 189. The reason for the statement that Ramsey received the information from a correspondent is because the names are garbled to some extent, *e.g.* William Christie, instead of Gilbert Christian; John Dunham, instead of John Duncan. Dr. Ramsey was too familiar with these names to have so miscopied them himself.

151

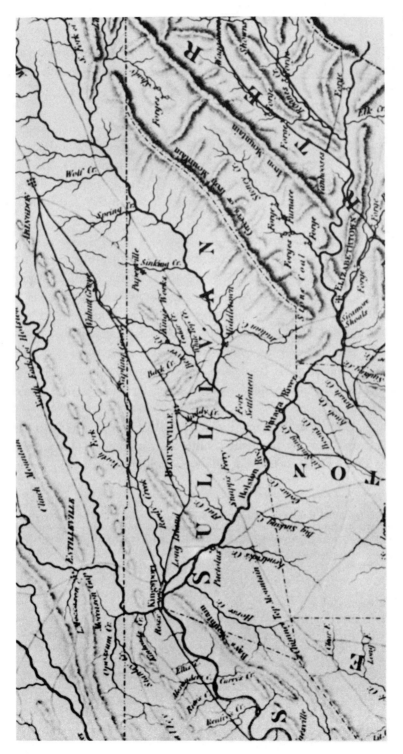

Sullivan County

A detail from the Matthew Rhea Map, 1832

in 1825 by a brick building with a jail adjoining. The third courthouse, located between the sites of the first two, was erected in 1853. After being burned by Federal troops in 1863, it was rebuilt in 1866 and remodeled in 1920.[4]

The system of assessing and collecting public taxes in Tennessee was established by an act passed by the territorial assembly on September 30, 1794. The act prescribed the manner of taking the taxes and designated what property was taxable: "All lands held by deed or entry . . . or by lease, or right of dower, all free males and male servants between the age of ten and fifty years, all stud horses, and all town lots within this territory."[5]

The following lists were transcribed from a microfilm copy of the original certified copy returned by Matthew Rhea, Sullivan County court clerk, to the Tennessee general assembly, now on file in the Tennessee Archives. It is not of record in Sullivan County. Also in the Archives are lists for 1797 and 1811-12. All of these lists were microfilmed by the compiler in 1949, through the courtesy of Mrs. John Trotwood Moore, then Tennessee state librarian and archivist. The films are available in the McClung Collection, Lawson McGhee Library, Knoxville.

As previously stated, many of the Sullivan County records have been destroyed, among them the county court minutes. The county tax rate for 1796 is unknown due to the loss of these records.

---

[4] *Inventory of County Archives . . . Sullivan County,* 5.
[5] George Roulstone (comp.), *Laws of the State of Tennessee* (Knoxville, 1803), 54-56. The legal and constitutional bases of taxation in Sullivan County, 1796, and the methods of collecting, were the same as those for Carter County as described in *Publications,* No. 30 (1958), 104-06.

SULLIVAN COUNTY, TENNESSEE
TAX LISTS
1796

Key to Column Numbers[6]
[1] Acres of Land
[2] White Polls
[3] Black Polls

"Copy of the Tax Roll of Sullivan County for the year 1796"

Names	[1]	[2]	[3]	Names	[1]	[2]	[3]
Ashworth, John	177	1		Bas, Benjamin			1
Anthony, William	500	1		Bishop, Thomas			1
Arwine, James		1		Bishop, Peter			1
Ackyard, Jacob	200	1		Bishop, William			1
Acoff, Timothy	904		3	Bradshaw, Thomas			1
Adams, Macajah	292	1		Buchannan, William			1
Acoff, John		1		Buckner, Presley		1	
Adwell, John	160			Boyd, James	84	1	
Allen, Charles	198			Browning, Roger	125	1	
Allen, James		1	1	Brooks, John	142	1	3
Allen, Daniel	283	1		Bowser, John		1	
Amos, Thomas		1		Birdwell, Robert	250		3
Anderson, Stuart	100	1		Birdwell, Joseph	60	1	
Agee, William	200	1		Birdwell, Mary	195		
Anderson, William	97	1		Baker, Morris	100	1	
Arrants, Harmon	400	1		Basket, Richard	80	1	
Armstrong, William	200	1	2	Billing, John	614	2	2
Anglin, Aaron		1		Birdwell, John		1	
Adams, Elisha		1		Birdwell, Benjamin		1	
Anderson, John	400	1		Bond, Henry	122	1	
Abbot, James		1		Barnes, William	120	1	
Allison, John	200	1	1	Bowry, Margaret	640		
Allison, John Sr. decd.	200		1	Bond, William		1	
in Washington				Bryan, Ambrose		1	
Allison, Robert esqr	450	1		Baker, Charles	240		3
				Beard, John		1	
Beaty, Andrew		1		Beard, Thomas		1	
Bear, Peter	100	1		Bowyer, Michal		1	
Bear, Matthias	60	1		Beachboard, Benjn		1	
Brittain, Abraham	350			Beaver, Christn	100	1	
Bear, George		1		Beelor, Daniel	100	1	
Brittain, Nathl		1		Barton, Thomas	100	1	
Brittain, Abraham		1		Bowen, Joseph		1	
Burk, John			1	Barber, Simon	100		
Beaty, James		1		Beelor, John	200		
Brigham, James	670		1	Beeler, Peter	200	1	
Brigham, John			1	Beelor, Joseph		1	

[6] There are two additional columns in the original, "Stud Horses" and "Town lots." Six individuals were designated as owning one stud horse each: Thomas Beard, Samuel Crockett, John Musgrove, Jr., James Pickins, Thomas Titsworth, and James Wheeler. Six individuals were listed as owners of town lots, with one owning two: John Burk (2), Samuel Crockett, Edward Cox, Richard Gammon, Robert Rutledge, and John Shelby, Jr.

Names	[1]	[2]	[3]
Blevins, William	312		10
Buckles, John	100	1	
Blevins, James		1	
Blevins, William		1	1
Boy, Jacob	470	1	
Brightbill, Peter	100	1	
Beelor, Joseph	348		
Beelor, Jacob	720	1	
Bougher, John	200	1	
Beelor, Woolery	150	1	
Beelor, George	267		
Blevins, Dillon			3
Blevins, Armstead		1	1
Brittain, Richard	300	1	
Bradley, Jonathan	20	1	
Bishop, John	400		
Barnard, John	300		
Bragg, Thomas	320		
Bragg, David	100	1	
Bucknel, William	200		
Butler, Elisha	300		
Bachman, Samuel	840	1	
Bryant, William	50	1	
Bragg, Charles		1	
Barber, Liff		1	
Crawford, Hugh	640	1	2
Copland, John		1	
Copland, William	300		
Craft, Thomas		1	1
Childress, William	306	1	1
Carrithers, Samuel	100	1	2
Cooke, Joseph	105	1	
Cooper, Caleb		1	
Chester, John	225	1	1
Carson, Samuel	187	1	
Clarke, James	195		
Chote, Benjamin		1	
Cowan, Robert	180		1
Crockett, Samuel	138	1	2
Cawood, John Jr.		2	3
Chrisman, John		1	
Citciller [?], William	150		
Chance, Ezekiel	30	1	
Creagan, Patrick	240		
Creeley, Patrick	100		
Cooper, John	180		
Cooper, Thomas		1	
Cooper, Andrew		1	
Coffill, John		1	
Curten, John		1	

Names	[1]	[2]	[3]
Carr, Gilbert	357	1	
Cox, Greenberry	100	1	
Cox, Jesse	100	1	
Craft, Michael Sr.	192		
in Long island	740		3
Christian, George		1	
Craft, Michael		1	
Christian, Robert	400	1	
Cloud, Jeremiah	300	1	
Craft, Jesse		1	
Childress, David		1	
Crum, Henry		1	
Christian, William		1	
Condry, Richard	400	1	
Caffray, Richard		1	
Christian, Margaret	400		
Coppiner, Higgins		1	
Combs, Nicholas	140	1	1
Claiborne,			
William C. C.	300	1	1
Cavitt, John	100	1	
Chase, Sarah	200		4
Cotterell, Lemuel		1	
Conkin, George	150	1	
Christian, John		1	
Cotterell, John	50	1	
Crowder, William		1	
Combs, Nicholas	140	1	
Cox, Jeremiah	416	1	
Crumley, George	574		
Crumley, Daniel		1	
Crockett, Andrew	300	1	
Cabbage, Adam		1	
Cabbage, John		1	
Carr, William	240	1	
Crumley, George		1	
Chrisman, John	228		
Chrisman, David		1	
Cox, Joshua	290	1	
Cross, Acquilla	118	1	
Cole, Joseph Jr.	355	1	1
Cross, Elijah	600	1	
Cross, Joel	72	1	
Cross, William	86	1	
Cross, Abram	182	1	
Cole, Elisha	260	1	1
Cox, Edward	360	1	1
Carroll, William		1	
Crockett, Joseph	176	1	
David, Richard	163	1	

Names	[1]	[2]	[3]	Names	[1]	[2]	[3]
Dolton, Timothy		1		Fink, George	42	1	
Dryden, David	450	1	1	Fleenor, Jacob	200	1	
Dunn, Thomas	150	1		Funkhouser, John	280		
Delany, William	780	1	3	Feltnor, John		1	
Dearman, George	618	1		Fulkerson, John	283	1	
Devault, Michael	150	1		Flin, George	95	1	
Davies, John		1		Frazier, James	180	1	
Downs, Benjamin	117	1	1	Ford, Dye		1	
Downs, William	146	1		Field, Stephen	300		
Dinnel, Richard	200	1		Ford, John	290	1	
Denton, James	400			Funk, John		1	
Denton, Joseph	100	1		Foster, Benjamin		1	
Davies, John	100	1		Frame, William	150		
Dunsmore, Samuel	150	1					
Dyer, David	18	1		Gifford, Jabez		1	
Davison, John		1		Ginnings, John	87	1	
Davison, Samuel		1		Gammon, Richard	1100	1	5
Davison, William		1		Ganes, Ambrose	200	1	2
Davison, Agness		1		Goad, John		1	
				Goad, Gabriel	79	1	
Easterlin, Thomas		1		Goad, Peter	200	1	
Erwin, David	540			Goad, Margaret	100		
Elmore, William		1		Goad, William	450	2	1
Edgman, Samuel	200	1		Gallimore, Abram		1	
Easley, Peter	300	1		Grubb, Jacob	200		
Easley, Stephen	520	3		Grubb, John	200	1	
Edgman, William	100	1		Gross, John	300	1	
Easley, Robert	720	1	1	Gross, George		1	
ditto for Moody's				Goodson, John		1	
orphans	200			Greer, Andrew, Jr.		1	
Edgee [?], Daniel	100	1		Goddard, William		1	
Elya [?], John		1		Goddard, William, Sr.	195		
England, John		1		Goodner, Conrad	150	1	
Emberson, John		1		Goddard, Thomas	178	1	
Egrim, John		1		Gaines, James T.		1	
Evans, William	216			Gaines, Francis H.		1	
Eldridge, William		1		Gaines, James esqr	3000	1	
Emberson, Walter		1		Giddins, Clark		1	
Etsley, Joseph		1		Grubb, John		1	
Ellor, Jacob	150	1		Jacobs son			
Edwards, John		1		Grubb, John		1	
Edwards, Abel	210			Gamble, Samuel	248	1	
Emmert, Jacob	378	1	2	in Hawkins County	227		
Emmert, George	150			George, James	50	1	
				Gregg, Nathan	390	1	1
Frost, John	100	1		Gregg, James	400	1	
Ford, Alexander	200	1		Graham, John		1	
Fagan, John	625	1	1	Gamble, Moses		1	
Foust, John	85	1		Giffeler, Adam	300	1	
Foust, Philip	216	1					
Foust, Peter		1		Hamilton, Abram	131	1	

Names	[1]	[2]	[3]	Names	[1]	[2]	[3]
Hamilton, Joshua	590	1		Hughes, Abner	100	1	
Hamilton, John		1		Hicks, Isaac	100	1	
Hilton, Charles	200	2		Hunt, John	328		
Hicks, Stephen	250	1		Harriss, James	320	1	2
Havron, James	92	1		Huls, William	68	1	
Harbert		1		Hodge, Francis	500	1	2
Huffman, Peter	312	1		Hughes, William	480	1	
Hannah, Andrew	100	1		Hodges, William	73	1	
Hallon [?], William	300	1					
Hughes, David	200	1		Iseley, Conrod	202	1	
Hartleroad, Henry	1035	1	1	Iseley, Conrod	202	1	
Hughes, Thomas	100	1		Iseley, Jacob	142	2	
Hacker, John		1		Isbel, Hickman		1	
Hacker, Julius, Sr.	640						
Hartleroad, Martin		1		Johnston, Philip	100	1	
Hacker, Julius		1		Johnston, Thomas		1	
Holloway, John	70			Jolliff, William		1	
Hawke, John	200			Joffill, Dudley	125		
Hicks, Isaac	40	1		Jackson, Joshua		1	2
Hamilton, Thomas		1		Jones, Henry	75	1	
Hamilton, Thomas		1		Johnston, Walter esqr	260	1	3
Houser, Nicholas	300	1		Jones, Solomon	240	1	
Hethaway, Leonard		1		James, Walter	35	1	
Houser, John	189	1		Joab, Jacob	230		
Hail, Alexr	212	1		Joab, Nathan	75		
Hamilton, Richd		1		Jackson, Peter	155		
Hamilton, Benjn		1		Joab, Samuel		1	
Hagan, Arthur		1		Jones, John	50	1	
Hitterick, William	400	1		Jones, Thomas		1	
Hitterick, John		1		James, Bennet	93	1	1
Hawkins, Henry		1					
Hatcher, William	75	1		King, Thomas	640	1	
Hughes, David	348			Knight, John		1	
Holt, Simon	100			King, Walter	2322	1	1
Hicks, Shedrach	317	2		King, William	100		
Hughes, Thomas	312	1		King, James esq.	490	1	9
Hewitt, William		1		Kite, Philip		1	
Hilton, Arnold		1		Kinchloe, John	233		
Hilton, John		1		Keywood, John	940		6
Houseley, Robert		1		Kniseley, John		1	
Hicks, Henry		1		Kaler, Frederick	150		
Hampton, Samuel	91	1		Key, Joas	59	1	
Hymns, George	275	1		King, Thomas	197	1	1
Hicks, Jacob		1		King, John	150	1	
Hawkins, John	290	1		King, James	300	1	
Hawkins, Nicholas	400	1					
Hawkins, Nathan		1		Low, George		1	
Harriss, Jeremiah	200	1		Lite, William	300		
Hart, Leonard	301	1		Lite, Vitchel	100	1	
Hicks, Richard	140	1	1	Large, Robert		1	
Hicks, Isaac	200		5	Little, George	400		
				Little, Matthias	455	1	

Names	[1]	[2]	[3]	Names	[1]	[2]	[3]
Lane, James		1		McNaley, John		1	
Lowry, John	200	1		Mercer, Nicholas	200	1	
Lite, Henry		1		Mercer, Edward	264	1	
Lewis, David		1		Moore, Alexander	281		
Lewis, Nathan	758			Myars, Jacob		1	
in Washington	642			Miller, Samuel	140		
Lewis, George		1		Miller, George		1	
Lewis, William		1		McBride, William		1	
				Musgrove, John	200		
McClarn, James	300	1	1	Musgrove, John Jr		1	1
Meade, Mahlon	180	1		Morrell, Edmund		1	
McElderry, John	218	1		Morrell, Thomas	100	1	
Morget [?], Henry	427	1		Morrell, Jonathan	100		
Maxwell, John		1		Morrell, John	87		
Moore, Samuel	500	1	2	Morrell, Daniel		1	
Molton, William	175	1	1	McCorkle, Samuel	400	1	1
Morrison, Thomas		1		Malone, Michal	280	2	
Murrell, Richard	285	1	1	Morgan, William	100		
ditto for Page, John	293			Miller, John	353	1	
Morrison, James	230	1		Miller, Thomas	295		
Miller, Henry	175	1		McClellan, Abram	500		3
McClain, Thomas		1		McClellan, John		1	
Matlock, Luke	50	1		Morriss, James		1	
Morelock, George	403	1		Morgan, Abel	33	1	
Morelock, James	155	1		McCormick, William	100	1	
Matlock, Jason	150	1		Massingall, Henry	100		
Moyer, Jacob	140	1		McKeymey, Robert		1	
Miller, George	65	1					
Moyer, John	100			Nash, William esq	679		3
Miller, Jacob		1		Norkett, John		1	
Moyer, Daniel		1		Nidiver, Jacob	600	1	
Milhorn [?], George	200			Nidiver, George	100	1	
Motton or Molton [?],				Offill, James	600	2	
Nicholas	100	1		Ozborne, Jnac.	164	1	
McKinley, Willm Sr.	375	1		Owen, Jonathan	400	1	
McKinley, Saml	150	1		Odle, William	100	1	1
McKinley, William		1					
Miller, Christian	100	1		Porterfield, Seth	200	1	
Miller, Isaac	200	1		Pope, Mary	550		
Mitar, Jacob W		1		Pawlett, Ann	147		
Moore, Samuel		1		Pawlett, Abram		1	
Mackay, John	200	1		Pawlett, Robert		1	
Moyer, Gasper	100	1		Prigmore, Drury	100	1	
Moyer, Jacob	100			Pilcher, John		1	
McAntire, David		1		Patterson, Sarah	870	1	
Miller, Adam	100	1		Peoples, Nathan	400		
Moseley, John	150			Pemberton, John	606	3	1
McGuire, Thomas	175	1		William	64	1	
McKaughan, Archd	50	1		Rachal	50		
Moore, Garrett	200	1		Punch, John		1	
McIntosh, Peter	156	1		Profit, David	377		

Names	[1]	[2]	[3]
Perry, Rowland	100	1	
Perry, David Esqr	322		2
Peters, Conrod	278		1
Peters, John		1	
Petre, George	60	1	
Phillips, Charles	180		
Price, Thomas	110	1	
Peirce, Absalom	50	1	
Parker, Hannah	100		
Perkins, Edward	170	1	
Pickins, James	300	1	1
Parker, William	220	1	
Prothro, David		1	
Prothro, John	270	1	
Roller, John	440	1	
Roller, Martin	750		2
in Knox County	200		
Roberts, William	485	1	
Robinson, Moses	417	1	1
Rogers, Abraham		1	
Roller, Jacob		1	
Richards, Joshua	150	1	
Rhea, William	300	1	1
Rutledge, George		1	2
Rhea, John			
in Sullivan	640	1	
Also on waters of			
Indian Creek	640		
Robinson, Catharine	125	1	
Ruby, Henry	190	1	
Rutledge, Robert	450	1	2
Rystone, Benjamin	400		4
Richeson, John	380	1	
Rogers, Nicholas	250	2	
Reyley, John	350		
Rowler, Martin Jr.	412	1	
Reyley, Joseph		1	
Rhea, Matthew	400	1	4
Spurgin, John	635	1	3
in Sumner County	320		
Shoemaker, John	200	1	
Shipley, Richard	480	2	
Smith, William	168	1	1
Shipley, Eli	400	1	
Shipley, John	100		
Stott, William	200	1	
Stephens, Edmund		1	
Shoemaker, William		1	
Stoke, Adam	200		
Stevenson, William	340	1	3
Shoemaker, John		1	
Smith, Joseph	402		
Stuart, John	437	1	
Stoke, Adam	161	1	
Seavers, George	200	1	
Sullivan, Henry	107	1	
Simpson, Mary	200		
Sharpe, John	546		4
Saunders, John	200	1	
Schell, Frederick	66	1	
Smith, William		1	
Smith, Solomon	440		
Smith, Daniel		1	
Smith, Samuel		1	
Scott, John esq	1000	1	2
Schell, Arnold	450		
Smalling, Solomon	100	1	
Schell, Joseph	250	1	
Schell, Andrew	100	1	
Sigler, Henry	225	1	
Smith, Samuel, Sr	900	1	1
Shelby, Catharine	200		3
Sircle [?], George	150	1	
Sells [?], Solomon	165	2	
Shaw, Michal		1	
Shelby, Isaac		1	
Shelly, Peter	250	1	1
Snodgrass, William	1100	1	2
Shrite, Henry	528	1	
Smith, George	201		
Slaughter, Jacob	125	1	1
Smith, George, Jr.		1	
Stevenson, Nicholas	203	1	
Sylvester, Joseph		1	
Snider, Michal	133	1	
Sands, Michal		1	
Shelby, John, Jr.	500	1	3
Shipley, Samuel	224	1	1
Shelby, John Sr.	640		4
Stipes, Jacob		1	
Shoemaker, Thomas		1	
Smith, Joseph	200	1	
Sampson, Emanuel	118	1	
Smalling, Thomas	105	1	
Schultz, Jacob	100	1	
Sharpe, John	97	1	
Smith, James		1	
Taylor, Joseph B Smith		1	
Taylor, Joseph	82	1	

Names	[1]	[2]	[3]	Names	[1]	[2]	[3]
Taylor, Jeremiah, Jr.	200	1	2	Weaver, Jacob	313	1	2
Tally, John	603	1		Ware, James		1	
Taylor, Isaac	33	1		Weeks, John	146		
Taylor, Stephen	300	1		Wolf, Charles	100	1	
Taylor, Archibald		1		Warden, David		1	
in Sumner county	1200			Warren, John	35		
Tabury [?], Thomas	257	1		Wright, David			2
Titsworth, Thomas	347		3	Weaver, Frederick	643	1	
Thomas, George		1		Warring, Edmund	300	2	
Taylor, John	107	1		Waggener, Henry		1	
Taylor, Daniel		1		Wallin, Stephen	100	1	
Tynor, Lewis		1		Webb, David	28½		
Titsworth, Thomas		1		Webb, George	306½	1	
Thomas, John		1		Webb, Benjamin	306½	1	
Thomas, James		1		Webb, Jonathan	287½	1	
Tussey, Jacob	200	1		Wallace, Joseph esq.	300	1	
Thomas, Jacob	250	1		Williams, Peter		1	
Tredway, Allan		1		Wadley, Thomas	100	1	
Torbet, John	435	1		Webb, Moses		1	
Torbet, Alexander, Jr.		1		Williams, Thomas		1	
Torbet, Alexander	100	1		Williams, Balis		1	
				Wiseman, Samuel		1	
Vincent, George	404	1	1				
Vincent, Thomas	136	1		Yokeley, John	481		
Vance, John esqr	400	1	1	Yancey, esqr	450		2
Vandeventer, Abram	116	1		Young, James	350		2
Waggener, Michal	200	1		Omitted			
Wolfe, George	269	1		Allison, Robert esqr			
Weeks, Zachariah	143	1		for Francis Allison	200		
Wyley, William	150	1		Total amount of this			
Whitlock, Alexander	260	2		Roll	118,135	516	196
Wheeler, James	600		1	Taxes			
Waggener, John		1		276 Dollars			
Weaver, Christian	300	1		64 Cents			
Webb, Benjamin	440	1		3 Mills			
Wartmiller, John	200	1					

I certify the above is a

A copy from the original Roll and agreeable to the returns delivered to me except a Small omission in some part of Mr. John Rhea's Tax which cannot be rectified for want of the original roll.

Matthew Rhea   C.S.C.
16 August 1797

Errors except

EARLY EAST TENNESSEE TAXPAYERS

Compiled by Pollyanna Creekmore

VIII. Hawkins County, 1809-1812[1]

Hawkins County, the sixth in order of creation in Tennessee, was created January 6, 1787,[2] out of Sullivan County by an act of the North Carolina general assembly. Sullivan County had been formed in 1779[3] from Washington County.[4]

Hawkins County was organized at the house of Thomas Gibbons on June 4, 1787, about six miles from the present county seat, Rogersville. The following officials were elected: John Hunt, sheriff; Thomas Hutchings, clerk; William Marshall, register; Joseph McCullah, surveyor; and Nathaniel Henderson, coroner. In the founding act commissioners named to locate a place for the courthouse and prison were: Lewis Widener, John Miller, Hutson Johnston, Francis Doherty, Joseph Cloud, William Reid, and John Carns. They reported and recommended that the courthouse, prison, and stocks be built at Joseph Rogers' on Crockett Creek. This became the town of Rogersville, incorporated by the North Carolina general assembly on December 22, 1789.[5]

Part of the original territory of Hawkins County was removed in 1792 in the formation of Knox County;[6] in 1796 Grainger County was created from Hawkins and Knox;[7] in 1801 part of Hawkins went into Claiborne County; in 1844 Hancock County[8] was created from Hawkins

---

[1] For introduction to this series see *Publications*, No. 23 (1951), 115-16. Previous installments have been: I. Anderson County, 1802, in No. 23; II. Blount County, 1801, in No. 24; III. Knox County, 1806, in No. 26; IV. Grainger County, 1799, in No. 27; V. Jefferson County, 1800, in No. 28; VI. Carter County, 1796, in No. 30; VII, Sullivan County, 1796, in No. 31. The compiler is indebted to Prentiss Price of Rogersville for supplying copies of the Hawkins County lists.

[2] Edward Scott (comp.), *Laws of the State of Tennessee Including Those of North Carolina Now in Force From the Year 1715 to the Year 1820, Inclusive,* 2 vols. (Knoxville, 1821), I, 378-79. Hereafter cited as Scott, *Laws.*

[3] *Ibid.,* 248-49.

[4] *Ibid.,* 221-22.

[5] Walter Clark (ed.), *The State Records of North Carolina,* 14 vols. continuing earlier series of *Colonial Records* (Goldsboro, 1905), XXV, 49.

[6] Henry D. Whitney (comp. and ed.), *The Land Laws of Tennessee* . . . (Chattanooga, 1891), 684-85.

[7] *Ibid.,* 687.

[8] *Ibid.,* 697-98, 785-86.

and Claiborne; and in 1870 the old 13th civil district of Hawkins County became part of Hamblen County, created that year out of Jefferson and Grainger counties.[9]

Many of the early Hawkins County records, including county court minutes, marriage register, estate books, guardians' accounts, from the county court clerk's office, were destroyed in November, 1863, when Federal soldiers invaded the office, carried the records to the center of adjacent Depot Street, and set them afire.[10]

The wills were re-recorded from the surviving original instruments. The marriage records were never recopied. The present marriage registers begin in June, 1865. In 1932 Mr. Prentiss Price of Rogersville copied the surviving original loose marriage bonds and licenses. His copy was checked twice, the last time in 1954, and in 1958 was published as Volume 2 of *Tennessee Marriage Records* (Knoxville, Clinchdale Press, 174 p.)

Mr. James Woods Rogan (1823-1891) was keenly interested in the history of the county and used many of the records before the Civil War. He wrote two series of articles which were published in the *Presbyterian Witness* in 1859 and 1860, and in the *Rogersville Review,* December 19, 1889, to November 27, 1890. The latter series was reprinted in the same newspaper from May 14 to August 13, 1953.

The following lists were copied by Prentiss Price from loose manuscripts, but are incomplete for each year covered. Presumably there were once books of recorded lists in the county court clerk's office, which were destroyed during the war. Microfilm and typewritten copies of the original lists are in the McClung Collection, Lawson McGhee Library, Knoxville. The library also has lists for companies commanded by Gillenwaters in 1809 and 1811 and by Lucus in 1811.

The county courts in Tennessee were authorized to levy taxes on property by a legislative act passed October 25, 1797,[11] in which types of taxable property were listed and the method of taking the taxes was prescribed. Other acts were passed amending minor provisions of this act. An act passed November 7, 1803, imposed taxes on additional types of property and made some changes in the method of taking the

---

[9] *Ibid.,* 870-71.
[10] Information from Prentiss Price, Rogersville.
[11] Scott, *Laws,* I, 585-91.

lists.[12] By the second section of this act, the tax rate was set at the following:

For each 100 acres of land 12½ cents; for each town lot 25 cents; on each free poll and male servant 12½ cents; on each slave 25 cents; on each stud horse kept for the season of mares, the sum equal to the season of one mare; on each billiard table $1,000; on each retail store $25.00; on each pedler or hawker $25.00. According to the census of 1810 the population of Hawkins County was 7,643, including 930 slaves.[13]

HAWKINS COUNTY, TENNESSEE
TAX LISTS
1809-1812

Key to Column Numbers[14]
[1] Land
[2] White Polls
[3] Black Polls

Names	[1]	[2]	[3]	Names	[1]	[2]	[3]
Capt. Lucus's Company, 1809				Ephraim Andrews	100	1	2
Wm Armstrong				Wm Alexander	400	1	
(Little)	200	1	1	Geo W Alvis			
John Armstrong				Spencer Altom			
(big)	100	1		Isaac Amicks		1	
Thomas Armstrong				Thos C Anderson			
Shff	200	1		Stephen Cole			
Jas Armstrong Jun		1		Henry Blevins		1	1
Thomas Armstrong				Jonathan Bannister			
(Shr)	250	1	1	Mason Bishop		1	
Wm Armstrong				Thomas Brooks			
(Sen)	100	1		Jacob Black			
John Armstrong				George Beets Jun	220	1	
Son to James	300	1	2	Joseph Bishop	388	2	1

---

[12] *Ibid.*, 762-69.

[13] *Aggregate Amount of Persons Within the United States in the Year 1810* (Washington, D. C., 1811), 77.

[14] There were two other columns in each of the lists: town lots and stud horses. All of the 32 town lots listed were in Lucus's company, 1809, and were distributed as follows: Wm. Alexander, 10½; Andrew Campbell, 6; Francis Dalzell, 2; King's Exors (Executors?), 4; Neil & Simpson, 1; Joseph Parks, 4½; Samuel Powel, 2; Jacob Hackney, 1; Alexander Nelson's Estate, 1.
Each of the following (in addition to John Cooper of McWilliams' company) was recorded as owning one stud horse: William Armstrong, Esq., of McCoy's company; Epps Gibbons and Wm. Gillenwaters of Gillenwaters' company; William Nichols, James Walling, Tiry Gibson, and David Denham of Looney's company; Joseph Anderson, Andrew Galbraith, and Stephen Smith of Mores (Moore's) company; and Thomas Johnston, Isham Mills, and William Slavins of Allen's company. Andrew Galbraith was listed in Smith's company (1811) as owning a stud horse, but he probably was the same man listed in Moore's company in 1810.

Names	[1]	[2]	[3]
Thomas Bright		1	
John Bowen		1	
Hugh Chesnut	100	1	
John Cockram	300	1	1
Samuel Coen	100	1	
John Coen	20		
Andrew Chesnut		1	
Andrew Campbell	400	1	2
Hugh Campbells Estate	400		
Dennis Cary		1	
James Davies		1	
Francis Dalzell		1	2
Raleigh Dodson			
John Eishford [?]			
Ralph Elkins	100		
John Elkins	100	1	
George Elkins		1	
William Everett			
William Fisher		1	
Daniel Flora Jun		1	
Daniel Flora Sen			
Herod Grizzel			
Daniel Grisry [?]		1	
Hezekiah Hamblin	365	1	4
George Hale for self & W			
King's Exors		1	4
William Hedrick			
Jacob Huntsinger		1	
Marvil Helton		1	
Harry Jones [?]		1	
John Johnson	150	1	
Pleasant Johnson	1200		1
Thomas Jackson			
George Kerns Sen	300		
John Kerns	110	1	
George Kernes Jun	90	1	
Jacob Kerns		1	
Robert Kile	1400		7
Rodham Kenner	600	1	5
William King			
George Kizer [?]			
William Long			
Daniel Lipe	170	1	1
[Do Do]	200		
John Lucus	100		
Dennis McCairy [?]		1	
Alexander McCanse	120	1	
Samuel Milligan	120	1	
John Morris		1	
Edward Morris	100		
David Martin		1	

Names	[1]	[2]	[3]
William Morris S. C.	100		
William McCarty	200	1	3
William McCulloch	100	1	
Henry McCulloch	100	1	
Thomas Moony		1	
William Moony	150	1	
Richard Mitchell			
George Moody	120	1	
James Nugent			
Neil & Simpson	100	2	1
John Nugent			
Robert Nall	300	1	7
Henry Orth	1920		
Daniel Owens		1	
Joseph Parks	100		
Lawrence Pearson			
Levy Panther		1	
John Pilant	300		
Joseph Pilant		1	
Henry Prices Estate	200		
Peter Pearson		1	
Samuel Powel		1	
Benjamin Powel		1	
Christian Pearson			
Wm Roseberry &			
Absalom Roseberry			
Jeremiah Rowland			
Michael Rorke Jun			
Willson Roach			
John Rhea	500		
Do do	640		
Christian Shanks	38	1	
John Smith			
John Stakely	200	1	
Adam Shanks			
John Tibbs	256	1	1
George Winterbower Jun		1	1
Do Do Sen	175		
Edward Williams		1	
John Woods		1	
F Dalzell returns one cotton machine			
Jacob Hackney		1	
Walter Sims	28800		
Joseph Painter		1	
Samuel Harlen [?]		1	
Wyet Coleman		1	
Samuel Myers		1	
Alexr Nelsons Estate,	300		
returned by Robt	300		
Nelson	100		

Names	[1]	[2]	[3]
	100		
James Hagan	519	1	6
Richard Mitchell	1240	1	2
	1140		
	640		
	80		
	48021	74	56

McWilliams Company, 1809[15]

Names	[1]	[2]	[3]
Arnold, Mary widow	170	[torn]	
Aikerd, John		1	
Austen, Sam		1	
Buris, John	100	1	
Branum, Thomas	100	1	
Brandun, Wm		1	
Beaty, Walter	100		
Cooper, James	700		3
Cooper, E[l]izabeth	500		
Cooper, John, 1 stud horse	480	1	
Cleck, Mikle	275		
Crew, Jacob	140	1	
Critz, John	567	1	
Crobarger, George	158		1
Currey, Sam	181	1	
Cox, Jacob	699	1	5
Cooper, John for M Daughertys Act	400		
Davis, John Jr		1	
Derrick, Mikle	233	1	
Dollins, David		1	
Derrik, John		1	
Davis, Jonathan	150	1	
Davis, Willi[a]m	100		
Epperson, Charls		1	
Epperson, William		1	
Elis, John	300	1	
Foster, Winkfeild		1	
Guyn, David		1	
Gentri, Joseph		1	
Gibbons, John	250	1	1
Hensley, Temple		1	
Hensley, Trent		1	
Hamilton, Robbert	965	1	
Hensley, Edmond		1	
Jones, Aquilla	200	1	
Jones, Walter		1	

Names	[1]	[2]	[3]
Kincade, D[a]vid Esq	820	1	
K[in]cade, David, Cr Valley	700	1	9
King, John	500		3
Liaht [Light], John		1	
Light, Joshua		1	
Lairkins, Thomas	150	1	1
Lee, Robbert		1	
McPheeters, Sam	150	1	
McPheeters, John	300	1	
Marshall, John	316		
Murphey, Joseph		2	1
Mitchell, John		1	
Mcanulley, Elijah	100	1	
Mcanully, John		1	
Morrison, James		1	
Morryson, Thomas		1	1
Morrison, Sam	350	1	1
Mill[e]r, Mathies	50		
Mann, Ebenezer		1	
Mann, Joseph		1	
McMinn, John		1	
Phillips, Waid		1	
Pannil, Beny		1	
Pairks, Jos. Lee C. where Mcanelley lives	100		
Ross, David, T Hopkins	7948		4
Rice, Dannel	640	1	1
Richards, John Sen	600		
Roberts, Josa		1	
Richard, John Jun		1	
Richard, Mikle		1	
Hopkins, Thomas, Bot of Stuart	380		
Smith, Elizabeth	160		3
Skelton, Wm	280	1	
Skelton, James		1	
Smith, John	200	1	1
Skelton, Thomas		1	
Smith, Alexr	300	1	
Skelton, Ruben		1	
Talor, Thomas	200	1	
Weaver, John	150		
Walker, Wm		1	
Wineger, John Jr	400		
Wineger, George		1	
Wilfee, Christopher	300	1	2

[15] "This list," according to Prentiss Price on his typewritten copy, "has been through a fire. One corner when folded is slightly charred and torn."

Names	[1]	[2]	[3]
Wilflee, John		1	
Winger, Wm			
(C valley	100	1	
Hicks, James	200	1	
Hains, Zachariah		1	
Woods, Zachariah		1	
Williams, Ginney	590		
Patterson, John	898	1	
Severs, Wm		1	
Beiard, John		1	
Horn, Fredrik Jun [?]		1	
Cleck, John		1	
Reynoulds, Mikle		1	
Patterson, Alexr	440	1	
Wells, Aaron	191	1	
Morrison, Peter	330		
Burnit, Jerremiah	140	1 [torn]	
Jones, Martin		1 [torn]	
Leek, John		1 [torn]	
McMinn, Robbert Esq	130	1 [torn]	
Gains, James		1	
Morrison, William		1	
McMinn, Joseph	400	5[?]	
McWilliams, Hugh	150	3	4[?]
	18381	85	43

Capt Lawrence's Company 1809

Names	[1]	[2]	[3]
Anderson,			
Mr. Joseph	1480	1	5
Austin, Natheneil		1	
Aikin, Harrison		1	1
Aikin, Ezekiel		1	3
Amis, Williss	82	1	2
Bryan, Joseph	160		
Bassett, Nathl	200	2	4
Baxter, Stephen		1	
Bond, Wright Senr		1	
Bond, Wright Junr		1	
Bragg, William Senr	150		
Bragg, Wm Junr		1	
Boykin, Eli	279	1	9
Bare, Peter			
Cloud, Benja	160	1	3
Cloud, Wm		1	
Cotral, Hiram		1	
Connor, Archibald		1	
Connor, Julius	640	1	3
Cain, Hugh			
Carpenter, Yelverton	50	1	
Conway, George	300	1	5

Names	[1]	[2]	[3]
Childers, Wm P.	120	1	
Do Do	29		
Cocke, Thomas	640	1	
Cocke, Jno,			
Cocke, Thos	25		
Connor, Thomas		1	1
Coolley, Isaac		1	
Dawson, John		1	
Davis, Lewis			
Davis, Benja			
Durham, John		1	
Evans, William	147		1
Do Do	40		
Evans, James		1	
Enis, William			
Galbraith, Andrew	421	1	3
Green, Francis	66 1/3		
Hill, John S.	440		4
Henderson, George	70	1	
Haywood, Wm			
Johnson, James Senr			7
Johnson, James Junr	157	1	2
Johnson, Wm	150	1	
Jack, William	100	1	
Jago, Abraham	200	1	
Lathim, James	170	1	
Lathim, Moses	180	1	1
Lawrence, Randolph			
Lebo, John	300		
Lay, Bartlet		1	
Lovin, James			
McAnelly, John	200	1	
McCraw, Gabriel	100	1	1
McClemore, Presley		1	
Moffett, William			
Mills, Hardy	162	2	
Moore, Hugh	238	1	5
Miller, John		1	
Miller, Robt		1	
Miller, Jacob		1	
Moore, Lemuel		1	
Martin, William	100	1	
Do Do	100		
Orick, Benja		1	
Orick, Saml		1	
Orick, James		1	
Owens, Wm	300	1	1
Do Do	480		
Do Do	50		
Owens, Farr		1	
Potter, Paul		1	

Names	[1]	[2]	[3]	Names	[1]	[2]	[3]
Poindexter, John	100			Brown, Jesse	200	1	
Permenter, Theophilus	50	1		Biggs, Benjamin	450	1	
Robertson, Hezekiah				Brown, John		1	
Ramsey, Richard		1		Childs, Paul		1	
Rigz, Saml				Charles, James Jr	89	1	
Stubblefield, R Lockly	300			Coldwell, John	298	1	2
Do Do	215			Cobb, Joel	75	1	
Stubblefield, Wiot	350			Coldwell, Benoni	540	1	2
Stubblefield, Thomas		1		Chambers's, E &			
Stubblefield, Wiot Junr		1		Daniel (admr)	480		
Smith, Jackson				Christian, Lewis	174		
Timmons, Charles	150	1		Christian, Allen	200	1	
Timmons, Wm		1		Collins, George Sr	100		
Thompson, Nathan	200	1		Christian, John	90	1	
Wendel, David				Coldwell, David	280	1	2
Willis, David				Clipper, Peter		1	
Wells, John S.		1		Clipper, Frederick		1	
Williams, Margaret	300	1	6	Childs, John	200	1	
Webb, Theodorick		1		Christian, Lewis Jr	152	1	
Cocke, William				Collins, George Jr	100	1	
the heirs of Thos Dodson,				Collins, James	100	1	
Deceasd by James				Clipper, George		1	
Anderson	250			Chambers, William		1	
Ballard, Alexd				Coldwell, Thomas	570	1	1
Grizal, Herod		1		Caldwell, James Esq	160		2
Meritt, George		1		Caldwell, John			
Patrick, Jessee		1		(Carters Valley)		1	
Patrick, John		1		Coldwell, Ballard	300	1	2
Richardson, Henry W.		1		Church, Christian	100		
the heirs of John Creed,				Chappel, Henry	100	1	
decd by Hugh Moore	742		6	Campbell, John		1	
Lard, William		1		Carrington, Asia		1	
Moore, John		1		Church, Henry		1	
Anderson, Thos		1		Davis, Lilburn		1	
Gaylard, James		1		Drury, William		1	
Flower, James		1		Eaton, William		1	
				Eaton, Alexander		1	
	11143 1/3	72	73	Felkner, Jacob & Salley			
				admrs of Lewis	150		
McCoys Company 1809				Felkner, Henry	600	1	
Armstrong, William				Forgey, Hugh		1	
Esq	1740		8	Finley, William	145		
Do for Marsteller	700			Finley, James (Doctor)	50		1
Do for Saml Gamble	226			Finley, Samuel		1	
Argenbright, George	78	1		Felkner, Phillip		1	
Armstrong, Thomas	100	1	4	Ferguson, Elijah		1	
Armstrong, John	150		3	Forgey, Andrew Sr	400		1
Brown, Henry	100	1		Forgey, Andrew Jr		1	
Bradley, William	1400	1	3	Finley, Reuben		1	
Bean, Mordecai	223	1		Francisco, John	130	1	1
Barret, Thomas	150	1		Forgey, James	663	1	2

Names	[1]	[2]	[3]	Names	[1]	[2]	[3]
Felkner, George	50	1		Langford, Jordan		1	
Felkner, Jacob		1		Long, Isaac		1	
Godard, Francis	200	1		Miller, John	500	1	
Groves, David	112	1		Maxwell, David		1	
Galbreath, Joseph	100	1	1	Maxwell, George Esq	600		4
Galbreath, Arthur	340		3	McCullah, Joseph		1	
Hensley, Robert		1		Miller, Michael		1	
Hagood, Elizabeth	100		1	Mason, Yelverton		1	
Hagood, James	89	1	1	Myers, Lewis		1	
Hiler, David	70	1		McVay, James		1	
Harrel, Hazel	100	1		Messer, Jacob		1	
Harrel, John Sr			5	Messer, James		1	
Harrel, John Jr	200	1		McVay, Patrick		1	
Harrel, Enoch	200			McCullah, Farmer		1	
Hamilton, William		1		Norman, Matthew		1	
Henderson, Nathaniel				North, Edward	237		
Esq	400	1	1	North, John		1	
Henderson, Samuel		1		Patterson, James		1	
Humble, Mary				Phipps, William	350	1	4
(widow)	350			Pheagens, William	50	1	
Humble, Joseph		1		Reece, Joseph	100	1	
Hicks, Isaac	200	1		Richards, Joshua		1	
Holland, Shadrick		1		Rice, Reuben	300	1	
Jackson, Micajah		1		Richards, John Sr	650		
Judkins, James	60	1	1	Rice, John Jr	84	1	
Johnson, George		1		Rice, Drury	150	1	
K[i]ncheloe, Elijah	757	1	3	Rice, Edmond		1	
Kline, Jacob		1		Sissum, William		1	
Kirkpatrick, James		1		Smith, Nathan		1	
Long, Alexander		1		Sproul, Thomas	100	1	
Long, James		1		Skelton, John		1	
Lyons, William	160	1	1	Sensebough, Henry	194	1	
Lockmiller, Jacob	100	1		Saunders, Mary Arther		1	
Lyons, James		1		Sensebough, Jacob	200	1	1
Long, John (river)	100	1		Stubblefield, William	350	1	
Lockmiller, Jonas		1		Stubblefield, Coleman		1	
Lockmiller, John Sr	548			Stubblefield, Fielding		1	
Lockmiller, John Jr		1		Surguine, James	1240	1	3
Livingston, Jacob		1		Stewart, Hamilton	250	2	
Leaper, James, Francis				Skelton, William		1	
& Hugh	640	3	2	Snider, William		1	
Leaper, Francis	300			Saunders, Richard		1	
Leaper, Mathew		1		[These three names out of order			
Lockmiller, John				at the end of list]			
(over river) —	117	1		Thurman, William		1	
Long, Joseph Jr	320	1	3	Vaughn, James	200	1	
Larkins, Henry	200	1	1	Waterson, Edward	200		4
Loney [sic], Isham	72	1		Woods, Joseph	140	1	
Looney, Michael	138		3	Walters, Solomon		1	
Looney, Absolom		1	3	Woods, James		1	
Looney, Mary (widow)	164		1				

Names	[1]	[2]	[3]
Williams, Elizabeth			
(widow)			3
Williams, Darling		1	
Williams, Theophilus		1	
Winstead, Francis	400	1	
Winegar, Phillip	100	1	
Winegar, Frederick		1	
Winegar, Peter		1	
Warren, William		1	
Winstead, Ezekiel		1	
Winegar, John	416	2	
Winegar, William	100	1	
Wilson, Jesse	100	1	
Winegar, Andrew	316		
Wright, George	500	1	
Warren, James		1	
Young, John	1306	1	3
Young, William	500	1	2
Young, Robert	270	1	2
	28553	146	88

Gillenwaters Company, 1810[16]

Names	[1]	[2]	[3]
Wm Gross	456	1	
John McBroom	382		1
Fanny Groves	397		2
Epps Gibbons	31		1
Wm Gillenwaters	340	1	5
Spencer Acuff	50	1	
Corl Carmack	993	1	
James Charles	236	2	
Jacob Creese	100	1	
John Gilbreath	220	1	1
Joseph Gilbreath	100	1	1
Wm Gibbons	300	1	2
Jacob Millar	200	1	2
Peter Millar	125		
Wm More	52	1	1
Wm Mee	150	1	
Zachariah Ingram		1	
James Simmons	145		
Saml B. Hawkins	200		
John Howell	400	1	1
Jacob Wright		1	
Joel Gillenwaters	150	1	3
Thos Gillenwaters	320	1	1
Wm Shropshire	54	1	
John Green		1	

Names	[1]	[2]	[3]
William Loony		1	
John Grosse		1	
	5411	22	21
Robt Mallery	72	1	
Wm Spires		1	
John Shanks	103	1	
Francis Younge		1	
Andw Ingram Senr	300	1	1
Jos Pilant		1	
Thos Mee		1	
Fanny Glespy			3
Samuel Wilson	504	1	
Thos Ingram	550	1	
John Cox	135		
Amasa Howell	355	1	3
Philip King		1	4
Jos Russell	400		3
John Carmack		1	
Danl Henry	25	1	
Wm Bradford	53	1	
Wm Carmack		1	
Benjn Hutcher[s]on	100	1	
David Sensabaugh	200	1	1
Daniel Flora		1	
Christan Simmons	220	1	
	3017	19	15
	5411	22	21
	8428	41	36
Wm Armstrong	552		4
Ira Ball	35		
Wm Brice	709	1	
George Cox		1	
Jacob Clepper	100		
Robert Campbell	670	1	
James Y Campbell	100	1	
Groce, Christopher	150		
Hinch Gilliam	75	1	
Thomas Henly	50	1	
Saml Kirk		1	
John Kensinger	240	1	
Sampson Larkin	150	1	
Benja Looney		1	
George Myers	100	1	
Thos McBroom		1	
Alexander McBroom		1	

---

[16] "In a good many instances this list shows the amount of tax paid. It is scribbled all over with names and figures." *Ibid.*

Names	[1]	[2]	[3]
Wm Molsby	250	1	
Martin Shaner	346	1	1
Hardin Sanders	75	1	
Phillip Clepper	65		
Jonas Lockmiller	400	1	
David Kasner		1	
Franklin Denham		1	
John Tebbs	30	1	
Lewis Stirgeon		1	
Thos Ingram	400	1	
	150		
Jessey McWilliams	130	1	1

Loudebacks Company 1810

Names	[1]	[2]	[3]
Bright, William		1	
Barnett, John		1	
Beal, George		1	
Barrott, Stepen		1	
Breaden, James	1000	1	1
Cox, James		1	
Coward, James		1	
Coward, Joel Jnr		1	
Cyster, Daniel	150		
Chesnut, Henry		1	4
Counsel, Cyrus		1	
Cox, Tabitha	300		2
Dodson, John	350		
Day, William		1	
Everhart, Jacob	300	1	
Everhart, Christley		1	
Finney, William	160	1	
Farmer, James		1	
George, Harbert	150	1	
Gollihorn, John		1	
Grigsby, John Snr	550		6
Henton, William			2
Haskins, John		1	
Hoard, William Snr	270	1	
Hoofmaster, Goodlef	200		
Haynes, Thomas		1	1
	3430	20	16
Jeffres, William		1	
Kite, John	180	1	
Kite, George Snr	320		2
Kite, William		1	
Kite, George Junr	200	1	
King, Andrew	600	1	
Kenner, Winder	370	1	
Lawson, Jacob	290	1	1
Lea, Samuel		1	

Names	[1]	[2]	[3]
Lawson, Elijah		1	
Loudeback, Isaac	124	1	
Lawson, Isham	100	1	
Lawson, Peter	100	1	
Lawson, William	200		
Long, Nicholas		1	
Loudeback, Henry	166	1	
Manes, Daniel	50	1	
Manes, Bartlett	150	1	
Maples, William		1	1
Manes, Seth		1	
Manes, William		1	
Manes, George	50		
Manes, Ephraem	150	1	
Pain, William Junr	250	1	
Paine, Charles		1	
Parton, Charles		1	
Pope, Adkin		1	
	3300	24	4
Right, Hance	270	1	
Rork, John		1	
Rork, Michael Snr	290		
Rutherford, John		1	
Reynolds, Isham	300		
Reynolds, William Snr	180		
Reynolds, George		1	
Reynolds, Henry		1	
Robertson, Hezekiah	400	1	
Smith, Anthony G.	50	1	
Smith, John		1	
Short, Henry		1	
Self, Thomas	200		
Smith, Samuel		1	1
Smith, Joshua		1	1
Stewart, Elisha		1	
Smith, Lauther	44		
Smith, James		1	1
Henry & Lindenberger	397		
Smith, Robert	100		
Willis, John	100	1	
	2331	14	3
	3300	24	4
	3430	20	16
	9061	58	23

Capt Looney Company 1810

Names	[1]	[2]	[3]
Anderson, Swinfield	100	1	
Anderson, James	50	1	

Names	[1]	[2]	[3]	Names	[1]	[2]	[3]
Bloomer, John	50	1		Nichols, William	50	1	
Begly, Hennery		1		Prat, Thomas		1	
Brooks, Littleton	600	1	1	Roberts, William	60		2
Bloomer, Daniel	100	1		Roberts, James Esq	50	1	
Bleavins, James		1		Roberts, Joseph		1	
Brisco, Thomas		1		Rogers, Doswell	50	1	
Begley, John	300	1		Roberts, John	40	1	
Briant, William		1					
Brisco, John	86	1			3240	24	3
Cox, Absolum	150	1					
Colings, Bengamon	90	1		Rogers, Thomas	50		
Collings, Vardemon	100	1		Anderson, William	100		
Collings, James	100	1		Sisemore, Gorge		1	
Collings, Hennery		1		Vaughn, William	100		
Denham, John		1		Vaughn, John	100	1	
Baker, Andrew	200	1		Weddle, Daniel	100	1	
Burtain, Jess	150	1		Weddle, Amos	30	1	
Evins, James	50	1		Walling, William	300	1	
Evines, Mark		1		Walling, James	530	1	1
Frost, Robrt	250	1		Wilbourn, Stephen	195	1	
Goodmon, Obedah	100	1		Weddle, Elias	50	1	
Goodmond, Jurdan		1		Walling, Thomas		1	
Gray, Edward		1		Weddle, David	25	1	
Garrison, John		1		Weddle, John	50	1	
				Swiliven, Ezekiel		1	
	2476	26	1	Munnahon, Thomas		1	
				Munnahon, John		1	
				Rogers, Gorge		1	
Garrison, Isaac	350			Munke, Shadrick	30		
Garrison, David		1		Rogers, Thomas		1	
Gallian, Thomas	100	1		Monke, John		1	
Gonce, Isaac	200	1		Smith, Gorge		1	
Goodman				Fields, John		1	
Gibson, Gerden	100	1		Cotten, Burel		1	
Stapleton, William		1		Gibson, Yearby		1	
Hubbord, John	100	1		Gibson, Shepard	50	1	
Hurd, Elijah		1		Gibson, Charles		1	
Helton, Anald	100	1		Gibson, Tiry	50	1	
Johnson, Moses	100			Gibson, Royal		1	
Johnson, Gorge	50	1					
Johnson, Moses [again]	100				2030	25	1
Johnson, Thomas	50	1					
Joanes, Thomas		1		Vallingtine Collings	100	1	
Johnson, James		1		James Bird		1	
Kile, Robert	600			Samuel More		1	
Looney, John	300	1		Mckgee, William		1	
Lawson, John	50	1		John Wilson		1	
Looney, Absalum Esq	640	1	1	Clemment Lawson		1	
Lawson, Thomas		1		Philisom Howel		1	
Mendingall, Isaac	50			Birton, Robing		1	
Mosley, William		1		Nichols, Surril		1	
Neal, Adam	100	1		Qualls, Rolen		1	

Names	[1]	[2]	[3]	Names	[1]	[2]	[3]
Mckiney, James		1		Jacke, William	100	1	
Denham, David				Jaygo, Abraham	200	1	
				Ireland, John	100		
	100	11		Lathem, James	170	1	
	2476	26	1	Lathim, Moses	288	1	1
	3240	24	3	Lebo, John	400		
	2030	25	1	Laurence, Randolph	362		
				Loven, James			
	7846	86	5	McAnally, John	140	1	
				Mills, Hardy	162	1	
Capt. Mores Company, 1810[17]				Mills, Henry		1	
Anderson, Joseph M.	1880	1	5	Moore, Lemual		1	
Amis, Willis	92	1	2	Meritt, George		1	
Akin, Harrison		1	1	Moore, John		1	1
Boykin, Eli	279	1	9	Moore, Hugh G.		1	4
Bryan, Joseph	160			McCraw, Gabriel	100	1	1
Bragg, William Senr	150			Owens, William	330	1	1
Bragg, William Junr		1		Owens, Far		1	
Bare, Peter Senr	100			Owens, James			
Bare, Peter Junr		1		Potter, Paul		1	
Bond, Wright		1		Poidexture, John	100		
Childers, Wm P.	149	1		Permenter, Theophlus	50	1	
Cloud, Benjamin	160			Robertson, Thos		1	
Conway, Thos Senr	274	1	4	Stubblfield, Wiett Senr	350		
Conway, George		1	1	Stubblefield, Wiett		1	
Car, Samuel		1		Stubblefield, Thos.		1	
Conner, Archabald		1		Stubblefield, R Lockly	515		
Connor, Thomas		1	1	Smith, Henry			1
Carpenter, Yelverton	50	1		Smith, Stephen		1	
Creeds, Johns (Heirs)	742		6	Timmons, Charles	150	1	
Cocke, Thos	898	1		Timmons, William		1	
Cocke, William				Thompson, Natham	269	1	
Cocke, John & Thos	25			Willis, David		1	
Dawson, John		1					
Dodson, Thos (Heirs)	150				4586	25	12
Evans, William	187		1	Wilson, William		1	
Easley, Daniel		1		Wells, John S.		1	
Evans, James		1		Webb, Theoderick		1	
Galbraith, Andrew	421	1	3	Williams, Margaret	300		4
Grizzle, Harrod		1		Williams, William		1	
Hill, John S.	500		4	C[l]oud, Isaac		1	
Henderson, George	70			Shadoe, Joseph		1	
Hicks, Wm.		1		Bassett, Nathaniel	200		4
Haywood, William				Baxter, Stephen	120	1	
				Yow, Peregrine G.		1	
	6787	23	37	Littleton, Charles		1	
Johnson, James	150	1	3	Breeding, Thos.		1	
Johnson, William	150			Seels, Solomon		1	

[17] The list for this company has an additional column headed "Situation," which gives for most of the members the location of the land, e.g. "Holsten [Holston] river," "on the county line," "poor valey [*sic*] creek," and whether gained by deed, grant, or occupation.

Names	[1]	[2]	[3]
Huchenson, Daniel		1	1
Willabough, Matthew	200		
Cummens, James		1	
McVey, James Senr			1
	820	13	10
	4586	25	12
	6787	23	37
total	12193	61	59

Hale's Company, 1810[18]
[fragment]

Names	[1]	[2]	[3]
Robert Philips		1	
Lewis Tharp		1	
John West	300		
William Hedrick		1	
John Hedrick		1	
Joseph White	300		
Nathan White	398 1/3	1	
William Grigsbey		1	1
John Hamblen	500	1	5
	2		
	75		
	45		
Nathan Vernon		1	
Abraham Vernon	270	1	
	275		
	170		

The foregoing is A list of the Taxable
Property Taken by me in Capt Hales
Company for the year 1810

John Hamblen

[on back]

Names	[1]	[2]	[3]
Mooney, George	300	1	
Barger, Jacob	87		
Ferguson, James		1	
Long, Jonathan	450		
Long, John		1	
Moreland, Wm	280	1	
Mooney, Edward	275	1	
Patrick, John		1	
Long, George	100	1	
	1492	7	
[above]	2335	9	6
[missing]	5584	20	16
[missing]	3378	24	4
	12789	60	26

Capt. N. Smith's Company, 1811

Names	[1]	[2]	[3]
Anderson, Joseph M.	1880	1	7
Anderson, James		1	
Amis, Willis	114	1	2
Austen, Joseph		1	
Boykin, Eli	279	1	9
Bryant, Joseph	160		
Bragg, Wm Senr	150		
Bragg, Wm Junr		1	
Bair, Peter Junr		1	
Bair, Peter Senr	100		
Bond, Wright		1	
Bassett, Nathaniel	200		4
Baxter, Stephen	120	1	
Cocke, Thos	1113	1	2
Cocke, Thos & John	25		
Cain, Hugh	100		
Carpenter, Yelverton	50	1	
Creed, John, Heirs	742		6
Cloud, Benjamin	160		
Connor, Thomas		1	1
Cummins, James		1	
Dobtsen, Thos, Heirs	250		1
Davis, Lewis Senr	200		2
Davis, Lewis Junr		1	
Davis, Benjamin		1	
Davis, Wm		1	
Evins, William	187	1	1
Easley, Daniel		1	
Ennis, Wm		1	
Galbraith, Andrew	420	1	3
Grizzle, Herrod		1	
Gray, William		1	
Hill, John S.	500		5
Haywood, Wm		1	
Henderson, George	70	1	
Harrell, John		1	
Ireland, John	100		
Johnson, James	150	1	4
Johnson, Stephen	150		
Jacke, Wm	50	1	
Jayco, Abraham	200	1	
Lathim, James	170	1	
Lathim, Moses	288	1	1
Lebo, John	520	1	
Littleton, Charles		1	

[18] This list has three additional columns headed "No. of pieces," "How Gained," and "Situation." John Hamblen and Abraham Vernon had 4 and 3 pieces, respectively. Under "How Gained" the word "Entry" is used instead of grant. Under "Situation" such locations as "Holston R," "Bent C," "Carter's V," and "Robisons C" are given.

Names	[1]	[2]	[3]
Littleton, Mark		1	
McAnally, John	160	1	
Miles, Hardy	162	1	
Miles, Henry		1	
Miller, Jacob		1	
Meritt, George		1	
McCraw, Gabl	100	1	1
McCraw, Maddox		1	
Moore, John		1	1
Moore, Hugh G.	586	1	5
McVey, James Jr		1	
Owens, Willim	670		1
Owens, Far	160	1	
Potter, Paul		1	
Poindexture, John	100		
Permenter, Theophilus	50	1	
Robertson, Thos		1	
Stubblefield, Wyett	100	1	
Stubblefield, R. Locke	515		
Stubblefield, Thos		1	
Stubblefield, Wyett [again]	470		
Smith, Jackson	200	1	1
Smith, Henry			1
Shadeh [Shadow?], Joel		1	
Timmons, Charles	150	1	
Timmons, Wm		1	
Timmons, Thos		1	
Thompson, Nathan	265	1	1
Willis, David		1	
Wilson, William		1	
Williams, William		1	
Williams, Margaret	300		5
Willoughby, Wallace	150		
Webb, Theodoricke		1	
Wells, John S.		1	

Names of those that has not [been] Given in on the other side of the River

Names	[1]	[2]	[3]
Riggs, Samuel			
Robertson, Richard	62	1	
Ballard, Alexander			
Deadericke & Windel			
Sugars, Nathan			
Lay, Bartlett			
Flowers, John Senr		1	
Flowers, John Junr		1	
Pharis, Jacob		1	
Ramsey, Richard		1	
Cocke, John			
Cocke, William			

Names	[1]	[2]	[3]
Cooley, Isaac		1	
Carter, Silus		1	
Henderson, Thos		1	
Lott, Arthur		1	
Yow, Peregrine G.		1	
Short, Samuel		1	
Gaylard, James		1	
Beets, John		1	
Hicks, William		1	
Miller, Robert		1	
Evan, Young		1	
Floyd, Estis		1	
Edward Cox		1	
Harman, Miller		1	
John Miller		1	
William Martain			
Pharaoh Cobb	860		13
William Cobb		1	1

[Given twice as Capt Nathaniel Smith's Company]

Capt. Allen's Company 1811

Names	[1]	[2]	[3]
Alford, Jacob		1	
Blakeman, Moses		1	
Brewer, Jacob	50	1	
Bird, Betsy	200		
Beshears, John		1	
Barnat, George	50	1	
Butcher, John		1	
Bray, John		1	
Berry, Thomas		1	
Boyd, William		1	
Bennat Coffee		1	
Creech, Jesse	40		
Coffee, Benjamin	250		
Cloud, Joseph		1	
Davis, William		1	
Davis, Joseph	50		
Davis, Archibald		1	
Day, David		1	
Epperson, Thomas	100		
Epperson, Jesse	300	1	
Epperson, Joseph	100		
Giddings, James	200		
Greene, Jeremiah	100	1	
Hutchison, Lewis		1	
Hutchison, William	100	2	2
Hurly, Nehemiah	40		
Hawk, John	200		
Hawk, Abraham		1	
Jones, Cherry		1	

Names	[1]	[2]	[3]	Names	[1]	[2]	[3]
Johnston, Asahel	100	1		Disarn, Francs		1	
Johnston, Thomas	104	1		Gibson, Jesee	30	1	
Jones, Elizabeth	75			Guttary, William	50	1	
Jones, James		1		Roberts, James	150	1	
Kidwell, John	400			Denham, John	30	1	
Long, William	50			Robarts, William	60		1
Lawson, Thomas	50	1		Hubart, John	118	1	
Mitchell, Solomon			2	Sisemore, Owen	100		
Mitchell, John		1		Click, Matthias	640	1	
Mills, Isham	800	1		Evins, James	50	1	
Mills, John	240	1	1	Walling, James	530	1	1
Martin, Thomas	50	1		Johnson, Moses	100		
Martin, William	100	1		Johnson, James		1	
McKoy, Archibald	150	1		Baker, William		1	
McDaniel, Alexander	200	1		Monk, John	35	1	
Mathes, Enos		1		Weddle, Daniel	80	1	
Murrell, James	30	1		Weddle, James	75	1	
Orrick, Benjamin		1		Weddle, John Sinor	75	1	
Odunnahoo, Patrick	500			Roreark, Barnabas	50	1	
Ogin, John	100			Umphres, Moses	150		
Orrick, Samuel		1		Bloomer, Daniel	150	1	
Orrick, James		1		Vaughn, William			
Province, Thomas		1		Sinior	100		
Pearson, Christian, Junr		1		Gray, Hamonas		1	
Rhea, Joseph		1		Vaughn, John	100	1	
Seals, Peter		1		Vaughn, William Junor		1	
Sullavin, John		1		Galion, John	80	1	
Slaten, John	200	1		Wilson, John		1	
Seals, Solomon		1		Galion, Thomas	100		
Stewart, William	50	1		Monahon, Thomas		1	
Slavins, William				Weddle, Robart		1	
Trent, William		1		Joans, Ambers		1	
Tucker, James		1		Anderson, Gorge	130	1	
Wolf, Charles	200			Rogers, Thomas	75	1	
Wolf, Peter		1		Rogers, Douswell	75	1	
West, Moses		1		Heard, James	25	1	
Wolf, Jacob		1		Heard, Eligah		1	
Wolf, George	200	1		Helton, Arnold		1	
West, John		1		Walling, William	350		1
Wilder, William		1		Weddle, John Junor		1	
West, John [again]		1		Walling, Thomas		1	
Wilder, James		1		Robarts, Joseph		1	
Wolf, Adam	50	1		Stephens, James		1	
Young, Jeremiah		1		Stepleton, William		1	
				Weddle, Elias	50	1	
Tax List taken by Wm. Nichols				Weddle, Thomas	100		
1812				Blevens, James		1	
Cury, Eligah		1		Weddle, Amos	30	1	
Cury, William		1		Nichols, William	50	1	

EARLY EAST TENNESSEE TAXPAYERS

Compiled by Pollyanna Creekmore

IX. Greene County, 1805[1]

Greene County was established by an act of the North Carolina general assembly on April 18, 1783,[2] the third established in the territory now the state of Tennessee. The act provided that Washington County, established six years before,[3] should be divided into two counties by

> ... a line beginning at William Williams, in the fork of Horse Creek, at the foot of the mountain, thence a direct line to George Gillespie's house at or near the mouth of Big Limestone, thence a north course to the line which divides the counties of Washington and Sullivan, thence a direct line to the mouth of Cloud Creek on Holston river—and all that part of Washington county westward of said line is declared to be a distinct county by the name of Greene.

The county was named in honor of General Nathanael Greene, prominent Revolutionary war leader.

Part of the original territory was removed in the formation of Knox and Jefferson counties;[4] in 1797 Cocke County was created out of Jefferson[5] and in 1799 part of Greene County was attached to Cocke County.[6]

The earliest settlement of the territory which became Greene County was in the late 1770's when settlers pushed down the Nolichucky River from the Watauga settlement.[7]

---

[1] For introduction to this series see *Publications* No. 23 (1951), 115-16. Previous installments have been: I. Anderson County, 1802, in No. 23; II. Blount County, 1801, in No. 24; III. Knox County, 1806, in No. 26; IV. Grainger County, 1799, in No. 27; V. Jefferson County, 1800, in No. 28; VI, Carter County, 1796, in No. 30; VII. Sullivan County, 1796, in No. 31; VIII. Hawkins County, 1809-1812, in No. 32.

[2] Edward Scott (comp.), *Laws of the State of Tennessee Including Those of North Carolina Now in Force From the Year 1715 to the Year 1820, Inclusive,* 2 vols. (Knoxville, 1821), 282. Hereafter cited as Scott, *Laws.*

[3] *Ibid.,* 221-22.

[4] George Roulstone (comp.), *Laws of the State of Tennessee* (Knoxville, 1803), iv-v.

[5] *Ibid.,* 124-26.

[6] *Ibid.,* 168.

[7] Goodspeed Publishing Co., *History of Tennessee,* East Tennessee edition (Nashville, 1887), 881.

The first court was held at the home of Robert Kerr (Carr) at the site of present Greeneville. The first justices of the peace were Joseph Hardin, John Newman, George Doherty, James Houston, Amos Bird, and Asahel Rawlings. Daniel Kennedy was chosen clerk; James Wilson, sheriff; William Cocke, attorney for the state; Joseph Hardin, Jr., entry taker; Isaac Taylor, surveyor; Richard Woods, register; and Francis Hughes, ranger.[8]

The surviving Greene County records are available in the courthouse at Greeneville. There has been no serious loss of any records except loose papers, which were probably lost through carelessness. The county court minutes, estate books, will books, deeds, etc., have all been preserved. Many of the original marriage bonds and licenses were lost before being recorded, there being no mandatory law before 1838. The late Mrs. Louise Wilson Reynolds published the 1783 tax lists in the *D.A.R. Magazine* for April, 1919. The earliest tax lists available in the Greene County Clerk's Office are those for 1809. A copy of some of the early marriage bonds contributed by Mrs. Z. R. Peterson was published in the *Detroit Society for Genealogical Research Magazine.*

The following list was transcribed from a microfilm copy of the original certified copy return by Valentine Sevier, Greene County court clerk, to the Tennessee general assembly, now on file in the Tennessee Archives. This and early tax lists of other Tennessee counties were microfilmed by the compiler in 1949, through the courtesy of the late Mrs. John Trotwood Moore, Tennessee state librarian and archivist. The films are available in the McClung Collection, Lawson McGhee Library, Knoxville.

The county courts in Tennessee were authorized to levy taxes on property by a legislative act passed October 25, 1797,[9] in which types of taxable property were listed and the method of taking the taxes was prescribed. Other acts were passed amending minor provisions of this act. An act passed November 7, 1803, imposed additional types of property and made some changes in the method of taking the lists.[10] By the second section of this act, the tax rate was set at the following:

---

[8] *Ibid.,* 885.

[9] Scott, *Laws,* I, 585-91.

[10] *Ibid.,* 762-69. The list which follows, however, merely gives the names of the free inhabitants without the usual statistics as to the number of polls and amount of property owned.

For each 100 acres of land 12½ cents; for each town lot 25 cents; on each free poll and male servant 12½ cents; on each slave 25 cents; on each stud horse kept for the season of mares, the sum equal to the season of one mare; on each billiard table $1,000; on each retail store $25.00; on each pedler or hawker $25.00.

A Copy of the List of free taxable Inhabitants of Greene County in the Year 1805, as returned by James Patterson, Sheriff of said County.

Thomas Robinson	John Bailey	Michael Gurtner
William Bowers	Frethias Loyd	Stephen Alexander Senr
Samuel McGill	Philip Everet	William Brotherton
George Andes	Thomas Graham	William Reeves
John Weems	Josiah Frisby	James Pratt
Thomas Prathar	John Painter	Isaiah Harrison
Michael Neese	John Frushour	Solomon Reese
Daniel Bails	Rudolph Boo	Philip Smathars
James Weems	Joseph Babb	John Wolliver
David Tate	Jacob Linebough	David Gurtner
Benjamin Yeates	John Boils	Robert McGill
Alexander Prethero	George Phann	Andrew Stephens
Dutton Lane	John Phann	Thomas Watson
John Neese	Isaac Frisby	John McCurty
Abraham Hood	Andrew Luckey	John Alexander
Benjamin Vanpelt	Jeremiah Harrison	Ephraim Wilson
Young Landrum	Adam Painter	Benjamin Williams
John Broiles	John Copeland	James Penney
Patrick Ross	Joseph Reynolds	David Carter
John Willer	Samuel Lain	William Ramsey
Dutton Lane Junr	Abraham Peters	Henry White
John Carter Senr	John Woolsey	Nicholas Trobough
John Weems Senr	John Pogue	John Lane
Jacob Gray	Israel McBee	John White
Peter Harmon Senr	Charles Killgore	John Jones
Thomas Wyatt	Jacob Miller	Samuel Dinsmoore
Daniel McClellin	Peter Ricker	William McCormick
Ezekiel Broyles	Michael Neese	Philip Babb
Jeremiah Broyles	John Yerrick	John Glass Senr
John Farnsworth	Sebastian Smith	Thomas Greene
Jesse Huffman	William Harrison	James Neil
Jonathan Brown	John Killdea	George Jones
James Graham Senr	Thomas Williams	Benjamin Drue
Ezekiel Frazier	Jacob Smith	Christopher Winters
John Macky	Joseph Brown	Enos Pickering
Thomas Brown	Benjamin Pickering	Henry Dyke Junr
Martin Lentz	George Farnsworth	James Morrison
Michael Miers	Isaac Sherrill	Hezekiah Russell
Paulser Hawk	Henry Mantooth	James Johnston
Henry Stonecypher	William Ford	Charles McGill
Daniel Dunn	John Kelly Junr	Daniel Coulee
John Allen	William Wilson	John Mitchell

Thomas Mitchell
William Mitchell
Thomas Brown
Robert Burnett
Jacob Fellow
James Cotter
Michael Baysinger
Alexander Wilson
Benjamin Brown
Abraham White
Christopher Kerby
Phineas Jones
Samuel Brewer
Thomas Antrim
Samuel Varner
Philip Phann
Isaac Justis
Evan Jones Junr
John Vansandt
John Kyle
Daniel Cremer
Andrew Hixson
Absalom Haworth Sr
Ellis Pickering
Henry Trobough
Shadrach Cross
Henry Miers
John Davis
James McCurry
Ezekiel Carter
Daniel Kellar
John McMacken
John Linebough
Harris H. Hutchison
George Moyers
William Houston
Reuben Allen
Felix Earnest
Joseph Wright
John Glass Junr
David Adams
James Pearce
William Wilson
Philip Brewer
Peyton Randolph
James Guin
Solomon Edmondson
Abraham Williams
Isaac Doty
Capt John Stanfield
William McBride
John Coulson

Daniel Walker
David Huffstadler
James Gass
Philip Howel
Moses Moore
Even Evens Senr
John Jones
Abraham Carter Senr
James Houston
Edmund Strange
Jesse Wright
Solomon Bailes
Philip Brown
William McBroom
Henry Long
John Headrick
Adam Moyers
Robert Gamble
Thomas Thompson
Christian Dearstone
Philip Chance
Solomon Wilhoit
Alexander Russell
Thomas Perry
Thomas Harmon
Henry Farnsworth Sr
Shobal Ellis
John Kelsey Senr
Joseph Dugger
George Weems
William Moiers Junr
George Shields
Maurice Morriss
Edward Gray
Nicholas Long
Thomas Warren
Jesse Carter
Daniel Linebough
William Weems
Thomas Russell
William Miller
Stephen Brooks
William Headrick Senr
Edward Luster
Robert Farnsworth
Jacob Friese
Robert Johnston
Thomas Johnston
Alexander Kelsey
David Rice
Thomas Randolph
Isaac Davis

Josiah Temple
Jesse Willia
Joel Dryden
David Malick
William Greene
Alexander McAlpin
James Moore, Junr
William McGill
John Garvin
James Smith
Robert Carson
Evan Guin
Asahel Rawlings
Thomas Frazier
Samuel Frazier
William Wilson
Nathaniel Hall
Andrew Hall
Thomas Ripley
John Williams
Hezekiah Balch
Robert Maloney
Crafford Jones
John Ross
Robert Dobson
Samuel Craig
John Balch
William Pratt
Matthew Cox
William Hood
William McPheran
Ewen Allison
John Newman
John Guin
Moses Reeves
William Anderson
Randolph Guin
William Killgore
Benjamin Jameson
James Haworth
Samuel Ramsey
Andrew Gamble
William Ellis
James Temple
Samuel Davis
Henry Earnest
Giles Parman
Valentine Callihan
James Gibson
Reuben Biggs
Thomas Kennedy
Holden Shanks

John Bartley
John Moore
Thomas Lamb
John Bitner
Hugh Guin
John Henderson
Samuel Edmondson
Peter Dillon
David Parkins
John Temple
John Kerbough
Abraham Sherrill
Valentine Sevier
James J. Wilson
Thomas Alexander
John Bennett Junr
Jacob Bowman
John Reid
John Hall
William Bell
James Wright
William Likens
William Alexander
Robert Stuart
Thomas Southerland
Isaac Harmon
Joseph Gaston
Asahel Rawlings
James Jones
Leonard Ettleman
Robert Hall
James McPheran
Joseph Dobson
Isham Randolph
Robert Daniel
Jonathan Brown
Henry Shields
Henry Headrick
Samuel Y. Balch
John Shaw
James Kenney
John Stinson
Thomas McCollum
David Farnsworth
John Bowers
David Copeland
John Brown
William Hall Junr
Benjamin Neil
Robert Smith
William Crawford
Hezekiah W. Balch

Jacob Johnston
Samuel Henderson
Robert Samples
William Milburn
Harrison Johnston
Thomas Murray
John Hughes
Thomas Temple
William Hall Gent
James Galbreaith
Jesse Johnston
John Morriss
Benjamin McNutt
Samuel Sutton
Joseph Johnston
Thomas Davis Senr
John Neise
William Neil
Abraham Collet
Daniel Smith
Charles Smith
Lawrence Earnest
Thomas Denton
William Goforth
William Matthias
Isaac Brumley
Robert Wyly
Augustin P. Fore
Peter Castle
Robert Gray
Moses Johnston
Thomas Hunter
James Shields
Samuel Denwody
William Smith
James Dinwiddie
Robert Allen
Samuel Milligan
George Gordon
Griffith Rutherford
James Kelly
John Kifer
Eden Humbard
John Miers
David Keller
John Graham
Thomas Batt
Stephen Harmon
James Allen
Isaac Baker Senr
Joseph Kiser
George Brown

John Hunter
James Loyd
George Burkheart
Evan Jones Senr
Absalom Haworth
James Haworth
David Logan
George Harmon
Thomas Whennery
Frederick Shaffer
John Bennett Senr
Sperling Bowman Jr
Philip Babb
Dennis Harty
Joseph Finney
Samuel Ellis
William Dewoody
Samuel Vance
Ephraim Lane
Francis Johnston
Jacob White
Ezekiel Baldwin
Thomas Ellis
Thomas Humbert
Isaac Jones
Caleb Carter
John Stinson
Henry McBroom
Daniel Pierce
Thomas Shields Junr
William Alexander
Jacob Hennegar
Charles Lowrey
Joseph Lackland
Arthur Sloan
James Maloy
John Uttinger
David Key
Jacob Cook
James Jones
Isaac Carter
George Harrison
Benjamin Williams
Samuel Hannah
David Holt
Bloomer White
Abraham Haines
Henry Kellar
Robert Smiley
Philip Eaker
Benjamin Rose
Christian Dyke

Andrew Fox
Saymor Catching
James Matthias
John Wilson Senr
James Davis
Joseph Vanpelt
Hugh Neilson
Thomas Love
Alexander Brown
James Wilson
James Ramsey
Adam Smelser
William Ross
Benjamin McGeehon
Claudius Buster
Jacob Earnest
Thomas Oliphant
Jacob Hoyal
Richard Scruggs
Ezekiel Stanberry
Thomas Stanfield Junr
John Parks
William Parker
James White
James Bird
John Gamble
James Dillon
William Dillon
John Miller
A. Jones
Henry Conway
James Hampton
George Jameson
Stephen Cotter
Thomas Loyd
William Wall
George Ely
John Allison
Absalom Stonecypher
Thomas Wilson Junr
John Loyd
William Moore Sen
John Love
Henry French
John Jones Senr
John Pierce
Robert Smith
Thomas Gorrell
Philip Bible
Moses Gamble
Thomas Babb
Abel Loyd

George Pierce
Adam Fraiker
Leonard Symons
William Long
George Crosby
William Crosby
Simon Weston
George Brown
James Loyd
Derby Ragan
Peter Baker
Robertson Loyd
Philip Easterly
Anthony Kelly
James Kallewon
William McDonald
John Campbell
Henry Kelldea
John Cotter
Jacob Havely
George Hutchison
Joseph Henderson
Robert Henderson
Chrisley Harmon
Robert Campbell
William Rankin
Samuel Crawford
Jacob Teel
Nicholas Hays
Christopher Houts
James Moore
John Moore
Thomas Starnes
Bable Benson
Leonard Huff
Daniel McCoy
William Holloway
John Ragan
Jepthah Billingsley
John Oxen [?]
John Key
Isaac Johnson
Charles Lane
Robert Hays
Isariah Doty
Joseph Dunkin
Christian Fraiker
Joseph Allen
John Dodd
Christian Bible
Samuel Russell
William Wattson

William Black
Henry Thompson
David Allison
James Hays
Charles Coffin
Matthias Broyles
James Robertson
Ezekiel Howard
H. Smith
Vincent Jackson
Philip Harmon
Elijah McNew
John Glasscock
John Wilson
Anthony Moore
David Dugger
John Robertson
William Hankins
Thomas Jones
Joseph Kimmons
F. Burkheart
Frederick Reasor
Abraham Smith
Henry Yeakley
Christopher Baker
Benjamin Ishmael
William Davis
Daniel Alinger
John Crawford
Jacob Linebough
Thomas Davis
William Guin
William Kelly
John Ingram
Lewis Curington
Richard Pearce
Thomas Ishmael
Thomas Collier
Valentine Pauley
John Robertson
John Ledgerwood
John Feuston
Michael Fraiker
Isaiah McNees
Thomas Curton
John Fuston Junr
Philip Smith
Samuel Pickering
Elijah Coulson
David Frazier
William Dodd
William Johnston

Jacob Harmon
Richard Curton
Henry Cross
James Oliphant
John Bird
Jacob Paysinger
Charles Mayberry
Thomas Billingsley
George Conway
John Keller
Michael Dittimore
Garrett Dillen
John Newberry
Michael Freese
John Delaney
Samuel Caldwell
Andrew McFarlin
Thomas Johnston
Gabriel North
James Bailey
Henry Williams
John Ragan Junr
George Neilson
William Graham
James Glass
David Milburn
Christian Busley
Henry Bowman
William Cooley
Leonard Dell
John Simpson
Frederick Smith
John Long
John Blackburn
Barrott Holt
Daniel Bowman
George W. Woods
Martin Foster
Alexander Newberry
Nathaniel Patterson
Henry Dyke Senr
Maxwell Brown
George Gass
John Gibson
Frederick Fraiker
Jesse Mosley
James Reynolds
Andrew English
Thomas Justis
William Brown
Thomas McCollum
Thomas Caldwell

Joseph Hays
Zachariah Loveall
Stephen Bailes
Elijah Hurst
John Mismer
William Malone
John Collier
Samuel King
Major Temple
Thomas Self
William Tunnell
Jeremiah Dunkin
Thomas Walker
Christopher Laughiner
Patrick Powers
Solomon Stonecypher
John Baker
Richard Kerr
James Stinson
Frederick Souder
Cornelius Smith
John Smith
Henry Evens
William McNees
Henry Garrett
Rodger Browning
Christopher Cooper
Jonathan Davis
James Hays
Martin McBride
David Gray
H. Williams
William Finley
Isaac Walker
William Shields
Anthony Copeland
James Walker
James Bailes
John Ryan
Henry Morris
Francis Register
James Falls
Christian Hunsley
Henry Surbor
Absalom Templeton
Jacob Surbor
Adam Wilson
John Thornton
Peter Bitserburgy
John Rodgers, Jr.
Alexander Frasier
John Troy

Abner Gray
James Thompson
James Shields
James Scott
Samuel Rogers
James Campbell
Absalom Howath
James Anderson
John McCollum
Jesse Rush
Edward Gray
James Kelly
William Cox
John McAmis
William West
Timothy Hixson
Conrad Barnheart
John Malone
James Shelly
Shadrach McNew
Peter Casteel Junr
Aaron Newman
Barnet Crabtree
Walter Clark
John Fooshee
William Crumbley
David Rankin
Anthony Hoggatt
James Trim
John Carter Junr
William McNew
Daniel Coffman
Jonathan Milburn
Jacob Reesor
William Patterson
Alexander Williams
James Brown
John Bowers
James Rodgers, Senr
Owen Mycelf
Adam Kauble
Thomas McCullough
William McPheran
Stephen Tunnell
Josiah Clawson
Robert Foster
William Gibson
James McMurtry
James Hughes
Michael Myars
Daniel Small [? blurred]
John Kesterson

William Hopper
Samuel Hill
Robert Hutson
William Shannon
Nicholas Spring
Henry Hair
Alexander Dugger
Robert Rankin
John Fraiker
Robert Burns
William Wattson
John Thompson
Benjamin Parker
David Hutson
John Kirk, Senr
John Biggs
John Horton
James McAmis
David Carter
David Hays
Abraham Marshall
Jacob Bowman
Abraham Miller
Thomas Stanfield
John Whitehead
Hugh Carter
Samuel Stanfield
Thomas Wilson
Jacob Souder
Nathaniel Davis
Samuel Rhea
Absalom Gray
James Baxter
John Davis
Daniel Henderson
James Robinson
John McPheran
David Moore
Thomas Murphey
George Thompson
William Skyles
Harkins Davis
John Young
Alexander Armstrong
Jeremiah Smith
Thomas Donica
John Lackland
Philip Hale
Paulser Ruble
Michael Woods
Leonard Starnes
Joseph Carter

Robert Jameson
James Carson
Lewis Stults
Jacob Kyle
Christopher Bible
John Ellis
William Alexander, Sr
James Morrow
Stephen Woolsey
Thomas Alexander
William Woolsey
Claudius Bailey
Jeremiah Laney
William Hutson
Hugh Cavner
Abraham Hurst
Benjamin Farnsworth
Jacob Bird
John Wilson
Malachi Click
William Skiles
James Laird
John Oliphant
Andrew Dobbins
Thomas Stockdon
Robert Russell
Peter Earnest
Sperling Bowman
Andrew Huffman
Thomas McAmis
David Wilson
Julius Scruggs
James Rutlege
Jesse Linsey
Hugh Maloney
Thomas Hutson
Enoch Doty
Purnell Walker
Peter Bleak
John Bell
John Morrow
William Alexander
George Alexander
James Dinwiddie
John Bell Junr
James Wright
David Davis
David Robinson
Reese Prathar
William Hannah
David Copeland
James Copeland

George Rinker
Enos Rambough
Abner Frazier
Samuel McKemy
Claiborne Dugger
Abraham Fellows
John Kennedy
William Madcap
Joseph Weston
Daniel McKoy
John Casteel
Jeremiah Smith
Peter McCain
William McAmis
Robert Guin
Zebedee Dennis
William McGahee
Nathan Cooper
Conrad Kimes
Daniel Carter
John Rodgers
Thomas Blackburn
Thomas G. Brown
David Sample
Daniel Bordon
William Chandley
Thomas Peel
George Graham
Robert Wilson
William Dickson
John Maloney
Joseph Todhunter
John Maclin
Daniel Jackson
James Davis
David Paulsell
Frederick Trobough
Stephen Alexander
John McGeehon
George Alexander
David Allison
James McAmis
James Luckey
Nathaniel Hood
Nathan Carter
Anderson Walker
Michael Kauble
William Davis
John Litler
William Temple
Isaac Crump
Eathern Burgey

Benjamin Stuart
Daniel Armstrong
John Ramsey
John Lescollect
James Guthrie
William Bratcher
John Gragg
Isaac Armitage
Joseph Hixson
Ephraim Skiles
David Wilson
John Dobson
John Richmond
Seth Babb
John Hull
Jacob Linginfelter
William Britten
Jonathan Evens
James Newberry
Gravener Marsh
Stephen Alexander
James Moore
Daniel Kerby
William Hixson
James Steel
David Copeland
Alexander Wilson
Levi Carter
Christopher Lotspeich
John Lotspeich

James Witherspoon
Martin Click
Ellet Rutherford
William Bratcher
Britain Cross
Loveal Coffman
Lewis Gulley
John Guthry
Lewis Gulley
John Gentry
Lazarus Gulley
Phillamore Green
John Keel
John McConnal
John Rawlings
William Chapman
Robert Bell
Elijah Balch
John Keel Jun
James Keel
William Keel
John Long
Anny Martin
Joseph McCullough
Levi Moore
James Moore
Zadok Moore
Joseph Holt
Michael Burgar
Adam Starnes

Isaac McAmis
James Reece
William McCullough
William McCullough
Samuel McCullough
Jonathan Moreland
Gabriel Philips
Lewis Rue
William Smith
John Walker
James Walker
James Dugger
William Reece
Thomas Hurny [?]
Margaret Purdom
Mary Mismer
Thomas Wyatt
Solomon Wyatt
Nathan White
William White
Thomas White
Samuel White
Rachel Anderson
James Patterson Senr
James Patterson
Margaret McGehon
Ann Armstrong
Elizabeth Reves
Mary Brumley
Margaret McElroy

Total number 996

[Endorsed]

Enumeration from Greene County 1805

EARLY EAST TENNESSEE TAXPAYERS
Compiled by Pollyanna Creekmore

X. Washington County, 1778[1]

Washington County, the oldest county in the state of Tennessee and named in honor of George Washington, was created out of Washington District by an act of the North Carolina general assembly on December 18, 1777.[2] The bounds of the county as given in the act were:

> Beginning at the most North Westerly Part of the County of Wilkes, on the Virginia Line; thence running with the line of Wilkes County, to a Point Thirty Six Miles South of the Virginia Line; thence due West, to the Ridge of the great iron Mountain which heretofore divided the Hunting Grounds of the Overhill Cherokees, from those of the Middle Settlements and Valley; thence running a South Westerly Course, along the said Ridge, to the Unacoy Mountain, where the trading Path crosses the same from the Valley to the Overhills; thence South with the Line of this State, adjoining the State of South Carolina; thence due West, to the great River Mississippi; thence up the said River the Courses thereof, to a Point due West from the Beginning.

Thus, the boundaries of the new county were almost as extensive as the present state. The county was made a part of Salisbury District.[3]

The county was organized at the home of Charles Robertson, near present Jonesboro, on February 23, 1778. The justices, composing the court were: John Carter, who was elected chairman, John Sevier, Jacob Womack, Robert Lucas, Andrew Greer, John Shelby, George Russell, William Bean, Zachariah Isbell, John McNabb, Thomas Houghton, William Clark, John McMahon, Benjamin Gist, John Chisholm, Joseph Willson, William Cobb, James Stuart, Michael Woods, Richard White, Benjamin Willson, James Robertson, Valentine Sevier.[4]

---

[1] For the introduction to this series see *Publications*, No. 23 (1951), 115-16. Previous installments have been: I. Anderson County, 1802, in No. 23; II. Blount County, 1801, in No. 24; III. Knox County, 1806, in No. 26; IV. Grainger County, 1799, in No. 27; V. Jefferson County, 1800, in No. 28; VI. Carter County, 1796, in No. 30; VII. Sullivan County, 1796, in No. 31; VIII. Hawkins County, 1809-1812, in No. 32; IX. Greene County, 1805, in No. 33.

[2] Walter Clark (ed.), *The State Records of North Carolina*, 14 vols. continuing earlier series of *Colonial Records* (Goldsboro, 1905), XXIV, 141-42. Hereafter cited as N.C.S.R.

[3] *Ibid.*, 141.

[4] *Ibid.*, Washington County Court Minutes (Courthouse, Jonesboro); "The Records of Washington County," *American Historical Magazine* (October, 1900), 326-81. Many of the original manuscript minutes beginning May 24, 1779, through November, 1797, are in possession of the Tennessee Historical Society, Nashville.

The first officials of the county elected by the court were: John Sevier, clerk; Valentine Sevier, sheriff; James Stuart, surveyor; John Carter, entry taker; John McMahon, register; and Jacob Womack, stray master.[5]

The act which established the county appointed John Carter, Andrew Greer, William Cobb, Jacob Womack, George Russell, John Sevier, and James Stuart, Esquire, commissioners to lay out the county seat. Jonesboro, named in honor of Willie Jones (1741-1801), North Carolina Revolutionary leader, was established in 1779.[6] To defray the expense of the buildings a tax of two shillings and six pence for every hundred pounds was levied on all taxable property in the county, and also a poll tax of two shillings and six pence on every free man in the county who did not have property worth at least one hundred pounds. Soldiers in the continental service or the service of the state were exempt.

The laws governing taxation in the new county were those in force in the state of North Carolina enacted at the April and November sessions, 1777, of the general assembly.

"Whereas the levying a tax by General Assessment on Property will tend to the East of the Inhabitants of this State, and will greatly relieve the poor People thereof; and as the Mode for assessing Property, and collecting Public Taxes in this State, should be appertained and established by Law."[7]

The law specified what property was liable to be taxed. "That all Lands and Lots, with their Improvements, Slaves, Money, Money at Interest, and Stock in Trade, wherever the same may be, all Bonds, Notes, or other Obligations for Value on Interest, all Horses and neat Cattle."[8]

The county was laid out in districts by the county courts, and a justice of the peace was appointed in each district to receive "from every Inhabitant thereof a just and true Account, on Oath, of all the taxable Property which such Person had in Care, or was possessed of in his own

---

[5] *Ibid.*

[6] *Ibid.*, 141-42; Samuel C. Williams, "The Founder of Tennessee's First Town: Major Jesse Walton," East Tennessee Historical Society's *Publications*, No. 2 (1930), 70-80.

[7] *N.C.S.R.*, XXIV, 109-13.

[8] *Ibid.*, 109.

Right, or as Agent, Factor or Attorney, or in Trust for any other Person."[9] An oath was prescribed for the justice to administer each person making a return.

The court appointed three "honest and intelligent persons" in each district to assess the property in their district. The court also appointed a tax gatherer in each district who made his return to the sheriff. Oaths were prescribed for the tax gatherer and the sheriff.

The act provided "that every Freeman in this State of the Age of Twenty One Years and upwards (other than Soldiers in the Service of the Continent, or of this State) who shall not possess the value of One Hundred Pounds in taxable Property, shall pay annually in Lieu of Assessment on Property, a Poll tax equal to the Tax for that Year on One Hundred Pounds taxable Property . . . ."

This was the system of taxation initiated in the new county of Washington. When the court met on February 25, 1778, assessors were appointed, and at the session on August 26, the collectors were ordered to collect the following tax:

For every hundred pounds worth of property by general assessment	16	8
For Building Court House prison and stocks	2	6
For Building Court House in Salisbury		4d
For the Contingent charges of the County		1
Amounting in the whole to twenty shillings and six pence[10]		

The first tax lists of Washington County have survived and are on file in the County Court Clerk's office in the Courthouse at Jonesboro. These lists, along with other lists, some fragmentary, were discovered some years ago by Mrs. L. W. McCown, of Johnson City, and the late Mrs. Robert H. Stickley, of Memphis. Much credit is due to Mrs. McCown for her pioneer efforts in preserving the early Washington County records.

Other early records in the possession of Mr. Paul M. Fink, of Jonesboro, will be published in *Publications*, No. 35.

---

[9] *Ibid.*, 109-10.

[10] Minutes, August 26, 1778.

Key to Column Numbers

[1] Poll Tax

[2] Amount of their estate

[3] Sum to pay

Figures used indicate English currency (pounds, shillings & pence)
Assest by James Maulden, Josiah Hoskins and John Higgans
Retd. by B. Wilson Esq.

	[1]	[2]	[3]
Richard White		1346- 0-0	
Richard Woolridge		841-11-0	8-12-42
Andrew Bunton		465-10-0	4-13-11
Jo Certain	P.T.		1- 0-6
C. S. Hoskins	ditto		1- 0-6
George Tidwell	ditto		1- 0-6
Nath'l Durram	ditto		1- 0-6
Zekel Brown	ditto		1- 0-6
John Grimes	ditto		1- 0-6
—on Maulden		338-10-0	3- 9-3
William Flanary		465-11-2	4-13-9¾
Phillip Shelly		534- 1-0	5- 9-7½
Samuel Tate		1055- 0-0	10-16-3
Samuel Denny		170- 8-0	1-15-0
Amos Garrott	P.T.		1- 0-6
Leonard Morgan	ditto		1- 0-6
John Higgans		190- 9-0	1-19-0
James Maulden		499- 0-0	5- 2-3½
Edward Sweeten		119- 4-0	1- 5-0
Charles Asher		130- 0-0	1- 6-7½
James Colesen	P.T.		1- 0-6
James Coward		138-10-0	1- 8-2
John Hoskins		1001-16-0	10- 5-4
Richard Collett		252-10-0	2-11-8
Joseph Gentry	P.T.		1- 0-6
Elijah Abbott	P.T.	100- 0-0	1- 0-6
Josiah Hoskins		181- 0-0	1-17-1½
Henry Grimes		426- 8-0	4- 7-4½
Jesse Hoskins		417-16-0	4- 9¾ -
James Certain		140- 0-0	1- 3-10½
William Griffin		250-14-6	2-11-4
Ning Hoskins		295	3- 0-6
Richd Willson		295- 2-6	3- 0-7
Benjamin Willson		224- 0-0	2- 6-11½
John Davis		343-10-0	3-10-6
Henry Rains	P.T.	100- 0-0	1- 0-6
Benjamin Ward		356-10-0	3-12-0
Charles Asher Sen		102-17-0	1- 1-1
David Hicks		253-12-0	2-12-10½
Thomas Asher		130- 0-0	1- 6-0½
John Asher	P.T.	100- 0-0	1- 0-6

Washington County 1778

	[1]	[2]	[3]
Hueins Heatherly	P.T.	100- 0-0	1- 0-6
Joshua Curtis		154-12-0	1-12-9
David Curtis		206- 4-0	2- 2-3
George Hatherly		175- 1-0	1-15-11
Samuel Hatherly	P.T.	100- 0-0	1- 0-6
James Oweings		137-10-0	1- 8-2¼
John Arnold	P.T.	100- 0-0	1- 0-6
Wm Renolds		189-10-0	1-16-0½
Timothy Holdway	P.T.		1- 0-6
John Tidwell	P.T.		1- 0-6
Wm Asher	P.T.		
David Hicks		100- 0-0	1- 0-6
Wm Sawyer		100- 0-0	1- 0-6
Jonas Palestine		100- 0-0	1- 0-6
		12127- 7-2	143- 9-3¼

Assest by Henry Lyle, Samuel Henry and William McNabb
Retd. to Jno. McNabb, Esq.

		[2]	[3]
John McNabb		480-10-2	4-18-6¾
Joseph Culberson		114- 1-0	1- 3-6
Christopher Cunningham		626-12-6	6- 9-4½
James Stuart		2014- 4-0	20-13-0
John Carter, Esq.		3572- 8-0	36-12-9
Baptist McNabb		731-19-4	4- 8-4
Teter Nave		439- 8-8	4-10-0¾
Matthew Talbert		2050- 0-0	21- 0-3
Samuel Culberson		788- 0-0	8- 1-5¼
Wm Cocke		870- 0-0	8-18-4
Joseph Denton		376-14-8	3-17-1¾
John Moore		229- 0-0	2- 6-11½
James Henry		649- 8-3	6-13-2
John Casedy	P.T.	100- 0-0	1- 0-6
Lewis Jones		369-14-0	4- 1-10
Patience Cooper		408-18-4	4- 2-2
Jaramiah Dunging		575- 4-0	5-17-10½
Joseph Tipton		310- 0-0	3- 3-6
Robert Young Jnr		385- 0-0	3-19-1¼
Wm Duggar	P.T.	100- 0-0	1- 0-6
James Pearce		295-13-4	3- 0-8
Wm Parker		446-13-4	4-12-3
John Shelby Esq		920- 4-0	9- 8-7¼
Michael Hider		358-10-0	3-13-5
James Wray		330- 0-0	3- 7-7½
James Grism		185- 0-0	1-16-11
Samuel Denton		210- 6-0	2- 3-2
Hail Talbert	P.T.	100- 0-0	1- 0-6
Matthew Talbert Jr.	P.T.	100- 0-0	1- 0-6
John Gilleland		255- 0-0	1- 0-6
Matthew Arthura	P.T.	100- 0-0	3-17-10½
John Kenner		380- 0-0	1- 4-7½

	[1]	[2]	[3]
Valentine Sevier Sr.		125- 0-0	3- 4-8
James Denton		315-12-0	9- 5-6
Clevers Barksdill		905- 0-0	3-12-9
Emanuel Carter		360- 0-0	1-16-10½
William Ward		185- 0-0	1- 0-6
David Hickey	P.T.	100- 0-0	2- 0-0
Charles Robertson Jr.		194- 0-0	4-11-3
Robert Sevier		440- 0-0	18-12-0
Robert Young Sr.		1815- 0-0	1- 0-6
William Reeves	P.T.	100- 0-0	5-11-0¾
Valentine Sevier		541- 4-0	1- 0-6
Ambrose Hodge	P.T.	100- 0-0	1- 0-6
William Overall	do	100- 0-0	1- 7-11½
John Hughes		136-10-0	3- 3-8
Howell Doddy		310- 8-0	4- 6-1
Drury Gooding		420- 0-0	1-15-10
George Reeves		174- 4-0	1- 0-9¼
Jorden Reeves		101- 5-8	1- 0-6
Lewis Lain	P.T.	100- 0-0	5-13-10
Jonas Little		560- 0-0	1-10-9
Chris Cunningham Jr		150- 0-0	1- 0-6
Joseph Greer	P.T.	100- 0-0	1- 0-6
James Mullican	do	100- 0-0	1- 0-6
David McNabb		100- 0-0	1- 0-6
Jacob Chamble		191- 4-0	1- 9-4
Julis Robertson		138- 5-6	1- 8-4
John Oduel		242- 0-0	2- 9-6½
Isaac Taylor		589-16-0	6- 0-11
John Brown	P.T.	100- 0-0	1- 0-6
Wm Brown	P.T.	100- 0-0	1- 0-6
Wm McNabb Esq.		566- 1-0	5-16-1
Samuel Henry Senr		253-17-4	2-12-0
Thomas Houghton Esq.		1431-14-0	14-13-7½
Joshua Houghton		2926-13-1	30- 0-0
		47061-11-2	478-12-4¼

Assest by Benj. Cobb, Solomon Smith and Wm Asher
Retd. to John Chisholm Esq.

	[1]	[2]	[3]
Arthur Cobb		1379-10-0	14- 2-10½
Samuel Smith		654-12-6	6-14-3
Arnol Shells		476-15-0	4-17-9
Richard Choate		391- 0-0	4- 0-2
John Cawood in Virgn		10- 0-0	0- 2-1½
Charles Chasons		574- 0-0	5-17-10
Austin Choate		234- 0-0	2- 8-0
Jonathan Webb		616- 0-0	6- 6-4
Henry Massengill		260- 9-0	2-12-4
Edward Choate		523- 0-0	5- 5-0
Jesse Vawter in Virgn		10- 0-0	0- 2-1½
Abraham Cox		878- 1-6	9- 0-0

	[1]	[2]	[3]
Wm. Gris'om		465- 0-0	4-15-3¾
Valentine Little		101-12-6	1- 0-8½
Christian Weaver		300- 0-0	3- 1-6
John Matlock	P.T.	100- 0-0	1- 0-6
Jesse Maxsey		346- 0-0	3-11-1
Andrew Little		449-16-0	4-12-0
James Mallock	P.T.	100- 0-0	1- 0-6
Wm Bayley		192- 0-0	1-19-9
Calib Oduel		264- 0-0	1-13-5
Mathias Little		200-16-0	2- 1-2
John Cox		600-13-7	6- 3-2
John Ryley		326-13-0	3- 6-9
Samuel Hutton	P.T.	100- 0-0	1- 0-6
Samuel Underwood	do	100- 0-0	1- 0-6
Henry Massengil Senr		628- 0-0	6- 8-9
Jorden Roach		304- 0-0	3- 2-4
Thomas Choate		1280- 0-0	13- 2-4½
John Hill		300- 0-0	3- 1-6
Hosea Stout		198- 0-0	2- 0-8
Roger Top (Virgn)		200- 0-0	2- 1-0
Retd to Wm. Bean			
Henry Hickky		250- 0-0	2-11-9
Edward Bridges	P.T.	100- 0-0	1- 0-6
Andrew Thompson	do	100- 0-0	1- 0-6
Tho Williams	do	100- 0-0	1- 0-6
Danl Walker		121- 0-0	1- 4-9
John Vance		117-10-0	1- 3-11
Henry Clark		904-16-0	9- 5-5
John Bayley		227- 0	2- 6-6
James Whitter		121- 3-8	1- 4-4
Geo Gray		516-12-0	3- 4-11
Wm. Been, Esq.		1254-16-0	12-17-3
John Calliham		224-16-0	2-11-2
Joel Calliham		150- 0-0	1-10-9
Joseph Duncome		151- 8-0	1-11-1
John Been		311-17-0	3- 4-0
Clement Dixon Senr	P.T.	100-	1- 0-6
John B. McMahon		283- 5	2-18-0½
John Dunken	P.T.	100	1- 0-6
Absolom Thompson		173-12	1-16-0
James Cooper		120- 0	1- 4-7½
Andrew Thompson	P.T.	100- 0	1- 0-6
Isaac Titsworth		316-12	3- 4-10
Moses Laird		474-16	4-17-4
John Drake		199-12	2- 0-11
James Abbott		176- 0	1-16-0
James Kelley		225- 0-0	2- 5-3½
Charles Parker	P.T.	100- 0-0	1- 0-6
Demsey Ward		171-10-9	1-15-3

1. Be it enacted by the general Assembly of the State of North Carolina and by the Authority of the same, that the late District of Washington and all that Part of this State comprehended within the following Lines shall be erected into a new and distinct County by the Name of Washington County, viz: Beginning at the most North-westerly Part of the County of Wilkes on the Virginia Line, thence running with the Line of Wilkes County to a Point thirty Six Miles South of the Virginia Line thence due West to the Ridge of the great Iron Mountain which heretofore divided the hunting Grounds of the Overhill Cherokees from those of the Middle Settlements & Valley, thence running a South-westerly Course along the said Ridge to the Unacoy Mountain where the trading Path crosses the same on the Way from the Valley to the Overhills, thence South with the Line of this State adjoining the State of South Carolina thence due West to the great River Mississippi thence up the said River the Courses thereof to a Point due West from the Beginning thence due East with the Line of this State to the Beginning; and it is hereby declared that all that Part of this State comprehended within the Lines aforesaid shall from hence forth be & remain the County of Washington and shall be and is hereby declared to be Part of the District of Salisbury.

And be it further enacted by the Authority aforesaid and it is hereby declared, that all that Part of this State lying ~~west of~~ South of the County of Washington shall be & is hereby declared to be Part of the County of Burk —

—Courtesy North Carolina State Department of Archives and History, Raleigh

Bill for the Creation of Washington County

	[1]	[2]	[3]
John White	P.T.	100- 0-0	1- 0-6
John Duncome	do	100- 0-0	1- 0-6
Thomas Fletcher		134- 0-0	1- 6-7½
James Hollis		347-18-9	3-11-9
Delany Carrole	P.T.	100- 0-0	1- 0-6
Charles Thompson		107- 0-0	1- 2-0
John B. McMahon		153- 2-0	1-11-5
Thomas Jonackin		327- 8-0	3- 6-1
[Jarnagin]			
Jesse Been		254- 0-0	2-12-7
Joseph Davison	P.T.	100- 0-0	1- 0-6
James Walden		125- 0-0	1- 4-7½
Wm. Been Junr		257- 2-0	2-12-2
Geo. Richardson	P.T.	100- 0-0	1- 0-6
Robert Lucas Esq.		1192-16-8	12- 6-0
Christopher Choate		209- 0-0	2- 2-10½
Peter Hufman	P.T.	100- 0-0	1- 0-6
Alex Cairl ?		217- 7-0	2- 4-6
Leonard Adcocks		100- 0-0	1- 0-6
Wm. Anthony	P.T.	100- 0-0	1- 0-6
Nathan Davis		172- 0-0	1-15-10
Peter Renfro		471-14-0	4-17-4
George Russell		114- 0-0	1- 2-4½
John Clark		217- 6-3	2- 4-0
Jacob Hufman	P.T.	100- 0-0	1- 0-6
Thomas Titsworth		203- 0-0	2- 1-7
Vachworth Dillenham		1147- 0-0	11-15-7
Morgan Moray [Murray]		139- 4-0	1- 7-6½
Henry Gotcher		132-16-0	1- 6-1½
John Crawford	P.T.	100- 0-0	1- 0-6
John Wheeler	do	100- 0-0	1- 0-6
William Stringer	do	100- 0-0	1- 0-6
Benjamin Drake		523- 7-0	5- 6-6
John Russell		100- 0-0	1- 0-6
Richard Walker		138- 0-0	1- 8-2
George Martin		140- 0-0	1- 8-7
John Chis'm esq		353- 9-4	3-12-5¾
John Russell		265- 8-0	2-14-9
Elizabeth Duncome		157-12	1-12-2
Joab Mitchell		325- 0	3- 4-7½
Richd Fletcher		223-12	2- 6-0
Uriah Hunt	P.T.	100- 0-0	1- 0-6
John Rice		163- 4	1-13-3
Samuel Fain		157-16	1-12-5
George Russell esq		244-12	2-10-0
Robert Been		150- 0	1-10-9
Henry Richardson		115- 3-6	1- 3-8
Michael Massingell	P.T.	100- 0	1- 0-6
Bradley Gambrel		102- 4-0	1- 0-11½

	[1]	[2]	[3]
Wm Young		187-12-0	1-18-5
Mary Richardson		450- 0-0	4-12-3
Charles Dunkin		120-19-6	1- 5-8
Wm & Pharoah Cobb		2001- 0-0	20-10-2½
Retd to Michl Woods, Esq.			
Alex Chasewood	P.T.	100	1- 0-6
Robert Bayley	do	100	1- 0-6
Wm. Cannon	do	100	1- 0-6
John Brown	do	100	1- 0-6
Jonathan Tipton		104- 1-0	1- 1-4
Humphry Gibson		142- 2-0	1- 9-1
Hosea Roase		119- 3-4	1- 4-6
Joseph England		214- 2-0	2- 4-0
John Nave		559- 8-4	5-14-0
Charles England	P.T.	100- 0-0	1- 0-6
Thomas Shurley	P.T.	100- 0-0	1- 0-6
Wm English		130-10-0	1- 6-9
Aron Pinson	P.T.	100- 0-0	1- 0-6
Henry Nave	P.T.	100- 0-0	1- 0-6
John Smith	do	100- 0-0	1- 0-6
John Reding	do	100- 0-0	1- 0-6
Wm Johnson	do	100- 0-0	1- 0-6
Joseph English		25- 0-0	1- 0-6
Godfrey Isbell	P.T.	100- 0-0	1- 0-6
Joseph Pinson	ditto	100- 0-0	1- 0-6
Zacha Isbell		30- 0-0	0- 6-3
Martin Webb		102- 0-0	1- 1-0
Edward Shurly	P.T.	100- 0-0	1- 0-6
Wm Thornton	do	100- 0-0	1- 0-6
Michl Woods		358- 8-0	3-13-5
Joseph Leech	P.T.	100- 0-0	1- 0-6
James McAdams	do	100- 0-0	1- 0-6
Phillip Jones	do	100- 0-0	1- 0-6
Benja Gibson	do	100- 0-0	1- 0-6
Surrel Lewis	do	100- 0-0	1- 0-6
Edward Smith	do	100- 0-0	1- 0-6
John Oneal	do	100- 0-0	1- 0-6
John Shurley	do	100- 0-0	1- 0-6
Benja Johnston	do	100- 0-0	1- 0-6
James Jones	do	100- 0-0	1- 0-6
Thomas Pinson	do	100- 0-0	1- 0-6
Richd Trevillian		158- 0-0	1-12-5
Jeremiah Vaich	P.T.	100- 0-0	1- 0-6
Jacob Brown		1171- 0-0	12- 0-6
Charles Atkins	P.T.	100- 0-0	1- 0-6
Jonathan Tipton	do	100- 0-0	1- 0-6
Saml Crawford		126- 2-0	1- 5-10
John England	P.T.	100- 0-0	1- 0-6
Jesse Bond	do	100- 0-0	1- 0-6

	[1]	[2]	[3]
Assest by Saml Williams, Robert Box & Francis Hughes			
Retd to Zacha Isbell, esq.			
John Wood		218-18-8	2- 4-10
Henry Earnest		186- 1-0	1-18-0½
Benjamin Williams	Tax 4 fold		3- 6-8
Phillip Sherrill	ditto	1872- 8-8	3- 6-8
John Sevier		1872- 8-8	19- 4-0
John Waddel	P.T.	100- 0-0	1- 0-6
John Vance	ditto	100- 0-0	1- 0-6
Samuel Sherill Sen.		277- 0-0	2-16-9½
Michael Border		186- 6-8	1-18-0½
Danl Hair	P.T.	100- 0-0	1- 0-6
Joshua Williams	do	100- 0-0	1- 0-6
George Reed	do	100- 0-0	1- 0-6
Henry Baits Senr	ditto	100- 0-0	1- 0-6
Joseph Dunham		358-12	3-13-5
Oldhum Hightower	P.T.	100- 0	1- 0-6
Emanuel Seduxas	do	100- 0	1- 0-6
Jesse Walton esq		592- 5	13- 2-10½
	ditto	695- 5	-
Edward Rice	P.T.	100- 0	1- 0-6
Leonard Rice	ditto	100- 0-0	1- 0-6
Thomas Evans	ditto	100- 0-0	1- 0-6
Thomas Price		293-10	3- 0-6
William Clark Esq.		619- 0-0	6- 6-10
Joseph English		240- 0-0	2- 9-3
Isam Ireby	P.T.		
Samuel Sherrill, Jr	ditto		
Charles Bond	ditto		
Henry Baits, Jr.	ditto		
John Evans	ditto	to pay	
Patrick Murphy	ditto	ditto	
William Clawson	ditto		
Phillip Conway	ditto		
Jonathan Holley	ditto		
Edward Box	ditto		
James Box	ditto		
Zachariah Isbell Esq.		412-13-0	4- 4-0½
George Underwood		174- 0-0	1-15-6
Retd to Jacob Womack			
James Bradley	P.T.	100- 0-0	1- 0-6
David Cradduck	ditto	100- 0-0	1- 0-6
Aron Burleson		310- 0-0	3- 3-7
Thomas Burleson		166- 0-0	1-14-1
James Buchanan		271-15-0	2-15-7½
John Allison		269- 0-0	2-15-4
Thomas Gillespie		342-12-0	3- 9-8
William Trimble		215- 0-0	2- 4-0
Robert Blackburn		146- 0-0	1-10-1

	[1]	[2]	[3]
Charles Allison		255- 0-0	2-11-9
Elisha Nelson	P.T.	100- 0-0	1- 0-6
John Gibson		825- 0-0	8- 8-1½
Edmund Roberts	P.T.	100- 0-0	1- 0-6
Robert Willson		140- 0-0	1- 8-8
Charles Gentry		233- 0-0	2- 6-9½
William Campbell		123- 4-0	1- 4-7½
John Blackwell	P.T.	100- 0-0	1- 0-6
Michael Bacon		160- 0-0	1-12-10
Barnaba Anderson	P.T.	100- 0-0	1- 0-6
Jacob Hamilton	ditto	100- 0-0	1- 0-6
Southy Nelson	ditto	100- 0-0	1- 0-6
Moses Moore		132- 0	1- 6-1
Isaac Wilson		344- 4-0	3-10-6
Joseph Wray	P.T.	100- 0-0	1- 0-6
David Hughes		234- 4-0	2- 7-0
Joseph Martin		186- 2-0	1-17-3
Josiah Martin		372-16-0	3-16-7
Henry Dunham		406- 4-8	4- 3-3
Andrew Martin		113- 0-0	1- 3-2
Charles Harrington		845- 0-0	8-13-3
Geo. Hudson	P.T.	100- 0-0	1- 0-6
James Murrey	ditto	100- 0-0	1- 0-6
John Robertson	ditto	100	
John Webb	ditto	100	
Hugh Blair		165-10-0	1-13-11
Samuel Handley	P.T.	100- 0-0	1- 0-6
James Grymes		367- 3-4	3-15-3
Evan Edwards		401-16	4- 2-5
John Carrack		308- 2-0	3- 3-3
Alexr Campbell		130- 1-4	1- 5-7½
John Ritchie		145- 6-0	1- 9-9
Aron Pinson		256- 4-4	2-12-3
James Miller		207-11-0	1- 2-0
[torn] Willson		336-19-6	3- 8-0
John Gillahan		169-13-10	1-14-9
Adren Anglehand	P.T.	100- 0-0	1- 0-6
Francis Hamilton	do	100- 0-0	1- 0-6
John Bullard		308- 6-0	3- 3-2
Asael Rawlings		308- 6-0	3- 3-2
Reuben Dunham		226-10-0	2- 5-4
Farill Magahan	P.T.	100- 0-0	1- 0-6
Robert Shurley		154- 0-0	1-11-7
Robert Gentry		173-10-0	1-15-6
James English		532-19-8	5- 8-1
Christopher Taylor	P.T.	100- 0-0	1- 0-6
John Trimble		148-16-0	1-10-4
Samuel Lyle		204- 7-4 to pay	2- 1-10
John Howard		250- 0-0	2-11-3

	[1]	[2]	[3]
Joseph Gest		141- 0-0	1- 8-9
John Morrison		262- 0-0	2-13-9
Isiah Hamilton		164-16-4	1-13-9
Henry Jones	P.T.		
Wm Allison		125- 0-0	1- 4-7½
Joseph Bullard		636- 1-0	6- 9-2
Benj Gest		211- 0-0	2- 3-3½
Edward Hobson		1548- 0-0	15-17-8
Robert Allison		256- 4-0	2-12-6
James Stephenson		151- 8-0	1-11-0
David Chambers		215- 0-0	2- 4-2
John Dunham		251- 3-8	2-12-0
John Chambers	P.T.	100	1- 0-6
Phillip Mulchy		453-16-0	
Samuel Weaver		332-16	[torn]
James Michael	P.T.		
Thomas Brown		241- 0-0	2- 9-4½
Benjamin Pyburn		311- 8-0	3- 3-10
Adam Sherrill		165-16-0	1-13-8
Solomon Coal	P.T.		
David Campbell		129-16-0	1- 5-8
Alexr Murrow		173-16-0	1-15-2
William Hutton		173-16-0	1-15-2
Thomas Barker		1052-16-0	10-15-8
James McCartney		156- 0-0	1-12-0
Sandofar Gozach		144-10-8	1- 9-6
Joseph Willson		425-15-2	4- 6-3½
William Storey		121-15-0	1- 5-8
Charles McCartney		133- 8-0	1- 6-3
David McCord		254- 0-0 to pay	2-12-1
James Randol		114- 9-0	1- 3-5
Francis Hamilton	P.T.	100- 0-0	1- 0-6
George Karr	Ditto	100- 0-0	1- 0-6
William Nelson		240- 0-0	2- 9-3
Bartholomew Woods		232- 0-0	2- 6-7½
William Chambers	P.T.	100- 0-0	1- 0-6
Joseph Fowler		171-14-8	1-14-10½
William Ritchey		224-12	2- 6-1
John Pinson	P.T.	100- 0-0	1- 0-6
John Patterson		227- 0-0	2- 6-9
Peter McMamee		205- 6-0	2- 2-1
Jonathan Bird	P.T.	100- 0-0	1- 0-6
[torn] Robertson		148-10-0	1-10-7
David Posey		169-10-0	1-14-9
Jarrett Williams		189- 0-0	1-17-10
Moses More		145- 0-0	1- 9-9
Thomas Scott		113- 0-0	1- 3-2½
Jonathan Denton		168-10-9	1-17-7½
Jacob Womack		671- 8-0	6-17-7½

	[1]	[2]	[3]
Daniel Dunham		221- 2-0	2- 6-3½
Adam Willson		525-16-0	2- 6-9½
Daniel Kenedy		265-19-2	2-14-7½
Isaac Johnson		325- 2-4	3- 6-8
Retd to Court			
Gideon Morress		936- 4-0 to pay	9-11-0
John Holley Junr		263-19-0 ditto	2-13-11½
Joseph Cole	P.T.	100- 0-0	1- 0-6
Charles Phillips	Ditto	100- 0-0	1- 0-6
John Malone	Ditto	100- 0-0	1- 0-6
Jacob Holley		135- 0-0	1- 7-8½
Henry Cross	P.T.	100- 0-0	1- 0-6
John Holley		753- 0-0	7-14-4½
Shadrick Morress	P.T.	100- 0-0	1- 0-6
John Pebley	Ditto	100- 0-0	1- 0-6
Francis Holley	Ditto	100- 0-0	1- 0-6
James McCord		125- 0-0	1- 5-7
David Robertson	P.T.	100- 0-0	1- 0-6
Daniel Keith	ditto	100- 0-0	1- 0-6
Delgt Retd by Thos Houghton Colr			
Amos Bird		1093- 0-0	torn
John Clarke		553- 5-0	"
James Crawford		669- 5-0	"
John Stuart		692- 6-0	7- 1-10
Nathl Clark		326-14-0	3- 7-8
John McFarling		147- 5-0	1-10-2
Francis Hughes		1155- 5-5	11- 6-10
Samuel Williams		873- 4-0	8-19-0
Alexr Eroin in Burk		150- 0-0	1-10-9
James Howard	ditto	75- 0-0	0-15-4½
Benjamin Cobb		2006-13-4	20-11-3
Solomon Smith		256- 4-6	2-12-6
William Ashurt		266- 0-0	2-14
Charles Robertson Esq		2382-13-14 to pay	24- 8-4
Henry Lyle		1891- 5-8 to pay	19- 7-8
Austin Honycutt		352- 0-0	3-12-2
William Whood		181-17-0	1-17-4½
William Cornealious		192-10-0	1-18-5
John Dunham		130- 0-0	1- 6-9¾
John Prator		148- 0-0	1-10-4½
Isaac Thomas		942-12-0	9-13-2
Ezekiel Smith		792- 0-0	8- 2-5
John Honeycutt		1257-17-2	12-17-9
William Fauling Decd		1399- 4-0	14- 6-9¾
Andrew Greer Esq		4865- 0-0	49-17-4½
By John Coward			0- 2-1½
By Jesse Vawter			0- 2-1½
By Timothy Holdway			1- 0-6
By Ezekel Brown			1- 0-6

	[1]	[2]	[3]
Nathaniel Durram	ditto	ditto	1- 0-6
Samuel Denny	ditto	ditto	1-15-0
Leonard Morgan	ditto	ditto	1- 0-6
Richard Collett	ditto	ditto	2-11-8
Elijah Abbott	ditto	ditto	1- 0-6
Henry Rains	ditto	ditto	1- 0-6
Elias Lain	ditto	ditto	1- 0-6
Matthew Arthur			
By Edward Bridges Delgt Retd by Benj. Gest Colr			1- 0-6
By Thomas Williams	Ditto	Ditto	torn
By John Bayley	Ditto		
John Dunkcome	Ditto	Ditto	1- 0-6
Moses Laird or	Ditto	Ditto	4-17-4
Charles Parker	Ditto	Ditto	1- 0-6
Delaney Carroal	Ditto	Ditto	1- 0-6
Peter Hufman	Ditto	Ditto	1- 0-6
Jacob Hufman	Ditto	Ditto	1- 0-6
Isam Ireby	ditto	Ditto	1- 0-6
James Howard	ditto	ditto	0-15-4
		148701- 6-0	1497-12-10

EARLY EAST TENNESSEE TAXPAYERS

Compiled by Pollyanna Creekmore

XI. Washington County, 1787

From the Private Collection of Paul M. Fink

The following tax lists, copied from the original manuscripts, were made available to the compiler for exclusive use in the East Tennessee Historical Society's *Publications* by Paul M. Fink, of Jonesboro, Tennessee, an active member for many years and a frequent contributor to the *Publications*. These lists are unique; no copies are in the Washington County Courthouse or elsewhere.

Washington County, the oldest county in the state of Tennessee, was created out of Washington District by an act of the North Carolina general assembly on December 18, 1777; its government was organized on February 23, 1778.

Washington County being a part of North Carolina, the laws governing the county were those of the state as prescribed by legislative acts. The law prescribing what property should be taxed, in effect in 1787, was enacted by the general assembly on November 18, 1786. This act amended an earlier act passed in April, 1784, but the method of taking and returning the taxes was retained. Property taxable was:

> All land held by deed or entry, where there is no caveat or by lease, or in right of dower, all town lots with certain improvements, all free males and servants between the ages of twenty and sixty years within this State . . .

By provision of the same act, the clerk was required to transmit to the comptroller of the state attested copies of the amount of taxable property and polls subject to pay a public tax setting forth in such return the quantity of each species of property subject to be taxed and the number of poles within the county.

The first list following appears to be a composite list of the taxable property and polls, probably compiled by the clerk to return to the comptroller. The list is undated, but a comparison with the original list of Captain William Cox's Company for 1787 proves, without doubt, that the date of the composite list is 1787. While there are 103 names missing, 10 additional names are found on Captain Cox's list, while none of the 30 names on Captain Fain's is included in the composite list. In addition to Captains Cox and Fain's lists, two undated lists, those of Captains William Hughs and Adam Reader, were located which are thought to be returns for the year 1787. While the names on Captain Hughs' lists are found on the composite list, the list is printed in its entirety because of the additional statistical data. None of the 23 names on Captain Reader's list is included in the composite list. Therefore, if the compiler's deductions are correct, the captains' original lists supply 63 out of the 103 missing names of the composite list. At any rate, here is an impressive list of the residents of Washington County, Tennessee, in what is thought to be the year 1787. A recapitulation of the tax returns for 1787 gives a total of 172,322½ acres of land, 782 white polls and 223 black polls.

WASHINGTON COUNTY, TENNESSEE
TAX LISTS
1787

Key to Column Numbers
[1] Number
[2] Persons' Names
[3] Acres of Land
[4] White Poles (Polls)
[5] Blacks　from 12 to 60 Years

[1]	[2]	[3]	[4]	[5]	[1]	[2]	[3]	[4]	[5]
104	Jacob Hooss	700	1		124	John Hammer Esqr	510	1	
105	Peter Miller	200	1		125	John Alison Senr	920		
106	Thomas Carney	520		8	126	Edward King	440		
107	John Hodges	330	2	2	127	George Emmert	250	1	
108	Thomas Ensor	45	1		128	William Frame	150	1	
109	Robert Stone	240	1	1	129	Thomas King	200	1	
110	Samuel Moore	224	1		130	John King	175	1	
111	Richard Burch		1		131	Jonathan King	200	1	
112	Thomas Melvin	300			132	Henry King	200	1	
113	John Melvin		1	1	133	Capt. James Gregg	350	1	
114	Michael Mesingale	200	1	1	134	John Tarbott	500	1	
115	John Beverly		1		135	David Hughs	350	1	1
116	Saml Witherington		1					hired	
117	James Cox	50	1	1	136	Alexr Tarbot	100	2	
118	Henry Long	40	1		137	Nathan Gregg	400	1	1
119	Peter Starnes	200	1		138	William Hughs	339	1	
120	Waters Williams	Discharged			139	Robert Hughs	200	1	
121	William Cox	500	1	2	140	Jacob Hetrick	300	2	
122	William Stone	240	1	1	141	James Price	151	1	
123	Joseph Crouch	250	1		142	George Millhorn	200	1	

[1]	[2]	[3]	[4]	[5]	[1]	[2]	[3]	[4]	[5]
143	William Dyer	150	1		194	William Whittington		1	
144	Jeremiah Prathro	238	1		195	Thomas Linvill	100	1	
145	Michl Waggoner	17½	1		196	Joshua Perkins Sr.		1	
146	Joseph Schuyler		1		197	Joseph Gentry	100	1	
147	Peter Hickman		2		198	Shadrach Eastepp	50	1	
148	John Sanders		1		199	Rowland Genkins	250	1	
149	Christian Shoults	250	1		200	Richd White Esqr.	765	1	5
150	James Hunter	58	1		201	Willm Oddel	100	1	
151	Robt Alison	400	1	1	202	Charles Neilson		1	
152	Robt Alison Esqr.	108	1		203	John Neilson	103	1	
153	Saml Tarbot	100	1	1	204	David Joab	280	1	2
154	William Bullington	200	1		205	Jean Nilson	103		3
155	Anty Apperson	250	1		206	Joseph Denton Senr	200	1	1
156	James Owen	100	1		207	William Ward	250	1	
157	William Evans	220	1		208	Jacob Waggoner	150	1	
158	Elizabeth Dunkin	300			209	William Watson	600	1	
159	John Austin	150	1		210	John Moore		1	
160	John Gyllim		1		211	David Moore		1	
161	Abner Davis		1		212	Robt Lusk	460	1	
162	Philip Workman		1		213	Jonathan Tipton Jr.		1	
163	Peter Workman		1		214	John Campbell		1	
164	Ninion Hoskins	200	1		215	John Blackwell		1	
165	Gilbert Kellems Sr.		1		216	Dawson Rockwell		1	
166	William Griffen	353	1		217	Willm. Wood	177	1	
167	Danl Oldhans		1		218	Charles Reno	150	1	
168	William Sweny		1		219	Philamon Lacey		1	
169	Benjn Brown	50	1		220	Nathen Davis	230	1	
170	George Brown	300	1		221	Jonas Little	321	1	
171	John Wilson Senr	70	1	1	222	John Peoples	100	1	
172	Evins Hetherly	80	1		223	Francis McFall	300	1	
173	Saml Wilson		1		224	Robt English	300	1	
174	Jacob Perkins	200	1		225	Elijah Cooper	200	1	
175	Charles Ashurt	250			226	Andw. Taylor, Jr.		1	
176	Henry Ryan		1		227	Thomas Milsaps		1	
177	Baker King	100	1		228	James Milsaps		1	
178	George Perkins	200	1		229	Wm. Edmondston		1	
179	Thomas Parker	125	1		230	Robt Taylor	205	1	
180	Elisha Hoskins	100	1		231	Anthy Moser		1	
181	William Wilson		1		232	Tho Gourley		1	
182	Nathan Arrundil		1		233	Matt Talbott		1	
183	John Graves	92	1		234	Richd Postle		1	
184	Thomas Majors		1		235	John Carrol		1	
185	William Runnels		1		236	John McIntorf	200	1	
186	Aaron Wallace		1		237	Richd Kite	150	1	
187	Richd Hains		1		238	Willm Shannon	150	1	
188	Silus Flanery	100	1		239	Henry Bottles		1	
189	Joshua Perkins, Jr.		1		240	John Shannon		1	
190	Wyatt Vanderpool		1		241	John Wallace		1	
191	James Guinn	252	1		242	George Brown		1	
192	Champness Guinn		1		243	John Humbert	172	1	
193	Peter Guinn		1		244	James Cash	428	1	4

[1]	[2]	[3]	[4]	[5]	[1]	[2]	[3]	[4]	[5]
245	James Wallace		1		296	James Range	270	1	
246	Nicholas Starns	201	1		297	George McCormick	200	1	
247	Saml Bailey	1005	1		298	Tho Maxwell	194	1	
248	Colvin Finch	143	1		299	Tho Hudeburg	50	1	
249	Abram Riffe	150	1		300	John Polland	200	1	
250	George Burkhart	130	1		301	Godfry Carager	3709	1	
251	Henry French	50	1		302	Jacob Boiles		1	
252	John Steger	350			303	Gutridge Garland	138	1	
253	Willm Nodding Jun.	200	1	1	304	Charles Longmire		1	
254	Edwd Million	162	1		305	John Garland	250	1	
255	Willm Nodding Sr.	300		5	306	Joseph Hedrick		1	
256	Saml McCaman	200			307	William Baldwin	340	1	
257	James Campbell	125	1		308	John Worley	140	1	
258	Adam Herman	100	1		309	Landon Carter	2040	1	5
259	Willm Fain	500	1		310	Saml Garland	300	1	
260	Edmund Williams	1540		2	311	Richd Cox		1	
261	James Chambers	140	1		312	Robt McCormick	50		
262	Garret Reasonor	203	1	1	313	John Lynch	100	1	
263	David Medlock	540	1		314	Jeremiah Dungan	1000	1	2
264	James Edden	530	1		315	Mesach Hale	460	1	
265	Michael Hider	420	2		316	Thos Price	210	1	
266	Timothy Tracey		1		317	Zebulon Smith		1	
267	Mary Cuningham	590			318	Elisha Humphrys		1	
268	Joel Cooper	150	1		319	Leonard Bowers	100	1	
269	Coln. John Tipton	2015	1	1	320	John Simerley	400	1	
270	Revd. Saml Huston	912	1		321	James Ivey		1	
271	John Fentress	200	1		322	John Reno	500		2
272	Willm Moorland	600	1	1	323	Joseph Tipton	743	1	
273	Isaac Grindstaff	200	1		324	Caleb Oddle	205		
274	Danl Vincent		1		325	Saml Blyth		1	
275	James Russel		1		326	Joab Cooper		1	
276	Cornelius Bowman	260	1		327	Edwd Cooper		1	
277	Joseph Ford	150	1		328	Wm Peoples	100	1	
278	John Bowman		1		329	Wm Forehand		1	
279	Julies Dugger	50	1		330	Saml Oddel		1	
280	Jacob Smith	100	1		331	Jesse Whitson	161	1	2
281	William Dugger	50	1		332	Joab Oddel	120	1	
282	Wm Flanery	90	1	1	333	Nehemiah Oddel		1	
283	Solomon Hendricks	170	1		334	Charles Taylor	Cleared by Court		
284	Thomas Leckey	130	1		335	Margt Taylor	169		
285	Jacob Hedrick	220	1	1	336	Joseph Denton Jr.	185	1	
286	Joshua Kelly	200	1		337	Isaac Taylor	700	1	
287	Humphry Garland			1		Do	400		
288	Saml Tipton	520	1				Cumberland		
289	James Philips		1		338	Resen Robeson	200	1	
290	Oliver Wallace		1		339	David McNabb	258	1	
291	Joseph Brown		1			Do	500		
292	John Brown		1				Cumberland		
293	Isaac Tipton	200	1		340	Solomon Combs		1	
294	Howel Ivey	75	1		341	Casper McIntorf	100	1	
295	Joseph Garland	200	1		342	Josiah Clark	270	1	

[1]	[2]	[3]	[4]	[5]
343	John Hendricks	200	1	
344	Isaac Denton	70	1	
345	Cotrail Bailey	400	1	
346	Isaac Lincoln	573	1	
347	Christian Peters		1	
348	Willm Hammonds		1	
349	Henry Bigs		1	
350	George Mitchel		1	2
351	Andw Greer Junr		1	
352	Nicholas Grindstaff	100	1	
353	Zech. Campbell	100	1	
354	Tho Dunkin	50	1	
[No. 355 was omitted.]				
356	Abrm Boorghauss		1	
357	Adam Rainbolt		1	
358	Robt Tate		1	
359	Thomas Hoskins		1	
360	John Potter	100		
361	Moses Reynolds		1	
361	John Tate		1	
362	Peter Parkison	200	1	
363	John Anderson	50	1	
364	Lewis Jones	350	1	
365	Edwd Smith	550	2	
366	John Arnold	400	1	
367	Willm Dunkin		1	
368	George Parkison		1	
369	Tho Lindvil	100	1	
370	Michal Grindstaff	100	1	
371	James Cumberford		1	
372	Teter Knave	350	1	1
373	John Hopkins	300	1	3
374	Jacob Grindstaff		1	
375	Joab Wilder	50	1	
376	Reuben Roberts		1	
377	Danl Kellems	50	1	
378	Robison Asher		1	
379	Saml Tate	872		1
380	John Grimes	100	1	
381	John Asher	150	1	
382	Jeremiah Campbel	100	1	
383	Solomon Campbel	200	1	
384	John Collins		1	
385	Nich. Smith		1	
386	John Smith	200	1	
387	Patt Dunkin		1	
388	Tho Carder	150	1	
389	Danl Nicholas		1	
390	William Davis	478	1	
391	Saml Smalin	100	1	
392	Ezekiel Abel		1	
393	Jonathan Pugh	450	1	
394	Joseph Whitson	127½	1	5
395	Henry Neilson	103	1	1
396	Abrm Cox	375	1	
397	Barnaby Eagen	200	1	
398	Andw Thompson	156	1	
399	Joseph Taylor	300	1	
400	Jas Campbell	360		
401	John Ferguson	300	1	
402	Wm Glass	339	1	
403	John Stanton		1	
404	Isaac Depue	100	1	
405	Wm Pursley Senr	250	1	
406	John Campbel		1	
407	John Trotter	264	1	1
408	Robt Alison	290	1	
409	Ninion Chamberlain	735		
410	Joseph McCorkle	200	1	
411	Willm Bell	80	1	
412	Willm Dale		1	
413	John Alexander	250	2	
414	James McWhorter	200	1	
415	David Shields	100	1	
416	George Shields	150	1	
417	David Steuart	260	1	
418	Isaac Davis	325	1	
419	James Mitchell	157	1	
420	Robert McCain	200	1	
421	James Bell	100	1	
422	Thomas Bell	166	1	
423	Willm Hannah	96	1	
424	John Hannah		1	
425	John Blair Senr	250	1	
426	Moses Carson	350	1	
427	Joseph Duncan	700	1	
428	Willm Fowler	230		
429	Willm Pursley Jur		1	
430	John Campbell Senr	300	1	
431	Hugh Campbell	200	1	
432	Robert Gambol	350	1	
433	Nathl Jones	100	1	
434	David Carson	100	1	
435	Thos Rogers	500	2	
436	Abraham Campbell		1	
437	Willm Kelso	300	1	
438	Patrick Shields	200	1	
439	Willm Stephenson	300	1	
440	Jacob Alexander		1	
441	Revd John Cason	250	1	
442	Willm Houston	200	1	
443	Noah Hawthorn		1	

[1]	[2]	[3]	[4]	[5]	[1]	[2]	[3]	[4]	[5]
444	James Kirkindol	489	1		494	Abrm. Hastings	173	1	
445	Thos Brandon	235			495	Saml Hastings	50	1	
	inhabitant of Greene County				496	Danl McCray	100	1	
446	Robert Blackley	570	1		497	Isiah Phips	80	1	
447	James Irwin	200	1		498	Wm Calvert	127	1	
448	William McNabb	507	1		499	Reuben Bailey	178	1	
449	Latcher				500	James Keele	200	1	
450	Benjn Nolland	460	1	2	501	Francis Baxter	130	1	
451	Peter Holland			2	502	Peter French	200	1	
452	George Gray	500	1		503	John Lemons	250	1	
453	Uriah Hunt	250	1		504	Issiah Lemons		1	
454	John Crouch Sr	150				[No. 505 was omitted.]			
455	Geo. Nowland	290	1		506	Robt Atchson		1	
456	Reubin Paign [?]	200	1		507	Hezekiah Bailey	200	1	
457	Jesse Crouch		1		508	John Young	637	1	1
458	Saml Epperson	250	1		509	Saml Woods	300	1	
459	John Ellis	100	1		510	Christ Taylor	305	1	2
460	William Davis		1		511	John Crecelius	76	1	
461	James Barron	225	1		512	Arshs Blackburn	200	1	
462	Anthony Gott	690	1		513	Hugh Rodgers		1	
463	Joshua Hale	200	1		514	Benjn Blackburn	200	1	1
464	James Chamberlin	110	1	1	515	Willis Gray		1	
465	Richd Hale	210	1		516	Charles Robeson	350	1	5
466	Abednego Hale	836	1	1	517	Ambrose Mayfield		1	
467	Richd Shot	100			518	Alexr Matthews	500	1	3
468	Green Shot		1		519	Danl Benner	100	1	
469	Shadrach Murray	150	1		520	Henry Kilburn	100	1	
470	Benjn Shipley	170			521	Joseph Rodgers	50	1	
471	William Brittain	100	1		522	Richd Keel		1	
472	Peter Shipley		1		523	Col John Sevier	1220	1	7
473	Robert Gray		1		524	Alexr Moffet	150	1	
474	Tho Shipley	160	1		525	David Hughman	146	1	
475	Saml Shipley	700	2		526	Thomas Goar	335	1	
476	Benjn Ford	120	1		527	Tho. Talbott	586	1	1
477	Loyd Ford Junr	122	1		528	John Love		1	
478	Loyd Ford Senr	100		1	529	Hugh Cuningham	375	1	
479	Mordicai Ford	220	1		530	George Davis		1	
480	Thomas Ford	120	1		531	Alexr Anderson		1	
481	Morgan Murray	200	1		532	Wm Moore	350	3	
482	Abrm Brittain	136			533	Andw Beard	250	2	
483	Robert Been	200	1	2	534	John Houston		1	
484	Saml Kelsey	265	1		535	Joseph Greer	415	1	
485	Jacob Pugh		1		536	Do James Taylor			
486	Isaac Thomas		1	5		South Carolina	1032		
487	Tho. Millar		1		537	Andw Greer Sr	2175		3
488	Saml Neel	100	1		538	Wm McCloud	200	1	
489	Elisha Butler	200	1		539	John Nowland		1	
490	John Lyon	206			540	Michal S[mith] Petter		1	
491	Acton W[hite] Cotton		1		541	Wm Clark	300	1	3
492	John Crouch Jur	100	1		542	John Clark	200	1	
493	Little B. Medlock		1						

[1]	[2]	[3]	[4]	[5]
543	Robt Young Junr	640	1	
[No. 544 was omitted.]				
545	Nathl Hall	220	1	
546	John Been	840	1	
547	Mark Mitchel	2300		12
548	Mary Mitchel			6
549	Patience Cooper	300		
550	Adam Horn		1	
551	Alexr Frosher	340	1	
552	Joseph Sevier		1	
553	John Carrol		1	
554	Benjn Lindsay		1	
555	Abrm Sevier		1	
556	Henry Mesingale	400	1	1
557	Wm Hodges		1	
558	Joseph Crouch	255	1	
559	Zechy McCubbin	200	1	
560	Geo. Brittain	136	1	
561	David Dunnom	100	1	
562	John Medlock		1	
563	Luke Medlock		1	
564	Wm Ellis	325	1	1
565	Geo Been		1	
566	Lydia Been	400		2
567	John Carney		1	
568	Edmd Been		1	
569	Benjn Shaw	200	1	1
570	Wm Been	100	1	
571	Benjn Cobb	470		6
572	Henry Masingale Jr		1	2
573	John Stern	1		
574	Wm Cobb	600	1	10
575	Pharoah Cobb	600	1	6
576	Archd [?] Evans		1	
577	Solomon Massingale	200	1	
578	Wm McCloud Junr		1	
579	John McCloud		1	
580	Jesse Humphrys	125	1	
581	Andrew Maiden	100	1	
582	Nathal Boman	200	1	
583	Kerbey King		1	
584	John Galt	100	1	
585	John Walker	68	1	
586	Eliz. Lane	250		2
587	Tho Grissam	164	1	
588	Tho. Findley	118	1	
589	Bartly O neal	200	1	
590	Patt. Kilpatrick	230	1	
591	John English	100		
592	Wm Barn	125	1	
593	Joseph Barn	170		
594	Robt Demit	200	1	
595	Richd McTeer	108		
596	Geo. Kinchelo	250		
597	Antho. Dunkin	153	1	
598	Leeroy Taylor	300	1	
599	Nathl Davis	500	1	
600	Wm Randol		1	
601	John Allison		1	
602	John Anderson	200	1	
603	Wm Jefferson		1	
604	John Barn	125	1	
605	Wm Hall	860	1	
606	Geo Crukshanks	136	1	
607	Henry Shields		1	
608	Benjn Sands	175	1	
609	Tho. Dale	100	1	
610	Shadrach Hale	160	1	
611	Shadrach Hale Jur	100	1	
612	Mesach Hale		1	
613	Joshua Green	170	1	
614	Tho Miller		1	
615	James Reed	100	1	
616	Tho. Smith	300	1	
617	Wm Leech	100	1	
618	Moses Chambers		1	
619	Tho Richey		1	
620	James Dale	250	1	
621	Francis Allison	150		
622	John Houston	1000	1	
623	Rowland James	50	1	
624	Wm Pursley Junr	400 Green		
625	James Rees	1100	1	6
626	Adam Wilson	890	1	3
627	James Carmichael	500	1	
628	John Shields	350	1	
629	Wm Carson Senr	212	1	
630	John Brandon		1	
631	Joseph Blair	1500		
632	Hugh Blair	600	1	
633	Joseph Wilson	100	1	
634	Wm Holloway Junr		1	
635	Philip Crawford	262	1	
636	Isaac Hill		1	
637	Danl Dunn	200	1	
638	Peter Namee	225	1	
639	Geo. Hous		1	
640	Wm Richey	555		
641	Andw Richey		1	
642	Amos Richeson		1	
643	John Giles	100	1	

[1]	[2]	[3]	[4]	[5]	[1]	[2]	[3]	[4]	[5]
645	Isaac Christapher	200	1		696	Tho Henderson		1	
646	Wm Doddson	165	1		697	John Branshaw	675	1	
647	Richd Emberton	150	1		698	Richd Rankins	300	1	
648	Wm Humphrys	790	1		699	Tho Rankins Sr	150	1	
649	James Dunn		1		700	Tho Rankins Jr		1	
650	Wm McPike	140	1		701	Wm Rankins	100	1	
651	James Shanks	625	1		702	Reubin Riggs	200	1	
652	David Brown	200	1		703	James Bowers	100	1	
653	David Thompson	100	1		704	Andw Chamberlin		1	
654	George Bell	150	1		705	John Archer		1	
655	John Bell	100	1		706	Wm Archer		1	
656	John Ford	250	1		707	Joseph Newel		1	
657	Anderson Smith	250	1		708	Jesse Bounds Sr	300	1	2
658	Hezekiah Lyons	100	1		709	John Wear	300	1	
659	Thomas Petit	150	2		710	Geo. Hanley		1	
660	John Wheellock	450	1	1	711	John Emery		1	
661	Nathl Hale	200	1		712	Joseph Bounds	100	1	
662	Nichs Hale	200	2		713	Aaron Tredaway		1	
663	Wm Hale	200	1		714	Alexr McKee	400	1	
664	Benjn Petit	200	1		715	James Bounds		1	
665	Saml Blair		1		716	John McKee	100	1	
666	Saml Thompson	62	1		717	Evan Dobbin	100	1	
667	John Smith	100	1		718	John Edwards	230	1	
668	Wm Stroud		1		719	Southy Neilson	100	1	
669	Abner Barnet	100	1		720	Alex Montgomery	100	1	
670	Issiah Standford	50	1		721	Missrs Brown	4263/4	4	
671	Patt. Kerr	140	1					Her	Third
672	John Watson	60	1		722	Jacob Brown	853	1	
673	Jacob Warren	40	1		723	John Hannah		1	
674	Wm Carson Junr	150	1		724	Tho Brown		1	
675	David Robeson	245	1		725	John Rodgers	100	1	
676	Wm Bryan	155	1		726	Patt. Murphy	372	1	
677	James McCord	400	1		727	Julias Robeson	130	1	
678	Elisha Haddon	300	1		728	Patt Dorrel		1	
679	Robt Carson	130	1		729	Moses Emery	150		
680	Holdon Shanks		1		730	Charles Robeson Jr.		1	
681	John Strain	100	1		731	Andw Hains		1	
682	Abednego Inman	450	1	1	732	Wm Lewis		1	
683	John Blair	249	1			[No. 733 was omitted.]			
684	Wm Carson	130	1		734	Jacob Casiner	100	1	
685	James Rain	110	1		735	Willm Adams	200	1	
686	Joseph Barn Junr	200	1		736	Cyrus Broyls	400	2	
687	Wm Holoway Senr	500	1		737	John Gann		1	
688	John Moseby	49½	1		738	Andw Hannah	275	1	
689	Jesse Hunt	306	1		739	Jeremiah Robertson	200	1	
690	John Combs		1		740	Nathan Gann		1	
691	Hardin Dunam		1		741	Henry Roads		1	
692	Tho. Randols	100	2		742	Michl Woods	1340	3	
693	Patt Morrison	300	1		743	Archd Woods		1	
694	Tho. Robeson	300	1		744	Richd Humphrys	307	1	
695	James Rodgers	400	1		745	Saml Doak	180	2	

[1]	[2]	[3]	[4]	[5]
746	Lewis Jordan	200	1	
747	Casymore May		1	
748	Saml Handly	150	1	
749	Wm Beard		1	
750	Jacob Collet		2	
751	Danl Haston		1	
752	James Miller		1	
753	Thomas Scott	200	1	
754	Jonathan Denton	100	1	
755	James Brading	60	1	
756	Robt Cowan	150	1	
757	John Roberts		1	
758	George Kindle		1	
759	John Miliken	239		
760	Ebenezer Scroggs	203	1	2
761	James Davis	150	1	
	Green			
762	Moses Kelsy		1	
763	Robert Kirkpatrick		1	
764	Robt Blackburn	227	2	
765	George Willson		1	
766	Danl Harrison	250	1	
767	Charles Hill		1	
768	Tho. Biddle	500	1	
769	Robt Willson	588	1	
	Green Co.			
770	Ann Moore	240		
771	Jean Dunlop	640		
772	Ephraim Dunlap		1	
773	Tho. Gilespy	1300	1	

[1]	[2]	[3]	[4]	[5]
774	Geo. Gilespy	1505		6
775	John Gilespy		1	
776	Jas Montgomery	200	1	
777	Joseph Alexander		1	
778	Tho. Weolum	500	1	
779	Joseph Wilson	500		
780	Robt Henry	150	1	
	Green Co.			
781	Edwd Ross	200	1	
	Green Co.			
782	Alexr Moore		2	
783	Clement Gann	100	1	
784	James Carter		1	
785	Conrod Willhoit	205	1	
786	James Galaher	400	2	
787	Nichols Broyls	120	4	
788	Solomon Yeagor	100	2	
789	Isaac Wilson	350	1	
790	Abrm Broyls	100	1	
791	Willm Breading	100		
792	Lewis Clerk	200	2	
793	Jasper Lott		1	
794	Adam Gann	100		
795	Mathias Broyls		3	
796	Michael Broyls		1	
797	Wm Trimble	420	1	
798	John Waddle	770	2	
799	Val Sevier Junr			
800	Alexr Greer			

Ye Returns for Cpt William Cox Comy of this year 1787

[1] Land No of acres
[2] Poles
[3] Black Poles
[4] Males above 60 years
[5] Widdos
[6] Fame Covert
[7] Fame Sole
[8] Male Miners
[9] Male Infints
[10] Female infints
[11] Black male infints
[12] Black female infints

	[1]	[2]	[3]	[4]	[5]	[6]	[7]	[8]	[9]	[10]	[11]	[12]
James Cox	30			1		1						1
Henry Stone			1	1								
Charles Dungeth		1				1			2	1		
Dannl Lane		1				1			2	2		
George Engle	250	1				1			3	1		
James Allsup	115	1				1		1	3	1		
John Corvin	109	1				1						
John Crabtree	100	2				1	3	1	1			
Thomas Pearce		1				1		1	4	2		
Jacob Bull	225	1	1			1			2	3	Fains Co.	

[1]	[2]	[3]	[4]	[5]	[6]	[7]	[8]	[9]	[10]	[11]	[12]
Jacob Hoose	700	1				1	2	1	5	1		
Peter Miller	200	1				1			1	1		
Thomas Carny	520		3			1	3		2			
John Hodges	330	2	2			1	2	1				
Thomas Ensor	45	1				1	1		2			
Robert Stone	240	1	1									1
Samuel Moore	224	1				1			1	4	Do Cpy	
Richard Burch		1				1			1		Do Cpy	
Thomas Melvin	300					1	3	2				
John Melvin		1	1			1			3			
Michel Masengil	200	1	1			1			2			
John Beverly		1				1						
Samuel Wetherington		1				1			3	4		
James Cox	50	1	1			1	1		3	4		
Henry Long	40	1										
Peter Starns	200	1				1						
Waters Williams	discharged					1						
William Cox	500	1	2			1	2		3			2
William Stone	240	1	1			1			3	1		
Joseph Crouch	250	1				1			2	2		
John Hammer Esqr	510	1				1	2	2	2	1		

Endorsed: John Hammers Esqr Return
            of Capt Willm Cox's Comp
            Taken off

A list of Ye Taxables of Ct Fains Company For the Yr 1787

Key to Column Numbers

[1] Names
[2] Land No acres
[3] Poles
[4] Black Poles
[5] Males above 60 Years
[6] Widdos
[7] Faime Covert
[8] Faime Sole
[9] Male Miners
[10] Male Infants
[11[Female Infants
[12] Black Males above 60 Years
[13] Black male infants
[14] Black femal infants
Taken in by me
          Jon Hammer

[1]	[2]	[3]	[4]	[5]	[6]	[7]	[8]	[9]	[10]	[11]	[12]	[13]	[14]
Samuel Bogart	640	1		2		1	2	1	2	3			
Samuel Denten	250	1				1			3				
Samuel Underwood		1											
Jacob Hammer	100	1				1							
Henry Bogart		1				1			2	2			
Kinchin Kelley	discharged				1				1				
John Thomas	250	1				1		1	2	1			
John blear McMacken	348	1	1			1			4				1
John White	640	1				1			2	1			
Adam Mitchel	300	1				1	1	2	3	3			
Peter Range	200	1				1			1	5			
Jonathan Tulles	400	1				1			2	2			

[1]	[2]	[3]	[4]	[5]	[6]	[7]	[8]	[9]	[10]	[11]	[12]	[13]	[14]
Michael Tulles 280	1				1				3	2			
Andrew Miller	1				1				2	3			
Charles Duncon 432	1				1	1	2		2	2			
Joseph Morrison 200	1				1				2				
Samuel Fain 400	1	1			1				3	2			
John Fain 240	1				1				2	1		1	
David Grate 100	1												
William Nelson 500	1	1			1	1			3	4		1	1
John Carr 250	1	2			1	2	1		3	3		1	
William Dannil 200	1				1	2			1	2			
William McBee 150	1				1				1	3			
Thomas Gibson 100	dis Charged				1				1	1			
John Humphrey 100			1		1		2	1					
Francis Hodge 348	2				1	3	1				of Capt Grayes Coy		
Joseph Collins 100	1				1				6	1	Do		
Henry Oldham 100	1				1				1	5	Do		
William Grisom 300	1	1			1				2	4			
John Alison 75	1										Gregs Com		

The return of the Taxable Property of the Inhabitants of that part of Washington County in the Fork between Holston and Wataughah Rivers, the District of Capt. William Hughses Company & State of No Carolina, also a return of Every Sac and Condition

Key to Column Numbers*

[1] Land Acres   [6] Male Minors
[2] White Poles   [7] Male Infants
[3] Black Poles   [8] Female Infants
[4] Feme Covert   [9] Whites above 60
[5] Feme Sole

	[1]	[2]	[3]	[4]	[5]	[6]	[7]	[8]	[9]	Note
John Alison Senr	920			1			1			Sd Jno Alison
Edward King	440			1	3	2	1			Sd Ed King
George Emmert	250	1		1			3	1		Sd Geo Emmert
William Fream	150	1								
Thomas King	200	1		1	1		1	2		
John King	175	1		1	1					
Johnathan King	200	1								
Henry King	200	1		1			2	3		
Capt James Gregg	350	1								
John Tarbet	500	1					2	3		
David Hughs	350	1		1 hierd Mrs. Bass						
Alexander Tarbet	100	2								
Nathan Gregg	400	1	1	1			1	1		
William Hughs	339	1		1	1			5		
Robert Hughs	200	1								
Jacob Hetrick	300	2		1		1	2	2		
James Price	150	1		1			1			

*Column, "Black Infants," omitted.

	[1]	[2]	[3]	[4]	[5]	[6]	[7]	[8]	[9]
George Millhorn	200	1		1		2	1	4	
William Dyer	150	1		1			2	2	
Jeremiah Prothro	238	1		1		1	2	4	
Michael Waggoner	17½	1		1				2	
Joseph Schuyler		1		1				1	
Peter Hickman		2		1	1	2	3	2	
John Sanders		1		1	1	1	3	4	
Christian Shoults	250	1		1	3	2	1	2	
James Hunter	58	1		1			3		
Robert Alison	400	1	1	1	1		1	3	4 Black Infants
Francis Hodges	345	1							

A List of Taxable Property Belonging to Captn Readers Company in Washington County

Key to Column Numbers*

[1] Land No. Acres
[2] Poles No.
[3] Males above 60
[4] Fame Covert

[5] Fame Sole
[6] Male Minors
[7] Male Infants
[8] Female Infants

	[1]	[2]	[3]	[4]	[5]	[6]	[7]	[8]
Captn Adam Reader	600	1		1			1	2
Jonathan Watson	115		1	1	2	1	1	1
John Hunter	939	2		1	1	2	2	2
Fredrick Anderson	150	1		1				3
Solomon Goodpasture	200	1		1	1	2[?]	3	3
Elias Walker	270	1		1			1	3
Jeremiah Compton		1		1			1	
George Fitzgerald		1		1			1	
Abraham Goodpasture	200	1		1			2	
John Goodpasture		1		1			1	
In Care of Mr John Hunter								
350 belonging to Peter Ruble								
George French	250	1		1				
Ambrose Hodges		1		1	2		2	1
Philip Azamis	200		1	1	2	1	4	2
John Mayfield			1	1		2	1	1
Robert Rodgers	200	1		1	2	2	2	1
Thomas Rodgers	200	1						
Joseph Cooper	69	1		1	1			

Continued for the Company of Captain Rife

Abraham Rife

	[1]	[2]	[3]	[4]	[5]	[6]	[7]	[8]
John Smith	300	1		1	1	3	1	1
Saml Pearcefull	200	1		1	1	1	1	4
John McMachen	4[torn]		1					
John Hunter		1		1			1	4

Endorsed: John McMahon Esq. Return

---

*Five additional columns, Land Owners Absent, Number of Souls White & Black, Widows, Black Male Infants, and Black Female Infants, appear in the original and are omitted here since no statistics were included except in one instance, e. g. Peter Ruble was an absentee land owner.

EARLY EAST TENNESSEE TAXPAYERS

Compiled by Pollyanna Creekmore

XII. Campbell County, 1818[1]

Campbell County was created by a legislative act of September 11, 1806, from parts of Anderson and Claiborne counties.[2] Anderson County had been created from parts of Grainger and Knox counties in 1801,[3] at the same session of the general assembly which created Claiborne County from parts of Grainger and Hawkins counties.[4] Grainger County had been created from parts of Hawkins and Knox counties in 1796,[5] Knox from Hawkins and Greene in 1792,[6] Hawkins from Sullivan in 1786,[7] and Greene from Washington in 1783.[8]

The bounds of the new county were described as

> Beginning at a point to be ascertained by running a direct line from the town of Burrville [now Clinton], in Anderson county, north, forty-five degrees west, to the Kentucky state line, or the northern boundary line of the state of Tennessee, from thence east, with the said boundary line, to a point on the same, from whence a line to be run at the angle of forty-five degrees, southeast, shall cross Powell's Valley, at or near where James Davis formerly lived in said Valley, leaving said house in Campbell county not more than fifty poles, thence the same course continued, to the line of Grainger county, on the right bank of Clinch, thence down the said river of Clinch, agreeably to its various meanders, to a certain point that shall intersect the lines of Anderson and Claiborne counties, immediately on the said right bank of Clinch river, thence crossing said river, and running southwardly with the line that divides the counties of Anderson and Claiborne counties [*sic*], immediately on the said right bank of Clinch river, thence crossing said river, and running southwardly with the line that divides the counties of Anderson and Grainger, to the Chesnut

---

[1] For the introduction to this series see *Publications*, No. 23 (1951), 115-16. Previous installments have been: I. Anderson County, 1802, in No. 23; II. Blount County, 1801, in No. 24; III. Knox County, 1806, in No. 26; IV. Grainger County, 1799, in No. 27; V. Jefferson County, 1800, in No. 28; VI. Carter County, 1796, in No. 30; VII. Sullivan County, 1796, in No. 31; VIII. Hawkins County, 1809-1812, in No. 32; IX. Greene County, 1805, in No. 33; X. Washington County, 1788, in No. 34; ·XI. Washington County, 1787, in No. 35.

[2] *Acts*, 1806 (Ch. 21), 64-66.

[3] George Roulstone (comp.), *Laws of the State of Tennessee* (Knoxville, 1803), 274. Hereafter cited as Roulstone, *Laws*.

[4] *Ibid.*, 279-281.

[5] *Ibid.*, 95-96.

[6] *Ibid.*, iv-v.

[7] Edward Scott (comp.), *Laws of the State of Tennessee Including Those of North Carolina Now in Force From the Year 1715 to the Year 1820, Inclusive*, 2 vols. (Knoxville, 1821), I, 378.

[8] *Ibid.*, 282.

Ridge, thence along the extreme height thereof, to a point from whence a line shall be run at the angle of north, forty-five degrees west, to the point the place of beginning.[9]

Campbell County itself has been partitioned in the formation of other counties. Portions were removed when Scott County was created in 1849 out of fractions of Campbell, Anderson, and Morgan counties,[10] and in 1850 when Union County was created out of Claiborne, Grainger, Knox, Anderson, and Campbell counties; however, owing to a lawsuit Union County had to be re-established in 1852 and its government organized in 1853.[11]

Campbell County was organized at the house of Richard Linville on the first Monday of December 1806.[12] The act establishing the county appointed James Grant, William Hancock, Jason Cloud, Robert Glenn, Richard Linville, Sampson David, and John English as commissioners "to locate and layout a place for a county seat to be known by the name of Jacksborough," and in 1808 or 1809, Jacksboro was laid out, and a jail and courthouse were erected. About 1855 a new courthouse was built. This building was destroyed by fire in December, 1884,[13] and a new building was constructed upon the same site which was occupied until April 13, 1926, when it was destroyed by fire.[14] The present courthouse occupies the same site.

The earliest permanent settlement of the county by white persons within the present territorial limits was begun in the early 1790's.[15] Many settlers were encroachers upon Indian lands whose title was not extinguished until the treaties of 1798 and 1805.[16]

Some facts of the county's early history are unknown due to the loss of the county court minutes until 1813. None survive for the period 1817-1834. The marriage records are also missing before 1838, there being no mandatory law for their recording. Two of the

[9] *Acts,* 1806 (ch. 21, sec. 1), 64.
[10] *Acts,* 1849-50 (ch. 45, sec. 1), 145.
[11] *Ibid.,* (ch. 61, sec. 1), 181.
[12] Goodspeed Publishing Co., *History of Tennessee,* East Tennessee edition (Nashville, 1887), 844. Hereafter cited as Goodspeed, *History.*
[13] *Ibid.*
[14] *The Knoxville Sentinel,* April 13, 1926.
[15] Goodspeed, *History,* 844.
[16] See "List of Insolvents living within the Indian Boundary for the Year 1797 which the County Court of Grainger released the Sherriff [*sic*] from the Collection of. Certified by Am[brose] Yancey C.G.C." [Endorsed] "Allowed by the Committee of Finance Oct. 4, 1799 R. Weakley CK." Original Manuscript in Tennessee Archives, Nashville; microfilm copy in McClung Collection.

early estate books, 1806-1841 and 1860-1880, survive. All of the deeds are preserved and are available in the office of the register of deeds.

Before 1820 the northern part of Campbell County was included in territory claimed by both Kentucky and Tennessee. This was due to Dr. Thomas Walker's failure to establish the true parallel of 36 degrees and 30 minutes, when he ran the line dividing the western claims of Virginia and North Carolina as far west as the Tennessee River in 1779. His line fell from six to twelve miles north of the true parallel, but was allowed to stand under an agreement made in 1820.

According to the agreement reached in 1820 by the states of Kentucky and Tennessee, where the land fell into Tennessee, Kentucky was given the right to issue grants for all the territory lying north of parallel 36 degrees and 30 minutes and east of the northward flowing section of the Tennessee River.[17] Tennessee was not to tax those lands for five years. Thus, the titles to some early settlers' lands may be found in the grants on file in the secretary of states office at Frankfort. The tax lists of Knox and Whitley counties, Kentucky, on file in the Kentucky Historical Society, contain the names of the earliest settlers in the disputed territory.

The county courts in Tennessee were authorized to levy taxes on property by a legislative act passed October 25, 1797, in which types of taxable property were listed and the method of taking taxes were prescribed.[18]

According to the laws governing taxation in Tennessee in force in 1818, the date of the following lists, taxes were based on legislation enacted in 1815.[19] Taxable property and polls were specified as

> All lands to which the Indian title has been extinguished & not exempt from the payment of public taxes held by grant, deed, entry, dower, occupancy & pre-emption, and all free males between the age of twenty-one and fifty years; all slaves between the age of twelve and fifty years; all town lots, stud horses or jacks, kept for mares, all retail stores as well medicine as merchandize, all taverns or retailers of spirituous liquors, all pleasurable carriages, all pedlars and hawkers, except such as are exempt by law. . . .

The specified tax rate was

> on each hundred acres of land eighteen and three fourths cents; on each town lots [*sic*] thirty seven and one half cents; on each white poll

---

[17] Henry D. Whitney (comp.), *The Land Laws of Tennessee* . . . (Chattanooga, 1891), 643-46.
[18] Scott, *Laws*, I, 589-91.
[19] *Acts*, 1815 (ch. 201), 267-70.

twelve and one half cents; on each slave between twelve and fifty years old, twenty five cents; on each stud horse or jack, the price of the season of one mare; on each retail store fifty dollars; for license to keep an ordinary or house of entertainment, or to sell spiritous liquors by a less quantity than a quart, five dollars; on each four wheel carriage of pleasure five dollars; on each two wheel carriage of pleasure, two and one half dollars; on each deck of cards imported into this state twenty five cents; on each hawker and pedlar not exempt by law, fifteen dollars in each county.

Campbell County also levied a tax of fifty cents on each hundred acres of land, fifty cents on each free poll, seventy-five cents each on town lots and slaves, and five dollars each on stores and pedlars. Two other types of taxes, a jail, and a poor tax were also levied.[20]

The following lists were copied many years ago from the original manuscript book, containing the lists from 1818 to 1833, on file in the office of register of deeds in the courthouse at Jacksboro. The compiler has had a keen personal interest in the records of Campbell County; it is her county of birth and the home of her ancestors for six generations. Subsequently, through the kindness of Mr. J. T. Heatherly, then register, she microfilmed the book, and a copy of the film is available in the McClung Collection, Lawson McGhee Library, Knoxville. A printed list of the names, without statistics, is found in Dr. G. L. Ridenour's *The Land of the Lake: A History of Campbell County, Tennessee* (LaFollette, Tenn., 1951). The key to abbreviations was made by the compiler.

Key to Column Numbers
[1] Quantity of Acres
[2] Where situated
[3] What held by
[4] Free polls
[5] Town lots
[6] Bk. polls
[7] Stores
[8] Stud horses

Key to Abbreviations for Land Locations in Column 2
Buf = Buffalo Creek
BC = Big Creek
CC = Coal Creek
CF = Clear Fork of Cumberland River
CR = Clinch River
do = Ditto
EF = Elk Fork of Clear Fork of Cumberland River
H = Henderson and Co. land
IC = Indian Creek
LH = Lot H in Henderson & Company Survey
PR = Powell River
PV = Powell Valley
WC = Walnut Cove

20 Campbell county, Tenn., Tax Lists, 1818-1833, flyleaf.

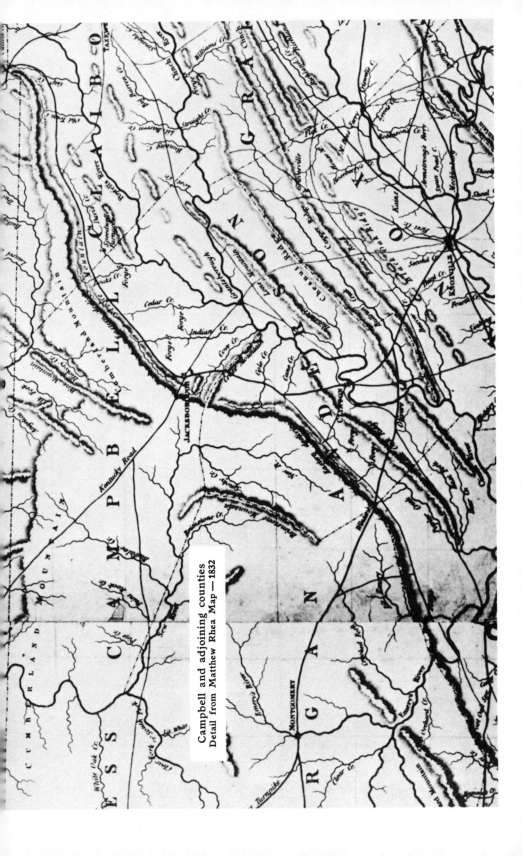

Campbell and adjoining counties
Detail from Matthew Rhea Map — 1832

LIST RETURNED BY JOSEPH PETERSON ESQR.

Names	[1]	[2]	[3]	[4]	[5]	[6]	[7]	[8]
Alvis, Walter	4468½							
Bell, John & Wm.	329							
Brown, Jh.	35							
Braham, Ephraim	20	Buf	Bond	1				1
Brumley, Wm.				1				
Barbee, Wm.				1				
Bowling, Absolom	125	CC	D	1				
Brown, Thoms.	16	CC	D					
Chaudoin, Jas.				1				
Chambers, Joshua				1				
Craven, Jos.				1				
Cuningham, David	60	PR	D	1				
Crismon, Gilbert				1				
Cravens, Joshua				1				1
Cross, Elizabeth	672							
Delap, Robert	500							
David & Simpson					2			
David, Sampson	2075	WC	Deed	1	1	6	1	
David & King	303	do	do		9			
Eisley, John				1				
Grady, John				1				
Geo.[rge], Reubin	50	IC	D	1				
Gray, James				1				
Gross, Edmd.	150	IC	D	1				
Gray, Joseph				1				
Gray, Nath'l.				1				
Graham, Spencer					1			
Henderson, James				1				
Hollingsworth, E. V.				1				
Harmon, John	200	CR	B					
Hays, Robt.				1				
Huckoby, John	100	IC	D	1				
Huckoby, William				1				
Harnis[?], John				1				
Hatmaker, Francis	644	IC	D	0				
Hughes, Francis	170	BC	D	1				
Hart, Joseph	1940			1	6			
Hart & Brown	113½	CF	G					
Houston, Robert	500	CR	D					
Johnston, William		CR	E	1				
Kinnet, Thomas				1				
Losson [Lawson], Joshua				1				
Lannon, Joseph	50	IC	D					
McClung, Charles	5987½							
Miller, Jacob	50	CC	B	1				
Miller, Wm.	5	CR		1				
Mozer, Adam	91			1				
Martin, Daniel	166	WC	Deed			1		
McCoy, Spruce	172½	EF	G					

Names	[1]	[2]	[3]	[4]	[5]	[6]	[7]	[8]
Martin & Inglish	30							
Montgomery, Lemuel P. heirs	906	WC	D		6	1		
McBride, James	35	CC	D	1				
Maysey, Charles	80	IC	D	1				
McCinny [McKinney], Henry	50	WC	D	1				
Moad, John	200	do	D					
McNealy				1				
McBride, Patience	55	IC	D					
Murray, James	100			1				
Noel, James				1				
Philips, John				1	2	1		
Brock, Elijah	30	CC	G	1				
Peterson, Joseph				1	5			
Prewet, Hardin	70							
Quenner, Jacob	550	CC	D	0	1			
Quenner, Dan'l	370	PV	D					
Quenner, Henry	139	do	do	1				
Quenner, Jacob Junr.				1				
Richardson, Brice				1				
Richardson, David	58			1				
Roark, John	25	CC	D	1				
Ready, Thomas				1				
Roark, John Junr.				1				
Roark, Joshua	50			1				
Smith, Robt.	149							
Simpson, John	200		B	1				
Smith, Wm. H.	123		B	1	8		1	
Sharp, Wm.				1				
Scruggs, James	108			1				
Smith, Sterling				1				
Sharp, John	78	IC	D	1				
Sharp, Aron	150			1				
Souders, Jacob	10			1				
Sharp, Aron	300	CR	D			3		
Sharp, John	100	do	do					
Sharp, George	126	CR	do	1				
Sharp, James	98			1				
Smith, Frederick	99			1				
Smith, John	25			1				
Sharp, Jacob				1				
Thomas, Mary Graves	1000							
Thompson, John	740							
Thomas, Adonijah	166	CC	D	1				
Umstead, John	3223½							
Thomas, Elisha				1				
Wilson, Eli	95		Deed	1				
White Cotton, Aron	50			1				
Wilson, Abraham	52			1				
Wilson, Wm.	20			1				
Whitton, Robt.	55							
Wiley, James				1				

Names	[1]	[2]	[3]	[4]	[5]	[6]	[7]	[8]
Whitmon, John	100							
Wheeler, Thomas	934	WC	D	1	3	3		
Warrener, Martha						1		
Warrener, Thomas	50			1				
Wheeler, Benj.	725			1	1	4		
Warren, Henry	10			1				
Warren, John	30							
Williams, Silas				1	1			
Warrener, John				1				
Williams, Abel	140			1				
Young, Samuel				1				

RETURNS MADE BY JAMES WALKER ESQUIRE

Names	[1]	[2]	[3]	[4]	[5]	[6]	[7]	[8]
Bundy, James	59	LH		1				
Burgis [Burgess], Wm.				1				
Braden, George				1				
Braden, John				1				
Basham, Wm.	150	LH		1				
Burgis, John				1				
Bowman, John				1				
Basham, Jonathan	209	H						
Basham, Johnson	89½	H	D					
Basham, Archibald				1				
Basham, Richard				1				
Basham, John				1				
Brannom, Joseph				1				
Bullock, Richd.	5975							
Bratcher, Charles	212					1		
Bratcher, John				1				1
Bratcher, Wm.				1				
Bratcher, John Sen.						2		
Barron, Joseph Sen.	50							
Coffett, Abraham				1				
Coffett, Isaac				1				
Coffett, George				1				
Cowan, Sam'l.	242			1				
Clebon [Claiborne, Cliburn, etc.], John				1		1		
Coffett, Daniel	200							
Doak, Thomas	245	LF	Deed	1				
Dauset, Edmond				1				
Dauset, Robt.				1				
Doak, John	80			1		1		
Evans, Walter				1				
Elliot, Robt.	130			1				
Furry, Daniel				1				
Furry, John				1				
Flemmon [Fleming], John W.				1				
Glenn, Robert	400							

Names	[1]	[2]	[3]	[4]	[5]	[6]	[7]	[8]
Glenn, James				1				
Goin, Isham	60			1				
Herren, Wm.				1				
Haines, Joshua				1				
Hunter, David				1				
Kincade, William	309							
Kincade, Thomas	140			1				
Meadors, Joel	99			1				
McNew, William	100			1		1		
Moad, Loadwick	222			1				
Moyers, Abrm.				1				
McClain, Thomas	950			1		7		
Miller, John	100			1				
Murray, Thos.				1				
McClary, Wm.	400			1				
McClary, John				1				
McCulley, Wm.				1				
Miller, James Sen.	278							
Miller, James Jun.	76			1				
Miller, Andrew				1				
McCulley, John	140							
McDonald, Aron				1				
Profit, William	130			1				
Parrot, James				1				
Parrot, Lewis				1				
Parrot, Joel	177							
Parrot, Elijah				1				
Petree, John				1				
Petree, George	410							
Robertson, Joseph, Jun.				1				
Rodgers, Jessee	33			1				
Raleigh, Vinson				1				
Robertson, Fielden				1				
Robertson, Joseph, Sen.	150							
Smith, Daniel				1				
Smith, Robert	400			1		5		
Smith, Jacob	230			1				
Smith, Thomas				1				
Smith, Anderson	174			1				
Smith, Benj. A.				1				
Smith, Ransom	250					1		
Scritchfield, Henry				1				
Sweet, Nathan				1				
Sweet, Wm.				1				
Shetter, Martin				1				
Shetter, George	100							
Skipper, Hardy	250							
Stanley, Page	75			1				
Sweet, Benjamin	100			1				
Walker, James	175	H	Deed	1	1	1		
Willoby, John	100							

RETURNS MADE BY THOS. MOAD ESQUIRE

Names	[1]	[2]	[3]	[4]	[5]	[6]	[7]	[8]
Alder, Barnabas	130			1				
Agee, James								
Agee, Isaac	200							
Archy, Richmond	150							
Anderson, William				1				
Burges, Wm.	120			1				
Buckland, Walter				1				
Barren, James	60			1				
Brown, John	62			1				
Ballard, Micajah				1				
Butcher, Elisha				1				
Barron, John	15			1				
Brooks, Philip	220							
Campbell, James	25			1				
Campbell, Joseph	58			1				
Craven, Richard				1				
Cunningham, James	100			1				
Carlock, Sarah	600							
Curtis, Elijah				1				
Cheek, Dauson	105							
Campbell, Thomas	200							
Campbell, Zachariah				1				
Doak, Robert	50			1				
Dagley, Elias				1				
Davis, Pallamon				1				
Davis, James				1				
Davis, Furklan				1				
English, Joshua	220					1		
English, James	162			1				
Edwards, Walter				1				
English, Joshua	162			1				
Edwards, John	18¾							
Griffeth, Wm.				1				
Griffeth, Wm.	100							
Grimes, Geo.	500			1				
Grimes, Sam'l.				1				
Heather, Thos.				1				
Hatfield, Jonathan	26			1				
Hanna, John	50			1				
Hatfield, Jeremiah	60			1				
Hayter, Abrm.	228					1		
Hatfield, James				1				
Holloway, Jeremiah	220			1				
Hatfield, Joseph				1				
Hatfield, Andrew	350			1				
Isaacs, Caleb				1				
Jones, William	20			1				
Lamb, Hannah	130							
Lamb, Josph.				1				

Names	[1]	[2]	[3]	[4]	[5]	[6]	[7]	[8]
Lamb, Gross				1				
Loe, Fielding	47			1				
Linville, Abrm.	100			1				
Mattonly [Mattingley], Walter	79							
Murray, David	300			1				
Murray, Thomas				1				
Murray, Morgan				1				
Moad, Thomas	150			1				
McCully, John				1				
Milstead, John	212½			1				
McCulley, Peter	208			1				
Poe, Linza				1				
Pewsley [?], Wm.	150							
Pearce, Robert				1				
Petree, Samuel				1				
Richardson, John				1				
Richardson, Amus	100							
Sealy, Jeremiah				1				
Starr, Francis	160			1				
Sharp, Richard				1				
Starr, James	200			1				
Stanley, Rewbin				1				
Skidmore, Thomas				1				
Stinson, Martin				1				
Statten or Slatten [?], Ambrose				1				
Sharp, Jacob	150							
Vanderpool, Wynant				1				
Vanderpool, Anthony	137			1				
Wheeler, Marget	150							
Williams, John	116			1				
Wheeler, Nimrod B.				1				
Wheeler, Benja. N.				1				
Wilhite, Simian	425			1	2			
Walker, Sam'l.				1				
Wilson, Isaac				1				
Williams, John Sen.	497							
Whitmon, Jacob	100			1				
Wilson, Levy				1				
Wilhite, Julius	50			1				

RETURNS MADE BY JACOB BREWTON ESQR.

Names	[1]	[2]	[3]	[4]	[5]	[6]	[7]	[8]
Allison, Hugh	100							
Angel, Archd.				1		2		
Anderson, John	72½							
Brown, James	25							
Brown, Eli				1				
Brewton, John	10							
Broils [Broyles], Aron	100				0 by order of Court			
Bowling, William				1				

Names	[1]	[2]	[3]	[4]	[5]	[6]	[7]	[8]
Baker, Samuel	120			1				
Baker, Edward	55			1				
Baker, Robt.	20			1				
Baker, Geo. Jun.				1				
Brewton, Jacob	40			1		1		
Branham, Jas.	100			1				
Branham, Martin, Sen.	20							
Beard [Baird], Lewis	5			1				
Crusenbery [Christenberry], Joseph	60			1				
Coffman, Joseph				1				
Chitwood, William	60			1				
Cox, Braxton	65			1				
Douglass, Mathew	20			1				
Douglass, Wm.	20			1				
Davis, Wilson	25			1				
Davis, Benja.	20			1				
Eyrs [Ayres], Baley				1				
Hays, Wm.	40			1				
Holt, Henry	20			1				
Hood, Hethpon	22½							
Jones, Mark				1				
Jones, William	47½			1				
King, William	80			1				
King, Murry T.	20			1				
Lawson, Jessee				1				
Lawson, David	20			1				
Lay, Jessee	57½							
Lay, John	30			1				
Lay, John Jun.				1				
McAnalley, Chas.	15							
Murray, Isaac	10			1				
Murray, Thos. Sen.	45			1				
Murray, Jabash				1		2		
Murray, Jonathan				1				
Murray, Christopher	6							
Murray, Wm.	25			1				
Percifield, Jeremiah Jun.	20			1				
Percifield, Jeremiah Sen.	20							
Perkins, Edwd.				1				
Perkins, Peter	103			1				
Pearce, Robt. D.	100			1				
Rustin, Jesse				1				
Powel, Riggins	20			1				
Stanley, Roads				1				
Shelton, Sam'l.				1				
Trammel, Peter	25			1				
Trammel, James	40			1				
Trammel, David	15			1				
Todd, Isaac				1				

Names	[1]	[2]	[3]	[4]	[5]	[6]	[7]	[8]
Todd, Loe	40							
Wright, Esau	10			1				
Wright, Wm.				1				
Wallen, Evan				1				
Total	831½			30	3			

RETURNS MADE BY SUGAR JONES, ESQR.

Names	[1]	[2]	[3]	[4]	[5]	[6]	[7]	[8]
Branham, James				1				
Branham, Talmon	60			1				
Branham, Sarah	190							
Brock, Sarah								
Black, John, Snr.	143							
Black, John, Jun.				1				
Brim, Lewis	382							
Brim, Henry				1				
Brim, Joseph				1				
Crowly, James	300							
Cuningham, Jonathan				1				
Craig, John	250			1				
Craig, Rewbin				1				
Dagley, Joseph	200			1				
Erwine, Francis	700			1				
Griffith, Thos.	273							
Grant, John Sen.	250							
Grant, Jno. Jun.				1				
Hancock, Geo.				1				
Hawn or Haws [?], Dan'l.				1				
Hancock, Martin				1				
Hancock, John				1		1		
Hunnycut, John				1				
Hansroe, John	100							
Hill, Matthew	100			1				
Jones, Sugar	200			1				
Langley, Joseph				1				
Lowery, John	260			1				
Loy, John	300							
Loy, Peter				1				
Lyon, Nathaniel				1				
Mozier, Geo.				1				
Mason, Solomon				1				
Millerbarger, Wm.	100			1				
Martin, John				1				
Malone, Richard	116					2		
Martin, Geo. Sen.				1				
Nations, Thos.				1				
Reader, Wm.				1				
Riley, Elisha				1				
Robts [Roberts], John				1				

Names	[1]	[2]	[3]	[4]	[5]	[6]	[7]	[8]
Read [?], Edward				1				
Robertson, Jas.	500							
Retherford [Rutherford], Wm.				1				
Sharp, Conrod	537					1	1	
Sharp, Henry				1				
Sharp, Wm.	50							
Snodderly, John	200							
Simons, Amon				1				
Stanley, Joseph				1				
Swafford, William	50			1				
Strader, Jacob	235			1				
Tuder, Harris	100							
Thomas, Joseph	27			1				
Vinson, John				1				
Williams, Jno. Jun.				1				
Young, Martin								

RETURNS MADE BY JNO. ANDERSON, ESQR.

Names	[1]	[2]	[3]	[4]	[5]	[6]	[7]	[8]
Acres, John	5			1				
Atkins, Sherrod				1				
Allen, Sam'l.	100			1				
Acres, Daniel				1				
Britten, Banja.	15			1				
Brown, Robert				1				
Briant [Bryant], John	4			1				
Chambers, Thomas	140			1				
Carter, Elijah	50			1				
Cox, Elisha				1				
Dunkin, Henry	100			1				
Dulin, Daniel				1				
Davis, James	25			1				
Davis, George	200			1				
Elswick, Stephen	120			1				
Elswick, Jonathan				1				
Fulkerson, William	50			1				
Gray, Jacob	60			1				
Griffey, Richard				1				
Howard, William	15			1				
Goad, Ayers	43			1				
Hewet, William				1				

Names	[1]	[2]	[3]	[4]	[5]	[6]	[7]	[8]
Goad, Joshua	4½			1				
Huckaby, John				1				
Jeffries, James				1				
Jeffries, William				1				
Kiberley, William	11			1				
Losson, David	20		G	1				
Lauson, David	20			1				
Lay, Jessee	30		Ent.					
Lawson, Randol	11							
Lawson, Elijah				1				
Lawson, Edward	40							
Lawson, Robert	30							
Litton, Rachel	16½							
Litton, James				1				
Ledgwood, John	100							
Lawson, William	34			1				
Lawson, Jacob	30			1		1		
Mathias, Thomas	20							
Massengale, John				1				
Martin, Nathal.	10							
Martin, Stephen				1				
McKehan, John				1				
Murray, Joshua	65			1				
Nestor, Fredrick				1				
Newman, John, Sen.	100			1				
Newman, John, Jun.				1				
Richardson, Lows				1				
Richardson, John, Sen.				1				
Richardson, John, Jun.				1				
Read, Isaac	50			1				
Read, Allen				1				
Read, John	100			1				
Richardson, George				1				
Sharp, Isham				1				
Sharp, Richard, Sen.	50							
Shoopman, Nicholass	20							
Stanley, Ellen	50							
Shoopman, Michael	30			1				
Simpkins, Robert				1				
Sartin, Write	60			1				
Stanley, Robert	87½							
Sartin, David	40							

Names	[1]	[2]	[3]	[4]	[5]	[6]	[7]	[8]
Sexton, Aron	10			1				
Shoopman, Jacob	100							
Shoopman, John	20			1				
Sowders, Jacob	10			1				
Thompson, William	10			1				
Thompson, Harmon				1				
Thompson, Lewis				1				
Thompson, Blag.	50			1				
Terry, Elijah				1				
Terry, Josiah				1				
White Cotton, Aron	50			1				

EXTRA RETURNS FOR THE YEAR 1818

Names	[1]	[2]	[3]	[4]	[5]	[6]	[7]	[8]
Alder, John	70							
Asher, Charles				1				
Asher, Amos				1				
Brumley, John, Sen.	25							
Brown, Samuel	75							
Cooper, Peter				1				
Campbell, James, P. V.	85	P. Valley		1				
Chambers, Elisha	200	EF	Ent.					
Daniel, William				1				
Ford, Joseph				1				
Gray, Robert				1				
Hollingsworth, James	189			1				
Hollingsworth, Dan'l.				1		1		
Hamson, Briant	2644							
McCorry & Overton	2000	EF	Deed					
Moss, Reubin					1			
Miller, William				1				
Moad, James	260			1				
Morris, Absalom	226							
Morgan, Joseph				1				
Noe, Berry	130			1				
Overstreet, Lewis	145			1				
Philips, John					1			
Ridenour, John				1				
Ryon, Harris	150							
Sharp, John P. Valley	130	PV						
Smith, Ransom								1
Salter, Robert, heirs	1345	PV						

Names	[1]	[2]	[3]	[4]	[5]	[6]	[7]	[8]
Sweeton, John				1				
Sharp, Jacob								1
Smith, Ali, Sen.	180							
Smith, Ali, Jun.				1				
Smith, Uricus	120			1				
Smith, Wm.				1				
Smith, James				1				
Todd, Jessee				1				
Tivis, Robert	2375							
Thomas, Mary G.	1000							
Warrener, William	180							

REPORTED PROPERTY & POLLS FOR THE YEAR 1818

	Quantity of acres	Free Polls	Town lots
Haynes, Sterling	50	1	
Hide, William	100		
King, Thomas	3000		
Linville, Richard			1
Shofner, Michael	100	1	
White, Dan'l. & Branscomb	135		

EXTRA RETURNS CONTINUED
Amount brought forward

Cox, John		1	
Huckoby, Thos.	143	1	
Phillips, Thos.	143	1	1 stud horse
Rukard, Jonathan	100		
Sexton, Timothy, Sen.	75		
Sexton, William	10	1	
Smedly, Jessee		1	
Shoolbrid, James pr. S. David	812½		

EARLY EAST TENNESSEE TAXPAYERS
Compiled by Pollyanna Creekmore

XIII. Cocke County, 1839[1]

Cocke County was created by an act of the general assembly on October 9, 1797, from a part of Jefferson County.[2] Jefferson County had been created in 1792 from parts of Greene and Hawkins counties.[3]

The act creating Cocke County, "an act to divide the county of Jefferson into two separate and distinct counties," established these boundaries:

> to begin on the North Carolina boundary line with this State, on the south side of French Broad River, one mile from said river, thence down said river one mile distance from the same to where it intersects the Greene County line; thence with said line to Nolichucky River, a small distance below Captain William White's house; thence down said river to French Broad, leaving all the islands to Jefferson County; thence down the river French Broad, in the same manner, to the bent of said river opposite Colonel Parmenas Taylor's and from thence a direct line to the top of English's Mountain within one mile of Sevier County line, thence parallel with that line to the uppermost house on Cosby's Creek, and from thence an easterly line, to a point on the North Carolina boundary line, as to leave six hundred and twenty-five square miles in Jefferson County, and from thence with the said boundary line to the beginning.

After its creation, the boundaries remained substantially the same except in 1799, when a small part of Greene County was added,[4] and in 1811, when "all the inhabitants on the waters of Cosby's Creek supposed to be in Jefferson County" were annexed to Cocke County.[5]

The county was named in honor of William Cocke (1748-1828), a prominent military and civil officer.[6] The same act which created the county attached it to Hamilton District.[7]

---

[1] For the introduction to this series see *Publications* No. 23 (1951), 115-16. Previous installments have been: I. Anderson County, 1802, in No. 23; II. Blount County, 1801, in No. 24; III. Knox County, 1806, in No. 26; IV. Grainger County, 1799, in No. 27; V. Jefferson County, 1800, in No. 28; VI. Carter County, 1796, in No. 30; VII. Sullivan County, 1796, in No. 31; VIII. Hawkins County, 1809-1812, in No. 32; IX. Greene County, 1805, in No. 33; X. Washington County, 1778, in No. 34; XI. Washington County, 1787, in No. 35; XII. Campbell County, 1818, in No. 36.

[2] George Roulstone (comp.), *Laws of the State of Tennesssee* (Knoxville, 1803), 124-26.

[3] *Ibid.,* iv-v.

[4] *Ibid.,* 168.

[5] *Acts of Tennessee,* 1811, pp. 128-29.

[6] *Dictionary of American Biography,* 20 vols. (New York, 1928-36), IV, 255-56.

[7] Roulstone, *Laws,* 126,

Henry Ragan, William Job, John Calfee, Peter Fine, John Keeney, Reps Jones, and John McGlothlen were appointed to select the site for a county seat and were authorized to contract a "court house, prison and stocks." They selected a site known as Fine's Ferry on the French Broad River about one and one-half miles below the present county seat. Fifty acres of land were donated by John Gilliland. A log courthouse and rock jail were constructed. This courthouse was used until 1828, when a brick building replaced it. The first court met at the house of Daniel Adams.[8]

For other details of the settlement and early history the reader is referred to Mrs. Ruth Webb O'Dell's *Over the Misty Blue Hills* (Newport, 1950) and to the Goodspeed Publishing Company's *History of Tennessee,* East Tennessee Edition (Chicago, 1887).

In 1867, the Cincinnati, Cumberland Gap and Charleston Railroad was completed to Cliffton (or Clifton), the site of present Newport, and there ensued a lengthy controversy over the removal of the county seat. One report states that the records were kept on a wagon, and that it burned consuming the records.[9] A more likely story is that Fairfield's store housed the county offices,[10] and it was this structure that burned on the morning of December 30, 1876,

> Destroying all of the records and papers belonging to the office of the Clerk of the County Court and nothing remains to refer to, the only source of information that can be obtained will be from the recollection of parties interested, memorandums [*sic*] they may have, and from recollection of the different officers of the County
> It being also reported to the Court that all of the Records and papers belonging to the offices of the Clerk of the Circuit Court, and Chancery Court of the County of Cocke, as well as all of the Records of the Registers office of Cocke County except Book No. 17 were burned at the same time, as well as a part of the Records of the Entry takers and Surveyors office of the county.[11]

In 1884 the county seat was fixed at Clifton and a new courthouse was completed in 1886. This building was used until 1930, when the structure burned; however, the records were saved. The present courthouse was completed in 1931. In addition to the few records that survived the fire of 1876, some legal documents were re-recorded.[12]

---

[8] Goodspeed Publishing Company, *History of Tennessee* . . ., East Tennessee edition (Nashville, 1886), 865.
[9] "Newport, Tennessee," in *Knoxville Tribune,* anniversary ed., 1896.
[10] Mrs. Emily Swanson, "Newport 70 Years Ago," *Plain Talk and Tribune* (Newport), June 10, 1940.
[11] Cocke County Court Minutes (Courthouse, Newport), January 1, 1877.
[12] Tablet on Courthouse, Newport.

Part of Cocke County was included in the 1806 District South of French Broad and Holston (the present Tennessee), and west of Big Pigeon rivers, originally reserved by North Carolina in 1783 to the Cherokee Indians, one of the seven districts created by the general assembly in 1806 when the compact of that year was concluded between the governments of the states of North Carolina, Tennessee, and the federal government.[13]

The titles to some of the settlers' lands were secured by grants from the state of Tennessee, based upon preemption and right of occupancy, at a price of $1.00 an acre, instead of the $2.00 minimum required before 1823 for other lands sold by the state.[14] The grants are recorded in the Archives Division of the Tennessee State Library and Archives, Nashville. After this price restriction in the Compact of 1806 was removed by an act of Congress in 1823, the Tennessee general assembly provided for the sale of waste land outside the Congressional and Cherokee reservations for a price of 12½ cents an acre. All the revenue received, both from the sale of the land and the subsequent taxes on it, were to be placed in the common school fund created by the same law.[15] Presumably, the "school lands" in the tax list below were of this type.

The state constitution as amended by the Convention of 1834 provided that "All lands liable to taxation, held by deed, grant or entry, town lots, bank stock, slaves between the ages of twelve and fifty years, and such other property as the Legislature may from time to time deem expedient shall be taxable. . . . But the Legislature shall have power to tax merchants, pedlars, and privileges, in such manner as they may, from time to time direct." The constitution also directed that civil districts be laid off in each county, the number in any one county not to exceed twenty-five, or four for every hundred square miles. Two justices of the peace and one constable were to be elected for each district, except districts including county towns, which were to have three justices and two constables.[16]

The general assembly on December 11, 1835, appointed commissioners to lay off the counties into districts of convenient size. John F. Fowler, George Nease, William Robinson, Abraham Fine, and

[13] Henry D. Whitney, *The Lands Laws of Tennessee* (Chattanooga, 1891), 58-61.
[14] *Ibid.*
[15] *Acts of Tennessee*, 1823, ch. 30.
[16] Article II, Section 28; Article VI, Section 15.

Alexander E. Smith were appointed for Cocke County.[17]

By an act passed February 5, 1836, the method of taking the lists of taxable property was prescribed. Beginning at the May term 1836 of the county court and from then on at the last term of the court, one justice or qualified person, was to be appointed in each district, to be known as the revenue commissioner, to take in a list of taxable property and polls within the magistrate's district. He was required to record separately the acres of lands in his district, the revenue arising from which is by law appropriated to common schools, from other lands. He was then to return an alphabetical list to the county court. The clerk then was to record the returns and in turn send a complete transcription of all lists to the Comptroller of the Treasury on or before the first day of October 1836, and after that date on or before the first of July of each year.[18]

The following lists are a copy of the certified lists returned by William McSween, county court clerk of Cocke County, to the Comptroller of the Treasury. The bound original lists are in the Archives Division of the Tennessee State Library and Archives, Nashville. At the present, these are the only known early tax lists of Cocke County and the most complete list of early residents and landowners exclusive of the population schedules of the federal decennial censuses of 1830 and 1840, which list the names of the heads of families, thus do not include names of many young men and some widows.

Key to Column Numbers

[1] Acres of land   [4] Slaves
[2] School lands   [5] Town lots
[3] White polls

		[1] [19]	[2]	[3]	[4]	[5] [20]
1	Allen, Mary	370			6	
2	Allen, Geo. W.		500	1		
3	Allen, Jas R		150			
4	Burnett, James	100		1		
5	Burnett, Wm. C.	255		1		
6	Burnett, James, Guard. for Jos. & Benj. Burnett	100				
7	Burnett, Jno M	200				

---

[17] *Acts of Tennessee,* 1835-36, Resolution No. III, p. 196.

[18] *Ibid.,* 62-71.

[19] Numbers in parentheses refer to number of tracts of land.

[20] Apparently the numbers refer to lot numbers. The only districts with town lots were districts 3 (Parrottsville) and 6 (Newport).

		[1]	[2]	[3]	[4]	[5]
9	Burnett, Elizabeth	200				
10	Brooks, Kaner		150	1		
11	Bell, John	227				
12	Brooks, John		100			
13	Brook, Royal			1		
14	Boydston, Wm.			1		
15	Black, Reuben	250	400			
16	Black, James			1		
17	Black, Matthew		100	1		
18	Black, Alexr		150			
19	Black, Jno		200	1		
20	Ball, Royal			1		
21	Ball, Mereman			1		
22	Ball, Osbourn		1680			
23	Ball, Adonijah		400			
24	Ball, Jno		96			
25	Ball, Ira		200			
26	Bugg, David		5,000	1		
27	Birdsey, Ezekiel	8	37,000			
28	Church, Allen	2	60			
29	Carson, Drucilla	130	100			
30	Carson, Andrew			1		
31	Cogdill, Frederick			1		
D						
32	Davis, Peter J [or I]	223	800	1	4	
33	Davis, James		50	1		
34	Davis, Benjamin	72	950	1		
35	Driskell, Davy		400			
36	Davis, William		50	1		
E						
37	Ellisson, John	50	350			
38	Ellisoon, Michael			1		
39	Ellisson, Wm			1		
40	Ellison, James	30	75	1		
41	Ellisson, Martin		100	1		
F						
42	Fugat, John	110			1	
43	Fugat, Noah			1		
44	Fugat, Jackson			1		
45	Ford, James		150	1		
46	Ford, Benjamin		150	1		
47	Ford, Evan	25	700	1		
48	Fowler, Jno T.		90			
G						
49	Green, Thomas			1		
50	Green, Washington		50			
51	Green, Jeremiah Senr		50			
52	Green, David		1000	1		
53	Green, Jeremiah Jun.		400	1		
54	Gillett, Wm. P		150			

		[1]	[2]	[3]	[4]	[5]
H						
55	Howel, Jno J		640			
56	Huff, Stephen	840	400	1	3	
57	Huff, David	30	300			
58	Harris, Wm. P.	144		1		
59	Holland, James	200	300	1	2	
60	Holland, Wm.	200	50	1		
61	Huff, Jonathan	100	80	1		
62	Henry, Reuben		300	1		
J						
63	Jones, Wyett			1		
64	Jones, Americus	25	238	1	1	
K						
65	Knight, Richard	25	700	1		
L						
66	Lea, Alfred	300	205	1	1	
M						
67	Moonyhan, Thos	60	25	1		
68	Moonyhan, Wm. Sen.	98	60			
69	Moonyhan, Wm. Junr	40	150	1		
70	Messer, Solomon		500	1		
71	Miller, Abraham	50		1		
N						
72	Nichols, Charles	100	25		1	
73	Nichols, Bury		400	1		
P						
74	Penland, Jno H			1		
75	Parker, Nicholas		200			
76	Penland, Abraham	75	25			
77	Penland, Jackson			1		
R						
78	Robinson, Wm.					
79	Russel, Wm.		50			
80	Rose, Green	15	510	1		
81	Rowland, Abraham			1		
S						
82	Swagerty, James					
83	Smith, Joel			1		
84	Sawyers, James		80	1		
85	Stokely, Royal	300	124		2	
86	Stokely, Jno H			1		
87	Stokely, Nathan	30	50	1		
88	Stephens, Charles		50	1		
89	Smart, Wm Junr			1		
90	Smart, Daniel		50	1		
91	Smart, Wm Senr	75				
92	Stuart, Jno		300			
93	Story, Wm C		50			

		[1]	[2]	[3]	[4]	[5]
W						
94	Wood, David		483		1	
95	Williams, Pleasant			1		
96	Williams, David	60	437	1		
97	Williams, Solomon		50			
98	Wooddy, John		100			
99	Wooddy, Achilles		3000	1		
100	Wooddy, Wm		100	1		
Y						
101	Young, Joseph	150	50	1	1	
	do Guardian J. R. Jones					
	Heirs	200	300			
[102]	Yeates, Samuel Senr		100			
[103]	Yates, Nathaniel		250	1		
[104]	Yeates, Samuel Junr		200	1		
District 2nd						
B						
1	Borden, John (Heirs)	415	68			
2	Borden, Danl	150	50			
3	Blazer, Aaron			1		
4	Blazer, Henry			1		
5	Benner, Christopher			1		
6	Bailey, David		50	1		
7	Baker, John			1		
8	Baker, James			1		
9	Busby, Reaves		60			
10	Bell, Jos E		1000	1		
11	Blazer, Christopher	50	150			
12	Blazer, Adam	90	78			
13	Borden, Archibale			1		
14	Borden, Elizabeth	50				
15	Blazer, Phillip			1		
C						
16	Chapman, Wm	366			2	
17	Cooper, Robt Sr.	311				
18	Cooper, James			1		
19	Chapman, Luna	100		1		
20	Clark Harris	146			3	
21	Cooper, John			1		
D						
22	Davis, Gransham			1		
23	Dockry, Balaans			1		
24	Dockry, Robt			1		
E						
25	Ebbs, John		300			
26	Ebbs, Greenberry			1		
27	Ebbs, Jno W			1		
28	Ebbs, Richard			1		
29	Erwin, James		195			

		[1]	[2]	[3]	[4]	[5]
F						
30	Faubion, Wm.		200			
31	Faubion, John	540	21		2	
32	Fabion, Henry			1		
33	Faubion, Jackson			1		
34	Freshour, Jacob			1		
35	Faubion, Spencer	50	150	1		
G						
36	Gragg, Geo W			1		
37	Gragg, Thos W			1		
H						
38	Huff, David	279		1	1	
39	Huff, Joseph	294	300	1	1	
40	Huff, Thomas B.	214		1		
41	Hale, Joseph			1		
42	Holland, H. L.	200	105		2	
43	Houston, Howel	340	72			
44	Headrick, Daniel			1		
45	Headrick, John		566	1		
46	Hickey, Isaac		68			
I						
47	Icenhoser, Phillip	200		1		
48	Icenhower, John	229	9	1		
49	Icenhower, Martin	294				
50	Icenhower, Peter		35	1		
J						
51	Justus, Martin	100		1		
K						
52	Kelly, Wm.		125			
53	Killian, Eli			1		
54	Kilgore Jane [blurred]	150				
55	Kilgore, Thomas			1		
L						
56	Linebarger, Catharine	219	25			
57	Love, Wm			1		
58	Love, Jno T	156	100			
59	Lea, Robt H	17	1,000	1	1	
M						
60	Maloy, Jacob	204		1		
61	McMurtry, Jos	79				
62	McMurty, Jno			1		
63	McNew, Shadrach		50	1		
64	Maloy, James	108	5			
65	McNabb, Geo			1		
66	Maloy, John	200	225	1	2	
67	Micalsane [?] John		100			
N						
68	Neas, Michael	245		1		
69	Neas, George	534	318			

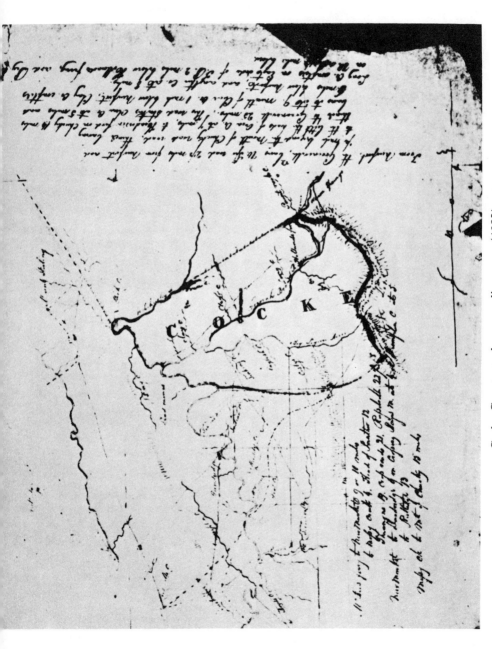

Cocke County and surrounding area (1832)

From Matthew Rhea's original sketch, Tennessee State Library and Archives

		[1]	[2]	[3]	[4]	[5]
70	Neas, Benjamin			1		
71	Neas, Ambrose			1		
72	Neas, Phillip	260	75	1		
73	Neas, Saml			1		
O						
74	Ottinger, Wm.			1		
75	Ottinger, Michael	245	83	1		
76	Ottinger, Adam			1		
77	Ottinger, Peter (of Mason)	100				
78	Ottinger, Peter (of Peter)	184	70			
79	Ottinger, Henry (Capt.)	503	83			
80	Ottinger, Jacob	150				
81	Ottinger, Henry (of Peter)	53		1		
82	Ottinger Jno (of Jonus)	100		1		
83	Ottinger, Lewis	276				
84	Ottinger, David (Jun?)	100				
85	Ottinger, Susannah	58				
86	Ottinger, David (of P)	83	63	1		
P						
87	Pack, Henry			1		
R						
88	Rener, John	75	575			
89	Reaves, Thos J.	300	50	1		
90	Reece, John	217		1		
91	Rener, Henry	75	575	1		
92	Ren, Joel			1		
S						
93	Spencer, Edward	100	60			
94	Shelton, N. K.		150	1		
95	Spencer, Alfred	50		1		
96	Smith, Wm			1		
97	Sheppard, Hiram			1		
98	Sheppard, Wm			1		
99	Swagerty, James	300	900		3	
100	Stuart, Wm	74		1		
101	Stokely, Jahu	296	50	1		
102	Sawyers, Archibald			1		
103	Smith, Charles	100		1		
104	Stuart, Hugh			1		
105	Smelcer, Frederick	350	129			
106	Smelcer, Jonathan			1		
W						
107	Winebarger, George			1		
108	Warden, David		153			
109	Winter, Catharine	242	100			

		[1]	[2]	[3]	[4]	[5]
110	Winter, Joseph			1		
111	Winter, Andrew		12	1		
112	Witt, Merril	117		1		
113	Williams, Isaac	200				
114	Williams, Lewis			1		
115	Welty, John		50	1		
116	Williams, Joseph	76	10	1		
Y						
117	Yett, Wm	300	100		3	

District 3rd

A

		[1]	[2]	[3]	[4]	[5]
1	Alexander, L. D.	181		1		
B						
2	Buckner, George	45	850			
3	Boyer, Lewis	270	100	1		
4	Bible, Lewis	76		1		
5	Black, James			1		
6	Boyer, Isaac	200	28	1		
7	Blanchet, John	50	50			
8	Baldridge, James			1		
9	Baloo, Leonard		150			
10	Baloo, Thomas			1		
11	Buster [?] or Basler Henry			1		
12	Basinger, George			1		1
13	Barnett, Meradith		284	1		
14	Brooks, William					1
15	Bryant, Saml	80	130	1		
16	Bryant, Benjamin	233	170			
17	Boyer, Henry	270	50	1		
C						Part of
18	Coffman, John		200			2
19	Cureton, Robert		50	1		
D						
20	Downs, Nelson			1		1
21	Dawson, Amos		450	1		
22	Davis, Jos H			1		1
E						
23	Easterly, George		164			
24	Easterly, Jacob Jr.		148			
25	Easterly, Jacob senr	342	218			
26	Eslinger, David	100	50			
27	Etherton, James	115	470	1		
28	Etherton, Pleasant			1		
29	Easterly, N. W.			1		
30	Easterly, Payne			1		
31	Easterly, Reuben			1		
F						
32	Fowler, Josiah	250	170	1		
33	Fowler, Isaac		184			

		[1]	[2]	[3]	[4]	[5]
34	Fowler, John			1		
35	Faubian, Jacob			1		4
36	Fansher, W. L.			1		
37	Fowler, Jno F	200	570	1	3	
38	Fowler, F. F.			1		1
39	Faubion, Jno	200		1		
40	Fowler, Thomas	324	474		1	1
41	Fowler, Wm.			1		
42	Faubion, Wm	1640	510		2(?)	
43	Fansher, Jno	265	130	1		
G						
44	Green, John		250	1		
45	Gammon, Ivy		60			
H						
46	Hughs, Saml M			1	2	2
47	Henly, Geo S			1		
48	Har? Job	12	30			
49	Hale, John			1		
50	Headrick, David			1		
51	Harned, David	310	550	1		
52	Hutson, Wm B		375	1		2
53	Hampton, Wayd			1		
J						
54	Jourdan, John		100			
55	Larew, Frances			1		
M						
56	McBee, Asa			1		
57	Mims, Alfred (Decd)	70	1,050			
58	Mims, Albert (decd)	109	259			
59	Miller, Charles		100			
N						
60	Nelson & Yearout		1,000			
O						
61	Ottinger, John Junr	30	25			
62	Ottinger, John Senr	20	25			
63	Ottinger, George	248	252			
64	Ottinger, Jno (George)			1		
P						
65	Parrott, George	416	194			
66	Parrott, Jacob	116	35	1		1
67	Parrott, Saml			1		1
68	Parrott, Bethany					1
69	Parrott, Elly			1		
70	Parrott, Henry	200		1		
71	Parrott, Job	180	50	1		
72	Palmer, Wm	300	866	1		
73	Pierce, George	800		1		
74	Pulliam, Robt W.					1

		[1]	[2]	[3]	[4]	[5]
R						
75	Redder, Robt	.		1		
76	Reece, Henry			1		
77	Roadman, Wm C	200				3
78	Reece, N. L.					2
79	Robinson, Wm	160				
80	Shields, David	100	100			
81	Shields, Wm			1		
82	Swagerty, S. H.			1		
83	Swatsell, Jacob					1
84	Swatsell John					
85	Swatsell, Isaac			1		
86	Swatsell, William [?]					1
87	Smith, Henry					1
T						
88	Teter, George			1		
W						
89	Worth, William		250	1		
90	Ward, Gabriel			1		
91	Wood, John		142			
92	Wikel [?] Joseph		260			
93	Wyatt, L. D.	80	120	1		
Y						
94	Yearout, Jno		240	1		
95	Young, L. B.			1		
96	York, Hannah		10 [?]			
Dist 4						
A						
1	Alway, Isaac		200			
B						
2	Bullman, Jno W.			1		
3	Buckner, Edward			1		
4	Broyls, Cyrus	40	640	1	1	
5	Brady, Nancy		45			
6	Buckner, Wm		275	1		
7	Brizendine, James			1		
8	Bragg, William	200	200		1	
9	Brizendine, Jno	25	90			
10	Bibee, Wm (Heirs)		168			
C						
11	Chunn, Joseph		220			
12	Cureton, Richard	229	348	1	5	
13	Cox, Sampson			1		
14	Conway, James T.	624		1	3	
15	Carter, Wm.	262	1,100			
16	Cureton, Robt		900			
17	Campbell, Jno	50				
18	Christian, Anthony		100			

		[1]	[2]	[3]	[4]	[5]
D						
19	Dawson, Isaac	100	400			
20	Davis, James			1		
21	Davis, Wm		40	1		
22	Driskell, Nancy	70	200		3	
23	Davis, Nancy	110	27			
24	Davis, Reps J	181	150			
25	Driskell, Moses	60	250	1		
26	Dickson, Thomas	149		1		
27	Driskell, Davy	200	330	1	1	
28	Easterly, Thos J			1	1	
29	Ellis, Elbert	55	175	1		
30	Fowler, Larkin			1		
31	Fox, John			1		
32	Fox, Absolum	242		1		
33	Fox, William			1		
G						
34	Gallaher, Wm			1		
35	Gragg, Thos M		100			
H						
36	Hale, Thos L		133			
37	Hale, Joseph	38	67			
38	Hale, Patrick H	20				
39	Holdway, Hezekiah			1		
40	Harrel, Baldwin	100	60			
41	Holt, Zebadee		85			
42	Hale, Hugh D		170			
43	Hudson, Jno	62	29	1		
44	Hudson, Sterling	48	14			
45	Holt, Josiah	50		1		
46	Holt, Paschal	30		1		
47	Holt, Asa	112	400			
48	Holdway, Wm		200	1		
49	Harvey, James			1		
50	Hurly, Zachariah	150	50			
51	Holt, Wm			1		
52	Hall, Wm	100	115	1		
53	Hickey, Saml H		72			
54	Holt, Edward		215			
55	Holt, Jas. S.		20			
56	Inman, Charles	46	[2] 320	1	1	
57	Inman, Lices		120			
58	Inman, Thos W.	327		1		
59	Inman, S. H.	222		1	6	
60	Jones, Daniel (Heirs)	125	70		6	
61	Jones, W. P.	54	100			
62	Jones, Daniel			1		
63	Jones, Thos. M.			1		
64	Jett, Edward			1		
65	Jones, James			1		

		[1]	[2]	[3]	[4]	[5]
66	Kesterson, Nancy	50				
67	Kelly, John Esqr		125	1		
L						
68	Lofty, Wm	71	50	1		
M						
69	Mayfield, Wm					
70	Mason, Joel	180	(2) 52		2	
71	Malony, W. C.		130			
72	Moore, Dempsey	8	(2) 600			
73	Myers, Allen	(3) 610	(2) 98	1		
74	Moore, William	800			8	
75	Martin, James W.	44	60	1		
76	Martin, James			1		
N						
77	Nowland, Wiley		(3) 327	1		
78	Nelson, W. D.					
O						
79	Odum, Tilmon			1		
80	Odum, John		(2) 120	1		
P						
81	Palmer, Wm		50			
82	Phillips, Martin [?]	108		1		
83	Pucket, Rice N.		400			
R						
84	Roddy & Jones	273	18	2	1	
85	Reams, Danl			1		
86	Roberts, John			1		
87	Roberts, Mark			1		
88	Reed, Geo		(2) 275			
89	Ragle, Wm K		(3) 375	1		
S						
90	Stuart, John		250	1		
91	Smith, Nancy (Heirs)	100				
92	Solomon, John			1		
93	Solomon, James	116	100			
94	Smith, Rebecca	100	75			
95	Smith, Wm C.	100		1		
96	Smith, Mariah				1	
97	Solomon, Nicholas			1		
98	Solomon, Owin			1		
99	Scruggs, Abijah	230	(4) 815			
100	Scruggs, Richd		2½			
101	Smith, Thos Senr	266	100			
102	Smith, Thos Junr			1		
103	Smith, Asa		200	1		
104	Still, James & Co.	15	325			
105	Smith, Wm	(2) 217				
106	Smith, Simon		200	1		

		[1]	[2]	[3]	[4]	[5]
107	Smith, Lewis	100				
108	Solomon, Wm	75	50			
109	Smith, Saml D	100	160	1	5	
110	Smith, Caleb W.			1		
111	Smith, David		20			
112	Smith, John	75				
113	Smith, Robert R			1		
T						
114	Tally, John		125	1		
115	Taylor, John		100	1		
116	Tally, Benoni			1		
117	Thomas, John		50			
118	Tally, James	46	200	1		
119	Tally, Carter	100			5	
120	Tally, Bradly W.			1		
121	Tally, James H.			1		
122	Turner, James	122	246			
123	Turner, John		250	1		
124	Tally, Dudly	134	75		1	
125	Turner, L. D.			1		
V						
126	Voils, Amos	135				
W						
127	Worth, John Sen.	50	32			
128	Worth, Wm		30			
129	Worth, Jessee			1		
130	Worth, John	75	30			
District 5						
A B						
1	Bibee, Wm W	30	178	1		
2	Bishop, Edward			1		
3	Beard, Allen			1		
C						
4	Christian, Thos. E. (2)	198	40	1		
5	Christian, James	79	800	1		
6	Christian, Anthony, Sr.	64	(2) 180		1	
7	Christian Anthony	250	65	1		
8	Colfee, Wm	100		1		
9	Coleman, Wm	170	100			
10	Clark, Shelton (Heirs)	232	100		3	
11	Clark, James	293	100	1	11	
12	Clark, John (Heirs)	191	180			
13	Crookshanks, G. M.	370	100	1	3	
14	Cooper, William			1		
15	Carter, Wm by H. Smith	100	310			
16	Cherrytree, Thomas			1		
17	Coleman, G. M.			1		
18	Edington, Martin			1		
19	Edington, James			1		

		[1]	[2]	[3]	[4]	[5]
F						
20	Fox, Ransom			1		
21	Franklin, L. D.	200		1	8	
22	Farles, William			1		
G						
23	Gooch, Wm	60	100			
24	Gooch, John			1		
25	Gooch, Austin	35		1		
26	Gillett, Jno	(3) 98	322	1		
27	Gillett, A. J.			1		
28	Graham, Wm	20				
H						
29	Hurly, James			1		
30	Hudson, Sterling			1		
31	Huff, Wm		(2) 104	1		
32	Haney, Haywood			1		
33	Haney, Lewis		45	1		
34	Holt, Jas S			1		
35	Hale, H. L.			1		
36	Hudson, Obadiah	180		1		
37	Hardin, John			1		
J						
38	Jarnagin, D. N.			1		
39	Jenkins, Washington			1		
40	Jones, William			1		
K						
41	Kelly, Bryson			1		
42	Kelly, Charles	10	250	1		
L						
43	Lovel, John	126	374			
44	Lovel, John H.			1		
45	Lenox, John Senr		550			
46	Lenox, John Jun			1		
M						
47	Morris, Howel			1		
48	Moore, Wm		235	1		
49	Moore, Wm Junr			1		
50	Moore, White [?]	125	277	1	2	
51	Maning, David	100		1		
O						
52	Ottinger, Joseph	200		1		
53	Oniel Jno & Henry			2		
P						
54	Paul, Sarah		50			
55	Patterson, John		158	1		
R						
56	Ramsey, Andrew	185	60			
57	Ramsey, John			1		

		[1]	[2]	[3]	[4]	[5]
58	Rodgers, Robt (He)	495	44	3	3	
59	Rodgers, I. W.	354			3	
60	Rodgers, Thomas	430	300		3	
61	Rodgers, J. A.	372	150		3	
S						
62	Smith, John B. M.	166	6	1		
63	Smith, Simon	26	200			
64	Story, Thomas	112	100	1		
65	Shaver, Stark			1		
66	Smith, John Junr	100	150	1		
67	Sartin, Allen			1		
T						
68	Thomas, John		330	1		
69	Wood, Jno	331	184			
70	Wood, David	136	266		3	
71	Wice, Simon		25			
72	Wice, John		150			

District 6

A

1	Allen, Daniel	270		1		
2	Anderson, Thos			1		
3	Allen, John					½ 35
4	Adcock, James			1		

B

5	Ball, Lunsford			1		
6	Baxter, Aaron					7
7	Bugg, Thomas			1		
8	Bryan, Jas M			1		
9	Birdseye, Ezekiel	8	500			

C

10	Cureton Wm			1		25
11	Chamberlain, D. C.			1	1	
12	Click, Wm	200		1		
13	Coleman, Mary	40	150			
14	Click, Geo L	150				
15	Clark, Aaron R.			1		
16	Carny, John	69				

D

17	Dameron, Wm B			1		
18	Dawson, James			1		12

E

19	Evans, Elijah	188				
20	Evans, D. T.			1		
21	Evans, Wm			1		
22	Evans, Jessee			1		
23	Evans, Thos C			1		
24	Edmonds, Wm			1		
25	Earnest, Amos			1		

		[1]	[2]	[3]	[4]	[5]
F						
26	Fox, Jackson			1		
27	Fox, Ezekiel	40	60	1		
28	Fout, Jacob					½-39
29	Faubion, Jacob	300	300	1		
30	Finchum, Wm			1		
31	Finchum, James			1		
G						
32	Graham, Wm	7				
33	Gray, George	13				
34	Gray, Geo & James					37
35	Gilliams			1		
H						
36	Hudlin, James			1		
37	Hall, Jno W	200		1		
38	Hall, Royal	115		1		
39	Hall, W. S.			1		
40	Hare, Peter	400				
41	Has [blurred] Saml	168				9
42	Hurley, Danl A.	50	200			
43	Hill, Eli			1		
44	Hollingsworth, Eli H.	40				½ 40
45	Howel, Jno J	10	45			36
46	Huff, Wm	342	168			
47	Henry, Spencer			1		
48	Henly, Thos O			1		
J						
49	Jack, Henry	203	133		11	
50	Jones, Calvin M.			1		
51	Jenkins, Augustine[21]					
52	Inman, Joshua			1		
53	Inman, Green	200		1		
54	Icenhower, Martin	400		1		
K						
55	Kendrick, Edom	(2) 327½	150		6	
56	Kendrick, Geo W			1		
57	Kendrick, Edom J.			1		
58	Kendrick, Fine P.			1		
59	Kelly, Jonathan			1		
L						
60	Lotspeich, Saml	408			2	
61	Lotspeich & Henry					11
M						
62	Miller, Jonathan			1		
63	McKoy, Jeremiah	241	25			
64	McKoy, Abraham	257	101		1	
65	McKoy, James			1		
66	McLain, Houston			1		

[21] Under town lots he was listed as owning "Back lots" numbered 49, 10, 11½.

		[1]	[2]	[3]	[4]	[5]
67	McLain, John			1		
68	Maning, Joseph	200		1	1	
69	Mathis, Alexr	5	25	1		
70	McMahan, Anderson	(2) 285		1	2	
71	McMahan, Allen	140		1		
72	McSween, Saml			1	½	23 40
73	McSween, Wm			1		
74	Mealer, Robert			1		
75	McFarland, Moses			1		
76	McFarland, Erasmus			1		
77	Milliken, Deborah Ad	100 1				
78	Moon, John			1		
79	Morris, Wm	125	153	1		
80	McCurry, Robt	20		1		
O						
81	Odell, Benjamin	145	15			
82	Odell, Lewis			1		
83	Odell, David			1		
84	Odell, Job			1		
85	Odell, Abraham			1		
86	Oneil, Harrison			1		
P						
87	Patterson, Edmond			1		
88	Porter, L. D.			1		10
89	Pulliam, Rosl W.			1	3	32; 31
R						
90	Rankin & Pulliam	40				
91	Rankin, Wm D	13		1	2	34
92	Robinson, Wm	200		1		
93	Rodman, W. C.[22]	(8) 670			5	
94	Roadman, Wm C Junr			1		
S						
95	Stuart, John	890		1	6	35; 36
96	Stanberry, Jno F			1		7
97	Story, Wm C	200	(2) 60	1	1	
98	Shields, Jno P			1		
99	Stinnet, James			1		
100	Stephens, Danl	472		1		
101	Sluder [?] Francis			1		
102	Shannon, Hugh			1		
103	Smith Alexr E.	1025		1	23	53
104	Swaggerty, James	500		1	3	
105	Sisk, Bartlet	175				
106	Thompson, Robt H			1		

[22] He was listed as owning lots numbered 13, 14, 15, 16, 42, 1, 2, 5, 6, 42, 28, 29, 30, 24, 3, 4, 5, 6, 7, 8.

		[1]	[2]	[3]	[4]	[5]
107	Thomas, Jno G.			1		
108	Thomas, George	466			1	
109	Turnmyer Saml	100		1		
W						
110	Wiley, Geo	368	200	1		
111	Wiley, Elijah			1		
112	Wiley, Geo Jr.			1		
113	Whitaker, Wm			1		
114	Wood, John					1
115	Womble, John			1		
116	Weaver, James	(2) 400			3	
117	Umstead, R. H.			1		

7th District

A

1	Allen, John		100	1		
2	Anderson, Joseph			1		
3	Anderson, James			1		

B

4	Boyer, John	42	220			
5	Brown, Elijah			1		
6	Bennett, P. M.			1		
7	Broderick, Hugh		50			

C

8	Carson, Saml	16				
9	Cody, Stephen			1		
10	Cody, Godfrey			1		
11	Chunn, Saml	555			4	
			50			
12	Cameron, Joseph		46			
13	Clark, James	542	135		6	
14	Carter, Geo & W	908	950	2	5	
15	Carter, E. C.			1		
16	Clevinger, Asa			1		
17	Chilton, Thos			1		
18	Coffee, Reuben		81¼	1		
19	Clark, Francis			1		

D

20	DeWitt, Richd B	400		1	3	

E

21	Epps, Geo		150			
22	Emry, Joel			1		
23	Evans, Edmond	50				

F

24	Francis, Burgess			1		
25	Francis, Edison		226			
26	Francis, Archibald		100	1		
27	Francis, Wm		200	1		
28	Fox, George		50			

		[1]	[2]	[3]	[4]	[5]
29	Fru, John	76½				
30	Fru, James		55	1		
31	Fine, Abraham	438		1	4	
32	Fine, Isaac		40	1		
33	Franklin, Wm			1		
34	Finry, Joseph					
G						
35	Gorman, John Junr		300	1		
36	Gann, John	80	74			
37	Gray, Wm	145	14	1	1	
			74			
38	Gorman, John Senr	364	29			
39	Gray, George	73	190			
40	Gorman, Thos			1		
H						
41	Hipps, Jno H.			1		
42	Howel, Jno J		517			
43	Holloway, Wm			1		
44	Holloway, Jos			1		
45	Hall, Saml			1		
46	Hightower, Allen			1		
47	Hewitt, Jno		100	1		
48	Henry, Robt		100	1		
49	Hunt Jno (Free negro)		110			
J						
50	James, Wm		184			
51	Jones, Thomas		167	1		
52	Jones, Henry	83				
53	Jones, John			1		
54	James, F. R.			1		
55	Jack, Wm	625		1	1	
L						
56	Larew, George	209¼	164			
57	Lain, Wm			1		
58	Lain, John		150			
59	Lain, Aza		150			
60	Larew, Francis			1		
61	Larew, James			1		
62	Lake, Jane		300			
M						
63	Milliken, Hiram or Alexr		100	1		
64	McSween, Murdock	169	90		1	
65	Milliken, Deberah		100			
66	Morell, Charles		140			
67	Maxwell, Matthew			1		
68	Mainos, Amos			1		
69	McKay, Geo G for Jane		50			
70	McKay, Geo G.			1		
71	McNabb, John			1		
72	McGinty, Abner ?			1		

		[1]	[2]	[3]	[4]	[5]
N						
73	Newcom, Levi			1		
74	Newcom, Jane		100			
75	Newcom, Wm			1		
76	Nichols, Richd (Free negro)		50			
77	Newcom, Thornton		500			
O						
78	Ogden, Wm	216½		1		
79	Oneil, Joseph	127	50	1		
P						
80	Porter, Geo M	187	150	1	2	
81	Do Guardian for A Cockran				4	
82	Prewit, Polly		100			
83	Prewitt, Saml			1		
84	Prewitt, Wm			1		
85	Prewitt, Danl		100			
Q						
86	Quarrels, Jonathan		37½			
R						
87	Roadman, Wm C Sen	300	142			
88	Rutherford, Joseph	100	20	1		
S						
89	Snead, Henly, Senr	340				
90	Snead, Henly Junr			1		
91	Snead, Pleasant			1		
92	Samms[?] Kerby			1		
93	Strange, Wm		150	1		
94	Sarrett, Allen		80			
95	Sims, Elliott Sen		170			
96	Sims, Elliott Jur	135		1		
97	Sims, Geo G.		300			
98	Sims, Wm K			1		
99	Seahorn, Wm G		300	1		
100	Samples, Josiah			1		
101	Smith, Alexr E.		320			
102	Singleton, James		1			
103	Sweatman, Josiah			1		
104	Seansell, John			1		
105	Townsend, Thos		250	1		
106	Taylor, Eleanor	16				
107	Taylor, James		150			
W						
108	Wood, John		180			
	Mill tract bot of McKay		200			
109	Ward, Cyrus	168½	75			
110	Wilson, Wm	454	330	1	3	
111	Wilson, Barnett	230	100	1	1	
112	Walden, Richd			1		
113	Wood, Jonathan		167			
114	West, Lewis			1		

8th District		[1]	[2]	[3]	[4]	[5]
A						
1	Allen, Jas R	360		1	3	
B						
2	Barton, Solomon			1		
3	Burk, Joseph	100				
4	Burk, John			1		
5	Brooks, David			1		
6	Brooks, Matthew	50				
7	Ball, Alfred			1		
C						
8	Clevinger, Elias	(5) 449½			1	
9	Clevinger, Samuel			1		
10	Clevinger, Allen			1		
11	Cameron, Martin			1		
12	Click, Geo W			1		
13	Click, P. W.	200		1		
D						
14	Dillon, Margaret	145			1	
15	Dillon, John			1		
16	Dillon, James	160				
17	Dewitt, Nancy	84				
18	Davis, John	150				
19	Davis, Martin			1		
E						
20	Ellis, John	125				
21	Ellis, Moses	60		1		
22	Ellis, Nathan	80		1		
F						
23	Fox, Jno Sr.	50		1		
24	Fox, James			1		
25	Fox, William			1		
26	Fox, Anderson			1		
27	Frasier, Martin			1		
28	Frasier, Ben.			1		
29	Fine, Vinet			1		
G						
30	Gray, James	144	87	1		
31	Gray, George	261		1		
32	Gray, Wm	63	20			
33	Gann, George	100		1		
H						
34	Hartsell, Isaac	100				
35	Humboard, Isaac	266		1		
36	Hall, Samuel		360			
J						
37	Johnson, Joseph	151		1	2	
K						
38	Kelly, Wm		50			

		[1]	[2]	[3]	[4]	[5]
L						
39	Lea, Agness	275			1	
40	Loyd, Pleasant		2	1		
41	Lea, Stephen		50			
M						
42	Mantooth, James		137	1		
[43]	Mantooth, James			1		
[44]	Mantooth, James			1		
[45]	Mantooth, Wm			1		
[46]	Mantooth, Elizabeth	200				
47	McNabb, George	414	250			
48	Morris, Wm		400			
49	McNabb, Garrett			1		
50	McNabb, Malcolm			1		
51	McNabb, Margaret	100	75			
52	Mantooth, Letty	130				
53	Markes [?] Alexr	50				
54	McNabb, James	125	15	1		
55	Morell, Charles			1		
56	McSween, Murdock		100			
57	McNabb, John	100		1		
58	McMillian, Saml			1		
59	McMahan, Sanders	150	25	1		
60	Mantooth, Jno Junr	344		1		
61	Mantooth, Thomas			1		
62	Mantooth, Samuel			1		
N						
63	Netherton, John			1		
64	Netherton, James			1		
65	Netherton, Enoch	100				
O						
66	Oniel, Joseph		31			
P						
67	Phillips, John			1		
R						
68	Runion, Henry		200	1		
69	Rutherford, Pleast			1		
70	Rutherford, Cal			1		
71	Rutherford, Eliz	200				
72	Roadman, Wm C	288				
73	Robinson, Isaac			1		
S						
74	Sisk, Tolover	311		1		
75	Sisk, Bartlet	60		1		
76	Swagerty, Ab			1		
T						
77	Thomas, George	160				
V						
78	Vinson, Wm	287	188			
79	Vinson, Wm.			1		

		[1]	[2]	[3]	[4]	[5]
W						
80	Wood, Ashly			1		
81	Wood, Wm			1		
82	Wood, Gipson			1		
83	Wood, John	794		1	3	
84	Wallace, Pleasant	150				

9th District

		[1]	[2]	[3]	[4]	[5]
A						
1	Allen, John	411			4	
2	Do of G. North Decd				3	
3*	Allen, Abraham	20	139	1		
4	Allen, William	70	50	1		
5	Allen, Calvin			1		
6	Allen, George			1		
B						
7	Butler, Isaiah	154	100	1		
8	Baxter, Aaron	280	100			
9	Bryant, Tarlton	291	625	1		
10	Breeden, Elijah	55	47			
11	Bailey, James F.			1		
12	Bryant, Brummit			1		
13	Bird, Dennis	66	50	1		
14	Bryant, James H			1		
15	Bryant, Polly		50			
16	Brooks, Wright			1		
17	Brooks, Mark			1		
C						
18	Caughron, Samuel		500	1		
19	Click, Lewis A.	160	115	1		
20	Click, Henry	50	159			
21	Click, James	218	50	1		
22	Click, H. J.	3	100	1		
23	Clevinger, John	63	72			
24	Clevinger, William		50	1		
25	Case, Saxton		300			
26	Case, John			1		
27	Cavender, F. A.		250	1		
28	Carr, Benjamin			1		
29	Carroll, Willis			1		
30	Clevinger, Jackson			1		
31						
32	Cross, Wm			1		
33	Clevinger, Alexd			1		
D						
34	Denton, Jonathan			1		
35	Denton, Alfred	111	110	1		
36	Denton, Abraham	132	12	1		
37	Denton, Jefferson		3910	1		
38	Denton, John			1		

		[1]	[2]	[3]	[4]	[5]
39	Denton, Jackson			1		
40	Duncan, Wm		30	1		
41	Davis, Wm	25				
42	Davis, Alfred			1		
43	Denton, Francis	395	12½			
44	Dennis, Cary	75		1		
F						
45	Fine, Thomas			1		
46	Fine, John			1		
47	Fine, Abraham (Blk)			16		
48	Felker, Wm	251	70	1		
49	Fru, William			1		
50	Fru, George			1		
G						
51	Garret, John	100	50	1		
52	Gray, Wm	10	160			
53	Gray, James Senr	175			5	
54	Gray, Willis	123	113	1		
55	Gilleland, John		20	1		
56	Gregory, Archibald	50	100	1		
57	Gregory, Samuel			1		
H						
58	Hickey, Joseph	124		1		
59	Hickey, Henry	123		1		
60	Hartgrove, Thomas	88	85			
61	Hicks, Moses Senr	17	35			
62	Hicks, James			1		
63	Hicks, Timothy			1		
64	Hicks, Joseph			1		
65	Henry, Wm			1		
66	Henry, Jno Junr			1		
67	Henry, Robert			1		
68	Hartsell, Charles	53	131	1		
69	Hartsell, Morris	100	50	1		
70	Hartsell, Jacob			1		
71	Huff, John	178	122			
72	Huff, Peter			1		
73	Huff, William	3	200			
74	Hatly, John			1		
75	Hatly, Elias			1		
I						
76	Irvine, Alfred	100		1		
L						
77	Lillard, James			1		
78	Lax, Elizabeth		90			
79	Lewis, Joel		52			
80	Lewis, Wm			1		
81	Lewis Jno (B)			1		
82	Lewis, Martin			1		
83	Lewis Richd			1		

		[1]	[2]	[3]	[4]	[5]
84	Lewis, Samuel			1		
85	Lane, Royal			1		
86	Lane, John	78	210			
87	Murr, Wm			1		
88	Murrel Job	80	183	1		
89	Murr, Jeremiah		100	1		
90	Millsaps, Peter			1		
91	McNabb, Wm.			1		
92	Mantooth, Jno Junr			1		
93	Murrel, Jno		40			
94	Norris, Hugh			1		
95	Miller, S. K.		150	1		
96	Odell, William	209				
97	Odell, Caleb	71	129	1		
98	Odell, Esther		70	1		
99	Odell, Rachel		30			
100	Roadman, Wm. C.	150				
101	Rutherford, Robt.			1		
102	Roberts, George	197	25			
103	Sims, Geo. G.			1		
104	Sisk, Bartlet Senr.	270			1	
105	Sisk, Blackburn			1		
106	Sisk, Elias	195		1		
107	Stuart, Thomas	130	50			
108	Sisk, Lawson			1		
109	Taylor, Jno. W.			1		
110	Templin, Jacob	81	186			
111	Watson, Jacob			1		
[112]	Wilson, Thomas	23	78	1		
[113]	Williams, Thos. L.	125		1		
[114]	Wood, John	153				

10th District

A

		[1]	[2]	[3]	[4]	[5]
1	Allen, John (L)	106	(3) 420		1	
2	Allen, Isaac			1		
3	Allen, Russel			1		
4	Allen, James Junr			1		
5	Allen, John (Capt.)	574¼	664¼			
6	Allen, John Junr			1		

B

		[1]	[2]	[3]	[4]	[5]
7	Baxter, James	(4) 172	(4) 1,091	1		
8	Baxter, Johns			1		
9	Broyls, Saml	147	200			
10	Balentine, Henry			1		
11	Bryant Mary		50	1		
12	Bates, Martin		15	1		
13	Baker, Gilbert		5000			
14	Barnes, John			1		
15	Brooks, David		50	1		

		[1]	[2]	[3]	[4]	[5]
C						
16	Clark, Jno H			1		
17	Coleman, Spencer			1		
18	Caton, Stephen			1		
19	Campbell, Joseph		50	1		
20	Clark, Moses			1		
D						
21	Dennis, Joel	(4) 173	(2) 65		1	
22	Dennis Robert	57	25	1		
23	Dennis, John	57	25	1		
24	Dennis, Mark			1		
25	Denton, Abraham		(3) 136			
26	Dewitt, Nancy	75				
27	Dennis, Cary		125			
28	Ellington, Saml			1		
29	Earps, Elijah			1		
30	Earp, Phillip			1		
31	Earp, Thos		2250	1		
F						
32	Fowler, Jno F		500			
G						
33	Gilleland, Wm		200			
34	Green, James			1		
35	Green, Wm	43	25	1		
36	Green, John		400	1		
37	Giles, Jessee	61	50			
38	Giles, Holloway			1		
H						
39	Harrison, John			1		
40	Harrison, Reuben	40	(2) 400			
41	Hicks, David		(2) 90	1		
42	Holder, John			1		
43	Harper, Wm.			1		
44	Howat, Jno J		75			
45	Huff, Sarah				1	
46	Huff, Elizabeth	189	50			
J						
47	Jenkins, Jessee			1		
48	Jenkins, Augustine			1		
49	Jenkins, Phillip	20	(6) 190			
50	Jenkins, Wm	49	2500	1		
51	Jenkins, Joel		50	1		
52	Jenkins, Delilah		(4) 95			
53	Jenkins, John			1		
L						
54	Large, John	34	100			
55	Large, Robt		(3) 100	1		
56	Lillard, John	(5) 216	(2) 77	1		
57	Leatherwood, Daniel	40		1		
58	Leatherwood, Willis		(2) 155	1		

		[1]	[2]	[3]	[4]	[5]
M						
59	McMahan, Eli	(3) 256	50			
60	McMahan, Wm Junr	15¼	50	1		
61	McMahan, Sevier			1		
62	McMahan, Redman	50	50			
63	McMahan, Wm		(3) 450	1		
64	Moore, John			1		
65	Mathes, Joel P.			1		
66	McGaha, Robert	(8) 595		1		
67	McGaha, Saml	115		1		
68	McMillian, Joseph			1		
69	McKoy, Geo G.		(2) 5100			
70	McCoy G. John			1		
71	Moore, William		1000			
72	Metcalf, Hezekiah		50			
73	McGaha, Isaac		(2) 475	1		
74	Miller, Elizabeth	(3) 73				
75	McMahan, Eli Junr	(2) 419				
76	McMahan, James			1		
P						
77	Prewit, James			1		
78	Paget, Joseph	84	(2) 375	1		
79	Peck, Talbert Isham & Adam		5000			
80	Peck, Wm R. & Wiley		5000			
R						
81	Robinson, Edward			1		
82	Rains, Wm		76			
83	Rains, James			1		
84	Rains, Joel	111	42			
85	Ramsey, Jno		25	1		
86	Ramsey, Geo		200	1		
87	Ramsey, Wm			1		
88	Ramsey, Jessee			1		
89	Robinson, Jno					
90	Rogers, Saml		(2) 200			
91	Roadman, Wm C		100			
S						
92	Styles, Zachariah			1		
93	Sams, Warren		300			
94	Smith, Giles		25			
95	Smith, Mitchel		45			
96	Smith, William		50			
97	Smith, W. N.		13	1		
98	Smith, Charity				1	
99	Shults, Jacob	65	65	1		
100	Shults, Martin	15	125			
101	Sutton, Cornelius			1		
W						
102	Webb, William	108		1		
103	Webb, John	75		1		

		[1]	[2]	[3]	[4]	[5]
104	Willhite, Keziah	184				
105	Webb, Joseph	(3) 107	(7) 556	1		
106	Webb, Eli			1		
[107]	Williamson, Reuben			1		
[108]	Williamson, Elizabeth		100			
[109]	Weaver, John	(2) 263	(3) 165			
[110]	Williams, Collins			1		
[111]	Williams, William		200			
[112]	Williams, Jourdan		25			
Y						
[113]	Youngblood	37	100	1		

Aggregate of Taxes for 1839 Cocke County

District	A. Land	Value	S. Land	Value	Town Lots	Value	Slaves	Value	White Polls
1st	4404	35745	62595	11379			23	9000	64
2nd	11513	52459	8663	11372			23	10800	77
3rd	7262	33159	12182	9248	36	5607	11	4900	61
4th	8148	56346	13571	12090			51	21800	75
5th	5692	61941	6818	11145			36	16800	57
6th	9209	83790	2685	3297	45½	16515	64	29500	87
7th	5121½	49335	8517½	7795			37	15700	70
8th	7256½	36625	1800	1515			11	3556	57
9th	6129	24405	9205	6295			13	5700	86
10th	3781	18494	35552	9700			3	1300	74

2 T Pike Roads on 1st district 8000[23]

| | 68516 | 461099 | 161588½ | 82836 | 81½ | 22122 | 272 | 119050 | 708 |

State of Tennessee
Cocke County

I William McSween Clerk of Cocke County Court Certeify that the foregoing is a correct duplicate list of the Taxes of Cocke County for the year 1839,
which Abraham Fine Sheriff and collector of the public Taxes for said County
is bound to collect and account for as directed by Act of Assembly
June 1st 1839

William McSween, Clerk

Value

Carriages Dist. 6-2   275

---

[23] There were also 2 carriages in district 6 with total value of $275.

EARLY EAST TENNESSEE TAXPAYERS
Compiled by POLLYANNA CREEKMORE

XIV. Greene County, 1783[1]

Greene County was established by an act of the North Carolina general assembly on April 18, 1783, the third established in the territory now the state of Tennessee. The act provided that Washington County, established six years before, (but reduced in size somewhat by the creation of Sullivan County in 1779), should be divided into two counties by

> . . . a direct line beginning at William Williams, in the Fork of Horse Creek, at the foot of the Iron Mountain, thence a direct line to George Gallespie's house, at or near the mouth of Big Limestone, thence a north course to the line which divides the counties of Washington and Sullivan, thence from the said line, to the Chimney-Top Mountain, thence a direct course to the mouth of Cloud Creek in Holstein River; and all that part of Washington county westward of the said line, . . . is declared to be a distinct county by the name of Greene.[2]

The county was named in honor of General Nathanael Greene, prominent Revolutionary War leader.

Since the western boundary of Washington County at that time was the Mississippi River,[3] it is obvious that Greene County also extended that far west. Part of the original territory was removed on the same day by the creation of Davidson County in Middle Tennessee.[4] By the formation of Knox and Jefferson counties in 1792 by Governor William Blount of the Southwest Territory additional territory was lost. In 1797 Cocke County was created out of Jefferson and in 1799 part of Greene County was attached to Cocke County.[5]

The Greene County's government was organized the third Monday in August, 1783, at the home of Robert Kerr (given as Carr) at

---

[1] For the introduction to this series see *Publications* No. 23 (1951), 115-16. Previous installments have been: I. Anderson County, 1802, in No. 23; II. Blount County, 1801, in No. 24; III. Knox County, 1806, in No. 26; IV. Grainger County, 1799, in No. 27; V. Jefferson County, 1800, in No. 28; VI. Carter County, 1796, in No. 30; VII. Sullivan County, 1796, in No. 31; VIII. Hawkins County, 1809-1812, in No. 32; IX, Greene County, 1805, in No. 33; X. Washington County, 1778, in No. 34; XI. Washington County, 1787, in No. 35; XII. Campbell County, 1818, in No. 36; XIII. Cocke County, 1839, in No. 37.

[2] W. L. Saunders and Walter Clark (eds.), *The Colonial and State Records of North Carolina*, 30 vols. (Raleigh, 1886-1907), XXIV, 539-40. Hereafter cited N.C.S.R.

[3] *Ibid.*, 141.

[4] *Ibid.*, 540.

[5] George Roulstone (comp.), *Laws of the State of Tennessee* (Knoxville, 1803), iv-v, 124-26, 168.

the site of present Greeneville. The first justices of the peace were Joseph Hardin, John Newman, George Doherty (or Dougherty), James Houston, Amos Bird, and Asahel Rawlings. Daniel Kennedy was chosen clerk; James Wilson, sheriff; William Cocke, attorney for the state; Joseph Hardin, Jr., entry taker; Isaac Taylor, surveyor; Richard Woods, register; and Francis Hughes, ranger.[6]

The next day the Court laid the county off into four districts, as follows:

> the first district beginning at John Tools from thence & direct course to Wm. Stocktons thence a to the mouth of plumb creek, thence up said Creek to Bay Mountain including the Northern part of this County.
>
> The Second district beginning at John Tools thence to the County line. thence with the Said line to Nolachucky [Nolichucky] River. thence down said River to the mouth of Richland Creek thence to Jas. Delaneys, thence to Richard Woods, thence to Isaac Bullards, thence a direct course to Bay Mountain, thence to the line of the first district.
>
> Third district including all the residue of Sd. County the North Side of Nolachuckey & French Broad River.
>
> Fourth District including all the South Side of Nolachuckey.[7]

Asahel Rawlings was appointed to record the inventory for the first district, James Houston for the second, Amos Bird for the third, and George Doherty for the fourth. At the same time assessors were appointed for each district: first, Lanty Armstrong, Owen Owens, and William Stockton; second, Alexander Gilbreath, Ebenezer Alexander, and Major Temple; third, Gideon Richey, James Dillard, and Henry Conway; fourth, Alexander Kelly, Jeremiah Jack, and Henry Earnest. Also, John Harmond, James Robinson, Joseph Box, and Robert Orn were appointed constables in each of the respective districts to notify the inhabitants to give in a list of taxable property.[8]

The assessors made their returns to the court the first week in February, 1784, and at the same time the constables were allowed one dollar per day for their services. At this session of the court, Asahel Rawlings was appointed tax gatherer for the first district, John Houston for the second, Amos Bird for the third, and James Kenny for the fourth.[9]

---

[6] Greene County Minutes of Court of Pleas and Quarter sessions (Courthouse, Greeneville; typewritten copy, transcribed by Historical Records Survey, McClung Collection, Lawson McGhee Library), 1.
[7] *Ibid.*
[8] *Ibid.*, 1-2.
[9] *Ibid.*, 4-5.

According to North Carolina legislation of 1782,

> . . . all lots and lands, with their improvements, slaves under the age
> of sixty years, horses, mules and cattle, from one year old and upwards,
> and stock in trade, shall be held and deemed taxable property. . . .

Also, the county assessors were required to "return into the clerk's office . . . a fair state of the taxable property in their districts respectively, distinguishing the quantity and valuation of taxable property," under the following headings: "Persons Names, Acres of Land, Negroes from one to seven, and from fifty to sixty years of age. Negroes from seven to sixteen, and from forty to fifty years of age. Negroes from sixteen to forty years of age. Horses and mules. Cattle. Stock in trade. Carriage wheels. Value of each persons property carried out." It was also provided in the same law that all cattle one year old or more should be "rated at twenty shillings per head"; slaves under seven and between fifty and sixty "at twenty pounds each"; slaves between the ages of seven and sixteen and between forty and fifty "at forty pounds each"; slaves between sixteen and forty "at eighty pounds"; and "every wheel affixed to any coach, chariot, phaeton, stage waggon or other carriage of pleasure, be taxed the sum of five shillings specie for each wheel." Finally, it was stated that "every unmarried free man in this State of the age of twenty-one years and upwards, other than soldiers . . . , who shall not possess the value of one hundred pounds in taxable property, shall pay annually, in lieu of assessment on property, a poll tax equal to the tax for that year on one hundred pounds."[10]

The following lists are copied from the original manuscripts in the Calvin Morgan McClung Historical Collection of Lawson McGhee Library. They are presented to the Collection by Professor Benjamin D. Meritt and the late Mrs. Meritt, of Princeton, New Jersey. The papers came down by inheritance from Mrs. Meritt's parents, Chancellor James H. Kirkland and his wife, Mary Henderson Kirkland. The latter was the daughter of Colonel William A. Henderson of Knoxville, long a prominent lawyer and a writer of historical subjects.

It cannot be determined how many original lists once existed, as the County Court Minutes do not record the returns other than the action of the assessors.

---

[10] *N.C.S.R.,* **XXIV,** 429-31.

The late Mrs. Louise Wilson Reynolds published a 1783 alphabetical list in the *D.A.R. Magazine* for April, 1919, presumably copied from documents in her possession.

The following list is endorsed: Assessors Return Third District 1783, Henry Conway, Gidon Richey, James Dillard. There are seven columns after the name with headings T, S, H, C, L, S, D. There are no assessments for any name in the first column; and, it is presumed that the other columns are:

S — Slaves   C — Cattle   S — Shillings
H — Horses   L — Pounds   D — Pence

Name	S	H	C	L	S	D
Robert Box	2	6	12	232	0	0
Joseph Box		12	16	136		
George Brock		3	9	39		
John [illegible]		6	8	68		
James Boyd		3	3	33		
Hugh Brison		1	8	18		
John Biggs		2	3	23		
Bryant Bryants [illegible]		2		20		
Amos Bird	3	24	29	4		
Henry Conway	4	8	16	336		
Jacob Clowers		2	2	22		
Thos Crafford		2		20		
				4		
John Camnass		4	7	27		
Joseph Dunham		21	20	230		
Abraham Duley		6	6	66		
Rebin Dunham		9	3	93		
Nicholas Davis		2	2	22		
Henry Dunham		23	8	238		
James Dillard	4	2	2	263		
Joseph Epperson		1	3	13		
Jonathan Evens		6	9	69		
Thos Eldridge		5	4	54		
Benjamin Goodman		4	4	44		
William Goforth		6	10	70		
James Galaspey		4		44		
John Gilles		3	11	41		
Benjamin Goodman Junr		8	8	88		
James Goodman		3	4	34		
Thos Goodman		6	4	64		
Lm Hubbard		4	4	44		
Drury Hodges		2	6	26		
Richard Hightower		3	1	31		
James Hill		7	13	83		

All numerals overwritten indistinct.

George Haworth		2	2	22
Smith Hutchings		4	4	44
Robert Himall		2	4	24
Welcom Hodges		5	12	62
Shadrick Inman	2	2	16	136
John Jones		3		30
Jacob Johnson		3	10	40
Harmon King		3	5	35
John Keney		14	9	149
Thomas Kilbrath		2	3	23
Robert King		2	4	24
Andrew Leper		5	11	61
		4		
Alexander McFarthing		12	10	150
James McGill		1		10
Robert McGill		1		10
John Murphey		2	9	29
James Mahan		2	7	27
Hugh More		2	12	32
Joseph McPeters		4	3	43
Joseph Nation		7	7	77
Gideon Richey		12	5	125
Isaac Running		2	2	22
James Ruddell		3	2	32
Henry Russell		3		30
Mical Reed		6	6	66
David Reed		2	1	21
Joseph Reed		5	2	52
Thos Ranking			2	2
John Reed		2	2	22
Hardy Skipper		4	1	41
John Smith		3	2	32
Reuben Simpson		3	6	36
Joseph Saratt		4	7	47
Richard Woods	1	3	7	
a Deduction on a Negro				77
Joseph Wilson		9	10	100
William Wiatt		4	7	47
Samuel Wiatt		5	4	54
Richard Webb		2	5	25
Absolom Pennington		2	1	25
				8
Jas Perie [?]	3	4	7	207
David Privet		3	6	36

[Endorsed]   Henry Conway
                     Gideon Richey
                     James Dillard

___

All numerals overwritten indistinct.

The following list is endorsed: Assessors Return 1783 Fourth District
Key to Column Numbers:

[1]	Men's Names	[6]	Bonds on Interest
[2]	Land	[7]	Horses
[3]	1t Rate Negroes	[8]	Neal Cattle
[4]	2d Rate Negroes	[9]	Total Sums
[5]	3d Rate Negroes		

[1]	[2]	[3]	[4]	[5]	[6]	[7]	[8]	[9]
Saml Sherril Senr	400	5		2	4	20	£	6
Saml Sherril Junr	300					3	10	6
James Cosbey		1				9	6	12
Ephraim McDowell	300					3	6	56
John Kelley	100				17-15	3	1	88
David Eagleton	200					7	2	73
Emanuel Seduscuss	296					8	6	123-10
Phillip Sherril	200					5	9	79-10
Thos Buckingham	200	6	1	3		9	15	820
Robert Miller	150					3	8	35
Wm English	400					3	14	70
John Russell	300	2				3	13	246
Shadrach McNew	200					4	11	56
John Johnston	300					4	8	70
Lewis Morgan	200					2	7	60-10
Joseph Dunn						4		Poll Tax
Joseph McMurtry	200					2	7	52
Sd McMurtry								
Orphans Estate	300							103
Abraham Hunt	100					1	1	13
Charles Robertson	400					4	12	90
Jacob McConnel	200					3	4	45
Frederick Swagerty	100					5	3	103-10
Saml Wilson	300					7	6	82
Elisha Sherril	100					4	7	63-10
John McNeil	400					4	4	73
Elisha Baker	300	1				4	1	137
Andrew Miller	350					3	6	74
Joseph Williams	200					3	3	32-10
James Henderson	200					3	6	66
Thomas Hart						2		Poll Tax
John Byrd						2		16
Thomas Davis	270	4	3			3	14	£5 6
Adonijah Morgan								Poll tax
Joseph Doherty	200					5	10	70
David Hickey	100					3	3	28
Abel Ritcheson	300					3	6	54
Wm Job						3	2	20
Nathaniel Curtice						7		7
Samuel Matthews						2	2	7
Thomas Vance						2	0	10
Robert Alison	150					6	9	8 10
William Williams	300					3	2	57

[1]	[2]	[3]	[4]	[5]	[6]	[7]	[8]	[9]
Peter Fine						3	5	30
Joel Mathew	200					2	2	36
James Anderson	200					6	6	66
John Fine	100					1	6	60
Robert O'Neal	550	1				7	14	252
Edward Box	110					2	5	48
Matthias Willhight						4	3	22
Charles Kilgore	200	1		1		7	13	200
Henry Runnells	300					4	10	100
Adam Willhight	200					4	3	63-10
Obadiah Matthews								Poll Tax
John Lee	180					4	6	60
Joseph Bumpers	100					2	0	10
William Hail	100					2	16	80
Joseph Newberry						1	3	10
Austin Hightower						1	4	10
Alexr Montgomery Senr						3	6	24
James Jonson	250					2	9	50
James Alexander					123	2	5	£44
Adam Scott	100					2	1	Poll Tax
Michael Borders	250					10	45	186-10
Henry Box	200					2	2	39
George Reed						2	4	24
Jacob Broyles	293					5	12	75
Lanseylot Armstrong						1		poll tax
Nicholas Neel	200					4	13	82-10
Benjamin Armstrong	250					3	7	57-10
John Web	250					1	6	42
Fethias Walls	300					4	5	66-10
Joseph Cyler [Siler]						2	8	24
Laurens Glaize	640	3				6	5	383-10
Thomas Preator						1		10
Thomas Fiels [torn]						4	7	30-10 [torn]
William Jonston						2	1	27
John Davis	300					8	4	90-10
Thomas Billands	200					3	6	70
Caleb Hubs								poll tax
John Duncan								poll tax
James Jonston [blurred]	400					5	8	117
Edward Eagins	200					4	5	60
Henry Willis	640							58
Alexr Pretherow						3	3	20-10
Cornelis McGuire	300					8	11	134-10
William Boyd						1	5	27-10
David Craig	200				3	3	8	79
Saml Gilberts	600					2	8	74
John Sherril						3	8	40
James Cravens								Poll tax

[1]	[2]	[3]	[4]	[5]	[6]	[7]	[8]	[9]
Joseph Bird	200	2	2	1		9	£11	280
John Kelley	100					3	5	45-10
John Chamberlin						2	6	22
Hoseah Stout	100					4	6	48
John Stephens	45					3	2	33
John Trimble	300					5	8	85
Joseph English	200					7	16	113
Robert Cravens	200					9	7	160
Thomas Gillespy	200					6	19	110-10
Job Runnells	400					2	5	50-10
Hugh Beard	200		1			8	5	200
David Runnells								Poll tax
Adam Peinter	200					2	7	50
Robert Armstrong	300	2				3	7	154-10
James Craig Senr						4		
James Craig Junr	200					2	5	47
John Upton	200					2	10	55
James Millican	200					14	15	130-10
Alexr Montgomery						2	2	9
William Doherty	156					10	9	97-10
James Brown						2	2	12
Adam Sherril	200					7	7	94-10
Joseph Keeney	200					2	3	25
Richard Prior						6	15	57
Wm Bigham	400					6	8	84
Wm Dunn						2	22	18
John Cunningham	100					2	5	23
Thomas Morgan						2	3	8
Francis Hughs	300	2		2	1	6	25	366
Alexr Miller						2	2	14
Elijah Veatch						3	2	17
James Cameron					5	6		£36

A list of poll taxables

Charles Adkinson	Stout Chamberlin
Thomas Rutherford	Thomas Christian
Ferril Megehe	Isam Christian
Cornelis ONeal	Thomas Dixon
Michael Halfacor	Matthew Nail
William Richeson	Abraham Swagertey
Phillip Feint	Jeremiah Veatch
David Jonston	William Robertson
Abner Lee	Saml Norris
George Lee	John Craig
Daniel Creamer	Sebert Sollars

A List of Delinquents

John Baskins	William Boydstun
David Fraim	William Mulholland
Henry Jones	James Ward
William Whitson	Charles Rorux
William Crowson	William Nelson
John Stephenson	William Runnells
Francis Rowan	James Crabtree
John Smith	John Faint
Phillip Conaway	Ephraim Wilson
Nathan Veatch	John Frior
William Bell	James Jervis
James Furman or Turman	John Totton
James Ritchardson	George Doherty [scratched]
Richard Gullet	

The following lists have no identification:

Key to Column Numbers:

[1] Names
[2] Land
[3] Negroes from 1 to 7, and from 50 to 60
[4] Negroes from 7 to 16, and from 40 to 50
[5] Negroes from 16 to 40
[6] Horses
[7] Cattle
[8] Value
[9] Pounds
[10] Shillings
[11] Pence

[1]	[2]	[3]	[4]	[5]	[6]	[7]	[8]	[9]	[10]	[11]
Saml McKighen					2	2	16		4	1½
Jonathan Hix					1	5	12		3	1
Jno Carson					6	12	54		13	10
Robt Carson					3	9	30		7	8½
Zophar Toncry					2	3	17		4	4½
Ben Jamison					7	10	59		15	1½
Henry Farnsworth					4	8	36		9	3
Alexr Wilson	200				6	9	111	1	8	6
Jno Colter					2	5	19		4	10½
Jno McAdow Ser	350				9	8	176	2	5	2
Jno McAdow					1		7	1	5	8
Wm Francis					3	3	24		6	2
John Castile Ser					5	1	36		9	3
John Castile					1		7	1	5	8
Ben. Ray				1	6	14	136	1	14	10½
Jos Ray Deceased					4	13	41		10	6½
Thos Ray				1	7	15	144	1	17	0

[1]	[2]	[3]	[4]	[5]	[6]	[7]	[8]	[9]	[10]	[11]
Samuel Sample					6	1	43	1	5	8
Geo. Jamison					2		14	1	5	8
Fredrick Whitinburg					6	17	59		15	1½
Jos Whitenburg	250				3	18	114	1	8	9¼
Wm Gilbreth					1		7	1	5	8
Jno Oliphant	50				3	2	38		9	8½
Thos Phlippen				1	12	10	164	2	2	1½
Thos Brumlow	200				6	10	112	1	8	9
Anty Bully	100				3	5	56		14	4½
Matthew Pate	100		1	1	7	15	214	2	14	11
Jno Edmunds					5	7	42		10	10
Henry Whitenburg	250				4	7	110	1	8	3
Robt Campbell					3	6	27		6	11
James Kerr		2		1	4	6	154	1	1	6
Jno McClung	200				2	4	78	1	0	0
Hugh McClung	200				6	9	111	1	8	6
Jno Mitchell	200				4	4	92	1	9	8
Wm Wilson					8	9	65		16	8½
David Rankin	500				3	9	180	2	6	3
Robt Paris	200				8	11	127	1	12	7
Jos Bullard	1000		3		43	21	742	9	10	6
Wm Robison					3	5	26		6	8
James Houston					2	5	19		4	10½
Alexander Kilbreth	250				3	4	100	1	5	8
Elizabeth Holly	100			1	6	11	163	2	1	10½
Jos Lusk				3	4	25		6	5	
Ephraim Cox	400				4	12	160	2	1	½
Edmund Crump	200				5	7	102	1	6	2
Wm Morrow	200				5	3	98	1	5	2
Jno McCosky	150				2	3	62		15	11½
Thos Beavers					4	6	34		8	8½
Solomon Reed					2	4	18		4	7½
Craven Duncan					2	3	17		4	4½
Jno Moore					3	3	24		6	2
Jno Gilbreth					3	5	26		6	8
Anty Moore	300				8	15	161	1	1	4½
Jno Hays					3	3	24		6	2
Robert Hood					3	4	25		6	5
David Campbell	200				4	14	102	1	6	2
Ebenr Alexander	100				4	4	62		15	11
Jno Corbit					1		7		1	9½
Jno Paterson	100				4	6	64		16	5½
Geo. Martin	125				2		51.10	1	5	8
Jas Delany	200				4	5	93	1	3	11
Alexr Campbell					3	3	24		6	2
Richd Martin					6		42	1	5	8
Wm McBroom	200				2		74	1	5	8
James Keele	200				2	7	81	1	0	10
Jehu Reese					3	6	27		6	11
James McFaren					4	5	33		8	5½
Wm Kerr					3	4	25	1	5	8

[1]	[2]	[3]	[4]	[5]	[6]	[7]	[8]	[9]	[10]	[11]
Andw Martin	100				4	5	63		16	2
Jos Alexander	400				2	5	139	1	15	7½
Jno Delany	600				8	10	246	3	3	2
Samuel Wallace	200				7	7	116	1	9	9
Francis Delany	100				2	6	50		12	10
Barns Brumlow	47				5	4	53.2		13	9
Augustine Brumlow	300				1	9	106	1	7	2½
James Berke					2	3	17		4	4
Joseph Hardin	700		1	1	8	9	395	5	1	5
Ebenr Byram					5	18	53		14	1
Abram Reed					2	1	15		3	10
Adam Kuykindal	150		1		6	3	130	1	13	4½
Isaac Barton	244				4	11	112	1	8	9
Jos Kuykindal	200	2		2	8	11	327	4	3	11
Saml Paxton	200				1	1	68		17	5½
Francis Hamilton					6	7	49		12	7
Jno Kuykindal			1		1	1	48		12	4
David Russel					7	11	60		15	4½
Saml Huston					4	14	42		10	9½
Robt Huston	350				1		112	1	8	9
Abr: Carter					5	11	46		11	10
Michl Carter					2	1	15	1	5	8
Wm Robison					1	2	9		2	4
Jno Richardson	150				3	12	78	1	0	0
Jno Anthony					1	1	8		2	½
Jacob Sertain					3	5	26		6	8
Jno Blackwell					4	7	35		8	11½
Uriah Acres	200				4	9	97	1	4	11
Richd Keele					1	2	9		2	4
Thos Woodward					3		21	1	5	8
Thos Stanfield					9	9	72		18	6
Thos Piercifull					3	1	22		5	8
David Linsey					6	4	46		11	10
Dutton Lane					1		7		1	9½
Jno Ligget	200				1		67	1	5	8
David Copeland					5	7	42		10	9½
Jos Lovelaty					2		14		3	7
Matt. Bishop					4	7	35		8	11½
Nathl McClur					4	2	30		7	9½
Wm Sample	250				5	6	116	1	9	9
Major Temple		2	2		4	13	241	3	1	10½
Hugh Wier					2	6	20		5	1½
Robt Carr Ser	100				5	5	70		10	0
Thomas Tate					5		35		8	11½
Wm Ryon	100				2	2	46		11	10
Jacob Smelser					3	6	27		6	11
Jno Lovelaty	230				5	11	115	1	9	6
Jacob Green					3		21		5	5
Andw McFaren					5	2	37		9	5½
Marshal Lovelaty	100				5	5	70		18	0
Hezekiah Balch			2	1	2	3	157	2	0	5

[1]	[2]	[3]	[4]	[5]	[6]	[7]	[8]	[9]	[10]	[11]
Edmund Roberts	300				3	10	121	1	11	1
Geo. Mooney					3	5	26		6	6
Jonathan Roberts					3	5	26		6	6
Jno Roberts					3	9	30		7	9½
Saml Vants [Vance]	200				6	6	108	1	7	8½
Saml Moor	250				6	5	122	1	1	4
Luke Shally	112				4	5	66½		17	11½
Barnabas Anderson					3	2	23		5	11
Wm Burney					8	10	66	1	5	8
David Kirkwood					1	2	9		2	3¾
Henry Foaly					3	3	24		6	2
Chas Dotson	300				4	7	125	1	12	1
Jno Dotson					1		7	1	5	8
Robt Kerr Jr.	200				2		74	1	5	8
David Alison					3	4	25		6	5
Wm McMurry					4	6	34		8	8½
Saml McMurry					4	8	36		9	2½
Wm McGaughy					4	10	38		9	9
Isaac Taylor	500				2		164	2	2	1
Wm Henderson	400				7	10	179	2	5	11
Chas McCartny	200				11	6	143	1	17	
Jno McCartny					4	3	31		7	11½
Wm Murphy				1	2	3	97	4	4	11
David Gamil					8	5	61		15	8½
Wm Johnston					7	9	58		14	11
Archd McCurdy					5		35		9	
Cornelius Ringo					2		14		3	7½
Isaac Bullard	340				15	13	220	2	16	5½
Saml Rentfro					4		28		6	4½
Moses Poor	200				6	7		1	9	2
Jno Price	200				4	4	92	1	3	7½
Jos Robison					1	0	7		1	10
Jas McCartny	150				9	15	123	1	11	7
Saml Gibson	100				3	3	57	0	12	8½
					4	11				4
Jas Moore	100				2	22	69	0	17	2½
								1		
Jas Hayworth					2			2	5	8
Moses Moore				1	2	3	90	1	3	2
Matthw Rhue [?]	200				2	2	75	0	19	3
								1		
Jos Davis	400				2	2	136	2	12	10½
Peter Dillard	100				6	6	78	0	19	9
Gabriel McCool	100				3	6	57	0	12	2½
										1
Jas Right	100				2	7	52	0	13	2
Wm Riece	200				6	11	113	1	9	0
Absom Hayworth	250				7	5	129	1	13	2
Jos Eaton	200				3	7	88	1	2	7

All numerals overwritten indistinct.

[1]	[2]	[3]	[4]	[5]	[6]	[7]	[8]	[9]	[10]	[11]
Evan Evans					2	3	17	0	4	4½
Jno Gillihand				1	4	2	110	1	8	3
									5	
Moses Tremble	100				3			1	3	8
Thos Bennett								1	5	8
Math Leeper					6	4	46		11	10
Benj. Gist	200				6	8	110	5	2	10
Thos Gist					2	2	64		17	0
Jno Gist								5	2	8
Evan Jones	160[?]				3	3	6	1	14	
Richd Howard	200				5	8	100	1	6	5

All numerals overwritten indistinct.

Abbot, James 15,153
Abbott, Elijah 190,201
  James 193
Abel, Ezekiel 207
Able, Cain 46,66
  John 66
Abner, Elisha 144
Acklen, Jeanette Tillotson
  58
Acklin, Samuel 118
Ackyard, Jacob 153
Acres, Daniel 229
  John 229
  Uriah 275
Acoff, John 153
  Timothy 153
Acuff, Cain 102
  Christopher 100
  John 102
  Spencer 169
Adair, Alexander 15
  David 88
  John 15,72,150
  Thomas 6
  William 59
Adams, Daniel 234
  David 180
  Elisha 153
  George 106
  James 134
  Jesse 144
  John 106
  Macajah 153
  Roberts 116
  Thomas 46
  Will'm 210
  Wm. 43
Adamson, John 127
  Jonathan 127
  Simeon/Simon 68,127
Adcock, James 251
Adcocks, Leonard 195
Adkins, James 14
  Thomas 105
Adkinson, Charles 272
Adwell, John 153
Ady, Loyd 100
Agee, Isaac 225
  James 225
  Eilliam 153
Aikerd, John 165
Aikin, Ezekiel 166
  Harrison 166
Aikman, William 89
Ailor, James 95
Airhart, Nicholus 43
Akin, Harrison 172
Akin, Sam'l 51
Albright...86
Alder, Barnabas 225
Aldridge, Nathan 12,18,71
  William 18,71
Aleson, James 51
Alexander, Benjamin 37
  Ebenezer 40,266
  Eben'r 274
  George 144,184
  Jacob 207
  James 271
  Jeremiah 41
  John 37,38,179,207
  Joseph 40,211,275
  L. D. 244
  Margaret 40
  Oliver 30,37
  Stephen 179,184,185
  Thomas 41,181,184
  William 41,181,184

Alexander, Wm 163
Alenson, Robert 51
Alford, Jacob 174
Alinger, Daniel 182
Alison, David 276
  John 204,213
  Rob't 205,207,214,270
Allen...59
  Abraham 259
  Barnet 116
  Benjamin 132
  Calvin 259
  Charles 153
  Daniel 153,251
  George 259
  Geo. W. 236
  Isaac 261
  James 51,153,181,261
  Jas. R. 236,257
  John 84,179,251,254,259,
  261
  Joseph 182
  Mary 236
  Penelope Johnson 7,38,
  57,66,97,109,122
  Reuben 180
  Robert 181
  Russel 261
  Sam'l 229
  William 259
Alley, Edward 126
  James 4,115
Allison, Charles 198
  David 182,184
  Ewen 180
  Francis 159,209
  Hugh 226
  John 153,182,197,209
  John Sr. 153
  Robert 153,159,199
  Wm. 199
Allstot, Robert 59
Allsup, James 211
Alred, Thomas 12
  Solomon 12
Alsop, James 103
  John 100
Alt, Charity 74
  Conrad 74
  Frederick 74
  George 74
  Jacob 74
  John 74
  Mary 74
  Michael 74
Altom, Spencer 163
Alves, Amelia 21
  Walter 21,74
  Walter Hogg 16
Alvis, Geo. W. 163
  Walter 221
Amicks, Isaac 163
Amis, Williss/Willis 166,
  172,173
Amonet, John 81
Amos, Thomas 153
Anderson, Alex'r 208
  Archibald 4
  Barnaba 198
  Barnabas 276
  Daniel 91
  Fredrick 214
  George 175
  Isaac 88
  Jacob 88
  James 47,132,170,173,
  183,254,271
  Joseph 2,132,163,166,254

Anderson, Joseph M. 172,
  173
  Nellie Pickens 35
  Rachel 185
  Samuel 91
  Stuart 153
  Swinfield 170
  Thomas/Thos. 91,251
  Thomas Jr. 144
  Thomas Sr. 144
  Thos. C. 163
  William/Wm. 74,79,115,
  153,171,180,225
Andes, George 179
Andrew, Samuel 66
Andrews, Ephraim 163
Angel, Arch'd. 226
Anglehand, Adren 198
Anglin, Aaron 153
Anthony, John/Jno. 59,275
  William 153
  Wm. 195
Antrim, Thomas 180
Apperson Anty 205
Arbuckle, James 4
Archer, Cornelius 111
  John 144,210
  Richmond 15
  William/Wm. 144,210
Archy, Richmond 225
Arehart, Henery 41
Argenbright, George 167
Armitage, Isaac 185
Armstrong, Alexander 184
  Ann 185
  Benjamin 271
  Daniel 185
  James 84,163
  Jas. Jr. 163
  John 6,81,163,167
  Joseph 70
  Lanseylot 271
  Lanty 266
  Martin 95
  Robert 6,81,272
  Thomas 163,167
  William 153,167,169
  Wm. 41,163
  Zella 8,36,60
Arnet, Jacob 103
Arno, Peter 109
Arnold, John 6,191,206
  Mary 165
  William 103
Arnwin, James 102
  John 102
Arrants, Harmon 153
Arrundil, Nathan 205
Arthur, Elias 106
  Matthew 201
Arthura, Matthew 191
Arwin, John 111
Arwine, James 153
Ashbrooks, George 144
Ashburn, Martin 98,103
Ashe, Thomas 144
Asher, Charles 190
  Daniel 111
  John 144,190,207
  Robertson 6,111
  Robinson 207
  Thomas 190
  William/Wm. 18,191,192
Ashley, Noah 123
Ashlock, William 6
Ashmore, Hezekiah 123
Ashurt, Charles 205
  William 200

Ashworth, John 153
  Joseph 77
Atchson, Robt. 208
Atkins, Charles 196
  Sherrod 229
August, John 116
Ausemus, Peter 105
Austen, Joseph 173
  Same 165
Austin, Archibald 132
  John 205
  Natheneil 166
  William 6
Auston, Nathaniel 117
  William 106
Averett, Jesse 88
Ayers, Chastity 70
  David 70
Ayres, Baley 227
Azamis, Philip 214

Babb, Joseph 179
  Philip 179,181
  Seth 185
  Thomas 182
Bachman, Samuel 154
Bacon, Michael 198
Baid, James 9
Bailes, James 183
  Solomon 180
  Stephen 183
Bailey, Charles 144
  Claudius 184
  Cotrail 207
  Cottril 144
  David 239
  Hazekiah 208
  James 183
  James F. 250
  John 179
  Reuben 208
  Richard 127
  Robert 47
  Sam'l 206
Bails, Daniel 179
Baird, Lewis 227
Baits, Henry 197
Baker, Abednego 15
  Andrew 171
  Charity 74
  Charles 51,91,153
  Christopher 182
  Edward 227
  Elisha 270
  Geo. 227
  Gilbert 261
  Henry 74,88
  Isaac 181
  James 127,239
  John 14,103,126,144,183,
  239
  Joseph 106,123
  Morris 153
  Peter 182
  Robt. 227
  Samuel 14,115,227
  Tilman 88
  William/Wm. 51,88.114,
  175
Balch, Amos 121
  Elijah 185
  Hezekiah 180,275
  Hezekiah W. 181
  John 123,180
  Samuel Y. 181
Baldridge, James 244
Baldwin, Ezekiel 181
  William 81,206
Balentine, Henry 261
Bales, Jacob 68
  John 68
  Purnell 68
Balinger, Lydia 127

Ball, Adonijah 237
  Alfred 257
  Ira 169,237
  James V. 16
  Jno. 237
  Lunsford 251
  Mereman 237
  Osbourn 237
  Royal 237
Ballard, Alex'r. 167,174
  John 144
  Micajah 225
Ballenger, Moses 138
Baloo, Leonard 244
  Thomas 244
Bane, Robert 136
Banneth, John 105
Bannister, Jonathan 163
Barbee, Wm. 221
Barber, Liff 154
  Simon 154
Barclay, Felix 81
  William 94
Bare/Bair, Peter 166
  Jr. & Sr. 172,173
Barlet/Bartlett, Joseph
  53,94
Barger, Jacob 66,173
Barkehouse, John 144
Barker, Thomas 199
Barksdill, Clevers 192
Barn, John 209
  Joseph 209,210
  Wm.209
Barnard, John 154
Barnes, James 123
  John 261
  William 153
  Wm. 46
Barnat, George 174
Barnet, Abner 210
Barnett, John 170
  Meradith 244
  William 91
Barnheart, Conrad 183
Barren, James 225
Barret, Thomas 167
Barron, James 208
  John 225
  Joseph 223
Barrott, Stepen 170
Bartholomew, Joseph 59
Bartlet, Nicholas 30
Bartley, John 181
Barton, Gilbreath 89
  Henry 113
  Isaac 117,129,275
  Martha 100
  Roger 89
  Sarah 117
  Solomon 257
  Thomas 153
Bas, Benjamin 153
Basham, Arcibald 223
  John 223
  Johnson 223
  Jonathan 223
  Richard 223
  Wm. 223
Basinger, George 244
Basket, Richard 153
Baskins, John 273
Basler, Henry 244
Bass, Jeremiah 144
Bassett, Nathl/Nathaniel
  166,172,173
Bates, Martin 261
  Mathew 132
Batt, Thomas 181
Baugher/Boyer, Jacob 53
Baldwin, Henry 127
Baxter, Aaron 251,259
  Francis 208

Baxter, James 184,261
  Johns 261
  Stephen 166,172,173
Bayles, Caleb 81
  George 64,93
  Daniel 64
  John 64
  William 88
Bayless, Hezekiah 64
Bayley, John 193,201
  Robert 196
  Wm. 193
Baysinger, Michael 180
Beachboard, Benjn. 153
Beal, George 170
Beames, James 144
Bean, Elizabeth 109
  George 109
  Jacob 68
  Jessee 109
  John 102
  John H. 102
  Mordecai 167
  Stephen 102
  William 187
Bear, George 153
  Matthias 153
  Peter 153
Beard, Allen 249
  And'w 208
  Arch 49
  George 36
  Henry 36
  Hugh 93,272
  James 49
  John 153
  Lewis 227
  Patrick 138
  Thomas 153
  Wm. 211
Beardon, Richard 59
Beaty, Andrew 153
  James 153
  John 49,100
  Samel 36
  Walter 165
Beaver, Christ'n 153
Beavers, Thos. 274
  William 135
Beelor, Daniel 102,153
  George 154
  Jacob 154
  /Beelar, John 102,118,
  153
  Joseph 153,154
  Peter 102,153
  Woolery 154
Been, Edmd. 209
  Geo. 209
  Jesse 195
  John 193,209
  Lydia 209
  Robert 195,208
  Wm. 193,195,209
Beeson, Amariah 127
  Thomas 127
Beets, George Jr. 163
  John 174
Begley, Hennery 171
  John 171
Beiard, John 166
Bell, George 210
  James 207
  John 33,184,210,221,237
  Jos. E. 239
  Richard 144
  Robert 185
  Samuel 82
  Thomas 207
  William 71,94,181,207,
  221,273
Benham, Daniel 47
Bennat, Coffee 174

Benner, Christopher 239
Danl. 208
Bennet, Jessy 138
Bennett, Daniel 75
Elizabeth 89
F. M. 254
John 181
Peter 89
Thomas 106,277
Benson, Bable 182
Chirchester 106
Thomas 19
Berke, James 275
Berry, James 106,111
John 105,123
Josiah 74
Nancy 74
Robert 123
Thomas 38,174
Beshears, John 174
Besley, Wm. 41
Beverly, John 204,212
Bibee, Wm. 246
Wm. W. 249
Bible, Christian 182
Christopher 184
Lewis 244
Philip 182
Bibles, John 47
Bice Wm. 46
Bickerstaff, Henry 19
Bickham, Gittig 59
Biddle, Tho. 211
Biggs, Benjamin 167
John 184,268
Reuben 180
Bigham, Natth. 42
Samuel 42
Wm. 41,272
Bigs, Henry 207
Billands, Thomas 271
Billing, John 153
Biillingsley, Jepthah 182
Thomas 183
Bird, Amos 178,200,266,268
Charles Lee 16
Betsy 174
Dennis 259
Jacob 184
James 171
John 103,183
Jonathan 199
Joseph 272
Birdsey, Ezekiel 237
Birdseye, Ezekiel 251
Birdsong, John 105
Birdwell, Benjamin 154
John 154
Joseph 89,154
Mary 153
Robert 153
Birton, Robing 171
Bishop...64
Edward 249
Jacob 64
John 154
Joseph 64,163
Mason 163
Matt. 275
Matthew 64
Peter 153
Samuel 144
Stephen 64
Thomas 153
William 153
Bitner, John 181
Bitserburgy, Peter 183
Black, Alexr. 237
Gavin 36
Jacob 163
James 237,244
John 100,111,132,228,237
Joseph 30

Black, Matthew 237
Nancy 77
Reuben 237
William 182
Wm. 85
Blackburn, Arshs 208
Benj./Benjamin 43,89,
208
Gidion 38,39
John 121,123,183
Robert 197,211
Thomas 184
William 123
Blackley, Charles 68
Robert 208
Blackwell, John 198,205,
275
Blackwood, William 102
Blagg, John 11
Blair, Alex'd 109
Hugh 198,209
/Bliar, James 98,109
John 36,109,207,210
Joseph 209
Robert 109
Saml. 210
Sarah 98.109
William 36,109
Blakeman, Moses 174
Blan, John 77
Blanchet, John 244
Blankenship, Isom 51
Blazer, Aaron 239
Christopher 239
Henry 239
Phillip 239
Bleak, Peter 184
Bleavins, James 171
Bledsoe, Anthony 150
Bletcher, William 73,86
Blevens, James 175
Blevins, Armstead 154
Dillon 154
Henry 163
James 154
William 154
Bliar, Jossiah 116
Blizard, Thomas 36
Bloomer, Daniel 171,175
John 171
Blount, Barbara 62
John G. 117
Mary 30,62,97
Mary Louisa 62
/Blunt, Governor,
William/Willie 12,23,
30,62,97,111,121
Blue, Douglass 68
Blyth, Sam'l 206
Boatman, George 103
Henry 103
Boatwright/Boterite,
Daniel 46
Bodkin, Hugh 79
Bodle, James 102
Bogan, William 82
Bogas, Bennett 123
Bogart, Cornelius 144
Henry 212
Samuel 144,212
Boghard, Cornelius 53
Bogle, Andrew 33
Eleanor 33
Elizabeth 33
Hugh 33
Jean McAntyre 33
Joseph 33
Margaret 33
Samuel 35
Boiles, Jacob 206
Boils, John 179
Bolu, James 38
Boman, Natha'l 209

Bond, Charles 197
Henery 47
Henry 153
Isaac 89
Jesse 196
Nicholas 95
Octavia Zollincoffer,
60
Stephen 66
William 66,153
Wright 172,173
Wright Jr. 166
Wright Sr. 166
Bonds, John 88
Bonham, Benjamin 47
Boo, Rudolph 179
Booker, Barnabas 116
Bookout, Charles 10
Boon, Solomon 144
Boorghauss, Abrm. 207
Booth, Alice 59
Edwin E. 59,80
Borden, Archibale 239
Dan'l. 239
Elizabeth 239
John 239
Border, Michael
Borders, Michael 271
Bordon, Daniel 184
Bottles, Henry 205
Bougher, John 154
Bounds, Francis 74,75
Jesse 75,210
John 12
Joseph 210
Bourden/Borden, Adon 46
Bowen, Henry 109
James 109
John 98,109,164
Joseph 153
/Boen, Wm./William 51,
74
Bowerman, John 33
Michel 51
Peter 46
Bowers, Daniel 40
James 210
John 181,183
Leonard 144,206
William 179
Bowling, Absolom 221
Benjamin 6
Joel 15
William 226
Bowman, Cornelius 206
Daniel 183
Henry 15,183
Jacob 126,181,184
John 9,64,79.96,206,
223
Samuel 68,79
Sperling 181,184
Wm. 105
Bowry, Margaret 153
Bowser, John 153
Bowyer, Luke 121
Michal 153
Box, Edward 197,271
Henry 271
James 197
Joseph 266,268
Robert 197,268
Boy, Jacob 154
Boyd, Alexander 51
George 42
James 42,137,144,153,
182,268
John 43,68
Robert 33,100
Thomas 66
William 33,68,136,144,
174,271
Boydston, Wm. 237

3

Boydstone, Thomas 105
Boydstun, William 273
Boyer, Henry 244
   Isaac 244
   John 254
   Lewis 244
Boykin, Eli 166,172,173
Boyle...97
Boyles, David 129
Bradberry, John 17
Braden, Edward 111
   George 223
   James 64
   John 111,223
Bradford, Benj. 113
   Benjamin 136,144
   Henry 123
   Wm. 169
Brading, James 211
Bradley, James 197
   John 36
   Jonathan 154
   William 86,167
Bradshaw, James 126
   Joseph 64
   Samuel 126
   Thomas 153
   William 126
Brady, Nancy 246
Bragg, Charles 154
   David 154
   Thomas 154
   William 246
   William Jr. 166,172,173
   Wm. Sr. 166,172,173.
Braham, Ephraim 221
Bran, John 126
Brandon, John 209
   Thos. 208
Brandun, Wm. 165
Braner, Michael 123
Branham/Brannam, Edward
   71,73
   Jas. 227,228
   Martin 227
   Sarah 228
   Talmon 228
Brannom, Joseph 223
Brannum, Daniel 89
   Pleasant 89
Branshaw, John 210
Branstetter, Peter 144
Branum, Thomas 165
Brassfield, Thos/Thomas
   88,94
Bratcher, Charles 126,223
   John 223
   William 185,223
Bray, James 19
   John 6,174
Brazle, George 19
   Robert 19
   William 18
Brazleton, Isaac 6
   John 137
   Samuel 138
   Will 138
   William 137
   William Sr. 138
Brazil, Richard 9
   Valentine 9
Breaden, James 170
Breading, Will'm 211
Bready, John 100
Breeden, Elijah 259
   Thos. 172
Breeze, James 75
   Thomas 49
Brevert, John 137
Brewer, Jacob 174
   Oliver, 91,131
   Philip 180
   Samuel 180

Brewton, Jacob 226,227
   John 226
Brian, Thomas 130
Briant, John 229
   Joseph 109
   William 171
Brice, Wm. 169
Bridges, Edward 193,201
   Thomas 113
   William 113
Brigham, James 150,153
   John 153
Bright, John 59
   Thomas 164
   William 170
Brightbill, Peter 154
Brigs, John 130
Brim, Edmond 53
   Henry 228
   Joseph 228
   Lewis 228
Brimer, Joseph 144
Brisco, John 171
   Thomas 171
Brison, Hugh 268
Bristo, John 98,102
Brittain, Abraham 153,208
   Geo. 209
   Nath'l 153
   Richard 154
   William 135,208
Britten, Banja. 229
   William 185
Britton, Benjamin 129
   James 129
Brizendine, James 246
   Jno. 246
Brock, Allen 100
   Elijah 222
   George 81,100,268
   Lewis 81
   Pearson 81
   Sarah 228
   Sherard 15
Broderick, Hugh 254
Broiles, George 46
   John 179
Broils, Aron 226
Brokis, William 111
Bromley, James 36
Brook, Royal 237
Brooks, Agnes 75
   Ann 66,75
   David 257,261
   John 666,75,154,237
   Joseph 66
   Kaner 237
   Littleton 171
   Mark 259
   Mary 66
   Matthew 257
   Moses 75
   Philip 225
   Samuel 66
   Stephen 180
   Thomas 163
   William 244
   Wright 259
Brooton, John 4
Brothers, Thomas 89,91
Brotherton, William 179
Brown, Alexander 182
   Benjamin 180,205
   Claiborne 136
   David 51,126,210
   Eli 226
   Elija 51
   Elijah 254
   Ezekel 200
   Feliz 68
   George 136,181,182,205
   & Hart 221
   Henry 167

Brown, Isaiah 38
   Jacob 196,210
   James 111,183,226,272
   Jesse 167
   Jh. 221
   John 15,36,68,79,107,
   167,181,192,196,206,
   225
   Jonathan 179,181
   Joseph 179,206
   Maxwell 183
   Missrs 210
   Philip 180
   Robert 229
   Sylvanus 77
   Thomas 82,111,179,180,
   199,210,221
   Thomas G. 184
   William/Wm. 59,68,107
   131,183,192
   Zekel 190
Brownen, James 81
Browning, Rodger 183
   Roger 153
Broyles, Aron 226
   Ezekiel 179
   Jacob 271
   Jeremiah 179
   Matthias 182
Broyls, Abrm. 211
   Cyrus 246,210
   Mathias 211
   Michael 211
   Nichols 211
   Saml. 261
Bruar, John 71
   William 71
Brumit, Owen 136
Brumley, Barnet 53
   Isaac 181
   John 10
   Mary 185
   Wm. 221
Brumlow, Augustine 275
   Barns 275
   Thos. 274
Brummitt, Susannah 17
Brummit, Thomas 17
   Wm. 17
Bruston, James 111
Bruton, Jacob 115
   James 115
   Samuel 115
Bryan, Ambrose 153
   Jas. M. 251
   John 135
   Joseph 166,172
   William 123
   Wm. 210
Bryant, Benjamin 244
   Brummit 259
   James H. 259
   John 229
   Joseph 173
   Mary 261
   Polly 259
   Saml. 244
   Tarlton 259
   William 154
Bryants, Bryant 268
Buchanan, Edward 40
   James 197
Buchannan, William 154
Buckingham, Thos 270
Buckland, Walter 225
Buckles, John 154
Bucknel, William 154
Buckner, Edward 246
   George 244
   John 73
   Presley 73,94,111,154
   Ricey 73
   William 144

4

Buckner, Wm. 246
Bugg, David 237
  Thomas 251
Bull, George 102
  Jacob 211
  John 94
Bullard, Isaac 276
  John 198
  Joseph 199,274
  Martha 127
Bullards, Isaac 266
Bullinger, Peter 144
Bullington, William 205
Bullman, Jno. W. 246
Bullock, L. H. 21
  Richard 21,223
Bully, Anty 274
Bumpers, Joseph 271
Bunch, David 102
  John 98
  Martin 102
  Thomas 109
Bundy, James 223
Bunton, Andrew 190
Burch, Richard 204,212
Burger, Michael 185
Burges, Wm. 225
Burgess, Wm. 223
Burgey, Eathern 184
Burgis, John 223
  Wm. 223
Buris, John 165
Burk, Abraham 144
  Arter 144
  Elihew 144
  Isaac 86
  Isham 59
  John 153,257
  Joseph 257
  William 38
Burkhart, George 206
Burkheart, F. 182
  George 181
Burleson, Aron 197
  Thomas 197
Burnett, Benjamin 79,236
  Elizabeth 237
  James 236
  Jeremiah 94
  J. J. 51,61
  Joseph 79,236
  Jno. M. 236
  /Bernett, Michael 131
  Robert 180
  Wm. C. 236
Burney, Wm. 276
Burnit, Jerremiah 166
Burns, Isaac 135
  James 135
  Robert 184
Burrus, Elijah 15
Burrville...215
Burtain, Jess 171
Burton, John 107
  Robert 4
Busby, John 107,113
  Reaves 239
  Thomas 109,113,126
Busley, Christian 183
Buster, Claudius 183
  Henry 244
Butcher, Barney 107
  Elisa 225
  John 174
  Samuel 135
Butler, Elisha 154,208
  Elizabeth 19
  Isaiah 259
  James 19
  Peter 18
  Thomas 12
Byram, Ebenr. 275
  Levi 71

Byrd, John 270
Byrum, Alden 10
  /Byram, Ebenezer 10,64

Cabbage, Adam 154
  John 154
Caffray, Richard 154
Cain, David 105
  Hugh 116,166,173
  John 145
  Peter 145
Cairl, Alex 195
Caismon/Crismon, Isaac 115
Caldwell, Alexander 64,138
  Anthony 138
  Benjamin 64
  David 48,49
  George 49
  James 167
  John 49,167
  Samuel 183
  Thomas 53,183
  William 138
Cales, James 130
Calfree, John 334
Calkahoon, James 115
Callahan, Charles 131
  William 131
Callaway, John 71
Callen, Charles 68
  John 68
Calliham, Joel 193
  John 193
  Valentine 180
Calvert, Wm. 208
Cambel, Duncan 127
Cameron, James 272
  Joseph 254
  Martin 257
Camnass, John 268
Campbel, Jeremiah 207
  Solomon 207
Campbell, Abraham 207
  Alexander 66,81,198,274
  Andrew 73,163,164
  Archibald 5
  Arthur 24,115
  David 66,67,109,199,274
  Elizabeth 33
  George W. 16,60,95,126
  Hugh 164,207
  Isaac 145
  /Campble, James 49,60,
  66,67,100,123,138,183,
  206,207,225
  James Y. 169
  Jeremiah 145
  /Campbel, John 36,89,
  127,167,182,205,207,
  246
  Joseph 225,262
  Lewis 72
  Patk./Patrick 16,60
  Prudence 76
  Rhoda 60
  /Campble, Robert 49,
  169,182,274
  Solomon 145
  Terence 16
  Thomas 5,225
  William 67,132,198
  Zachariah 141,225
  Zach. 207
  Zachariah Jr. 145
  Zachariah Sr. 145
Camron, Agness 68
  Ezra 105
  Samuel 36
Canady, Charles 126
  John 126
  Porter 126
Canedy, Walter 51
Cannon, Abner 134

Cannon, Bartlett 66
  Caleb 131
  John 66,116,131
  Joseph 131
  Robert 66
  Thomas 136
  Wm. 196
  Zachariah 66
Canterberry, John 105
  Zecheriah 105
Capish, Adam 102
  John 102
Caps, Jacob 111
  William 118
Car, Samuel 172
Carager, Godfrey 206
Carder, Tho. 207
Carelock, John 115
  Joseph 115
Carlock, Abraham 5
  Isaac 5
  Job 5
  Jacob 5
  Sarah 225
Carmack, Corl 169
  John 169
  Wm. 169
Carmichael, Hugh 64
  James 108,129,209
  John 64
  Pumery 96
Carnes, Michael 109
Carney, John 209
  Thomas 204
Carns, John 161
Carny, John 251
  Thomas 212
Carpenter, John 81
  Thomas 12,79
  Yelverton 166,172,173
Carr, Benjamin 259
  David 42
  Gilbert 154
  James 42
  John 213
  Robert 178,265,275
  Samuel 42
  Walter 16
  William 154
Carrack, John 198
Carrick, Samuel 59,60
Carriger, Godfrey Jr. 142,
  145
  Godfrey, Sr. 144,145
  Michael 145
  Nicholas 145
Carrington, Asia 167
Carrithers, Andrew 75
  Samuel 154
Carroal, Delaney 201
Carrol, John 205,209
Carrole, Delany 195
Carroll, William 154
  Willis 259
Carson, Alexander 91
  Andrew 237
  Caldwell 34
  David 33,123,207
  Drucilla 237
  James 136,184
  Jno. 274
  John 16,123,136
  Mary 136
  Moses 207
  Robert 123,180,210,273
  Samuel 123,154,254
  Wm. 209,210
Cart, Richd. 48
Carter, Abraham 180,275
  Caleb 181
  Clarence E. 14,29
  Daniel 184
  David 184,179

Carter, E. C. 254
  Elijah 229
  Elizabeth 50,142
  Emanuel 192
  Ezekiel 180
  Geo. 254
  Hugh 184
  Isaac 181
  James 211
  Jesse 180
  John 141,145,179,182,
  187,188,191
  Joseph 82,184
  Landon 60,141,142,145,
  206
  Levi 185
  Mcaja 53
  Michl. 275
  Nathan 184
  Nathaniel 131
  Peter 84
  Samuel 123
  Silus 174
  Vincent 134
  W. 254
  William 60,84
  Wm. 246,249
Carven, Thomas 145
Cartwright, John 64
  Thomas 48
  William 64
Carwiles, John 111
Cary, Dennis 164
Case, John 259
  Saxton, 259
Casedy, John 191
Casey, James 102
  John 102
  Samuel 102
Cash, Benjamin 60
  James 205
Casiner, Jacob 210
Cason, John 207
Castalor, Martin 46
Casteel, Abednigo 91
  Edward 48
  Francis 91
  John 48,184
  Joseph 46
  Mesheck 91
  Peter 183
  Shadrack 91
Castile, John 273
Castle, Peter 181
Caswell, Richard 150
Catchem, Edward 77
  Hugh 77
  Joseph 77
Catching, Saymor 182
Cate, Charles 131
  John 131
  William 131
Caton, James 19
  Stephen 262
Caughron, Samuel 259
Cavander, Alexander 123
  F. A. 259
Caves, John 14
Cavett, Agnes 89
  Moses 89
  Richard 89
Cavitt, John 154
Cavner, Hugh 184
Cawood, John 192
  John Jr. 154
  Moses 53
Cearle, George 102
Certain, David 10
  James 190
  Jo 190
Chaffin, Robert 43
Chainey, Jacob 19
Chamberlain, Betsy 86

Chamberlain, D. C. 251
  Jere 103
  Jeremiah 86,132
  Ninian 136,207
Chamberlan, Hanna 46
Chamberlin, Andw. 210
  James 208
  John 272
  Stout 272
Chambers, Daniel 167
  David 199
  James 206
  John 199
  Joshua 221
  Moses 209
  Thomas 229
  William 167,199
Chamble, Jacob 192
Chance, Ezekiel 154
  Philip 180
Chandler/Chanler, Rich'd./
  Richard 16,53
  Shadrack 16
Chandley, William 184
Chapman, Asahel 75
  Luna 239
  Miles 75
  Thomas 75
  William 185,239
Chappel, Henry 167
Charles, Isaac 53
  James 169
  James Jr. 167
Charter, James 60,61,62,63
Chase, Sarah 154
Chasewood, Alex 196
Chasons, Charles 192
Chaudoin, Jas. 221
Cheek, Dauson 102,225
  Jesse 135
  William 135
  Willson 135
Cherrytree, Thomas 249
Chesnut, Andrew 164
  Henry 170
  Hugh 164
  Robert 79
Chester, John 154
Childers, Wm. P. 166,172
Childress, James 82
  John 70,71,72
  Mitchell 72
  Robert 72
  William 72,154
Childs, John 167
  Paul 167
Chiles, John 70
  Roland 70
Chilton, Thos. 254
  Wm. 107
Chisholm, John 187
Chis'm, John 195
Chisum, Elijah 98.117,118
  James 118
Chitwood, Lazarus 13
  Pleasant 13
  William 227
Choat, Austin 13
  Christopher 13
Choate, Austin 192
  Christopher 195
  Edward 192
  Richard 192
  Thomas 193
Chote, Benjamin 154
Chrisman, David 154
  John 154
Christapher, Isaac 210
Christenberry, Joseph 227
Christian, Allen 103,167
  Anthony 246,249
  George 154
  Gilbert 150

Christian, Isam 272
  James 249
  John 154,167
  Lewis 167
  Lewis Jr. 167
  Margaret 154
  Robert 154
  Thomas 272
  Thos. E. 249
  William 24
Christie, William 150
Christmon, Isaac 14
Chunn, Joseph 246
  Saml. 254
Church, Allen 237
  Christian 167
  Henry 167
Churchman, Edward 100,103,
  117
  John 103,126
  Thomas 100
  William 126
Citciller, William 154
Claiborne, John 223
  William C. C. 154
Clap, David 86
  Laudewick 86
Clark, Aaron R. 251
  Edward 102
  Francis 254
  George Rogers 20
  Hannah 60
  Harris 239
  Henry 111,114,150,193
  Isham 118
  James 249,254
  John 195,208,249,262
  Josiah 206
  Letitia 63
  Moses 262
  Nathaniel 150,200
  Samuel 102,123
  Shelton 249
  Thomas 118
  Thomas Norris/N. 63,75
  Walter 23,149,161,183
  William 187,197,208
Clarke, James 154
  John 200
Claunch, Barnet 102
  John 102
Clawson, Josiah 183
  William 197
Claxton, Constatine 6
Clay, William 103
Clayton, Jesse 73
Clebon, John 223
Cleck, John 166
  Mickle 165
Cleek, John 106
Clemans, John 51
Clepper, Jacob 169
  Phillip 170
Clerk, George 138
  Lewis 211
Clevinger, Alexd. 259
  Allen 257
  Asa 254
  Elias 257
  Jackson 259
  John 259
  Samuel 257
  William 259
Cliburn, John 223
Click, Geo. W. 257
  Geo. L. 251
  H. J. 259
  Henry 259
  James 259
  Lewis A. 259
  Malachi 184
  Martin 185
  Matthias 175

6

Click, P. W. 257
  Wm. 251
Clift, Henry 89
  James 68
Clifton, Hardy 111
  William 111
Cline, Peter 107
Clinton...215
  George 3
Clipper, Frederick 167
  George 167
  Peter 167
Clodfelter, John 6
Clopton, Martha 16,62
  Patsy 16,62
Cloud, Benj./Benjamin 166,
172,173
  Isaac 172
  Jason 4,15,16,216
  Jeremiah 154
  Joseph 161,174
  Wm. 166
Clowers, Jacob 268
Cluck, Henry 136
  John 126
  Peter 126
Coal, Solomon 199
Coats, Charles 100
  Jessee 111
  John 34
Cobb, Arthur 192
  Benj./Benjamin 100,192,
  200,209
  Dred 144,145
  Isabella 100
  Joel 167
  Joseph 109,118
  Martha 100
  Pharoah 82,100,144,174,
  196,209
  Pharoah Boone 109
  Richard 96
  Sarah 84,109
  Sally 84,100
  William 84,100,109,174,
  187,188,196,209
  William P. 84
  William Pharoah 100
Cobel, Daniel 17
Cochain, James 51
  John 53
Cocke, Jno. 166
  John 113,172,173,174
  Sarah 113
  Thomas 116,172,173
  William 109,113,122,167,
  172,174,178,191,233,266
Cockram, John 164
Cockran, A. 256
Cody, Godfrey 254
  Stephen 254
Coen, John 164
  Samuel 164
Coffee, Benjamin 174
  James 123
  Reuben 254
Coffelt, Daniel 105
Coffett, Abraham 223
  Daniel 223
  George 223
  Isaac 223
Coffey, Meredith 103
Coffill, John 154
Coffin, Charles 182
Coffman, Daniel 183
  John 244
  Joseph 227
  Loveal 185
Cofman, David 129
  Isaac 123
  James 132
  Lovel 129
Cogdale, Joseph 118

Cogdill, Frederick 237
Coker, Demsy 82
Colboth, Jacob 145
Coldwell, Ballard 167
  Benoni 167
  David 167
  John 167
  Thomas 167
Cole, Alexander 7
  Elisha 154
  Joseph 150,200
  Joseph Jr. 154
  Stephen 163
Coleman, G. M. 249
  Mary 251
  Spencer 262
  Wm. 249
  Wyet 164
Colen, Joshua 102
Colesen, James 190
Colfee, Wm. 249
Colings, Bengamon 171
Colker, Charles 79
  Jude 91
  William 91
Colland, John 85
Colleson, James 103
Collet, Abraham 181
  Jacob 211
Collett, Richard 190,201
Collier, John 183
  Thomas 182
Collings, Hennery 171
  James 171
  Vallingtine 171
  Vardemon 171
Collins, Edward 134
  Elisha 118
  George Jr. 167
  George Sr. 167
  James 167
  John 134,207
  Joseph 213
Collinsworth, Coventon 123
Collison, Jonathan 114
Collums, George 106
Colville, George 49
  Joseph 49
Colyer, Charles 144
Combe, Philip 103
Combs, George 109
  Job 14,134
  John 138,210
  Nicholas 154
  Solomon 206
Compton, Jeremiah 92,214
Conaway, Phillip 273
Condrey, Benjamin 111
  Dennis 111
Condry, Richard 154
Conkin, George 154
Conley, John 103
Conner, Abner 114
  Archabald 172
  Joseph 123
  Julius 144
  Richard 126
  Terrance 46
  William 72
Connor, Archibald 166
  Julius 166
  Thomas 166,172,173
Conway, Charles 72
  George 166,172,183
  Henry 182,266,268,269
  James T. 246
  Jessey 36
  Joseph 36
  Phillip 197
  Thomas 36
  Thos. Sr. 172
Cood, William 111
Cook, Aron 111

Cook, George 48
  Jacob 181
  John 68
  Joseph 12
  Marcurious 114
  Michael 43
  William 111,116
Cooke, Joseph 154
Cooley, Isaac 174
  William 183
Coolley, Isaac 166
Coons, John 5
  Michael 123
Coontz, Margaret 33
Coope, Baracias 42
Cooper, Abraham 144
  Andrew 154
  Caleb 154
  Cornelius 114
  Edward 144,206
  Elijah 205
  Elizabeth 165
  George 43
  George T. 74
  Isaac 109
  Jacob 132
  James 165,193,239
  Joab 206
  Jobe 144
  Joel 144,206
  John 43,116,144,154,
  163,165,239
  Joseph 214
  Nathan 144,184
  Patience 144,191,209
  robt. 239
  Thomas 154
  William/Wm. 144,249,
  16
Cope, Andrew 5
Copeland, Anthony 183
  David 64,181,184,185,
  275
  Douglass 64
  James 184
  John 179
  Rickets 134
  Stephen 134
  Solomon 134
  William 64
  Zacheus 134
Copland, David 44
  John 154
  William 154
Coppiner, Higgins 154
Coppock, Isaha 138
  James 138
  Thomas 138
Corbett, Elizabeth 123
Corbit, Jno. 274
Cormack, Edward 60
Cornealious, William 200
Cornelius, John 100
Corrithers, James 116
Corvin, John 211
Cosbey, James 270
Cosby, Abigale 79
  James 79,83
  John 79
Cotral, Hiram 166
Cotter, James 180
  John 182,273
  Stephen 123,182
Cotterel, John 72
Cotterell, John 154
  Lemuel 154
Cotton, Acton White 208
  Jacob 103
Coulee, Daniel 179
Coulson, Elijah 182
  John 180
Coulter, Charles 49
  John 107

7

Couter, Richd. 49
Council, Hodges 70
   Isaac 70
   Jesse 70
   John 70
   Matthew 70
Counsel, Cyrus 170
Counts, John 109
   Nicholas 109
Courtney, John 77
   Jonathan 77
Cowan, Alexander 14,106
   Arch 51
   David 13
   J. 42
   James 42,67,123,131
   Jane 134
   John 42,134
   Joseph 67
   Nathaniel 60
   Robert 42,154,211
   Sally 13
   Samuel 107,223
Coward, James 170
   Joel Jr. 170
   John 200
Cox, Abraham 145,192,207
   Absolum 171
   Ambrose 47
   Braxton 227
   Curd 72
   Dudley 138
   Edward 154,174
   Elisha 229
   Emily 60
   Ephraim 274
   George 169
   Greenberry 154
   Harmon 116
   Henry 136
   Jacob 165
   James 82,170,204,211,
   212
   Jeremiah 116,154
   Jesse 154
   John 136,145,169,193,
   231
   Josiah 106
   Joshua 154
   Lewis 60
   Matthew 180
   Richard 103,114,145,206
   Sampson 246
   Samuel 73,98,116
   Solomon 136
   Tabitha 170
   Thomas 100
   William 121,132,136,138,
   183,203,204,212
Crabb, Francis 109
   John 109
   Joseph 109,118
Craboight, Charles 14
Crabtree, Barnet 183
   James 273
   John 211
Cradduck, David 197
Crafford, Thos. 268
Craft, Ezechiel 111
   Jesse 154
   Michael 154
   Michael Sr. 154
   Thomas 154
Craig, Alexander 46
   David 30,43,271
   James 43,272
   James W. 82
   John 30,43,228,272
   Rewbin 228
   Robert 82
   Samuel 180
   Wm. 43
Craighead, Hannah 60

Craighead, James Geddes
   60
   Margaret 60
   Mary 81
   Robert 60,81
   Thomas 60,81
   William 94
Crain, Benjamin 70
   James 4,9
Crank, Thomas 70
Craven, Jos. 221
   Richard 225
   William 10
Cravens, James 271
   Joshua 221
   Robert 272
Crawford, English 86
   Hugh 154
   James 40,200
   John 182,195
   Moses 75
   Philip 209
   Samuel 7,75,182,196
   William 181
Creagan, Patrick 154
Creamer, Daniel 272
Crecelius, John 208
Creech, Jesse 174
Creeds(Creed), John 172,
   173
Creeley, Patrick 154
Creely, William 11
Creese, Jacob 169
Cremer, Daniel 180
Cresswell, Henry 123
Crew, Jacob 165
Crippen, John 64
Crismon, Gilbert 221
Critz, John 165
Crobarger, George 165
Crocket, Alexander 6
Crockett, Andrew 154
   Joseph 154
   Samuel 153,154
Crookshanks, G. M. 249
Crosby, George 182
   William 182
Cross, Abram 154
   Acquilla 154
   Britain 185
   Elijah 154
   Elizabeth 221
   Henry 183,200
   Joel 154
   Shadrach 180
   William 154
   Wm. 259
Crosson, Samuel 144
Crosswhite, George 145
Crouch, Jesse 208
   John 208
   Joseph 204,209
Crowder, Greenham 75
   William 154
Crowly, James 228
   John 115
   William 115
Crowson, William 273
Crozier, John 59,62,87
Cruise, Allison 79
   Gideon 79
   James 79
Crukshanks, Geo. 209
Crum, Henry 154
Crumbley, William 183
   Daniel 154
   George 154
Crump, Edmund 274
   Isaac 184
Cruse, Walter 79
Crusenberry, Joseph 227
Cuckey, Zacariah 126
Cude, James 129

Culberson, Jospeh 191
   Samuel 191
Cull, William 17
Culton, James 40
   Robert 38
Cumberford, James 207
Cummens, James 173
Cummins, James 173
Cumpton, John 144
Cuningham, Mary 206
Cunningham, Aaron 144
   Chris/Christopher 191,
   192
   David 38,221
   Hugh 208
   Jacob 14
   James 11,116,134,225
   John 33,118,272
   Jonathan 16,228
   Joshua 109
   Mary 144
   Miles 38
   Moses 14
   Paul 95
   Rosannah 91
   Thos. 116
   William 79,145
Cup, David 33,34
   Jacob 34
Cureton, Richard 246
   Robert 244,246
   Wm. 251
Curington, Lewis 182
Curnutt, David 5
   John 5
   Reuben 5
Currey, Isaac 132
   Sam 165
Currier, James 89
   James A. 89
Curten, John 154
Curtice, Nathaniel 270
Curtis, Bolen 144
   David 191
   Elijah 255
   Joshua 191
Curton, Richard 183
   Thomas 182
Cury, Eligah 175
   William 175
Cusack/Cusick, John B.
   33
Cutberth, Benjamin, Jr.
   145
   Benjamin, Sr. 145
   Daniel 145
Cyler, Joseph 271
Cyster, Daniel 170

Dade, Townsend 61
Dagley, Elias 225
   Joseph 228
Dale, Abel 112
   Alexander 111
   James 209
   Tho. 209
   Willm. 207
Dallace, Joshua 132
Dalzell, Francis 163,164
Dameron, Christopher 135
   Joseph 135
   Wm. B. 251
Damewood, Henry 86
   Malachi 86
Dandridge, Martha 122
Danforth, Josiah 38
   Sarah 38
Daniel, Francis 114
   James 119
   John 114
   Robert 181
   Woodson 145
Dannil, William 213

Dardis, James 60
  Thomas 60
d'Armand, R. C. 80
Daugherty, M. 165
Dauset, Edmond 223
  Robt. 223
Davenport, William 81
David...21
  & King 221
  Richard 154
  Sampson 216,221
Davidson, Andrew 49
  James 34,127
  Samuel 116
  William 9,33,36
Davies, James 164
  John 155
Davis...18
  Abner 205
  Alfred 260
  Benj. 166,227,237
  Benjamin 132
  Charles 88
  Chesley 73
  Daniel 88
  David 114,132,184
  Elias 98
  Elijah 34
  Elnathan 111
  Furklan 225
  George 5,70,73,208,229
  Gransham 239
  Harkins 184
  Isaac 112,180,207
  James 34,35,75,91,115,
  124,182,184,211,215,225,
  229,237,247
  John 118,127,180,184,
  190,257,271
  John Jr. 165
  Jonathan 165,183
  Jos. 276
  Jos. H. 244
  Lewis 166
  Martin 257
  Michael 74
  Moses 105
  Nancy 74,247
  Nathan 145,195,205
  Nathaniel 19,184,209
  Nicholas 124,268
  Pallamon 225
  Peter 237
  Reps J. 247
  Richards 91
  Robert 127
  Samuel 34,180
  Thomas 36,84,181,182,
  270
  Walter 77
  William 7,114,132,145,
  165,182,184,207,208,237,
  247,260
  Wilson 227
Davison, Agness 155
  John 155
  Joseph 195
  William 155
Dawson, Amos 244
  Isaac 247
  James 251
  John 166
Day, Jesse 129
  John 11,135
  Levi 129
  Nathaniel 135
Dean, Benjamin 124
  Francis 122,127
  George 124
  John 124
  William 127
Dearman, George 156
DeArmand, David 53

DeArmand, Mary Flenniken
  53
  R. C. 53
  Richd. 53
  Saml. 53
  Thomas 53
Dearmon, Richard 42
  John 91
  Richard J. 91
  William 91
Dearstone, Christian 180
Deas, Eliza 17
Delaney, John 183
Delaneys, Jas. 266
Delany, Francis 275
  Jas. 274
  Jno. 275
  William 155
Delap, Robert 221
Dell, Leonard 183
Demit, Robt. 209
Denham, David 163
  Joseph 3,7
Denning, Matthew 38
Dennis, Cary 260,262
  Joel 262
  John 262
  Joseph 112
  Mark 262
  Robert 262
  Thomas 112
  Zebedee 184
Denny, Samuel 190,201
Denson, William 108
Dent, John 100
Denten, Samuel 212
Denton, Abraham 259,262
  Alfred 259
  Francis 260
  Isaac 207
  Jackson 260
  Jacob 134
  James 155,192
  Jefferson 259
  John 130,259
  Jonah 16
  Jonathan 199,211,259
  Joseph 134,155,191,205,
  206
  Samuel 191
  Thomas 181
Denwoody, Samuel 181
Depue, Isaac 207
Depus, Asher 91
Derick, Jacob 11
  William 11
Derrick, John 165
  Mikle 165
Derry luney, Michel 105
Devaul, Abraham 118
Devault, Michael D. 89
  Michael 155
Devees, Charles 115
  James 105
Dever, James 72
  John 19
Dewitt, Nancy 257,262
DeWitt, Richd. B. 254
Dewoody, William 181
Dick, Henry 127
Dickerson, Francis 127
Dickin, Thomas 136
Dickson, John 42
  Samuel 44
  Thomas 42,247
  William 184
Dillard, James 266,268,
  269
  Peter 276
Dillen, Garrett 183
Dillenham, Vachworth 195
Dillon, James 182,257
  John 257

Dillon, Margaret 257
  Peter 181
  William 182
Dilzill, John 44
Dinnel, Richard 155
Dinsmoore, Samuel 179
Dinwiddie, James 181,184
Dittimore, Michael 183
Dixon, Clement 193
  Thomas 272
Doak, John 223
  Robert 225
  Saml. 210
  Thomas 223
Dobbin, Evan 210
Dobbins, Andrew 184
  Reuben 134
Dobbs, William 16
Dobson, JOhn 185
  Joseph 181
  Robert 180
Dockry, Balaans 239
Dockry, Robt. 239
Dodd, James 75
  John 182
  Josiah 68
  Mary 68
  William 81,182
Doddson, Wm. 210
Doddy, Howell 192
Dodson, James 108
  Jessee 118
  Nimrod 118
  Raleigh 164
  Samuel 102
  Thomas 116
Doggett, Miller 132
Doherty, Francis 161
  George 95,122,124,178,
  266,273
  James 123
  John 53
  Joseph 138,270
  Joseph Jr. 138
  Wm./William 107,138,272
Dollins, David 165
Dolton, Bradley 9
  Timothy 155
Donahoe, Charles 38
Donald, John 89
  Matthew 89
Donaldson, Andrew 135
  Robert 38
  William 135
Donathan, Elijah 108
Donelson, Stockely 48,117,
  118
Donica, Thomas 184
Dorah, John 114
Dorrel, Patt. 210
Dothero, Michel 44
Dotson, Chas. 276
  Jno. 276
  Oliver 7
Doty, Enoch 184
  Isaac 180
  Isariah 182
Dougan, J. 90
  John 89
Dougherty, George 266
Douglass, Edward 68
  Jonathan 84
  Mathew 227
  Sarah 94
  Thomas 84
  Wm./William 67,227
Dowler, Francis 60
Downs, Benjamin 155
  Nelson 244
  William 155
Dowtherd, Evan 105
Doyl, Eve 94
  John 94

Doyle, Stephen 73
Dozier, Peter 79
Drake, Abraham 145
  Benjamin 145,195
  John 193
Drew, John 38
Driskell, Davy 237,247
  Mahal 132
  Moses 247
  Nancy 247
Drue, Benjamin 179
Dry...95
  Joel 180
Dryden, David 155
Duffell, William 72
Duggar, Wm. 191
Duggard, Julias 145
  William 145
Dugger, Alexander 184
  Claiborne 184
  David 182
  James 185
  Joseph 180
  Julies 206
  William 206
Dike, Pleasant 114
Duley, Abraham 268
Dulin, Daniel 229
Dullwitt, John 91
Dumvell, Robert 103
Dunam, Hardin 210
Duncan, Craven 124,274
  John 13,40,127,271,150
  Joseph 42,207
  Margaret 40
  Kolly 10
  Wm/William 104,207,260
Duncome, Elizabeth 195
  John 195
  Joseph 193
Duncon, Charles 213
Dugan, Jeremiah 206
Dungeth, Charles 211
Dunging, Jaramiah 191
Dunham, Daniel 200
  Henry 198,268
  John 150,199,200
  Joseph 197,268
  Rebin 268
  Reuben 198
Dunkcome, John 201
Dunken, John 193
Dunkin, Antho. 209
  Charles 196
  Elizabeth 205
  Henry 229
  Jeremiah 183
  Jesse 145
  John 116
  Joseph 182
  Laurence 145
  Patt 207
  Peter 116
  Samuel 106
  Tho./Thomas 17,207
Dunlap...74
  Adam 34
  Ephraim 150,211
  George 44,79
  Hugh 75
  James 34,81
  John 34,88
  Richard G. 75
  Samuel 79,145
  Susannah 75
Dunlop, Jean 211
Dunn, Daniel 179,209
  Francis 75
  James 210
  Joseph 270
  Thomas 102,155
  Wm./William 79,272
Dunning, Samuel 88

Dunnivan, John 9
Dunnom, David 209
Dunsmore, Samuel 155
Durham, John 166
  William 5,34,115
Durram, Nath'l. 190,201
Dyer, David 155
  James 100
  John 145
  William 205,214
Dyke, Christian 181
  Henry 179,183

Eagen, Barnaby 207
Eagins, Edward 271
Eagleton, David 270
Eaker, Philip 181
Eakin, John 42
Earls, Frederick 132
Earnest, Amos 251
  Feliz 180
  Henry 180,197,266
  Jacob 182
  Lawrence 181
  Peter 184
Earp, Philip 262
  Thos. 262
Earps, Elijah 262
Easley, Peter 155
  Robert 155
  Stephen 155
Easly, Samuel 73
Eastepp, Shadrach 205
Easterlin, Thomas 155
Easterly, George 244
  Jacob 244
  N. W. 244
  Payne 244
  Philip 182
  Reuben 244
  Thos. J. 247
Eaton, Jos./Joseph 104,
  276
Ebbs, Greenberry 239
  John 239
  Jno. W. 239
Echel, Charles 61
Edden, James 206
Eden, James 145
Edgar, Alexander 136
  /Adgar, Andrew 124
  George 136
Edgee, Daniel 155
Edgman, Samuel 155
  William 155
Edington, James 249
  JOhn 53
  Martin 249
  William 91
Edmond, John 131
Edmonds, Wm. 251
Edmondson, James 44
  John 42
  Samuel 72,181
  Solomon 180
Edmondston, Wm. 205
Edmunds, Jno. 274
Edward, Joshua 138
Edwards, Abel 155
  Evan 198
  Henry 126
  John 44,136,155,210,
  225
  Laben 126
  Mark 44
  Samuel 10
  Solomon 145
Egle, William Henry 68
Eishford, John 164
Eisley, John 221
Eldridge, Leila Mason 33
  Thos. 268
  William 155

Elis, John 164
Elkins, Abraham 145
  George 164
  John 164
  Ralph 164
Ellice, Lewis 130
Ellington, Saml. 262
Elliot(t), Amos 10
  Benj. 104
  Israel 65
  Jacob 64,104
  James 72
  Matthew 84
  Robt. 223
  Thomas 64
Elliott, William 124
Ellis, Elbert 247
  Francis 65
  James 136
  Jehu 127
  John 124,184,208,275
  Moses 257
  Nathan 257
  Nehemiah 127
  Robert 73
  Samuel 181
  Shobal 180
  Thomas 181
  William 138,180,209
Ellisson, John 237
  Martin 237
  Wm. 237
Ellison, James 237
Ellisoon, Michael 237
Ellor, Jacob 155
Elmore, David 126
  Joel 138
  William 155
Elswick, Jonathan 229
  Stephen 229
Ely, George 182
Elya, John 155
Emberson, John 155
Emberton, Richd. 210
Emery, John 210
  Moses 210
Emmerson, Littleton T. 75
  Thomas 75,76
Emmett, George 204
Emmert, George 145,155,213
  Jacob 155
Emry, Joel 254
England, Charles 196
  Ezekiel 77
  Jacob 4,13
  John 13,77,155,196
  Joseph 13,77,196
Engle, George 145,211
English, Andrew 183
  Henry 145
  James 198,225
  John 209,216
  Joseph 196,197,272
  Joshua 225
  Matthew 110
  Robt./Robert 145,205
  Wm. 196,270
Enis, William 166
Enson, Thomas 212
Ensor, Thomas 204
Ephland, Mary 88
  Sarah 86,88
Epperson, Charls 165
  Joel 94
  Joseph 268
  Saml. 208
  William 164
Epps, Edward 84
  Geo. 254
Eroin, Alexr. 200
Erwin, David 155
  James 239
Erwine, Francis 228

10

Eslinger, David 244
Essey, Thomas 48
Estes, Barnet 116
  Ezekiel 116
  JOhn 98,116
  John C. 116
  Micaijah 91,116
  Robert 116
  Thomas 116
Estridge, Richard 145
Etherton, James 244
  Pleasant 244
Etsley, Joseph 155
Ettleman, Leonard 181
Evans, Andrew 111,119
  Archd. 209
  Archer 145
  David 108
  Davis 108
  D. T. 251
  Edmond 254
  Edward 44
  Elijah 251
  Evan 277
  George 135
  Jacob 133
  James 127,166
  Jessee 251
  Joel 108
  John 97,114,197
  John B. 134
  John H. 134
  Joseph 68
  Mary 91
  Samuel 145
  Thomas 197
  Thos. C. 251
  Walter 16,223
  William 79,114,155,166,
    205,251
Evens, Even 180
  Henry 183
  Jonathan 185,268
Everet, Philip 179
Everett, William 164
Ewing, George 30,50
  James 50
  John 44,49
  Margaret 50
  Wm. 50
Eyrs, Baley 227

Fabion, Henry 240
Fagan, John 155
Fain, John 213,273
  Samuel 195,213
  Willm. 206
Falls, James 183
Fansher, James 136
  Jno. 245
  W. L. 245
Faris, Richard 81
Farles, William 250
Farmer, Andrew 7
  David 70
  Fredk. 7
  Henry 7,19
  John 7,145
  Thomas 145
  William 21
Farnsworth, Benjamin 184
  David 181
  George 179
  Henry 180,273
  John 179
  Robert 180
Farragut, George 47,90
  David 47
  David Glasgow 90
Faubion, Jacob 245
  Jackson 240
  Jacob 252
  John 240,245

Faubion, Spencer 240
  Wm. 240,245
Fauling, William 200
Feers, Jacob 100
Feint, Phillip 272
Felker, Wm. 260
Felkner, George 168
  Jacob 168
Fellow, Jacob 180
Fellows, Abraham 184
Feltnor, John 155
Fenley, James 105
Fentress, John 206
Ferguson, James 72
  John 207
  William 86
Ferguhason, Robert 61
Ferrel, Charles 16
Ferrill, James 124
Feuston, John 182
Field, Stephen 155
Fiels(torn), Thomas 271
Fillpot, Joseph 135
Filpot, Timothy 129
Finch, Colvin 206
Finchum, James 252
  Wm. 252
Findley, Tho. 209
Fine, Abraham 235,255,260
  Isaac 255
  John 260,271
  Peter 271,334
  Thomas 260
  Vinet 257
Fink, George 155
  Paul M. 189,203
Finley, John 36,79,85
  Joseph 40
  Robert 34
  Samuel 118
  William 183
Finn, Jesse 36
Finney, Joseph 181
Finry, Joseph 255
Fips, John 5
  Joshua 5
Fisher, Anthoney 145
  Daniel 81
  John 44
  William 81,145,164
Fitzgarald, George 214
Fitzgerald, Garrett 122
  Patrick 38
Fitzsimmons, G. D. 134
  Thos. 134
Flanary, William 145,190
Flanery, Silus 205
  Wm. 206
Fleenor, Jacob 155
Fleming, Betsy 89
  Esther Ann 75
  John W. 223
  Polly 90
  Samuel 75,90
Flemmon, John W. 223
Flenniken, James W. 91
  Samuel 91
Fleshart, Elizabeth 61
  Francis 61
Fletcher, Richd. 195
  Thomas 195
Flin, George 155
Flora, Daniel 165,169
Foaly, Henry 276
Folkner, James 48
  John 48
Folsom, Nathaniel 145
Fooshee, John 183
Forbis, Thomas 124
Ford, Alex 51
  Alexander 155
  Benjn. 208,237
  Dye 155

Ford, Evan 237
  James 237
  John 132,136,155,210
  Joseph 145,206
  Loyd 208
  Mordicai 208
  Thomas 208
  William 179
Fore, Augustin P. 181
Forehand, Wm. 206
Forguson/Forgeson, Benjn.
  103
  Henry 48
  Hugh 40
  James 100
  John 40
  /Forgeson, Robert 40
Forgy, Alexander 88
  Andrew 88
  Hugh 88
Formwalt, Eve 94
  Jacob 61
  /Formault, John 94,114
Forrice, James 129
Forrest, Richard 7
Foster, Austin P. 2
  Benjamin 155
  Martin 115,183
  Michael 72
  Robert 183
  Winkfeild 165
Fothergill, Augusta B. 2
Fournier, N. H. S. 61
Foust, Christian 88
  George 95
  John 86,88,155
  Peter 155
  Philip 155
Fouster, Robert 46
Fout, Jacob 134,252
Fowler, Agnes 75
  Esther Ann 75
  F. F. 245
  Isaac 244
  John 245
  John F. 235,245,262
  Jno. T. 237
  Joseph 199
  Josiah 244
  Larkin 247
  Robert 75
  Thomas 245
  Willm. 207,245
Fox, Absolum 247
  Anderson 257
  Andrew 182
  Ezekiel 252
  George 254
  Jackson 252
  James 257
  John 247,257
  Ransom 250
  William 247,257
Fraiker, Adam 182
  Christian 182
  John 184
  Frederick 183
  Michael 182
Fraim, David 273
Frake, Michael 65
Frame, William 155,204
Francis, Archibald 254
  Burgess 254
  Edison 254
  Wm. 254,273
Frank (negro) 117
Franklin, L. D. 250
  Wm. 255
Franks, John 48
  Richard 145
Frasher, Alexander 145
Frazer, Hugh 124
  Moses 127

11

Frazer, William 127
Frasier, Alexander 183
  Ben. 257
  Martin 257
Frazier, Abner 184
  Ann 65
  Barbara 65
  Beriah 65
  David 182
  Ezekiel 179
  James 155
  Julian 65
  Rebecca 65
  Samuel 65,180
  Thomas 65,180
Frazor, Abner 138
Fream, William 213
Freese, Michael 183
French, George 214
  Henry 75,182,206
  Joseph 90
  Peter 214
Freshour, Jacob 240
Frew, Archd. 53
Frier, John 36
Friese, Jacob 180
Friley, Caleb 5
Frior, John 273
Frisby, Isaac 179
  Joshia 179
Fristoe, Robert 85
Frosher, Alexr. 209
Frost, Edward 19
  John 19,155
  Joseph 19,70
  Micajah 19
  Samuel 19
  Thomas 19
Fru, George 260
  James 255
  John 255
  William 260
Frushour, John 179
Fry, Philip 11
Fryar, John 90,95
  William 95
Frye, Gabriel 102
Fugat, Jackson 237
  John 237
  Noah 237
Fulkerson, John 155
  William 229
Fulsher, Carson 77
Fulton, Hugh 68
  Thomas 9
Funk, John 155
Funkhouser, John 155
Furman, James 273
Furry, Daniel 223
  John 223
Fuson, Thomas 70
Fuston, John 182

Gailey, James 321
Gaines, Francis H. 155
  James 155
  James T. 155
  Robert 100
Gains, James 166
Galaher, James 211
Galaspey, James 268
Galbraith, Andrew 163,166
Galbreaith, James 181
Galbreath, Alexander 13
  Arthur 168
  James 13
  Joseph 168
Galbreith, Thomas 124
Gallagher, George 77
Gallaher, Peter 13
  Wm. 247
Gallespie, George 265
Gallimore, Abram 155

Galt, John 209
Gambell, Thomas 112
Gamble, Agnes 75
  A. Marion 50
  Andrew 50,51,180
  John 50,67,182
  John N. 61
  Josiah 50
  Josias 50
  Mary 66,75
  Moses 155,182
  Robert 66,67,75,180
  Samuel 155
Gambol, Robert 207
Gambrel, Bradley 195
Gamil, David 276
Gammel, John 9
  William 9
Gammon, Harris 65
  Ivy 245
  John 65
  Lewis 65
  Richard 150,153,155
Gamwell, Ann 50
Gandrud, B. W. 23,34
Ganes, Ambrose 155
Gann, Adam 211
  Clement 211
  George 257
  John 210,255
  Nathan 210
Garden, Parish 138
Gardener, John 38
Gardner, Obediah 139
Garen, John 65
Garland, Ambrous 145
  Guttredge 144,145,206
  Harper 145
  Humphrey 206
  John 145,206
  Joseph 145,206
  Samuel 145,206
Garnagan, Chesley 100
  Martha 100
  Mary 100
  Thomas 100
Garner, Elizabeth 34,50
  /Garnor, James 34
  John 19,34,75
  /Garnor, John F. 34
  Obediah 100
Garret, John 260
Garretson, John 145
Garrett, Henry 183
Garrison, John 38
Garrot, Absalom 104
  Isaac 105
Garrott, Amos 190
Garvin, John 180
Garvis/Jarvis, Suks Luke
  108
Gass, George 183
  James 180
Gastin, Alexander 19
Gaston, Joseph 181
Gauld, Samuel 44
Gault, Thomas 65
Gaut, John 46,131
  Wm. 46
Geiger/Giger, George 134
  John 134
Genkins, Rowland 205
Gentri, Joseph 165
Gentry, Ayrs 133
  Bartlett 124
  Charles 198
  John 185
  Joseph 145,190,205
  Martin 124
  Robert 124,198
George, Edward 124
  James 69,155
  Reuben 135,221

George, Samuel 53,73
  Silas 131
  Solomon 75
  Traverse 73
Geron, Joseph 65
Gess, John 16
Gest, Benj. 199,201
  Joseph 199
Ghormley, Joseph 51
Gibbons, Epps 163,169
  John 165
  Patrick 124
  Thomas 161
  Wm. 169
Gibbs, Barbara 65
  David 88
  George 75
  Jacob 88
  John 88,100
  Mary 88
  Nicholas 65,88
Gibson, Andw. 52
  /Gipson, Archeles 104
  Benja. 196
  /Gipson, Garret or
  Garrot 104,127
  Humphry 196
  Jacob 100
  James 180
  John 19,51,52,81,93,
  183,198
  Samuel 81,276
  Thomas 52
  Tiry 163
  William 183
Giddens, Randal 11
Giffeler, Adam 155
Gifford, Jabez 155
Gilbert, Felix 10
  John 118
Gilberts, Saml. 271
Gilbreath, Alexander 266
  Hugh 42
  John 67,169
  Joseph 169
  Thomas 42
  Wm. 40
Gilbreth, Jno. 274
  Wm. 274
Giles, Holloway 262
  Jessee 262
  John 209
Gilespy, Geo. 211
  John 211
  Tho. 211
Gilington, Nicholas 103
Gillahan, John 198
Gillam, John 145
Gillaspie, Alex 51,53
  James 46,50
Gilleland, John 191,260
  Wm. 262
Gillenwaters, Joel 169
  Thos. 169
  Wm. 163,169
Gilles, John 268
Gillespie, George 177
  Jacob 67
  James 44,79
  John 46
  Mary 81
  Pollie 44
  Robert 46
  Thomas 67,81,197
  Wm./William 46,53
  Zacharia 51
Gillespy, Thomas 272
Gillett, A. J. 250
  Jno. 250
  Wm. P. 237
Gilliam, Devereaux 62,75
  Deverix 81
  Hinch 169

Gilliam, Polly 62
  Spencer 65
  Susannah 75
  Thomas 65
Gilliams...252
Gillihand, Jno. 277,334
Gilmore, John 40,104
Ginkins, Aaron 19
Ginnings, Hezekiah 102
  John 155
  Royal 102
  Thomas 104
  Wm. 104
Ginnins, Danl. 19
Gipson, James 115
Gist, Benjamin 182,277
  Jno. 277
  Thos. 277
  William 124
Givens, Sam 93
  Samuel 67
  William 92
Glade, August 61
Glaize, Laurens 271
Glass, James 183
  John 95,128,179,180
  Samuel 30,53
  Wm./William 38,207
Glasscock, John 182
Glenn, James 224
  Robert 216,223
Glespy, Fanny 169
Goad, Ayers 229
  Gabriel 155
  John 155
  Joshua 230
  Margaret 155
  Peter 155
  Thomas 70
  William 70,155
Goar, Thomas 208
Goard, Ayers 19
Godard, Francis 168
Goddard, Thomas 155
  William 155
Goen/Goin, Daniel 132,133
  Ezekiel 133
  James 114
  John 114
  Thomas 100
  William 133
Goforth, William 181,268
  Zacharia 36
Gold, John 40
Gollaher, John 9
  Joseph 9
Golstein, Stephen 17
Golston, John 9
Gooch, Austin 250
  John 250
  Wm. 250
Gooding, Drury 192
Goodman, Benjamin 268
  James 268
  Stephen 36
  Thos. 268
Goodner, Conrad 155
Goodpasture, Abraham 214
  John 214
  Solomon 214
Goodson, John 155
  Joseph 127
  William 129
Gordon/Gorton, Elijah 79
  Geo./George 7,136,181
  Robert 7
Gore, Ambrose 134
Gorman, John 255
  Thos. 255
Gorrell, Thomas 182
Gotcher, Henry 195
Gott, Anthony 208
Gour, Thomas 67

Gour, William 67
Gourley, Tho./Thomas 145,
  205
Gozach, Sandofar 199
Grace, Richard 126
Grady, John 221
Gragg, Geo. W. 240
  John 185
  Thos. M. 247
  Thos. W. 240
Graham, George 123,134,184
  James 179
  John 155,181
  Nathaniel 86
  Spencer 5,221
  Thomas 179
  William 183,250,252
Grainger, Mary 30,62,97
Grant, Isaac 114
  James 15,16,21,216
  John 228
  Richard Rosey 61
  Thomas 69
Grantum, John 85
Grate, David 213
Grave, Daniel 86
  John 86
Graves, Betsy 86
  Bostian 88
  Boston 86
  James 145
  John 205
  Peter 88
  Sarah 86,88
  Stephen 34
  William 85
Gray, Abner 183
  Absalom 184
  David 183
  Edward 180,183
  George 193,208,252,255,
  257
  Jacob 136,179,229
  James 221,252,257,260
  Joseph 221
  Leven 65
  Nathl. 221
  Robert 181,208
  Wm. 52,255,257,260
  Willis 208,260
Grayson, Benjamin 77
  /Grason, Jesse 70
  John 77
  Joseph 3,19
Green, David 237
  Francis 129,166
  Funny 118
  Jacob 275
  James 7,75,112,262
  James I. 42
  Jeremiah 237
  Jesse 79
  /Greene, John 108,124,
  169,245,262
  Johua 209
  Joseph 112,127
  Pillamore 185
  Thomas 237
  Washington 237
  Wm. 262
Greenaway, James 48
Greene, Nathanael 177
  Thomas 179
  William 180
Greenley, John 126
Greenwood, Bailey 5
Greer, Alexr./Alexander
  145,211
Greer, Andrew 141,145,187,
  188,200,207,208
  Andrew Jr. 155
  Arthur 50
  John 138

Greer, Joseph 61,192,208
  Margery 63
  Thomas 126
Greeg, Isaac 129
  James 155,204,213
  Nathan 155,204,213
Gregory, Archibald 260
  Samuel 260
Grier, John 124
Griffen, William 205
Griffeth, Wm. 225
Griffey, Richard 229
Griffin, Jessee 13
  William 134,145,190
Griffis, William 90
Griffith, Thomas 16,228
  William 13,48
Grifith, George 105
  John 102
Grills, E. 77
  Eleanor 60
  Elliott 12,75
  John 75
Grimes, George 5,225
  Henry 190
  John 190,207
  Saml. 225
Grindstaff, Henry 145
  Isaac 206
  Jacob 207
  Michal 207
  Michael 145
  Nicholas 207
Grisham, Ezekial 124
  James 108
  Richard 124
  Thompson 124
Grism, James 191
Gris'om, Wm. 193
Grisom, William 213
Grissam, Tho. 209
Grissom, Robert 136
Grisry, Daniel 164
Grizzel, Herod 164
Grose, John 118
Gross, Edmd. 221
  George 155
  John 155
  Wm. 169
Grosse, John 169
Groves, David 168
  Fanny 169
  John 118
  Stephen 85
  Susan 85
  William 85
Grubb, Jacob 155
  John 155
Grymes, James 198
Guess, Samuel 124
Guffee, Ephim 108
Guin, Evan 180
  Hugh 181
  James 180
  John 180
  Randolph 180
  Robert 184
  William 182
Guinn, Champness, 205
  James 205
  Peter 205
  Wm. 104
Gullet, Richard 273
Gulley, Lazarus 185
  Lewis 185
Gurtner, David 179
  Michael 179
Guthrie, James 185
Guthry, Alexander 133
  Boyce 19
  George 9
  John 185
Guyn, David 165

13

Gyllim, John 205

Hack, Andw. 44
Hacker, John 156
   Julius 156
   Julius Sr. 156
Hackett, John 13,90,95
Hackney, Benjamin 69
   Hugh 52
   Jacob 163,164
Hackworth, Augustine 10,
   70
   Nicholas 10
Haddon, Elisha 210
Hagan, Arthur 156
   James 165
Haggard, Henry 124
Hagood, Elizabeth 168
   James 168
Hagler, Abraham
Hail, Alexr. 156
   Isom 48
   John 145
   William 271
Haile, Jonathan 129
   Nathan 9
   /Hail, Wm/William 47,
   129
Hailey, Barnebas 118
   Claiborne 86
   David 98,100,101
   John 86
Haines, Abraham 181
   Joshua 224
Hains, Andw. 210
   Israel 88
   Richd. 205
   Zachariah 166
Hair, Danl. 197
   Henry 184
Haislet, George W. 79
   Benjamin C. 92
Haislett, William 92
Halbert, Joel 86
   John 86
   Stephen 88
Hale, Abednego 208
   George 164
   H. L. 250
   Hugh D. 247
   John 245
   Joseph 240,247
   Joshua 208
   Mesach 206,209
   Nathl. 210
   Nichs. 210
   Patrick H. 247
   Philip 184
   Richd. 208
   Shadrach 209
   Thos. L. 247
   Wm. 210
Halfacor, Michael 272
Halfacre/Halfaker, Mich-
   ael 5,105
   Peter 107
Halfley...33
   Conrod 34
Hall...115
   Andrew 52,180
   David 19
   Hilard 67
   James 101
   John 104,181
   Jno. W. 252
   Nancy 65
   Nathaniel 180,209
   Robert 181
   Royal 252
   Samuel 70,255,257
   Thomas 19,65
   W. S. 252
   William 181,209,247

Hallaway, John 124
Hallon, William 156
Halmark, George 88
   Thomas 78
Hambleton/Hamilton, Isaiah
   73
Hamblin, Hezekiah 164
   John 106
Hambright, Benjamin 77
   John 77
   John H. 77
   Nancy 77
Hamer, Marguerite B. 63
   Philip M. 7
Hamilton, Abram 155
   Benjn. 156
   Francis 65,198,199,275
   Isiah 199
   Jacob 198
   James 65,101
   John 156
   Joseph 121,133
   Joshua 156
   Peter 101
   Richd. 156
   Robbert 165
   Thomas 156
   William 168
Hammer, Jacob 212
   John 204,212
Hammonds, Willm. 207
Hammuck, Isaac 128
Hamontree, James 44
   /Hammontree/Hammantree,
   Jeremiah 44
Hammantree, John 44
Hampton, James 182
   Joshua 47
   Samuel 156
   Wayd 245
Hancock, Geo. 228
   Joel 11
   John 16,228
   Martin 228
   William 16,216
Handley, Samuel 198
Handly, Saml. 211
Hanes/Haynes, Christopher
   126
   George 145
   John 126
Haney, Haywood 250
   Lewis 250
   Samuel 83
   Spencer 83
Hankins, Able 85,101
   Abraham 73
   Absalom 88
   David 73
   Edward 101,139
   John 73
   Margaret 75
   Richard 139
   Thomas 139
   William 100,101,182
Hanley, Saml. 42
Hanna, Andw. 54
   Jhn. 19,44
   Joseph 42
   Robert 54
   Wm. 44
Hannah, Andrew 156,210
   John 207,210,225
   Samuel 181
   William 184,207
Hanson, Jonathan 72
Hansroe, JOhn 228
Har, Job 245
Harbert...156
   David 107
Harbison, James 86
Harden, William 146
Hardin, Amos 78

Hardin, Benjamin 78
   Gibson 9,78
   James 77
   John 250
   Joseph 77,178,266,275
   Sarah 77
Hare, Peter 252
Harelson, John 112
   Wm. 112
Hargas, William 38
Hargrove, Benj. 133
   Eli 133
   Joseph 133
Harlas, David 17
   George 17
   Henry 17
   Philip 17
Harlen, Samuel 164
Harmon, Chrisley 182
   Christopher 126
   George 181
   Isaac 181
   Jacob 83,126,183
   John 221,266
   Lewis 126
   Paril 11
   Peter 179
   Philip 182
   Stephen 181
   Thomas 180
   Wm./William 11,112
Harned, David 245
Harness, John 12
Harnis, John 221
Harper, Thomas 133
   Wm. 262
Harralson, James 69
   Major 85
   William 61
Harrel, Baldwin 247
   Enoch 168
   Hazel 168
   John 168
Harrington, Charles 198
Harris, Even 104
   John 40,112
   Jonathan 40
   Madison Monroe 87
   Peter 117,118
Harris(s), Richard 102
Harris, Robert 104
   Samuel 54,117
   Simon 87
   Wm. 40
   Wm. P. 238
Harrison, Benjamin 133
   Danl. 211
   George 181
   Isaiah 179
   James 133
   Jeremiah 179
   John 137,262
   Reuben 262
   William 133,179
Harriss, James 156
   Jeremiah 156
Hart & Brown 221
Hart, Alexander 38
   David 12,21
   Hardy 106
   Joseph 38,221
   Leonard 156
   Robert 61
   Susannah 17
   T. 70/Thomas 12,17,270
Hartleroad, Henry 156
   Martin 156
Hartgrove, Thomas 260
Hartsell, Charles 260
   Isaac 257
   Jacob 260
   Morris 260
Harty, Dennis 181

14

Harvey, James 247
  John 131
Hasket, John 128
Haskins, Thomas 107
Hastings, Abrm. 208
  Saml. 208
Hastler, Michal 13
Haston, Danl. 211
  David 70
Hatcher, William 156
Hatfield, Andrew 225
  James 225
  Jeremiah 225
  Jonathan 225
  Joseph 225
  Richard 16
Hatherly, George 191
  Samuel 191
Hatley, William 69
Hatly, Elias 260
  John 260
Hatmaker, Francis 221
Hatter, Michael 136
  Phillip 136
Haun, Abraham 145
  Christopher 145
  Mathias 145
  Sebaustein 145
Havely, Jacob 182
Hevenridge, John 65
Havens, James 137
  John 137
  William 12
Havron, James 156
Hawk, Paulser 179
Hawke, John 156
Hawkins, Henry 100,156
  John 100,156
  Matthew 13
  Nathan 156
  Nicholas 156
  Samuel B. 116,169
  Thomas 100
Hawn, Danl. 228
Haworth, Absalom 180,181
  George 269
  James 138,180,181
  Richard 138
  Willi 138
Haws, Danl. 228
Hawthorn, Noah 207
Haygood, Tapley 109
Hayne...60
Haynes, Richard 14
  Stephen 61
  Sterling 231
Hays, David 184
  James 182,183
  Jno. 274
  John 124
  Joseph 5,183
  Nancy 65
  Nicholas 182
  Robert 182,221
  Wm./William 114,227
Hayter, Abrm. 225
Haywood, Wm. 166
Hayworth, Absom 276
  Jas. 276
  Stephen 126
Headrick, Daniel 240
  David 245
  Henry 181
  John 180,240
  William 180
Heard, James 9
  Stephen 4,20
Heath, William 73
Heather, Thos. 225
Heatherick, Jacob 145
Heatherly, Hueins 191
  John 146
  J. T. 218

Heaton, John 146
Heavins, James 88
Hedrick, Jacob 206
  Joseph 206
  William 164
Hellums, John 77,78
  William 78
Helms, Jonathan 17
Helton, Marvil 164
  Peter 145,146
  William 126
Henderson, Andrew 121,122,
  124
  Archibald 4,12,21
  Daniel 83,184
  David 137
  George 166
  James 221,270
  John 47,124,146,181
  John Fr. 146
  Joseph 47,182
  Nathaniel 161,168
  Peter 63,146
  Richard 62,118
  Robert 122,124,182
  Samuel 92,168,181
  Thomas 97,98,109,118
  Tho. 210
  Wm. 47,276
  William 109
  William A. 267
Hendricks, John 145,207
  Solomon 145,206
Hendrex, Garret 70
  Luke 70
  Morgan 70
Hendrix, Esquire 10
Henery, Charles 44
Henley, David 61,95
Henly, Geo. S. 245
  Thomas 160
  Thos. O. 252
Hennegar, Jacob 181
Henry...252
  Abraham 145
  Elizabeth Garner 50
  Danl. 169
  James 44,50,191
  Jno. 260
  Rachel 34
  Reuben 238
  Robt. 211,255,260
  Samuel 30,34,44,50,191,
  192
  Spencer 252
  /Henery, Wm./William
  50,124,260
Hensley, Edmond 165
  George 79
  Robert 168
  Temple 165
  Trent 165
Henson, Pall 101
Herman, Adam 206
Herren, Wm. 224
Herse, John 36
Hesse...36
Hethaway, Leonard 156
Hetherly, Evins 205
Hetrick, Jacob 204,213
Hewet, William 229
Hewitt, Jno. 255
  Nathaniel 61
  William 156
Heziah, Richard 103
Hibbard, Lemuel 117
Hibbert, Jedidiah 124
  John 98
Hichland, John 47
Hickey, Cornelius 83
  David 192,270
  Henry 260
  Isaac 240

Hickey, John 83
  Joseph 260
  Saml. H. 247
Hickky, Henry 193
Hickman, Benjamin 124
  Francis 124
  James 104,128
  Peter 205,214
Hicks, Abraham 92
  Charles 92
  David 190,191,262
  Henry 156
  Isaac 156,168
  Jacob 156
  James 166,260
  John 93
  Joseph 260
  Moses 260
  Richard 156
  Shedrach 156
  Stephen 156
  Timothy 260
Hide, William 231
Hider, Adam 145
  Elizabeth 145
  John 145
  Michael 145,191,206
Higgans, John 190
Higgins, John 73
Hightower, Allen 255
  Austin 271
  Joshua 78
  Oldhum 197
  Richard 268
Hiler, David 168
Hill, Abraham 137
  Charles 211
  Daniel 136
  Edward 90
  Eli 252
  Henry 72
  Hill 137
  Isaac 209
  James 11,114,268
  Joab 114
  John 79,86,118,134,145,
  193
  John S. 166
  Joseph 130
  Lewis 89
  Matthew 228
  Robert 136
  Samuel 184
  Samuel Jr. 137
  Samuel Sr. 136
  Thomas 14
  William 110,130
Hillsman, John 61
Hilton, Arnold 156
  Charles 156
  John 156
Himall, Robert 269
Hincha, William 128
Hindman, James 61
Hinds, John 88
  Joseph 95
  Levi 65,95
  Samuel 88
  Sylvanus 88
  William 79
Hinkle, George 126
  Henry 12
Hinshaw, John 104
  William Wade 51
Hippingstall, Joseph 69
Hipps, Jno. H. 255
Hipsheer, Henry 109
Hipsheers, Mathias 109
Hitterick, John 156
  William 156
Hix, Jonathan 273
Hixson, Andrew 180
  Joseph 185

15

Hixson, Timothy 183
  William 185
Hoan, Jacob 92
Hobbs, James 14,19
  Joel 19
Hobson, Edward 199
  George 75
Hodge, Ambrose 192
  Francis 156,213
Hodges, Ambrose 114,214
  Charles 128
  Drury 268
  Edmond 135
  Francis 214
  James 101
  John 204,212
  Martha 117
  Moses 114
  Welcom 269
  Wm./William 156,209
Hogg, James 16,21
  Obediah 101
  Reubin 101
  Saml. 44
Hoggatt, Anthony 136
Hogget, Solomon 136
Hogahead, William 7
Hoke, Michael 83
Holaway, John 44
  William 131
Holdaway, Timothy 135
Holder, John 262
Holdway, Hezekiah 247
  Timothy 191,200
  Wm. 247
Holland, H. L.240
  James 238
  Peter 86,208
  Shadrick 168
  Wm. 238
Holley, Francis 200
  Jacob 200
  John 200
  Jonathan 197
Hollingsworth, Eli H. 252
  E. V. 221
Hollis, James 150,195
Holloway, Jeremiah 225
  John 156
  Jos. 255
  William 182,209,255
Holly, Elizabeth 274
Holman, G. S. 134
  Peter 134
Holoway, Wm. 210
Holt, Asa 247
  Barrott 183
  David 102,181
  Edward 102,247
  Emily 60
  Henry 227
  Irby 90
  Jas. S. 247
  Joel 78
  Joseph 185
  Josiah 247
  Michael 17
  Paschal 247
  Robert 60,90
  Simon 156
  William /Wm. 17,247
  Zebadee 247
Holten, Daniel 44
Holton, John 50
Honeycutt, Ezekiel 200
Honycut, Austin 200
Hood, Abraham 179
  Andrew 92
  Aron 92
  Hethpon 227
  John B. 61
  Nathaniel 184
  Robert 274

Hood, Soloman 92
  Thomas 92
  William 180
Hooke, John 61
Hooker, William 146
Hooks, Robert 38
Hoose, Jacob 212
Hooser, John 145,146
Hooss, Jacob 204
Hopkins, John 207
  Thomas 165
Hopper, Archeble 112
  Charles 131
  William 184
Hord, William 112
Horn, Adam 209
  Fredrik, Jr. 166
  Jacob 83
  Thomas 9
Hornback, John 126
Horner, George 129
  James 104
  John 104
Horton, John 184
  William 13,129
Hoskins, C. S. 190
  Elias 11,107
  Elisha 205
  Jess/Jesse 129,190
  John 190
  Josiah 190
  Ning/Ninion 190,205
  Thomas 207
  William 124
Hoslar, George 7
Houghton, Joshua 192
  Thomas 187,192,200
Hous, Geo. 209
House, William 133
Houseley, Robert 156
Houser, John 156
  Nicholas 156
Houston, Elizabeth Mc-
  Croskey 44
  Elizabeth Paxton 40
  Ester 41,44
  Howel 240
  J. 54
  James 31,44,53,178,180,
    266
  John 40,208,209
  Margaret 33
  Martha Lyle 40
  Matthew 40,44
  Peter 83
  R. 76,94
  Robert 20,75,79,221
  Samuel 40,44
  Samuel Rutherford 33
  William 34,180,207
Houts, Christopher 182
Howard, Alexr. 133
  Ezekiel 182
  Henry 137
  James 135,200,201
  John 7,129,146,198
  Reason 78
  Richard 104,277
  Robert 105
  Samuel 78
  Thomas 78
  William 101,229
Howarton, Jackson 88
Howat, Jno. J. 262
Howath, Absalom 183
Howell, Benjamin 114
  Calip 114
  David W. 60
  /Howell, Henry 98,114
  Jno. J. 238,252,255
  /Howell, John 114,169
  Melchiah 114
  Philip 180

Howel, William 114
Howeth, William 102
Hoyal, Jacob 182
Hubbard, Lm. 268
Hubbs, John 73
Hubs, Caleb 271
Houcheson, Samuel 47
Huckaby, John 230
Huckoby, John 221
  Thos. 231
  William 221
Hudeburg, Tho. 206
Hudeburk, Thomas 145
Hudelton, John 112
Hudgings, Ambrose 108
  Robert 108
Hudiburgh, Thomas 83
Hudlin, James 252
Hudson...115
  Benjn. 112
  Burrel 9
  Ezekiel 112
  Geo. 198
  James 112
  Jno. 247
  /Hutson, John 13,112
  Obadiah 112,250
  Richd. 54
  Sterling 247,250
  Thomas 17
Huff, David 238,240
  Elizabeth 262
  John 260
  Jonathan 238
  Joseph 240
  Leonard 182
  Peter 260
  Sarah 262
  Stephen 238
  Thomas B. 240
  Wm. 250,252,260
Huffaker, Hugh D. 79
Huffer, Daniel 85
Huffman, Andrew 184
  Jesse 179
  John 135
  Peter 156
Huffstadler, David 180
Hufman, Daniel 145
  Jacob 195,201
  Peter 195,201
Hughes, Aaron 134
  Abner 156
  David 156,198
  Francis 178,197,200,221,
    266,272
  James 183
  John 134,181,192
  Thomas 156
  William 156
Hughman, David 208
Hughs, David 204,213
  Hardy 112
  John 112
  Moses 48
  Robert 48,101,204,213
  Saml. M. 245
  William 204,213
Hull, John 185
Huls, William 156
Human, Bazel 65
Humbard, Eden 181
Humberd, William 101
Humbert, John 205
  Thomas 181
Humble, Joseph 168
  Mary 168
Humboard, Isaac 257
Humes, Thomas 61,124
  Thomas W. 61
Humphrey, John 213
Humphreys, Jesse 145
Humphrys, Elisha 206

Humphrys, Jesse 209
    John 104
    Richd. 210
    Wm. 210
Hunicutt, Joseph 138
Hunnycut, John 228
Hunsley, Christian 183
Hunt, Abraham 270
    Jesse 210
    Jno. 255
    John 118,156,161
    Uriah 195,208
    Willson 61
Hunter, David 224
    George 130
    Henry 105
    James 65,136,205,214
    John 181,214
    Samuel 130
    Thomas 181
Huntsinger, Jacob 164
Huntsman, Jacob 69
Hurley, Danl. A. 252
Hurly, James 250
    Zachariah 247
Hurny, Thomas 185
Hurst, Abraham 184
    Elijah 183
    John 118
Husbans, Harmon 72
Huse, John 36
Husong, Jacob 92
Hussey, Christopher 52
Husse, Elija 52
Hutcherson, Charles 112
    Paul 112
Hutchings, Smith 269
    Thomas 161
    George 182
    Harris H. 180
Hutton, Josiah 44
Hutson, David 184
    Robert 184,275
    Saml. 206,275
    Thomas 184
    William 184
    Wm. B. 245
Hutton, Samuel 193
    William 199
Hymns, George 156

Icenhower, John 240
    Martin 240,252
    Peter 240
Icenhoser, Philip 240
Ingland, Thomas 40
Ingle, Peter 146
Ingles, Eleanor 60
    Rhoda 60
    Thomas 60
Inglish & Martin 222
Inglish, John 5,115
    Joseph 5,115
    Joshua 115
    Wm./William 16,110,115
Ingram, Andw. Sr. 169
    John 182
    Purnell 72
    Thos. 169
    Zachariah 169
Inman, Abednego 210
    Charles 247
    Green 252
    Joshua 252
    Lices 247
    S. H. 247
    Shadrick 269
    Shedrick 133
    Thos. W. 247
    William H. 130
Ireby, Isam 197,201
Irvine, Alfred 260
Irwin, Ann 66,75

Irwin, Francis 85
    George 129
    James 54,208
    Robert 54
    Samuel 133
Isaacs, Caleb 225
Isbel, Hickman 156
Isbell, Godfrey 196
    Zacha 196,197
    Zachariah 187
Iseley, Conrod 156
    Jacob 156
Ish, Elizabeth 52
    John 52
Isham, Goin 224
Ishmael, Benjamin 182
    Thomas 182
Isom, John 73
Ivey, Backster 114
    Henry 114
    Howel 206
    James 146,206
    Vandimon 114

Jack, George 81
    Henry 252
    Jeremiah 81,266
    John 94
    Samuel 122
    William 166
    Wm. 255
Jackson, Andrew 44,62
    Annis 81
    Churchwell 12
    Daniel 184
    David 5
    Jeremiah 65
    Joshua 156
    Josiah 133
    Micajah 168
    Nathan 112,128
    Peter 81,156
    Reubin 108
    Samuel 127,138
    Thomas 164
    Vincent 182
    William 88,114,146
Jacobs, Edward 20
    Greenberry 7
    Zachariah 7
Jago, Abraham 166
James, Bennett 156
    Jesse 98,112
    John 40
    Marquis 40
    Rawlings 146
    Rowland 209
    Samuel 52
    Thomas 112
    Walter 156
    Wm./William 107,112,
      255
Jameson, Benjamin 180
    George 182
    John 7,44
    Robert 184
Jamison, Ben 273
    Geo. 274
Jarman, John 137
Jarnagan, Drury 114
    John 114
    D. N. 250
    Lavinia 101
    Mary 101
    Noe 104
    Thomas 195
Jarnigan, Thomas 137
Jeffers, Thomas 118
Jefferson, Wm. 209
Jeffries, James 230
    William 230
Jenings, William 137
Jenkins, Augustine 252,262

Jenkins, Delilah 262
    Hugh 146
    Jessee 262
    Joel 262
    John 262
    Phillip 262
    Roland 146
    Wm. 262
    Washington 250
Jentry, Aaron 72
Jeoffery...6
    Jeremiah 7
    Joseph 7
Jervis, James 273
Jett, Edward 247
Jinings, Wm. 118
Joab, David 205
    Jacob 156
    Nathan 156
    Samuel 156
Job, William 121,234,270
Joffill, Dudley 156
Johnson, Craven 7
    Enus 127
    George 73,168
    Isaac 182,200
    Jacob 269
    James Jr. 166
    James Sr. 166
    John 164
    Joseph 257
    Margery 63
    Mary Lou 84
    Pleasant 164
    Smauel 124
    William 7,16,124,128,
      133
    Wm. 166,196
Johnston...67
    Ambrose 78
    Amelia 21
    Benja. 196
    Calvin 92
    Christopher 61
    Daniel 101
    David 272
    Francis 70,181
    Harrison 181
    Hutson 161
    Isaac 70,92
    Jacob 181
    James 79,93,179,271
    Jesse 181
    John 52,87,118,138,146,
      270
    Joseph 92,181
    /Johnson, Kinza 3,7
    Moses 181
    Noble 61
    Philip 156
    Robert 86,92,180
    Stephen 117
    Thomas 156,163,180,183
    Walter 156
    William 21,88,92,182,221,
      271,276
Jolliff, William 156
Jonackin, Thomas 195
Jones, A. 182
    Americus 238
    Ann 52
    Aqualla 110,165
    Calvin M. 252
    Crafford 180
    Daniel 247
    David 130
    Ebenezer 48
    Esther 75
    Evan 180,181,277
    Francis 52
    George 179
    George J. 81
    Harry 164

17

Jones, Harwood 101
  Henry 156,199,255,273
  Hester 85
  Isaac 71,118,181
  James 146,181,196,247
  Jane 52
  Jeremiah 79
  Jesse 65
  Joanne 52
  John 85,156,179,180,182,
  255,269
  Johnston 52
  Jones 124
  J. R. 239
  Levi 16
  Lewis 54,146,191,207
  Mark 227
  Martin 166
  Mary 92
  Matthew 13
  Nathl. 207
  Phillip 196
  Phineas 180
  Pistimas 52
  Reps 334
  Samuel 52
  Solomon 156
  Sugar 228
  Thomas 13,52,104,134,
  138,146,156,182,255
  Thos. M. 247
  Walter 165
  Wells 146
  William 110,118,225,227,
  250
  Willie 188
  W. P. 247
  Wyett 238
  Zephaniah 85
Jonson, James 271
Jordan, Ezekiah 107
  Lewis 211
  Weymouth T. 60
Jourdan, John 245
Journeygan, Elisha 95
Judkins, James 168
Jue, Robert 12
Juland, John 13
  George 65
Julian, Benjamin 65
  Rebecca 65
  Stephen 65
Julien, John 72
  Rene 72
Justice, Jacob 146
Justis, Isaac 180
  Thomas 183
  Martin 240

Kain, Jennie 85
  Kittie 85
  Mattie 85
Kaler, Frederick 156
Kallewon, James 183
Karr, George 199
Kauble, Adam 183
  Michael 184
Kean, John 17
Kearnes, Charles 75
  Henry 83
  James 85,87
  John 85
  Michael 83
  N. 59,63
  Nicholas 62
  Sarah 87
  Valentine 83
Keeble, Wm. 50
Keehill, Richards 92
Keel, James 185
  John 185
  Richd. 208
  William 185

Keele, James 208,274
  Richd. 275
Keener, Peter 80
  Woolrick 80
Keeney, John 334
  Joseph 272
Keeth, John 83
Kein, John 85
Keith, Daniel 200
  James 133
  Nicholas 133
Kelland, Thomas 95
Kellar, Daniel 180
  Henry 181
Kelldea, Henry 182
Kellems, Danl. 207
  Gilbert 205
Keller, David 181
  John 183
Kelley, James 193
  John 270,272
  Kinchin 212
Kellogg, Louise Phelps 10
Kelly, Alexander 30,48,87,
  266
  Anthony 182
  Bryson 250
  Charles 250
  Isaac 133
  Jacob 133
  James 181,183
  /Kelley, John 48,179,
  248
  Jonathan 252
  /Kelley, Joseph 87
  Joshua 206
  Michael 87
  William 182,240,257
Kelsey, Alexander 180
  John 180
  Saml. 208
Kelso, Alexander 124
  Hugh 42,122,124
  Willm. 207
Kelsy, Moses 211
Kenady, Henry 128
  Rebecah 128
Kendrick, Edom 252
  Edom J. 252
  Fine P. 252
  Geo. W. 252
Kenedy, Andrew 50
  Daniel 200
  John 44
  Rachel Penny 50
Keney, John 269
Kennedy, Daniel 178,266
  James 80
  John 34,184
  Thomas 180
Kenner, John 191
  Rodham 164
Kenney, James 118,181
Kenny, Jacob 83
  James 266
  John 134
Kensinger, John 169
Kepener, Elizabeth 52
Kerbough, John 181
Kerby, Christopher 180
  Daniel 185
  John 7,21
Kerns, George Jr. 164
  George Sr. 164
  Jacob 165
  John 164
Kerr, Andrew 67,124
  David 124
  James 274
  Patt. 210
  Richard 183
  Robert 178,265,276
  Samuel 80

Kerr, Wm./William 67,274
Kesterson, John 183
  Nancy 248
Key, David 13,181
  Joas 156
  John 182
  Peter 13
  Zachariah 13
Keywood, Benjn. 106
  John 156
  Stephen 106
Kiberley, William 230
Kidwell, John 98
  Josiah 117
Kifer, John 181
Kilbrath, Thomas 259
Kilbreth, Alexander 274
Kilburn, Henry 208
Kile, Robert 164
Kilgore, Jane 240
  Thomas 240
Killdea, John 179
Killgore, Charles 179,271
  William 180
Killian, Eli 240
Killion, Henry 70
Kilpatrick, Patt. 209
Kimberly...94
Kimbrel, Charles 75
  Paterson 75
Kimbro, Jesse 124
Kimbull, John 62
Kimes, Conrad 184
Kimmons, Joseph 146,182
Kimra, George 108
Kincade, David 165
  William 224
Kincaid, James 106
  John 10
Kinchelo, Geo. 209
Kincheloe, Elijah 168
  John 156
Kindle, George 211
King...163
  Baker 205
  Edward 204,213
  Harmon 269
  Henry 204,213
  James 117,156
  John 48,128,157,165,
  204,213
  Johnson 34
  Jonathan 204,213
  Kerbey 209
  Mary 139
  Murry T. 227
  Philip 169
  Robert 34,110,115,269
  Samuel 48,183
  Thomas 110,156,204,213
  Walter 156
  William 60,101,106,146,
  150,156,164,227
Kinkaid, Thomas 10
Kinnet, Thomas 221
Kirby, Francis 92
  Joseph 54,92
Kirbey, Richd. 54
Kerkpatrick, David 129
  Hugh 129
  Jacob 129
Kirk, Elijah 87
  John 184
  Saml. 169
Kirkkham/Curkham, Wm. 107
Kirkindol, James 208
Kirkland, James H. 267
  Mary H. 267
Kirklin, Moses 106
Kirkpatrick, Alexr. 20
  Charles 34
  James 34,112,129,168
  John 63,112

Kirkpatrick, Robert 211
  Thomas 34
Kirkwood, Dvaid 276
Kiser, Joseph 181
Kitchen, Jessee 101
  John 18
Kite, Isaac 146
  Philip 156
  Richard 146,205
Kizer, George 164
  Peter 73
Kline, Jacob 168
Knabb, Jacob 137
Knave, Jacobs 83
  Teter 207
Knight, John 156
  Richard 238
Kniseley, John 156
Knox, Joseph 52
  William 90
Kunse/Kounce...33
Kunse, Adam 34
  Henery 34
  /Kounce, John 11,34
Kykindal, Adam 275
  Jno. 275
Kyle, Jacob 184
  John 180

Lacey, Philamon 205
  William 138
Lackey, Andw. 52
  Arch./Archibald 47,48
  James 46
  James W. 45
  Thomas 146
  W. 37
  Wm./William 67,93
Lackland, John 184
  Joseph 181
Lacy, Hopkins 122
  James 146
  John 146
  Philimon 146
Lain, Aza 255
  Elias 201
  John 255
  Lewis 192
  Samuel 179
  Wm. 255
Laird, James 184
  Moses 193,201
Lairkins, Thomas 165
Lake, Jane 255
  William 128
Lamar, John 15
  William 12
Lamb, Gross 226
  Hannah 225
  John 5
  Joseph 225
  Thomas 181
Lambert, John 42
Lamor, James 128
Land, Newman 131
Landrum, Young 179
Lands, Joseph 141,142
Lane, Aquila 129
  Charles 182
  Dannl 211
  Dutton 179,275
  Eliz. 209
  Ephraim 181
  Isaac 118
  James 157
  John 179,261
  Richard 129
  Royal 261
  Tidence 129
  William 107
Lanes, James 112
Laney, Jeremiah 184
Langdon, Joseph 137

Langford, Jordan 169
Langham, Abel 118
Langley, Joseph 228
Lannon, Joseph 221
Lareau, Abraham 76
  George 62,76
Laremore, Hugh 117
Larew, Frances 245
  Francis 255
  George 255
  James 255
  Samuel 146
Large, John 262
  Joseph 85,146
  Robert 156,262
Larkin, Sampson 168
Larkins, Henry 168
Lassiter, Burrel 42
Latcher...208
Latham, Samuel 11,129
Lathim...118
  Elizabeth 119
  James 166
  Moses 166
Lathan, John 129
Laton, Patrick 62
Laudermilk, George 131
Laughiner, Christopher 183
Laughlin, Susannah 52
Laurence, Martin 47
Lauwon, David 230
Lavender, John 62,63
  Polly 62
Lavis, John 69
Lawler, John 11
Lawrence, James 131
  Randolph 166
Lawson, David 227
  Edward 230
  Elijah 230
  Hugh 77
  Jacob 230
  Jesse 227
  Joshua 221
  Malinda 77
  Mary 62,64,77
  Randol 230
  Robert 72,230
  William 72,230
Lax, Elizabeth 260
Lay, Bartlet 166
  James 65
  Jesse 146,227,230
  Joel 18
  John 146,227
  William 18
Layman, Daniel 130
  Joseph 130
  Jacob 136
Layne, John 14
Lea/Lee, Abraham 78
  Agness 258
  Alfred 238
  David 15
  James 107,121,130
  Jesse 8
  John 107
  Joseph 7
  Lavinia 101
  Luke 14
  Major 129
  Samuel 71
  Stephen 258
  William 3,15
  Zachariah 14
Leabo, Henry 110
  Jacob 110
  John 110
Leach, James 11
Leaky, John 69
  William 69
Leaman, David 130
Leaper, Francis 168

Leaper, Hugh 168
  James 168
  Mathew 168
Leatherwood, Daniel 262
  Willis 262
Lebo, John 166
Leckey, Thomas 206
Ledgerwood, John 182
Ledgwood, John 230
Lee, Abner 272
  George 272
  John 271
  Permit 78
  Robert 165
Leech, John 8
  Joseph 196
  Wm. 209
Leek, John 166
Leeth, Ebenezer 139
  George 131
  Joseph 131
Leeper, Gawen 68
  Math 277
Legg, Edward 85
  James 85
  John 85
  Jonathan 34
  Matthew 34,80
Leib, John 3,7
Lemons, Issiah 208
  John 208
Lenor, Young 112
Lenox, John 250
Lentz, Martin 179
Leper, Andrew 269
Lerue, Abraham 137
Lescollect, John 185
Lewallin, Richd. 118
Lewis, Abner 106
  Amos 134
  Andrew 124
  David 157
  Evan 128
  Fielding 112
  George 134,156
  Henry 78
  Jacob 134
  James 5,72
  Joel 260
  John 18,260
  Martin 260
  Nathan 156
  Richd. 260
  Samuel 78,261
  Stephen 18
  Surel 196
  Thomas 16
  William/Wm. 18,134,156,
    210,260
  Wm. T. 93
Liaght(light), John 165
Licans, John 42
Liddy, John 54
Ligget, Jno. 275
Light, Joshua 165
Likens, William 181
Lillard, James 260
Laillard, John 262
Linard, Jacob 7
Lincoln, Isaac 146,207
Lindar, Jacob 20
Lindsay, Benjn. 209
Lindvil, Tho. 207
Line, William 128
Linebarger, Catharine 240
Linebough, Daniel 180
  Jacob 179,182
  John 180
Linginfelter, Jacob 185
Linsey, David 275
  Jesse 184
Linvill...4
  Thomas 205

19

Linville, Abrm. 226
  Richard 5,216,231
Lion, John 85
  Thomas 85
Lipe, Daniel 164
Lisby, Moses 85
Lister, Reuben 76
Lite, Henry 156
  Vitchel 156
  William 156
Litel, Andrew 70
Litler, John 184
Little, Adam 83
  Andrew 193
  George 156
  Jonas 192,205
  Mathias 193
  Matthias 156
  Thomas 37
  Valentine 193
Litton, James 230
  Rachel 230
Lively, Jacob 130
  John 13
Livingston, Jacob 168
Lockhart, Robert 146
  William 146
Lockmiller, Jacob 168
  Jonas 168
  John 168
Lockwood, John 118
Loe, Fielding 226
Lofty, Wm. 248
Logan, Alexander 39
  David 181
  George 146
  Henery 44,180,204,212
  James 44
  Wm. 42
Lonas, Jacob 83
Loney, Isham 169
Long, Alexander 168
  Christian 34
  Edward 13
  Henry 31,40
  Isaac 169
  Jacob 34
  James 14,168
  John 8,168,183,185
  Joseph 104,168
  Moses 134
  Nicholas 180
  Robert 13,80,117
  Tobias 13
  William 62,164,182
Longacre, Benjamin 126
  John 126
Longmire, Charles 206
Longwith, Reuben 69
Looney...163
  Absalom 169
  Benaj. 169
  David 150
  Mary 169
  Michael 169
  Moses 83,84,150
  Peter 83
  William 169
Losson, David 230
  Joshua 221
Lotspeich, Christopher 185
  John 185
  Saml. 252
Lott, Jasper 211
Lough, Jacobs 134
Love, Charles I. 21
  J. 75
  John 76,78,90,208
  Jno. T. 240
  Joseph 73,76
  Robert 67
  S. A. 18
  Samuel 18,76

Love, Thomas 182
  Wm. 240
  William 137
Loveall, Zachariah 183
Lovel, John 250
  John H. 250
Lovelaty, Jno. 275
  Jos. 275
  Marshal 275
Loveless, David 54
Lovin, James 166
Low, Abraham 90
  Andrew R. 78
  Aquilla 71
  Caleb 71
  David 67,95
  George 156
  John 90,92
  Richard 71
  Robert 72
Lower, Henry 87
  Peter 112
Lowery, John 228
  Charles 181
Lowry, Adam 134
Lowry, Adam 134
  James 37,134
  John 33,38,39,156
  Robert 134
  Samuel 134
  William 30,37,42
Loy...88
  John 228
  Peter 228
Loyd, Abel 182
  Frethias 179
  James 146,181,182
  John 146,182
  Levy 146
  Owen 114
  Pleasant 258
  Robertson 182
  Thomas 182
Luallen, Richard 4,7
Lucas...163
  Abigail 72
  George 71,72
  Robert 72,187,195
Luckey, Andrew 179
  James 184
Lucus, John 164
Lumpkins, Robert 65
Luck, Jos. 274
  Robt. 146,205
  Samuel 107,146
Luster, Edward 180
Luttrell, James 81
  James C. 81,83,95
  John 17,81
  John King 81
  Laura E. 55,56,66
  Mary 68
  Richard 68
  Susannah 17
  William 81
Lyle, David 124
  Henry 191,200
  Samuel 124,198
Lynch, Jeremiah 106
  John 206
Lyon, James 133
  John 208
  Nathaniel 228
Lyons, Hezekiah 210
  James 168
  William 168

McAdams, James 196
McAdoo, Andrew 125
  John 12
  William Gibbs 12
McAdow, Jno. 273
McAffrey, Patsy 16,62

McAffry, Martha 16,62
  Terrence 62
McAllister, Charles 67
  Joseph 90
McAlpin, Alexander 180
McAmis, Isaac 185
  James 184
  John 183
  Thomas 184
  William 184
McAnalley, Chas. 227
McAnally, Charles 108
  John 85
McAnelly, John 166
McAntire, David 157
McAntyre, Jean 33
McAnulley, Elijah 165
McAnully, John 165
McBath, Robert 80
  William 39
McBee, Abigale 79
  Asa 245
  Isaac 112
  Israel 179
  Lemuel 85
  Saml. 112
  William 85,95,213
McBoon, Henry 181
McBride, James 222
  John 8
  Martin 183
  Patience 222
  Pleasant 74
  William 15,157,180
McBroom, Alexander 169
  John 169
  Thomas 110,169
  Wm./William 139,180,
    274
McCaffery, Terence 16
McCain, Peter 184
  Robert 207
McCairy, Dennis 164
McCaleb, Archibald 67
McCalister, John 52
McCall, John 80
McCaman, Samul 206
McCamey...12
  /McAmey, John 12,13
  Robert 12
  William 8
McCammon, John 80
  Samuel 35
  Thomas 35,92
McCamon, Robert 121
McCampbell, Andrew 74,76
  Isaac 88
  Sollomon 45,71
  William 76
McCandlys, John 92
McCanles, John 50
  Robert 41
McCallie...35
McCauley 59
McCanse, Alexander 164
McCarrel, James 92
McCart, Robert 78
McCartney, Charles 199
  James 199,276
  John 44
McCartny, Chas. 276
  Jas. 276
  Jno. 276
McCarty, Benjamin 98,113,
    115
  James 114,115
  John 115
  William 164
McCarver, Archd. 112
McCauley, Edward 85
McCauly, John 35
McCay, John 146
  Spruce 62

20

McCinny, Henry 222
McClain, Andrew 65
    Thomas 158
McClanahan, Alexander 134
    David 37.137
    James 37,39
    Robert 137
    William 134
McClarn, James 157
McClean, Stephen 72
    William 72
McCleary, Abraham 69,93
    Joseph 95
    Rachel 93
McClellan, Abram 157
    John 67,158
    Samuel 92
    William 92
McClellin, Daniel 179
McClemore, Presley 166
McClester, William 132
    James 133
McCloud, Andrew 65
    James 65
    John 209
    Robert 65
    Wm. 208,209
McClung, Charles 138,221
    C. M. 44
    Calvin Morgan 77
    Charles 8,20,37,90
    Hugh 274
    Jno. 274
McClur, Nathl. 275
McClure...67
    Charles 54
    Robert 69
McCollum, John 67,183
    Thomas 181,183
McComes, John 48
McComus, Stephen 8
McConald, James 45
McConnal, John 185
McConnel, Jacob 270
McCool, Gabriel 276
McCord, David 42.199
    James 200,210
McCorkle, Joseph 207
    Samuel 157
McCormack, Robert 146
McCormick, George 206
    Robt. 206
    William 157,179
McCorrey/McCorry, Thomas
    62
McCosky, Jno. 274
McCown, James 90
    Mrs. L. W. 189
McCoy...163
    Daniel 182
    John 92
    Samuel 16
    Spruce 221
McCrackin, James 6,116
McCraw, Grabriel 166
McCray, Danl. 208
McCree, William 94
McCubbin, Zechy 209
McCuistian, Andrew 125
    James 125
    Joseph 125
McCullah, Farmer 168
    Joseph 128,161,168
McCulle, John 132
McCulley, Peter 226
    Robert 52
    Solloman 52
McCulloch, Henry 164
    James 54,83
    John 50
    Saml. 50
    Thomas 54
    William 164

McCullock, James 90,94
McCullough, Joseph 185
    Samuel 185
    Thomas 183
    William 185
McCully, John 226
McCurdy, Archd. 276
McCurkin, Thomas 45
McCurry, James 180
    Robt. 253
McCurty, John 179
McDaniel, Archibald 12
McDonal, Michael 115
McDonald, Alexander 110,
    129,130
    David 126
    Isaac 108
    James 133
    Jane 101
    John 133
    Redmond 15,115
    Reuben 87
    Walter 131
    William 182
McDowell, Ephraim 270
    John 95
McElderry, John 157
McEldry, John 92
McElkeny, John 110
    Moses 110
    Robt. 110
McElroy, Margaret 185
    Mary 66,75
McFaddian, Joseph 39
McFall, Francis 205
McFaren, Andw. 275
McFarren, James 274
    Saml. 103
McFarland, Benjamin 125
    Duncan 107
    Erasmus 253
    James 136
    Moses 253
    Robert 121,133
McFarlin, Andrew 183
    John 125
McFarling, John 200
McFarson, Henry 104
McFarthing, Alexander 269
McFeeter, And. 112
McFeetrage, Matth. 112
McGaha, Isaac 263
    Robert 263
    Saml. 263
McGahee, William 184
McGaughy, Wm. 276
McGee, Richard 128
McGeehen, Brewer 146
McGeehon, Benjamin 182
    John 184
    Margaret 185
McGhee, Barcley 44
    James 62,136
    John 45,108,128
    Lawson 143
McGill, Charles 179
    David 67
    Robert 45
    James 269
    Robert 179,269
    Samuel 179
    William 180
McGinley, James 40
McGinty, Abner 255
McGirt, John 125
McGlothlen, John 334
McGriff, Thomas 11
McGuire, Cornelis 130,271
    George 130
    Isaac 130
    Patrick 62,125
    Thomas 157
    William 5

McHaffy, John 87
McIntorf, Casper 206
    John 205
McIntosh, Peter 157
McInturf, Casper 146
    Christopher 146
    Israel 146
    John Jr. 146
    John Sr. 146
McKain, Nancy 35
McKamie, J. 35
McKaughan, Archd. 157
McKay, Geo. G. 255
    Jane 255
McKee, Alexr. 210
    John 30,45,210
    Matthew 114
McKeehan, James 80
McKehan, George 15
    John 230
McKemy, James 45
    Samuel 184
McKeymey, Robert 157
McKiddy...83
McKighen, Saml. 273
McKinley, James 48
    Prudence 76
    Samuel 74,157
    William 157
    Willm. Sr. 157
McKinney, Henry 15,222
McKinzey, Daniel 48
McKiver, John 115
McKoy, Abraham 252
    Daniel 184
    Geo. G. 263
    James 252
    Jeremiah 252
McLain, Houston 252
    John 253
McLand, Joseph 131
McLane, Joseph 72
McLin, Joseph 142
McMachen, John 214
McMacken, John 180
    John blear 212
McMahan, Allen 253
    Anderson 253
    Eli 263
    James 263
    Redman 263
    Sanders 258
    Sevier 263
    Wm. 263
McMahon, John 69,187,188,
    214
    John B. 193,195
McMamee,'Peter 199
McMane, Dominy 108
McMeans, Isaac 130
    John 45
McMillan, Alexander 69
    Fay E. 2
McMillian, Joseph 263
    Saml. 258
McMillin, John 69
McMinn, John 165
    Joseph 166
    Robbert 166
McMore, Magnes 117
McMunn, William 85
McMurray, William 35
McMurry, James 35
    Robert 37
    Saml 35,276
    Wm. 50,276
McMurtry, James 183
    Jno. 240
    Jso. 240
    Joseph 270
    Sd. 270
McNab, Wm. 44
McNabb, Baptist 146,191

McNabb, David 141,192,206
  David Jr. 146
  David Sr. 146
  Garrett 258
  Geo. 240,258
  James 258
  Jean 50
  John 187,191,255,258
  Malcolm 258
  Margaret 258
  William 146,191,192,
    208,261
McNaley, John 157
McNealy...222
McNeely, Samuel 39
McNees, George 6
  Isiah 182
  William 183
McNeil, James 150
  John 270
McNeill, John 67
McNew, Elijah 183
  Shadrach 183,240,270
  William 183
McNutt, Alexander 39,75
  Benjamin 181
  George 63,64,76
  Isabella 64
  James 16
  John 81
  Rebecca 63
  Robert 81
McPeek, Ezekiel 8
McPeetur, Joseph 139
McPeters, Joseph 8,269
McPheeters, John 165
  Sam. 165
McPheran, James 181
  John 184
  William 180,183
McPherson, Samuel 74
McPike, Wm. 210
McQueen, Hannah 146
  John 146
McRanels, John 41
  Joseph 41
McRoberts, Samuel 134
McSpadden, Archibald 76
  Esther 125
  Samuel 131
McSween, Murdock 255,258
  Saml. 253
  William 236,253
McTeer, James 45
  Richd. 209
  Robert 35
  Wilson 35
  Will A. 26,35
McVay, James 168
  Patrick 168
McWhinney, Thomas 90
McWhorter, James 207
  John 12
  Moses 12
McWilliams...163
  Andrew 92
  Hugh 166
  Thomas 146

Macey, Robert 20
Mackay, John 157
Macky, John 179
Maclin, Elizabeth 60,142
  John 184
  Wm/William 8,62,93
Madcap, William 184
Magahan, Farill 198
Maggot, William 85
Mahan, James 269
Maid, James 5
Maiden, Andrew 209
Mainos, Amos 255
Magers, John 119

Majors, Abner 133
  Absolom 136
  Peter 136
  Smith 65
  Thomas 139,205
Malcom, Alexander 35
Malick, David 180
Mallery, Robt. 169
Mallock, James 193
Malone, John 183,200
  Michal 157
  Richard 228
  William 183
Maloney, Hugh 184
  John 184
  Robert 180
Malony, W. C. 248
Maloy, Jacob 240
  James 181,240
  John 240
Manerd, James 131
Manifee, Thos 72
Manifold, Benjamin 69
  George 69
Maning, David 249
Mankin, William 8
Mann, Ebenezer 165
  Joseph 165
Manning, Joseph 253
Mantooth, Elizabeth 258
  Henry 179
  James 258
  Jno. 258,261
  Letty 258
  Samuel 258
  Thomas 258
  Wm. 258
Manuel, Cudbert 87
  Valentine 37
Maples, James 138
  William 134
Marcum, Arthur 15
  Josiah 15
Mardick, Wm. 52
Marele, Laurence 106
  Peter 106
Margraves, John 138
Markes, Alexr. 258
Markham, Beverly 119
Markland, Nathan B. 85
Marlow, Thomas 112
Marsh, Gravener 185
Marshall, Abraham 184
  Bartley 98
  John 165
  J. W. 23
  Thomas 76
  william 161
Marshel, Bartlett 117
Martin, Andrew 198,275
  Anny 185
  Daniel 15,107,221
  David 164
  George 67,101,195,228,
    274
  Hugh 125
  James 42,67,150,248
  James W. 248
  John 76,90,104,228
  Joseph 150,198
  Joshua Lanier 35
  Josiah 198
  Luke 35
  Nathal. 230
  Richard 274
  Stephen 230
  Thomas 117
  Warner 35
  William 166
Masengil, Michael 212
Mash, John 92
Masingale, Henry 209
Mason, Edward 92

Mason, James 69
  Joel 248
  Michael 146
  Reuben 114,126
  Solomon 228
  Yelverton 168
Massengale, John 230
Massengil(1), Henry 192,
  193
Massey, Jonathan 110
  Peter 76
  Thos. 76
Massingale, Michael 76,98
Masangale, Mikel 110
Massingale, S. E. 76
  Solomon 3,18,209
Massingall, Henry 157
Massingell, Michael 195
Masterson, Aron 76
  William H. 23
Matheny, John 71
  Luke 71
  Robert 71
Mathes, Joel P. 263
Mathew, Joel 271
Mathias, Thomas 230
Mathis, Alexr. 253
Matlock, Jason 157
  John 193
  Luke 157
Matthes, James 52
  Jonathan 52
  Susannah 52
Matthews, Alexr. 208
  Jeremiah 121,132
  Obadiah 271
  Samuel 270
Matthias, James 182
  William 181
Mattingly, Walter 226
Mattocks, Danl. 10
Mattonly, Walter 226
Mattox, Valentine 85
Maulden, ___ on 190
  James 190
Maulsby, William 138
Maxey, Shadereck 80
Maxfield, Seth 104
  Thomas 146
Maxsey, Jesse 193
Maxwell, David 78,168
  George 150,168
  Hugh 65
  James 48
  John 47,78,137,157
  Mary 54
  Matthew 255
  Robert 47
  Tho. 206
  Thomas 45
May, Casymore 211
  David 5
  Francis 62
  Mary McConnell 62
  Reynolds 5
Mayben...45
Mayberry, Charles 183
  Isaac 12
  John 13
  Francis 85,101,119
Maybury, George 71
Mayfield, Ambrose 208
  John 214
  Wm. 248
Mayo, Valentine 48
Mays, Henry 114
  Sherod 114
  Thomas 114
  William 114,137
Maysey, Charles 222
Mead, Marston 100
  Sally 100
  Thomas 5

Meade, Mahlon 157
Mealer, Robert 253
Means, Robert 67
  Wm. 45
Mebane, Isabelle 62
Medley, James 126
  John 94
  Richard 85
Medlin...17
  Harden 18
  Richard 18
  Robert 18
  William 18
  Wm. Owen 18
Medlock, David 206
  John 104,209
  Little B. 208
  Luke 209
Mee, Thos. 169
  Wm. 169
Meek, Adam 95,129
  John 95
Megehe, Ferrill 272
Meigs, Return J. 16
Meire, James 138
Melcom, George 130
Meliçoat, James 101
Mellen, George F. 60
Melona, John 133
Meloney, John 20,78
Melvin, John 204,212
  Thomas 204,212
Mendingall, Abraham 119
Mendinghall, Jos'h 126
  Martin 128
  Mordica 126
  Stephen 128
Menefee, John 20,71,72
Menley, David 128
Mercer, Edward 157
  Nicholas 157
Meredith, Frederick 10
Meriot, John 47
Meritt, Benjamin D. 267
Merritt, Frank 141
Merryman, Francis 81
Mesingale, Henry 209
  Michael 204
Messer, Jacob 168
  James 168
  Solomon 238
Metcalf, Hezekiah 263
Metlock, George 146
  Gidian 146
  William 146
Micalsane, John 240
Michael, James 199
Michel, Mordecai 48
Mickle, Banzer 131
Midkiff, Isaiah 107,108
  John 110
Miers, Henry 180
  John 181
  Michael 179
  Peter 146
Milburn, David 183
  Jonathan 183
  William 181
Miles, Jacob 95
  John 138
Milhorn, George 158
Miligan, William 115
Miliken, John 211
Millar, Andrew 37,48
  David 42
  Jacob 169
  John 48,75,119
  Peter 169
  Saml. 44
  Tho. 208
Miller...88
  Abraham 184,238
  Adam 157

Miller, Alexr. 272
  Andrew 213,270
  Charles 245
  Chrisley 146
  Christian 157
  Daniel 146
  Elizabeth 263
  Eve 74
  Frederick 17,18,119
  George 104,146,157
  Harmon 103
  Henry 146,157
  Isaac 157
  Jacob 146,157,166,179,
    221
  James 83,198,211
  John 146,157,161,166,
    168,182
  John Jr. 146
  John Sr. 146
  Jonathan 252
  Martha 48
  Martin 104
  Mary Louisa 62
  Mathies 165
  Michael 18,168
  Peter 204,212
  Pleasant M. 62
  Robert 83,166,270
  Samuel 157
  S. K. 261
  Thos./Thomas 157,209
  William 180,221
Millerbarger, Wm. 228
Millhorn, George 204,214
Millican, James 72,272
  John 72
Milligan, Samuel 164,181
  William 98
Milliken, Alexr. 255
  Deberah 255
  Deborah Ad 253
  Hiram 255
Million, Edwd. 206
Mills, Asa 128
  Hardy 166
  Isham 163
  Jacob 128
  John 128
  Richard 128
  Samuel 128
  William 128
Millsaps, Peter 261
Milsaps, James 205
  Thomas 205
Milstead, John 226
Miltabarger, William 88
Milvany, Clary 69
Mims, Albert 245
  Alfred 245
  Daniel 67
Minatt, William 96
Minnis, John 39
Miser, George 47,83
Mismer, John 183
  Mary 185
Mitar, Jacob W. 157
Mitchel, Adam 212
  George 207
  Mark 209
  Mary 209
Mitchell, Benjn. 104
  Charles 85
  Isaac 115
  James 207
  Joab 195
  John 74,132,165,179,274
  Richard 110,164,165
  Thomas 180
  William 74,101,180
Moad, John 222
  Thomas 226
Moffet, Alexr. 208

Moffett, William 116,166
Moirs, William 180 (Moiers)
Molder, Henry 132
  John 131
  Polly 131
Molton, William 157
Monday, John 83
  Joshua 80
  William 80
Monkey, Henry 76
Montgomery, Alexander 37,
  44,210,271,272
  David 42
  George 42
  Hugh 3,15,21
  Humphrey 52
  James/Jas. 39,42,67,
    211
  John 39,42
  Lemuel P. 222
  Michael 138
  Samuel 80
  William 94,130
Moody...155
  George 164
Moon, Daniel 132
  Jonah 69
  John 253
  Joseph 131
  Nathaniel 131
Mooney, Geo. 276
Moony, Thomas 164
  William 164
Moonyhan, Thos. 238
  Wm. 238
Moor, Absolem 146
  Daniel 146
  Jacob 76
  James 80,92,131
  John 76
  John Parker 146
  Reuben 92
  Saml. 276
  Tenan 67
  Thomas 50
Moore, Abner 103
  Alexander 157,211
  Ann 211
  Anthony 183
  Anty 274
  David 184,205
  Dempsey 248
  Garrett 157
  James 98,104,180,182,
    185,276
  John 134,181,182,191,
    205,263,274
  John Trotwood 5,102
  Joseph 13
  Keziah 67
  Lemuel 166
  Levi 185
  Moses 180,198
  Nancy 85
  Phoebe 93
  Robert 112
  Samuel 104,157,204,212
  White 250
  William 134,182,208,
    248,250,262
  Zadok 185
Mooris, William 76
Moorland, Willm 206
Moray, Morgan 195
More, Alexander 37
  Hugh 269
  James 37
  Moses 199
  Wm. 169
Moreland, Charles 146
  Jonathan 185
  William 146
Morell, Charles 255,258

Morelock, George 157
  James 157
Morgan, Abel 157
  Adonijah 270
  Henry 108
  John 119
  Leonard 190,201
  Lewis 270
  Richard 131
  Silas 131
  Thomas 272
  Valentine 104
  William 128,157
Morget, Henry 157
Morrell, Daniel 157
  Edmund 157
  John 157
  Jonathan 157
  Thomas 157
Morress, Gideon 200
  Shadrick 200
Morris, Absalom 6
  Benjamin 15
  Edward 164
  Henry 183
  Howel 250
  Jean 133
  John 103,133,164
  Levin 146
  Nimrod 76
  Shadrach 15
  William/Wm 164,253,258
Morrison, James 157,165,
  179
  Joseph 213
  Patt 210
  Peter 166
  Sam 165
  Thomas 37,158
  Wm/William 166,199
Morriss, James 157
  John 181
  Maurice 180
Morrow, Alexander 85
  Isabelle 62
  James 184
  John 137,184
  Richard 85
  William/Wm 62,125,274
Morreyson, Thomas 165
Morton, Jesse 76
Moseby, John 210
Moseley, John 157
Moser, Anthy. 205
Moses, Poor 93
Mosgrove, John 112
Mosier, Absolum 116
  Geo. 228
Mosley, Jesse 183
Moswell, Nimrod 112
Motton(Molton), Nicholas
  157
Mower, Nathaniel 119
Mowrey, John 44
Mowry, Peter 69
  Valentine 15
Moyer, Daniel 157
  Gasper 157
  Jacob 157
Moyers, Adam 180
  Christopher 137
  David 137
  George 4,16,180
  Jacob 94
  James 137
  Joshua 137
Mozer, Adam 221
Mulchy, Phillip 199
Mulholland, William 273
Mulkey, Ann 146
  John 112
  Philip 146
Mullican, James 192

Mullins, John 101,146
Mulvany, William 69
Mumpouer, John 110
Munkas, John 106
Munrow, Robert 112
Murphey, John 269
  Joseph 165
  Martha 117
  Sarah 117
  Thomas 184
  William 117
Murphy, Alice 59
  David 136
  Dennis 59,80
  Patrick 197
  Patt 210
  Robert 76
  William/Wm. 104,138,
  276
Murr, Jeremiah 261
  Wm. 261
Murrah, Christopher 116
  Keaton 116
  William 15
  Christopher 227
  David 226
  Isaac 227
  Jabash 227
  James 222
  Jonathan 227
  Joshua 230
  Morgan 195,208,226
  Robert 83
  Shadrach 208
  Thomas 181,226,227
  Wm. 227
Murrel, Benjamin 128
  Jno. 261
  Job 261
Murrell, Richard 157
Murrey, James 198
Murrin, Robert 35
Murrow, Alexr. 199
Musgrave, Robert 146
  Samuel 146
Musgrove, John 157
  John Jr. 153,157
Myars, Jacob 157
  Michael 183
Mycelf, Allen 248
  Owen 183
Myers, George 169
  John 128
  Joseph 47
  Lewis 168
  Samuel 164
Mynatt, George 87
  John 87
  William 87

Nail, Frederick 94
  Matthew 272
Nall, Robert 164
Namee, Peter 209
Nanney, Patrick 130
Narramore, John 72
Nash, John 113
  William 157
Nation, Abraham 74
  Edward 74
  Joseph 104,119,269
  Thomas 74
Nations, Thos. 228
Nave, Abraham 146
  George 49
  Henry 196
  John 130,146,196
  Robert T. 143
  Teter 146,191
Neal, Benajamin 138
  Peter 119
  William 117
Neas, Ambrose 243

Neas, Benjamin 243
  George 240
  Michael 240
  Phillip 243
  Saml. 243
Nease, George 235
Neel, Nicholas 272
  Saml. 208
Neely, Andrew 137
  James 137
  John 137
Neese, John 179
  Michael 179
Neil...163,164
  Benjamin 181
  William 181
Neilson, Andrew 125
  Charles 205
  George 183
  Henry 207
  Hugh 182
  John 205
  Southy 210
Neise, John 181
Nelson, Alexander 163,164
  Elisha 198
  John 37
  Robt. 164
  Southy 198
  W. D. 248
  William 20,92,199,213,
  273
  & Yearout 245
Neston, Fredrick 230
Netherton, Enoch 258
  James 258
  John 258
Nethery, Thomas 94
New, James 179
Newberry, Alexander 183
  James 185
  John 183
  Joseph 271
  Stephen 94
Newcom, Jane 256
  Levi 256
  Thornton 256
  Wm. 256
Newel, Joseph 146,210
Newgin, Thomas 191
Newman...94
  Aaron 138,183
  Edmond 69
  Isaac 132
  Jacob 81
  James 138
  John 15,81,94,178,180,
  230,266
  Jonathan 126
Newport, Carana 106
  Richard 74
Nichol, William 94
Nicholas, Daniel 146,207
Nichols, Bury 238
  Charles 238
  David 117
  Richd. 256
  William 163
Nicholson, Jeremiah 125
  John 146
Nickoll, Josiah 62
Nicles, George 42
Nicolson, John 50
Nidiver, George 157
  Jacob 157
Nilson, Jean 205
Nobels, William 15
Noble, Lewis 8
Nodding, Willm. 206
Noe, John 110
  Joseph 108
  Peter 110
Noel, James 222

24

Noll, John 113
  Wm. 113
Nolland, Benjn. 208
Noradyke, Isariel 138
  Micaja 138
Norkett, John 157
Norman, Aaron 20
  Henry 20
  Isaac 20
  Matthew 168
Norris, George 113
  Hugh 261
  /Nooris, Samuel 16,83,
  272
North, Edward 168
  Gabriel/G. 183,259
  John 168
Norton, Nathan 108
  William 108
Norwood, John 47
  Samuel 42
Nosler, Bostian 87
Nothren, William 71
Nowland, Geo. 208
  John 146,208
  Wiley 248
  William 146
Nugent, James 67,164
  John 164
Null, Henry 82
  John 42,43
Nyman, Margaret 35
  Michal 33,35

Oatts, David 52
O'Conner, Thomas 47
Oddel, Joab 206
  Nehemiah 206
  Saml. 206
  Willm. 205
  Caleb 206
Odell, Abraham 253
  Benjamin 253
  Caleb 261
  Esther 261
  Job 253
  Lewis 253
  Rachel 261
  /O'Dell, Ruth Webb 234
  William 261
Odle, Jonathan 125
  William 157
O'Donal, John 113
O'Donald, Michael 87,104
Oduel, Calib 193
  John 192
Odum, Tilmon 248
Offill, James 157
Ogden, Wm. 256
Ogg, Daniel 72
Ogleby, David 39
Oldham, Henry 213
Oldhans, Danl. 205
Oliphant, James 183
  John 184,274
  Thomas 182
Oliver, Douglas 2,13
Oneal, Bartly 209
  Benjamin 130
  /O'Neal, Cornelius 272
  /O'Neal, Robert 271
Oneil, Joseph 256,258
  Harrison 253
  Henry 250
  Jno. 250
Ore, James 110
  /Orr, Joseph 43,104
Orick, James 166
  Saml. 166
Orn, Robert 266
Orth, Henry 164
Osborn, Alexander 52
Osburn, Daniel 86

Osburn, Solomon 135
Ottinger, Adam 243
  David 243
  George 245
  Henry 243
  Jacob 243
  Jno. 243,245
  Joseph 250
  Lewis 243
  Michael 243
  Peter 243
  Susannah 243
  Wm. 243
Outlaw, Alexander 121,122,
  125,233
Overall, William 192
Overstreet, William 92
Overton, John 62
  Mary McConnell 62
Oweings, James 191
Owen, James 205
  Jesse 20
  John 104,107
  Thomas McAdory 35
  William 107
Owens, Daniel 164
  Farr 166
  Jonathan 157
  John 66
  Joseph 126
  Owen 266
  Willis 16
  Wm. 166
Oxen, John 182
Ozborne, Jnac. 157
Ozburn, Charles 88
  Isaac 76

Pack, Henry 243
Page, John 157
Paget, Joseph 263
Paign, Reubin 208
Pain, Chesley 80
Painter, Adam 179
  John 179
  Joseph 164
Pairks, Jos. Lee C. 165
Palestine, Jonas 191
Palmer, Samuel 35
  William/Wm. 94,245,
  248
Pangle, Frederick 130
  John 130
Panken, Stephen 8
Pankey, John 8
  Stephen 8
Pannel, Thomas 110
Pannil, Beny 165
Panther, Alexander 39
  Levy, 164
Parham, W. E. 48
  Will E. 32
Paris, Robt. 274
Park, John 59,62,63
  William 62
Parker, Benjamin 184
  Benjn. C. 8,62
  Charles 193,201
  James 147
  Jesse 66
  Jonathan 66
  Nicholas 238
  Thomas 205
  William 158,182,191
  William E. 90
Parkes, Joseph 130
  William 130
Parkey, Jacob 130
Parkhill, David 49
Parkins, David 181
Parkison, George 207
  Peter 207
Parks, Jhon 11,45,182

Parks, Joseph 163,164
  Philip 113
Parman, Giles 180
Parrott, Bethany 245
  Elly 245
  George 245
  Henry 245
  Jacob 245
  Job 245
  Saml. 245
Parsons, Robert 147
  Thomas 10
Partin, Samuel 50
Pate, Anthony 10,70,74
  Jeremiah 95
  Joseph 14
  Stephen 78
Patten, John 147
Patterson, Alexr. 166
  Edmond 253
  James 168,179,185
  John 101,166,199,250,
  274
  Nathaniel 183
  Rhoda 82
  Robert 8,82,110
  Sarah 157
  William 8,183
Patton, Jacob 94
  John 132
  Matthew 12
  Robert 132
  Samuel 137
  Thomas 69,132
Pattrick, Jesse 147
  John 147
Paul, John 90
  Sarah 250
Pauley, Valentine 182
Paulsell, David 184
Pawlett, Abram 157
  Ann 157
  Robert 157
Paxton, Samuel 39,275
  W. M. 39
Payne, Rachel 93
  Thomas 147
Paysinger, Jacob 183
Payton, Joseph 146
Peak, Jacob 13
Pearce, James 54,180,191
  John 54
  Richard 182
  Robert 54,226
  Robt. D. 227
  Thomas 211
Pearcefull, Saml. 214
Pearson, Abel 86,147
  Christian 164
  Jacob 86
  Lawrence 164
  Peter 164
  William 20
Pebley, John 200
Peck, Adam 263
  Talbert Isham 263
  Wiley 263
  Wm. R. 263
Pedigrew, Matthew 39
Peek, Adam 138
Peel, Thomas 184
Peery, George 66
Peeters, Nathaniel 113
  William 113
Peinter, Adam 272
Peirce, Absalom 158
  George 88
Pelham, John 67,93
Pemberton, John 157
  Rachel 157
  William 157
Penaro, William 14
Penland, Abraham 238

Penland, Jackson 238
  Jno. H. 238
Penn, Richard 132
Penney, James 179
Pennington, Absolom 269
Penny, Rachel 50
Peoples, John 147,205
  Nathan 146,157
  Wm./William 147,206
Pepper, James 78
Percifield, Jeremiah 227
Perie, Jas. 269
Perkins, Edward 158,227
  George 147,205
  Jacob 147,205
  Joshua 205
  Peter 227
Permenter, Theophilus 167
Perrin, Joel 101
  Joseph 101
Perry, David 158
  Rowland 158
  Samuel 104
  Thomas 180
Peter (Negro) 117
Peters, Abraham 179
  Christian 207
  Conrod 158
  Genevieve E. 88,119
  Henry 10
  John 147,158
  (Smithpeters), John
  M. S. 147
  Nathaniel 87
  Samuel 147
  Tobias 10
Peterson, Joseph 222
  William 87
  Mrs. Z. R. 178
Peticord, Thomas 147
Petit, Benjn. 210
  Thomas 210
Petre, Adam 103
  Daniel 103
  George 103,158
  John 103
Petree, Adam 147
  Daniel 147
  Samuel 226
Petter, Michal S(mith)
  208
Petty, William 136
Peveehous, Abraham 107
Pewit, Joel 135
Pewsley, Wm. 226
Phann, George 179
  John 179
  Philip 180
Pheagens, William 168
Phibbs, Richard 67
Philips, Gabriel 185
  James 206
  John 222
  Thomas 20
Phillips, Charles 158,200
  Edmond 128
  Hezekiah 108
  John 258
  Martin 248
  Thos. 231
  Waid 164
Philpot, Isaac 11
  Richard 11
Phipps, John 78
  William 168
Phips, Isiah 208
Phlippen, Thos. 274
Pickens, John 35
  Lettitia Hannah 35
  Robert 90
Pickering, Benjamin 179
  Ellis 180
  Enos 179

Pickering, Samuel 182
Pickins, James 153,158
Pickle, Christian 82
  Henry 82
  John 82
Pierce, Daniel 181
  George 182,245
  John 182
  Robert 89
Piercefield, Saml. 103
Piercifull, Thos. 275
Pilant, John 164
  Joseph 164
Pilcher, John 157
Piles, Conrod 108
  Jesse 125
Pinson, Aron 196,198
  John 199
  Joseph 196
  Thomas 196
Poage, Robert 128
Pock, Thomas 106
Poe, Linza 226
Pogue, John 179
Poindexter, John 167
Poland, John 146
Polland, John 206
Pollock, John 6
  R. 4,14
  (Polk), Robert 15,121
  William 6
Pomfret, Elizabeth 89
Poor, Moses 276
Pope, Jahue 126
  John 133
  Mary 157
Pore, Peter 18
Porter, Charles T. 130
  Geo. M. 256
  James 13,83
  James L. 92
  L. D. 253
  Margaret 94
  Robert 13,83
Porterfield, Seth 157
Portwood, Page 20
Posey, Daniel 41
  David 199
  Joseph 45
Postle, Richd. 205
Potter, Benjamin 8
  John 207
  Paul 166
Potterfield, Richard 132
Powel, Benjamin 164
  Joseph 119
  Riggins 227
  Samuel 163,164
Powers, Jessee 106
  Patrick 183
Prather, Thomas 179
  Reese 184
Prathro, Jeremiah 205
Prator, John 200
Pratt, James 179
  Thomas 20
  William 180
Preator, Thomas 271
Pressgrove, George 104
Prethro, Alexander 179
Pretherow, Alexr. 271
Prewet, Hardin 222
Prewit, James 263
  Polly 256
Prewitt, Danl. 256
  Saml. 256
  Wm. 256
Price, Edward 86
  Henry 164
  James 92,147,204,213
  John 146,276
  Prentiss 97
  Ralph 125

Price, Reuben 87
  Solomon 147
  Thomas 146,158,197,206
Pride, Benjamin 90
  Burtin 49
Prigmore, Drury 158
  Joseph 62,67,125
Priggmore, Keziah 67
Primmer, Mary 147
Prior, Harris 80
  Richard 272
Pritchett, Ephraim 63
Privet, David 269
Profit, David 157
Prophit, John 147
Prothro, David 158
  Jeremiah 214
  John 158
Pruitt, Isaac 71,83
  Jacob 78,83
  Martin 83
Pucket, Rice N. 248
Puckett, Claiborne 8
  James D. 8
Pugh, David 147
  Jacob 89,208
  Jonathan 207
  William 147
Pulliam & Rankin 253
  Robt. W. 245
  Rosl. W. 253
Punch, John 157
Purdom, Margaret 185
Purris, John 63
Pursley, William/Wm. 69,
  207,209
Pyburn, Benjamin 199
Pyran, Joshua 83

Quarles, Robert T. 31
Quarrels, Jonathan 256
Queener, Verton M. 38
Quenner, Danl. 222
  Henry 222
  Jacob 222

Radle, John 110
Ragan, Derby 182
  Henry 234
  John 182,183
Ragin, Benj. 51
Ragland, Reuben 20
  William 20
Ragle, Wm. K. 248
Ragsdale, Britain 18
Rail, Saml. 108
Rain, James 210
Rainbolt, Adam 147,207
  Susannah 147
Rains, Henry 107,190,201
  James 263
  Joel 263
  John 6,108,139
  Jonathan 17
  Wm. 263
Rambough, Enos 184
Rambsy, Saml. 103
Ramsey, Andrew 250
  Francis Alexander 61
  Geo. 263
  James 182
  James Gettys McGready
  61
  Jessee 263
  J. G. M. 10,150
  John 185,250,263
  Richard 37,167
  Samuel 180
  S. G. 90
  Samuel G. 90
  William 179,263
Randol, James 199
  Wm. 209

Randolph, Henry 137
  Isham 181
  Peyton 180
  Sarah 125
  Thomas 180
Randols, Thos. 210
Range, James 147,206
  Peter 212
Rankin & Pulliam 253
  David 183,274
  John 54
  Richard 125
  Robert 184
  Thomas 125
  William 182
  Wm. D. 253
Ranking, Thos 269
Rankins, James 126
  Richd. 210
  Samuel 127
  Tho. 210
  Wm. 210
Ransbarger, John 69
Raper, Jacob 69
Rawlings, Asael 198
  Asahel 178,180,181,266
  John 185
  /Rawlin, Michael 45,83
  Moses 63
Ray, Ben. 273
  James 92
  John 15
  Jos. 273
  Joseph 105
  Thos. 273
  William 147
Read, Allen 230
  Edward 229
  Felps 97
  Isaac 230
  John 230
  Thomas 71
Reader, Adam 214
  Wm. 228
Ready, Thomas 222
Reagan/Regan, Ahimas 50
  /Regan, Charles 92
  James 92
  /Regan, John 50
Reames, Bartlett 74
Reams, Danl. 248
  John 133
Rearden, Thomas 128
Reardy, Joseph 86
Reasoner, Reasonor, Garret
  147,206
Reasor, Frederick 182
Reaves, John 11
  Thos. J. 243
Rector, George 107
  Maximilien 139
Redder, Robt. 246
Reddis, James 108
Reddish, William 136
Reding, John 196
Redman, Stephen 147
Redwell, Charles 127
Reece, Henry 246
  James 185
  John 243
  Joseph 168
  N. L. 246
  William 185
Reed, Abraham 92
  Abram 275
  Felps 98,117
  David 269
  George 197,248,271
  Henry 63
  James 209
  Jerimiah 80
  John 269
  Joseph 269

Reed, Lambert 33,34
  Margaret 33
  Mical 269
  Solomon 80,106,274
  William 21
Reedy, Sharack 17
Rees, James 209
  Thomas 139
  William 138
Reese, James 122,127
  Jehu 274
  Solomon 179
Reesor, Jacob 183
Reeves, George 192
  Jorden 192
  Moses 180
  William 179,192
Reid, Jacob 80
  John 181
  Samuel 53
  William 161
Register, Francis 183
Ren, Joel 243
Rener, Henry 243
  John 243
Renfro, James 107
  Peter 195
Renfrow, John 93
Renau, George 130
Renno/Reneau, John 121
Reno, Charles 205
  John 206
  Thomas 132
Renolds, Wm. 191
Rentfro, Saml. 276
  Stephens 84
Renshaw, John 72
  Moses 73
  William 73
Reser, John 147
Retherford, Wm. 229
Reves, Elizabeth 185
Revis, Henry 8
  Isham 8
Reyley, John 158
  Joseph 158
Reynolds, James 87,183
  John 63,89
  Joseph 179
  Mrs. Louise Wilson
  178,268
  Moses 147,207
  Thomas 87
Reynoulds, Mikle 166
Rhea, Archibald 80
  Hugh 50
  James 51
  Jessee 37
  John 8,35,37,39,63,98,
  122,127,150,158,159,
  164
  Margaret 94
  Matthew 152,158,159
  Robert 30
  Samuel 184
  William 158
Rhodes, George 53
Rhue, Matthw. 276
Rice, Daniel 165
  David 180
  Drury 168
  Edmund 168
  Edward 197
  Henry 105
  John 195
  John Jr. 168
  Leonard 197
  Reuben 168
Rich, John 11
  Thomas 108
Richard, John Jr. 165
  Mikle 165
Richards, John 101

Richards, John Sr. 165,168
  Joshua 158,168
  Lewis 6
Richardson, Amus 226
  Brice 222
  David 222
  Geo. 105,230
  Henry 195
  James 104
  John 35,226,230,275
  Lows 230
  Mary 196
  Obadiah 37
Richeson, Amos 209
  John 158
  William 272
Richey, Andrew 49,209
  Gideon 266,268,269
  James 43
  Tho. 209
  Wm. 209
Richmond, John 185
Ricker, Peter 179
Ricket, Stephen 18
Ricketts, Able 127
  Reuben 66
  William 66
Riddle, Barsdill 121
  Zacariah 130
Rider, John 50
Ridenour, George L. 4,115
  Henry 11
  John 17
  Joseph 17
  Martin 11
Riece, Wm. 276
Rife, Abraham 214
Riffe, Abram 206
Riggs, Clisby 133
  Edward 133
  Jessee 117
  Reubin 117,210
Right, Enock 86
  James 147
  Jas. 276
  Robert 147
  Thomas 147
  William 4,12
Rigz, Saml. 167
Riley, Elisha 228
  John 127
Rinehart, Michael 125
Ringo, Cornelius 276
Rinker, George 184
Ripley, Thomas 180
Rippeto, William 14
Richardson, James 273
Ritchee/Richey, Alexd. 107
Ritcheson, Abel 270
Ritchey, David 45
  Joseph 137
  Robert 137
  William 128,199
Ritchie, John 198
Roach, James 71
  John 83,86
  Jordan 128,193
  Willson 164
Roadman, Wm. C. 246,253,
  258,261,263
Roads, Henry 120
  John 73
Roan, John 130
Roane, Archibald 38,68,122
  Sarah 38
  William 71
Roark, John 222
  Joshua 222
Roase, Hosea 196
Robbins...11
  Isaac 12
  Jonathan 12
  William 12

27

Robenet, Moses 49
Robenson, Daniel 43
Roberts, Edmund 198,276
   George 135,261
   Henry 87,96
   Jacob 69
   John 128,211,228,248,
   276
   Jonathan 276
   Josa 165
   Mark 248
   Moses 8,69
   Nathan 8
   Phillips 135
   Reuben 207
   William 87,89,147,158
Robertson...199
   Charles 18,187,192,200,
   270
   Cornelius 18
   Daniel 110
   David 10,200
   Hezekiah 167
   Hughes 110
   Isaac 86
   James 10,101,182,187,
   299
   Jeremiah 210
   John 147,182,198
   Julis 192
   Townsend 18
   William 3,272
   Willoughby 82
Roberson, Joseph 20
   Stephen 14
   William 14
Robeson, Charles 208,210
   David 210
   Julias 210
   Resen 206
   Tho. 210
Robinson, Catharine 158
   David 184
   Edward 263
   Isaac 258
   James 184,266
   Jno. 263
   Moses 158
   Thomas 179
   William 235,238,246,253,
   275
Robison, Jos. 276
Rockhold, Dorson 147
Rockwell, Dawson 205
Roddy & Jones 248
   James 130
   Jessee 119
Roddye, James 121
   John 119
Rodgers, George 132
   Hugh 208
   I. W. 251
   J. A. 251
   James 183,210
   Jeremiah 92
   John 183,184,210
   Joseph 208
   Robert 147,214,251
   Thomas 251
Rodman, W. C. 253
Roe, Walter 63
Rogers, Abraham 158
   Isaac 54
   James 52
   John 54
   Joseph 43,68
   Josiah 121
   Nicholas 158
   Reuben 54
   Thomas/Thos. 47,78,207,
   214
   Samuel 183,263
Roller, Jacob 158

Roller, John 158
   Martin 158
Rorax, Martin 41
   William 133
Rorke, Michael Jr. 164
Rorux, Charles 273
Rose, Benjamin 181
   Green 238
Roseberry, Absalom 164
   Wm. 164
Rosicrans, Robert R. 61
Ross, Angus 17
   David 165
   Edwd. 211
   John 45,180
   Patrick 179
   William 182
Rothrock, Mary U. 8,29,
   57,59
Roulstone, George/G. 2,23,
   54,63,97,121,141,152
   Mathew 135
   Moses 135
   William 135
Routh, Edward 96
Rowan, Elizabeth 119
   Francis 273
   Henry 119
   Samuel 41
   Wm. Lackey 119
Rowland, Abraham 238
   Jane 117
   Jeremiah 164
Rowler, Martin Jr. 158
Royce, Charles C. 3,26
Roysden, Jesse 20
Roysdon, Robert 73
Ruble, Paulser 184
Ruby, Henry 158
Rucker, Austin 78
   Tiner 78
Rucknan, Isaiah 6
Ruddell, James 269
Rue, Lewis 130,185
Ruelle, Samuel 139
Ruhl, George 106
   Wm. 47
Rukard, Jonathan 231
Rule, Peter 110
Runion, Henry 258
Runnells, David 272
   Henry 271
   Job 271
   William 273
Runnels, James 108
   William 205
   John 6
Running, Isaac 269
Runnolds, John 110
   Richard 117
   William 119
Runyon, Freeman 135
Rusel, Elizabeth 110
Rush, Jesse 183
Russel, David 275
   James 115,206
   John 39
   Wm. 238
Russell, Alexander 180
   Andrew 68
   Brice 90
   David 130
   George 104,110,187,
   188,195
   Henry 18,269
   Hezekiah 179
   James 90,98,125
   John 76,115,195,270
   Jos. 169
   Mary 104
   Robert 184
   Samuel 182
   Thomas 147,180

Russle, James 52
   Vance 43
Russum, John 39
Rustin, Jesse 227
Ruth, Edward 69
   Samuel 128
   William 128
Rutherford, Absalom 87
   Cal 258
   Eliz. 258
   Ellet 185
   Ezekiel 87
   Griffin 181
   John 87,95
   Joseph 256
   Loyd 87
   Pleast 258
   Robt. 261
   Samuel 78
   Thomas 272
   Wm. 229
Rutledge, George 158
   Robert 153,158
   James 184
Ryan, Henry 205
   John 17,183
   Harris 17
   William 17
Ryley, John 193
Ryon, Henry 136
   Wm. 275
Rystone, Benjamin 158

Sadler, Fredk. 8
Saffell, Samuel 47
Sally, John 113
Salter, John 17,93
Samms, Kerby 256
Sample, David 184
   Mathew 125
   Moses 125
   Samuel 69,274
   William/Wm. 84,275
Samples, Josiah 256
   Robert 181
Sampson, Emanuel 158
Sams, Warren 263
Sanders, John 205,214
   Phillip 117
Sands, Benjn. 209
   Joseph 147
   Michal 158
Sapping, Betsy 72
Saratt, Joseph 269
Sarrett, Allen 256
Sartain, John 8
Sartin, Allen 251
   David 230
   Write 230
Saterthite, David 49
Saunders, Mary Arther 168
   John 6,63,158
   Richard 168
Savage, Michael 113
   William 119
Sawyers, Wm. 191
   Archibald 243
   James 238
   John 87
Scaggs, Charles 74
   Eli 74
   James 74
Scallions, Peter 15
Scarbrough, David 10
   James 10,78
   Robert 78
Schell, Andrew 158
   Arnold 158
   Frederick 158
   Joseph 158
Schmidt, C. D. H. 33
Schrader, Jacob 76
Schultz, Jacob 158

Schuyler, Joseph 147,205, 214
Scot, Absalom 147
Scott, Abraham 90
  Adam 271
  Ed/Edward 2,17,39,54,55, 63,97,161
  Garrett 71
  James 30,45,71,125,183
  John 150,158
  Laurence 71
  Thomas 199,211
  Willie 90
  William 94
  Wilson 69
Scritchfield, Henry 224
Scroggins, Henry 78
Scrogins, Barton 105
Scroggs, Ebenezer 211
Scruggs, Abijah 248
  James 222
  John 12
  Julius 184
  Richard 182,248
Seahorn, Wm. G. 256
Sealy, Jeremiah 226
Seansell, John 256
Seavers, George 158
Seduscuss, Emanuel 270
Seduxas, Emanuel 197
Seeber, Raymond C. 6
Seeburn, Edward 132
  John 132
Seehorn, Gabriel 135
  John 135
Self, Thomas 183
Sellardt, Nathan 139
  Samuel 139
Sellers, John 132
Sells, Solomon 158
Selvage, Jeremiah 113
Selvay, William 14
Selvidge, Michael 14
Sensabaugh, David 169
Sensebough, Henry 168
  Jacob 168
Senter, Willis 111
Sertain, Jacob 275
Severs, Wm. 166
Sevier, Abraham 147
  Abrm. 209
  John 24,25,42,52,79,98, 185,188,197,208
  John Jr. 147
  Joseph 147,209
  Robert 192
  Val./Valentine 147,178, 181,187,188,192,211
Sevoirs, William 12
Sewel, Abraham 147
Sexton, Timothy 231
  William 135,231
Shadden, Alexander 125
  James 125
  Thomas 125
  William 125
Shaddon, Joseph 10
Shaffer, Frederick 181
Shall...60
Shally, Luke 276
Shanks, Adam 164
  Christian 164
  Holden 180,210
  James 210
  John 169
  Nicholas 133
Shannon, Charles 10,78
  Hugh 253
  John 205
  William 184,205
Sharky, Thomas 63
Sharp...88
  Aron 222

Sharp, Conrad 18,119,229
  George 110,222
  Henry 18,119,229
  Isham 230
  J. A. 32
  Jacob 119,222,226,231
  James 222
  Jesse 63,75
  John 11,33,39,86,101, 222
  Joseph 6,116
  Margaret 39
  Moses 87
  Richard 6,226,230
  Samuel 87
  William/Wm. 11,147,222, 229
Sharpe, John 158
Sharpless, Jesse 63
Shaver, Stark 251
Shaw, Benjamin 103,209
  John 106,181
  Michael 158
  Samuel 53
Shawl, George 63
Shears, John 8
Shedderly, Michael 76
Sheerer, Peter 68
Sheets, Daniel 76
  Jacob 43
Shelby, Catharine 158
  David 150
  Evan 150
  Isaac 150,158
  John 150,187,191
  John Jr. 153,158
  John Sr. 158
Shell, Christian 66
Shells, Arnol 192
Shelly, James 183
  Jeremiah 139
  Nathan 136
  Peter 158
  Philip 190
Shelton, Cuthbert 78
  David 108
  Gabriel 20
  Nelson 110
  N. K. 243
  Palatiah 20
  Ralph 108
  Richard 108
  Saml. 227
  Thomas 137
  William 108
Shenall, Isaac 132
Shepley, Edward 117
Sheppard, Hiram 243
  Wm. 243
Sherill, Samuel 197
Sherrell, John 47
Sherril, Adam 272
  Elisha 270
  John 271
  Phillip 270
  Saml. 270
Sherrill, Abraham 181
  Adam 199
  Isaac 179
  Phillip 197
  Samuel 197
Shetter, George 224
  Martin 224
Shetters, George 18
Shewmake, Robert 14
Shields, David 207,246
  George 180,207
  Henry 181,209
  James 181,183
  John 128,209
  Patrick 207
  Robert 45
  Thomas 181

Shields, William 125,128, 183,246
Shinliver, Charles 8
Shipe, Adam 86
  Benjn. 208
Shipley, Eli 158
  John 158
  Peter 208
  Richard 158
  Samuel 158,208
  Tho. 208
Shockley, Richard 103
Shoemaker, Evan 66
  John 158
  Thomas 158
  William 158
Shofner, Michael 231
Sholley, Michael 107
Shook, Abraham 80
  Harman 80
  Isaac 80
  Jacob 80
  William 80
Shoolbird, S. David 231
  James 231
Shoopman, Michael 230
  Nicholass 230
Short, James 105,111
Shot, Green 208
  Richd. 208
Shote, Bagriel 108
Shoults, Christian 205,214
Shown, Leonard 147
Shrite, Henry 150
Shropshire, Wm. 169
Shulbred, Jas. 17
Shults, Jacob 119,263
  Martin 263
Shurley, John 196
  Robert 198
  Thomas 196
Shurly, Edward 196
Sidens, James 64
Sigler, Henry 159
Siler, John 11
  Joseph 271
Simerley, John 206
Simmerly, Adam 147
  John 147
Simmons, Christian 169
  James 10,169
Simes, James 119
  Matthew 113
Simms, James 35
  John 98
Simons, Amon 229
  John 45
  Wm. 41
Simpkins, Robert 230
Simpson...163,164,221
  Crisford 147
  John 183,222
  Mary 158
  Reuben 269
  Thomas 9,49
Sims, Elliott 256
  Geo. G. 256,261
  Littlepage 30
  Walter 164
  Wm. K. 256
Sinclair, John 11
  Joseph 6,9
  Robert 9
Singleton, James 256
  John 54,94
Sions, Nimrod 113
Sircle, George 158
Sisk, Bartlet 253,258,261
  Blackburn 261
  Elias 261
  Lawson 261
  Tolover 258
Sissum, William 168

Skean, James 35
Skeen, John 137
Skelton, James 165
  John 168
  Ruben 165
  Thomas 165
  Wm. 165,168
Skidmore, Henrix 106
  Thomas 226
Skiles, Ephraim 185
  George 43
  William/Wm. 43,184
Skipper, Hardy 224,269
Skippeth, Needham 147
Skyles, William 184
Slatery, Patrick 80
Slatten, Ambreose 226
Slaughter, Jacob 158
Slavins, William 163
Sloan, Alexander 45
  Archibald 45
  Arthur 181
  James 45
  John 45
  Robert 45
  William 45
Sloss, Joseph 41
Slover, Aaron 8,130
  Abraham 130
Sluder, Francis 253
Slymp, Michael 147
Smalin, Saml. 207
Small, Daniel 183
  William 53
Smallin, Samuel 147
Smalling, Solomon 158
  Thomas 158
Smart, Daniel 238
  Frances 53
  Wm. 238
Smathars, Philip 179
Smedley, Jesse 231
Smelcer, Frederick 243
  Jonathan 243
Smelser, Adam 182
  Jacob 275
Smiley, Robert 181
Smith A. 92
  Aaron 92,105
  Abraham 182
  Alexander 66,165
  Alexander E. 236,253,256
  Ali 231
  Anderson 210,224
  Andrew 51,116
  Asa 248
  Bartholomew 111
  Benjamin 17,21
  Benj. A. 224
  Brooks 147
  Caleb W. 249
  Charity 263
  Charles 108,181,243
  Cornelius 183
  Daniel 158,181,224
  David 249
  Deborah 139
  Edward 147,196,207
  Elijah 92
  Elizabeth 165
  Ephraim 17
  Ezekial 119,200
  Frederick 183,222
  Gedion 107
  George 158
  George Jr. 158
  Giles 263
  H. 182,249
  Harbert 110
  Henry 66,246
  Humphrey 147
  Jackson 167
  Jacob 147,179,206,224

Smith, James 10,78,158,
  180,231
  Jeremiah 184
  Jesse 95
  Joel 74,238
  John 37,68,69,87,111,
  119,127,147,164,165,
  183,196,207,210,214,
  222,249,251,269,273
  John B. M. 251
  Joseph 12,74,89,158
  Joshua 68
  Josiah 103
  Laton 20
  Lewis 249
  Mariah 248
  Mitchel 263
  Nancy 248
  Nich/Nicholas 147,207
  Philip 182
  Ransom 224
  Rebecca 248
  Richard 17,119
  Robert 66,74,95,181,
  182,222,224
  Robert R. 249
  Samuel 12,37,119,147,
  150,158,192
  Saml. D. 249
  Samuel Sr. 158
  Sarah 109
  Sebastian 179
  Simon 248,251
  Solomon 158,192,200
  Stephen 163
  Sterling 222
  Thomas 17,105,128,132,
  209,224,248
  Uricus 231
  William 98,115,117,147,
  158,181,185,231,243,
  248,263
  Wm. C. 248
  Wm. H. 222
  W. N. 263
  Zebulon 206
Snead, Henly 256
  Pleasany 256
Snider, George 51
  John 51
  Michal 158
  Peter 37,147
  William 168
Snodderly...88
  John 17,229
Snoddy, Thomas 137
Snodgrass, David 137
  Robert 137
  William 137,158
Snow, Morgan 84
Snuffer, John 127
Sollars, Sebert 272
Solomon, James 248
  John 248
  Nicholas 248
  Owin 248
  Wm. 249
Sommerville, John 110
Soree, Samuel 117
Sotherland, Daniel 101
  George 101
Souder, Frederick 183
  Jacob 184,222
Southerland, Thomas 181
Spence, James 89
Spencer, Alfred 243
  Edward 243
Spessard, John 8
Spilman, Thomas 90
Spires, Wm. 169
Spring, Nicholas 184
Sproul, Thomas 168
Spurgin, John 158

Stafford, Stephen 37,103,
  113
Stakely, John 164
Stanberry, Jno. F. 253
Stanbough, Jacob 136
Standefer, Israel 9
  James 14
  Samuel 9
  William 3,14
Standfield, Solomon 86
Standford, Issiah 210
Stanfield, John 180
  Samuel 184
  Thomas 182,184,275
Stanley, Ellen 230
  Garland 11
  Harris 6
  Joseph 69,229
  Page 6,224
  Reubin 6,226
  Thodes 11,227
  Robert 230
  Isaac 113
Stanton, John 207
Starnes, Adam 185
  Leonard 184
  Peter 204
  Thomas 182
Starns, Nicholas 206
  Peter 212
Starr, Francis 226
  James 106,226
Statten, Ambrose 226
Strawberry, Ezekiel 182
Steel, James 185
  John 78,95
  Ninian 78
  Peter 69
  Samuel 63
  William 78
Steele, George 15
Steger, John 206
Stelles, George 14
Stephens, Andrew 179
  Charles 238
  Danl. 253
  Edmund 158
  John 272
Stephenson, Edward 20,132
  James 199
  John 273
  Nicolas 49
  Robert 66,132
  Willm. 207
Sterling, Daniel 125
  Hannah 90
  Henry 90
  James 125
  John 125
  Samuel 90
  William 125
Stern, John 209
Sterns, George 68
Steuart, David 207
Stevenson, Edward 107
  Nicholas 158
  William 158
Stewart/Steward, Alexander
  47,101
  Hami Hon 168
  Hugh 61
  James 86
  Robert 86
Stickley, Mrs. Robert H.
  189
Stickly, Leva 84
Stiffee, John 115
Still, James 248
Stinnet, James 253
Stinnett, Benjamin 107
  Isham 20
  Ison 9
  William 9

Stinson, George 107
  James 183
  John 181
  Martin 226
  Robert 107
Stipes, Jacob 158
Stockdon, Thomas 184
Stockton, Marshall 54
  William 266
Stoke, Adam 158
Stokely, Jno. H. 238
  Nathan 238
  Royal 238
  Wm. 243
Stone, Edward 39
  Henry 211
  John 8
  Robert 101,204,212
  William 108,115,204,
  212
Stonecipher, Danl. 14
  Michael 14
  Absalom 182
  Henry 179
  Solomon 183
Storey, William 199
Storm, Coonrod 147
  Cornelius 147
  John 147
  Peter 147
Story, Thomas 251
  Wm. C. 238,253
Stott, William 158
Stour, Daniel 147
Stout, Abraham 76
  Hosea 193
  Hoseah 272
  Samuel 18
Stover, Christian 147
  Daniel 147
  John 147
Stowell, George 73
Strader, Jacob 17,229
Strain, John 210
Strange, Edmund 180
  Wm. 256
Street, Asa 115
Strewel, William 147
Stringer, Edward 125
  William 195
Stringfield, Rebecca 93
Strong, David 63
  Joseph C. 63
Stross, John 10
Stroud, William/Wm. 119,
  210
Stuart...165
  Benjamin 185
  Hugh 243
  James 187,188,191
  John 158,200,238,248,
  253
  Peter B. 72
  Robert 181
  Thomas 261
  Wm. 43,243
Stubblefield, Coleman 168
  Fielding 168
  Lock 119
  R. Lockey 167
  Robert Loxley 119
  Thomas 167
  William 168
  Wiot 167
  Wiot Jr. 167
Stults, Lewis 184
Sturm, Frederick 149
Styles, Azchariah 263
Suel, Dorson 147
  Joseph 147
Suirlock, Samuel 108
Sullavan, John 47
Sullivan, Henry 158

Sullivan, Jesse 94
  John 149
Summers, Lewis Preston 12,
  61
  William 128
Sumpter, Thomas 66
Surbor, Henry 183
  Jacob 183
Surquine, James 168
Sutherland, David 127
Suthon, Robert 119
Sutton, Cornelius 263
  John 133
  Samuel 181
Swafford, William 229
Swagertey, Abraham 272
Swagerty, Ab 258
  Frederick 270
  James 238,243
  S. H. 246
Swaggerty, James 253
Swain, Elisha 128
Swan, George 68
  Harvey 90
  Isaac 90
  James 90
  John 90
  Samuel 90,135
Swaney, John 135
Swanger, John 147
Swatsell, Isaac 246
  Jacob 246
  John 246
  William 246
Sweatman, Josiah 256
Sweet, Benjamin 224
  Nathan 224
  Wm. 224
Sweeten, Edward 190
Sweeton, Dutton 15,116
  John 6,116,231
  Robert 6
  William 119
Sweeney(Sweney), James C.
  135
Sweney, Joseph Mc. 135
Sweny, William 205
Swingle, George 135
  John 135
Swisher, Michael 80
Sylvester, Joseph 158
Symons, Leonard 182

Tablor, Michael 87
Tabury, Thomas 159
Tacket, Lewis 116
Taff, George 131
  Peter 131
Talbert, Hail 191
  Matthew 191
Talbot, Parry 125
Talbott, Matt 205
  Tho. 208
Tally, Benoni 249
  Bradly W. 249
  Carter 249
  Dudly 249
  James 249
  James H. 249
  John 159,249
Talor, Thomas 165
Tarbet, Alexander 213
  John 213
Tarbot, Alexr. 204
  Saml. 205
Tarbott, John 204
Tarwater, Frederick 93
  Jacob 37,93
  Lewis 37
Tate, David 179
  Isaac 37
  John 107,207
  Robt. 207

Tate, Samuel 107,190,207
  Thomas 275
Taylor, Andrew 69,147,205
  Ann 117
  Archibald 159
  Cawfield 91
  Charles 206
  Christ./Christopher 198,
  208
  Daniel 117,159
  David 47
  Elanor 256
  Henry 87
  Isaac 89,147,159,178,
  192,206,266,276
  James 9,47,51,117,125,
  147,208,256
  Jane 117
  Jeremiah 159
  Jno. W. 261
  John 39,159,249
  Joseph 158,207
  Leeroy 209
  Margt. 206
  Matthew 147
  Nathaniel 141,142,147
  Parmenas 135,233
  Robt. 205
  Stephen 159
  Thomas 49
Tedford, Alexander 45,46
  George 45
  John 45,46
  Joseph 41
  Mary 41
  Robert 45
  Thomas 45
Teel, Edward 76
  Jacob 182
  John 47
Temple, James 180
  John 181
  Josiah 180
  Major 183,266,275
  Thomas 181
  William 184
Templeton, Absalom 183
  James 119
Templin, Jacob 261
Tenan, Robert 20
Tenor, Jacob 82
Terford, William 147
Terrel, Benjamin 130
Terry, Jesper 147
  John 10,17,76
  Joseph 9
  Micaijah 71
  Moses 147
  Richard 103
  Samuel 9
  Sarah 147
Teter, George 246
Thairman, Joseph 39
Thatcher, Ellen 63
Thomas...33
  Adam 35
  Adonijah 222
  Elisha 222
  George 41,159,254,258
  Griffin 131
  Henry 41
  Isaac 200,208
  Jacob 34,41,159
  James 6,159
  Jno. G. 254
  John 9,41,135,159,212,
  249,251
  Joseph 229
  Mary G. 231
  Mary Groves 222
  Peter 133
  William 125
Thompkins, Joseph 147

Thompson, Absolom 193
  Andrew 193,207
  Charles 195
  David 90,210
  George 184
  Henry 182
  James 41,84,105,132,
  183
  John 35,43,89,125,184,
  222
  Joshua 147
  Nathan 167
  Richard 89,98
  Robert 90
  Robt. H. 253
  Samuel 90,91,210
  Temple 105
  Thomas 180
  Wm./William 11,84,90,
  98,127
Thomson, Garsham 147
Thorn, Reuben 141
Thornburg, Benjamin 139
Thornbery, Joel 129
  Richard 128
  Henry 128
  Joseph 128
Thornbury, Thomas 128
Thornhill, Armsted 54
Thornton, John 183
  Reuben 148
  Wm. 196
Thorp, John 132
Thurman, William 168
Thwaites, Reuben Gold 10
Tibbs, John 164
Tidwell, George 190
  John 191
Tillery, John 84
  Samuel 84
Tillman...88
Tilman, Tobias 18
Timberman, George 41
  Jacob 41
  Jonathan 41
  Matthew 41
Tiner, Lewis 78
Tindall, Jeremiah 71,73
  Samuel 73
  William 66
Tinley, John 63
Tipton, Abraham 93
  Benjamin 35
  Isaac 147,206
  John 147,206
  Jonathan 147,196,205
  Jonathan Sr. 147
  Jospeh 35,147,191,206
  Meshech 33,37
  Phoebe 93
  Reuben 93
  Samuel 141,142,147,206
  Shadrach 12
  Thomas 147
  William 93
Tirpin, Martin 78
Titsworth, Isaac 193
  Thomas 153,159,195
Tives/Tivis, Robert 21,73,
  231
Todd, Isaac 227
  Jessee 231
  Loe 228
  Martha 100
  Samuel 69
Todhunter, Joseph 184
Tolbert, Fredk. 15
Tomlin, John 86
Toncry, Zophar 273
Tooles, John 95
Tools, John 266
Top, Roger 193
Torbet, Alexander 159

Torbet, Alexander Jr. 159
  John 159
Tosh, Martin 130
Toten, Benjamin 116
Townsend, Taylor 68
  Thos. 256
Townsley, George 13
Tracey, Timothy 206
Tracker, Edward 105
Trammel, David 227
  James 227
  Peter 227
Travis, George 18
Treadaway, Aaron 210
Treadwell, Mae L. 84
Tredway, Allan 159
  Isom 113
Tremble, Moses 277
Trevillian, Richd. 196
Trim, James 183
Trimble, Arch 49
  James 61,63,93
  John 30,35,49,198,272
  Letitia 63
  William 197,211
Trippet, Jonathan 41
Trobough, Frederick 184
  Henry 180
  Nicholas 179
Trogdon, Ezechael 105
Trotter, James 136
  John 207
Trout, George 89
  William 89
Troy, John 183
Truder, Harris 229
Tucker, James 139
  John 113,139
Tulles, Jonathan 212
  Michael 213
Tullis, Samuel 147
Tunnel, John 14
  William 9
Tunnell, Stephen 183
  William 183
Turman, James 273
Turner, James 130,249
  John 129,249
  L. D. 249
  Robert 113,129
  Walter 129
Turnley, George 135
  John 135
Turnmeyer, Saml. 254
Tussey, Jacob 159
Tuttle, James 113
  Peter 113
Tye, John 115
Tyler, Thomas 66
Tynor, Lewis 159
Tyre, William 147

Umstead, John 14,21,222
  R. H. 254
Underhill, William/Wm. 86,
  105
Underwood, George 69,197
  John 69
  Samuel 193,212
  Wm. 10,11
Upton, David 93
  Isaac 36
  James 35
  John 272
Ussery, Saml. 20
  William 20
Utter, Abraham 43
Uttinger, John 181

Vaich, Jeremiah 196
Vall(Devault), Michael D.
  89
Vanbibber, James 106

Vanbibber, John 115
  Peter 106
Vanbiber, John 106
Vance, David 36
  Elizabeth 91
  James 129
  John 129,139,148,159,
  193,197
  Samuel 181,276
  Thomas 270
Vances, James 101
Vandegriff, Gilbert 148
  Jacob 148
Vanderpool, Anthony 226
  Wyatt 205
  Wynant 226
Vandeventer, Abram 159
Vandyke, Freeman 125
Vangriff, Garret 113
Vanhook, Aron 131
Vanhuser, Falts 132
Vanhooser, Jacob 98
Vanhuser, John 132
Vanoy, Jesse 15
  Jonathan 15
Vanpelt, Benjamin 179
  Joseph 182
Vansandt, John 180
Vants, Saml. 276
Varner, Samuel 180
Vaughn, James 168
  Reuben 74
  William 74,93
Vaught, Andrew 6,47,116
  John 141,148
Vawter, Jesse 192,200
Veatch, Elijah 272
  Jeremiah 272
  Nathan 273
Venoy, William 148
Vernon, Isaac 76
  Solomen 76
Vest, William 148
Vickers, James 68
Vincent, aDanl. 206
  George 159
  Thomas 135,159
Vinson, John 229
  Wm. 258
Vintreas, John 148
Vinyard, John 101
Voils, Amos 249
Vowel, Page 9

Waddel, John 197
Waddle, Daniel 101
  John 211
Wadley, Thomas 159
Waggener, Henry 159
  John 159
  Michal 159
Waggoner, David 148
  Jacob 205
  John 76
  Mathias 148
  Michl. 205,214
Walden, James 195
  Richd. 256
Walker, Anderson 184
  Buckner 78
  Daniel 180,193
  Elias 214
  George 9,70,78
  Isaac 183
  Isaiah 37
  James 59,183,185,224
  Jesse 78
  John 51,53,91,107,185,
  209
  Joseph 37
  Matthew 91
  Prudence 70
  Purnell 184

32

Walker, Richard 129,195
   Samuel 50,226
   Thomas 10,183,217
   West 94
   Wm. 165
Wall, William 182
Wallace, Aaron 205
   Adam 41
   Andrew 41
   Benj. 41
   David 41,43
   David B. 68
   James 206
   Joel 41
   John 12,41,43,205
   Joseph 160
   Matthew 42,43
   Oliver 206
   Pleasant 259
   Samuel 275
   William 30,39,43,41,
   150(Wallas)
Wallen, Elisha 107
   Evan 15,228
Wallin, Stephen 159
Walling, James 163
Walls, Fethias 271
Walter, Claiborne 86
   John 131,148
   Solomon 168
   Robert 148
Walton, Henry 91
   James 91
   Jesse 197
Wamble, Joshua 113
Ward, Benjamin 190
   Cyrus 256
   Demsey 193
   Gabriel 246
   James 273
   John 111
   William 119,192,205
Warden, David 159,243
Ware, James 159
   William 101
Waren, Michael 46
Warren, Charles 47
   Henry 223
   Jacob 210
   James 169
   John 159,223
   Thomas 180
   William 169
Warrener, John 223
   Martha 223
   Thomas 223
   William 231
Warring, Edmund 159
Wartmiller, John 159
Washam, Alexson 49
   Jeremiah 49
   John 49
Washburn, Sherord 49
Washington, George 16,122
   Martha 122
Wassom, Elijah 14
   John 14
Waterhouse, Richard G. 38,
   80
Waters, Obadiah 113
Waterson, Edward 168
Watson, Jacob 261
   James 53
   John 210
   Jonathan 214
   Thomas 179
   William 205
Watt, Joseph 70
Watterson, Elizabeth 61
   Henry 61
Wattson, William 182,184
Wayland, Charles F. 97
Wear, Abraham 30

Wear, John 89,210
Weatherly, Joseph 66
Weaver, Adam 136
   Christian 159,193
   Frederick 159
   George 136
   Jacob 159
   James 254
   John 106,165,264
   Jospeh 106
   Smauel 106,199
Web, John 271
Webb, Benjamin 159
   David 159
   Eli 264
   George 133,159
   Jesse 131
   John 63,198,263
   Jonathan 159,192
   Joseph 264
   Martin 196
   Moses 159
   Rebecca 63
   Richard 269
   William 263
Webster, Abbigal 117
   Reuben 117
Weeks, John 159
   Zachariah 159
Weems, George 180
   James 179
   John 179
   William 180
Weir, Abraham 41
   Esther 41
   Jonathan 41
Welden, John 9
Welker, Jacob 77
Wells, Aaron 166
   Lewis 148
   Rosegill 68
   Stephen 77
Welty, John 244
Weolum, Tho. 211
West, Lewis 256
   Samuel 127
   William 183
Western, Jospeh 148
   William 148
Weston, Casper 115
   Joseph 184
   Simon 182
Wetherington, Samuel 212
Wetzell, John H. 63
Whell, Benjamin 76
Wheeler, Benj. 223
   Benja. N. 226
   James 153,159
   John 195
   Marget 226
   Nimrod B. 226
   Peter 93
   Thomas 93,223
Wheelock, John 210
Wheller, Wm. 54
Whennery, Thomas 181
Whitaker, Wm. 254
White, Abraham 180
   Aron 222
   Benjamin 84
   Bloomer 181
   Caleb 84
   Cotton 222
   Daniel 6,231
   David 51
   Henry 76,179
   Hugh L. 77
   Isaac 93
   Jacob 181
   James 46,48,62,64,70,
   77,91,148,182
   Joel 15
   John 70,179,195,212

White, Joseph 115
   Martha 86
   Mary 62,64,77
   Mary McConnell 62
   Moses 64,77
   Nathan 185
   Reuben 98
   Richard 148,187,190,205
   Runa 23
   Samuel 130,185
   Thomas 130,185
   Westley 137
   William 185,233
Whiteaker, John 39
Whitechurch, William 77
Whitestton, Isaac 106
Whitefield, Neadom 113
Whitehead, John 184
   Robt. 105
Whiteman, John 68
Whitenbarger, Abrah 49
   Henry 47
Whitenburg, Henry 274
   Jos. 274
Whiteside, Jenkin 17,63,
   110
Whitinburg, Fredrick 274
Whitlock, Alexander 160
   James 105
Whitman, David 6,125
   Jacob 6
Whitmon, Jacob 226
   John 223
Whitnal, William 20
Whitney, Henry D. 97,121,
   141,161
Whitson, Abraham 148
   Charles 148
   Jeremiah 148
   Jesse 148,206
   John 148
   Joseph 207
   Thomas 148
   William 148,273
Whitter, James 193
Whitthell, Adam 132
Whittington, William 205
Whittle, Robert 119
   W. O. 35
Whitton, George 4,18
   Robert 18,222
   William 17
Whood, William 200
Wiatt, Samuel 269
   William 269
Wice, John 251
   Simon 251
Widbey, William 148
Widener, Lewis 161
Widner, Henry 113
   Lewis 113
Wier, Hugh 41,275
   James 40
   John 40,51
   Joseph 39
   Margaret 39
   Samuel 51
Wikel, Joseph 246
Wilcox, Isaac 46
Wilder, Joab 207
Wiles, John 148
Wiley, Alexander 43,131
   Elijah 254
   Geo. 254
   James 222
Wilfee, Christopher 165
Wilflee, John 166
Wilhight, Conrad 15
Wilhite, Bonard 116
   Elijah 6
   Julius 226
   Simian 226
Wilhoit, Solomon 180

Wilkerson, Sally 100
  Thomas 100
Wilkinson, John 39
Willcockson, George 125
Willer, John 179
Willhight, Adam 271
  Matthias 271
Willhite, Keziah 264
Willhoit, Conrod 211
Willia, Jesse 180
Williams...35
  Abel 223
  Abraham 180
  Alexander 87,183
  Allen 129
  Archibald 148
  Arthur 127
  Balis 159
  Benjamin 15,66,139,179,
  181,197
  Collins 264
  Darling 169
  David 11,139,239
  Edmund 206
  Edward 11,164
  Eleanor 33
  Elizabeth 169
  Francis 148
  George 86,142,143,148,
  165
  Ginney 166
  H. 183
  Henry 183
  Isaac 244
  Jarrett 199
  John 9,11,36,77,105,
  113,139,180,226,229
  Jonathan 73,105
  Joseph 77,95,116,127,
  244,270
  Joshua 197
  Jourdan 264
  Lewis 111,244
  Littleton, 127
  Lucreatia 148
  Melinda 77
  Peter 159
  Pleasant 239
  Rebeckah 77
  Reuben 14
  Richard 36
  Samuel 9,46,148,197,200
  Samuel C. 4,20,63,72
  Samuel Cole 24,141
  Silas 223
  Solomon 239
  Theophilus 169
  Thomas 159,179,193,201
  Thos. L. 261
  Waters 204,212
  William/Wm. 86,105,108,
  177,264,265
Williamson, Elizabeth 264
  Hugh 113
  Reuben 264
Willingham, John 9
Willis, Henry 271
  James 30,54
Willoby, John 224
Willson...198
  Abner 133
  Abraham 139
  Adam 125
  Benjamin 187,190
  George 107,211
  Isaac 80,133
  Jacob 133
  Jeremiah 74
  John 108,125
  Joseph 78,187,199
  Richard 71,190
  Robert 198,211
  Thomas 66

Willson, William 125
Wilson...10
  Abraham 6,222
  Adam 183,200,209
  Alexander 180,185,273
  Augustine 89
  B. 190
  Barnett 256
  Benjamin 11
  Daniel 131
  David 53,184,185
  Eli 6,222
  Ephraim 179,273
  Garland 148
  George 17,63
  Isaac 51,198,211
  James 39,131,178,182,
  266
  James J. 181
  Jesse 11,169
  John 182,184,205
  John Jr. 148
  John Sr. 148
  Joseph 121,148,209,211,
  269
  Josiah 121
  Levi/Levy 6,226
  Margery 63
  Mary 81
  Robert 46,184
  Samuel 148,205,270
  Samuel T. 88
  Thomas 21,71,182,184,
  261
  William 148,179,180,
  205,222,256,274
Windham Aaron 148
  Rachael 103
  Reuben 103
  William/Wm. 111,148
Winds, Enoch 105
Winebarger, George 243
Winegar, Andrew 169
  Frederick 169
  James 169
  Peter 169
  Phillip 169
  William 169
Wineger, John Jr. 165
Winger, Wm. 166
Winstead, Ezekiel 169
  Francis 169
Winter, Andrew 244
  Catherine 243
  Joseph 244
Winterbower, George Jr.
  164
Winters, Christopher 179
  Samuel 49
Winton, William 135
Wise, John 37
Wiseman, Samuel 159
Witherington, Saml. 204
Witherspoon, James 185
Witt, Abner 82,84
  Ayers 137
  Caleb 139
  Charles 84,100
  Elijah 137
  George 82
  Jesse 70
  Joel 117
  John 70,94
  Joseph 125,137
  Mary 100
  Merrill 244
  Noah 137
  Rhoda 82
Wolf, Charles 159
  George 63,82
Wolfe, George 159
Wolliver, John 179
Wolsey, Stephen 121

Womack, David 116
  Jacob 187,188,197,199
  Johnston 116
Womble, John 254
Wood, Ashly 259
  David 239,251
  Gipson 259
  John 111,197,246,251,
  254,256,259,261
  Jonathan 256
  Joseph 89
  Obadiah 20
  Samuel 87
  Willm. 205,259
Woodard, Aron 127
  Joseph 127
Wooddy, Achilles 239
  John 239
  Wm. 239
Woods, Archd. 210
  Bartholomew 199
  Eathern 63
  Enos 89
  Ephraim 73
  George W. 183
  James 168
  John 39,164
  Joseph 168
  Michael 184,187,196,210
  Richard 178,266,269
  Saml. 208
  Zachariah 166
  Zebulan 73
Woodward, Abraham 139
  Thomas 89,275
  William 139
Woody, John 53,54
  Joseph 54
  Patrick 54
Woolf, Jacob 43
Woolridge, Richard 190
Woolsey, John 179
  Stephen 184
  William 184
Woolton, Benjamin 71
  John 71
  Richard 71
  William 71
Wooten, John Morgan 77
Workman, Peter 205
  Philip 205
Worley, John 148,206
Worrick, John 18
  Wiley 18
Worth, Jessee 249
  John 249
  William 246,249
Worthington, James 14
  Samuel 3,4,14
  Thomas 14
Wray, James 191
  Joseph 198
Wright, David 159
  Edward 139
  Esau 228
  George 169
  Isaac 135,139
  Jacob 169
  James 119,181,184
  Jesse 180
  Joseph 180
  Joshua 139
  Nathan 129
  Robert 135
  Wm. 228
Wrinkle, George 80
  Jacob 80
Wyatt, L. D. 246
  Solomon 185
  Thomas 148,179,185
  William 148
Wyley, James 42
  William 159

Wyly, Robert 181
Wyman, Henry 148
Wysong, Elizabeth 61

Yancey...159
    Ambrose 98,99
Yancy, Ambrose 111
    Robert 111
Yarien, Frederick 46
    Michael 46
Yarnell, Daniel 71
    Joseph 71
    Michael 71
    Mordicai 73
Yates, Nathaniel 239
Yeagor, Solomon 211
Yeakley, Henry 182
Yearout, Jno. 246
Yearout & Nelson 245
Yeates, Benjamin 179
    Samuel 148,239
Yell, Moses 129
Yerrick, John 179
Yett, Wm. 244
Yoakum, George 106
Yokeham, Jacob 71
Yokeley, John 159
York, Hannah 246
    Jabez 113
    Jeremiah 119
    Semore 113
Young, Henry 12
    James 159
    John 10,21,46,84,169,
    184,208
    Joseph 84,239
    L. B. 246
    Martin 229
    Robert 169,191,192,209
    Samuel 223
    Wm./William 47,169,196
Youngblood...264
Youst, Francis 94

Associate Reformed Pres-
  byterian Church 78

Baker's Creek Presbyter-
  ian Cemetery 40
Ball Camp 81
Bartlett's Mill 53
Bay's Mountain 30,266
Bean's Station 62,109
Beaver Creek 62,69
Beaver Ridge 81
Bethel Presbyterian Church
  61
Bethesda Cemetery-Cheek's
  X Roads 117
Bigg Creek 218
Big Limestone 177,265
Big Pigeon River 23
Black's Blockhouse 36
Black's Station 41
Blount College 57
Bluff City 82
Bogle Settlement 26
Boyd's Creek 24,26
Buffalo Creek 218
Bull's Gap 97
Burnt Station 46
Burrville (Clinton) 215

Campbell's Station 64
Carter's Valley 82
Cedar Grove Baptist Church
  and Cemetery 36
Chamberlain Branch 46
Chesnut Ridge 215,216
Chimney Top Mountain 265
Chota Ford 26
Christiana 23
Clear Fork of Cumberland
  River 218
Cliffton 234
Clinch River 218
Cloud Creek 177,265
Clover Hill 48
Coal Creek 218
Cosby's Creek 233
Coyatee 26
Craig's Station 26,30,40,
  43
Crooked Creek 33,35
Cumberland Gap & Charleston
  Railroad 234

Day's Ford 11
Doe River 142
Dumplin Creek 25
Dutch Valley 6

Eagle Bend Farm 60
Eaton's Station (Eden's
  Ridge) 150
Ebenezer Academy 88
Elizabethton 58,142
Elk Fork of Clear Fork 218
Ellijoy Creek 35,44
English's Mountain 233
Eusebia Cemetery 26,33
Evangelical Lutheran Church
  33

Fairfield's Store 234
Fine's Ferry 234
First Presbyterian Church
  Cemetery-Knoxville 60
Flat Creek 97
Franklin Academy 5,16
French Broad River 23
Friends Cemetery 52
Friendsville 51

Galaher Creek 52

Gambles Station 50
Gilliam's Station 79
Grantsboro 16
Grassy Valley 64
Great Indian Warpath 24
Greenville 178

Hall's Cross Roads 63
Hamilton District 5,23,55
Headrick Cemetery 34
Henderson Branch 46
Henry's Station 44
Hesse Creek 36
Hickory Creek 2
Highland Memorial Cemetery
  63
Holly Hill 60
Holstein River 265
Holston River 23
Hopewell Presbyterian Ch.
  122
Horse Creek 177,265

Indian Creek 218
Indian Fork 2
Iron Mountain 265
Ish's Station 52

Jacksboro 216,218
Johnson City 189
Andrew Johnson Hotel 57
Jonesboro 187,188,189

Kingston 61
Kingston Pike 58

Lackey's Creek 47
Lebanon Presbyterian Ch.
  58
Lenoir City 23
Little River 30
Long Island Flats 77

Macedonia Methodist Church
  74
Maryville 26,30,32
Maryville Female Academy 38
McBee's Ferry 83
McPheeter's Bend 66
Methodist Church Cemetery
  Rutledge 113
Middlesettlements Metho-
  dist Episcopal Church
  and Campground 47
Militia Springs 42
Morganton 42
Mossy Creek 97
Mouth of Richland Baptist
  Church 76
Murphy's Cove 35
Murphy's Creek 36

Nails Creek 34
Newport 234,236
New Providence 26
New Providence Church 38
Nickojack, Cherokee Nation
  110
Nine Mile Creek 44
Nolichucky River 177

Oliver Springs 2,12,13
Overhill Cherokees Hunt-
  ing Grounds 187

Panther Creek 97
Parrottsville 236
Pistol Creek 41
Pleasant Forest Cemetery
  65
Point Pleasant 42

Poplar Creek 2
Porter Academy 39
Portville 42
Powell River 218
Powell's Valley 4,16,215,
  218

Raccoon Valley Station 63
Rice's Mill 105
Richland Creek 97,266
Rocky Spring 109
Russel's Valley, Ala. 62

St. John's Evangelical
  Lutheran Church 34
Sale Creek 82
Salisbury District 187
Scarborough (Village)10
Sequatchie Valley 109
Shook's Gap 78
Singleton's Station 54
Southwest Point 61
Stock Creek 53,89
Stoney Point Ferry 47

Turkey Creek 65

Unacoy Mountain 187
Union Academy 19,20

Wallen's (Walden's) Ridge
  2
Walnut Cove 218
Warrick's Cross Roads 18
Watauga 177
Watauga Old Fields 142
White's Creek 110
Wilkinson Pike 39

Yoakum's Station 106

#

Index to names found in the footnotes but also included in the master index. Names
of females indexed under both maiden and married names.

Albright...88
Alexander, Margaret 40
    Wm. 163
Allen...16
    Penelope Johnson 7,38,
    66,97,109
Alt, Charity 74
    Conrad 74
    Frederick 74
    George 74
    Jacob 74
    John 74
    Mary 74
Alves, Walter Hogg 16
Anderson, Isaac 88
    Joseph 2,163
    Nellie Pickens 35
Armstrong, William 163
    Zella 8,36,60

Baker, Charity 74
    Henry 74
Bartlett, Nicholas 53
Barton, Isaac 117
    Martha 100
    Sarah 117
Beard, Thomas 153
Berry, Nancy 74
Black, Nancy 77
Blackburn, Gideon 38,39
Blair, James, Jr. 98
    John 109
    Sarah Smith 109
Blount, Barbara 62
    Mary 62
    Mary Louisa 62
    William 12,23,62,100
Bogle, Andrew 33
    Eleanor 33
    Elizabeth 33
    Jean McAntyre 33
    Joseph 33
    Margaret 33
    Samuel 33,35
Bond, Octavia Zollincoffer
    60
Bonham, Benjamin 47
Booth, Alice 59
    Edwin E. 80
Brooks, Agnes 75
    Ann 66,75
    John 66,75
    Mary 66
Bullinger, Peter 144
Burk, John 153
Burnett, J. J. 51,61
Butler, Elizabeth 19
    James 19
Byrum, Ebenezer 10

Callaway, John 71
Campbell, Alexander 66
    Andrew 163
    David 66
    Elizabeth 33
    James 66
    Prudence 76
    Rhoda 60
Carringer, Godfrey, Sr.144
Carter, Clarence E. 14,29,
    121
    Elizabeth 60
Cavett, Moses 89
    Richard 89
Childress, John 71
Christian, Gilbert 150
Christie, William 150
Clap, Betsy 86
Clark, George Rogers 20
    Hannah 60

Clark, Letitia 63
    Walter 23,149,265
Clopton, Martha 62
    Patsy 16,62
Cobb, Benjamin 100
    Isabella 100
    Martha 100
    Pharoah 100,144
    Pharoah Boone 109
    Sally 100
    Sarah Smith 109
    William 84,100,109
    William Pharoah 100
Cocke, Sarah 113
    William 113
Coontz, Margaret 33
Cooper, John 163
Cowan, David 13
    Sally 13
Cox, Ambrose 47
    Edward 153
    Emily 60
Cozby, Abigale 79
    James 83
Craig, John 43
    Robert 82
Craighead, James Geddes 60
    Margaret 60
    Mary 81
    Robert 81
    Thomas 60
Creekmore, Pollyanna 143
Crockett, Samuel 153
Crozier, John 89
Cup, David 34

Dalzell,Francis 163
Danforth, Sarah 38
Davis, Michael 74
    Nancy 74
DeArmand, Mary Flenniken
    53
DeArmand(d'Armand), R. C.
    53,80,91
    Thomas 53
Dearmon, Richard 42
Dearmond...80,91
Denham, David 163
Dodd, Mary 68
Donelson, Stockley 48
Doyl, Eve 94
Draper, Lyman C. 24
Duncan, John 150
    Joseph 42
    Margaret 40
Dunham, John 150
Dunlap, Richard G. 75
    Susannah 75

Eakin, John 42
Egle, William Henry 68
Eldridge, Leila Mason 33
Elfland...88
English, Matthew 110
Ephland, Mary 88
    Sarah 86,88
Eppes, Edward 84
Ewing, Margaret 50

Farragut, David 47
    David Glasgow 90
    George 47
Fleming, Esther Ann 75
    Samuel 75
Fleshart, Elizabeth 61
Formwalt, Eve 94
    John 94
Foster, Austin P. 2
Fowler, Agnes 75
    Esther Ann 75

Fowler, Robert 75
Frazier, Ann 65
    Barbara 65
    Rebecca 65
    Samuel 65
Fristoe, Susan 85

Galbraith, Andrew 163
Gamble, Agnes 75
    A. Marion 50
    Josias 50
    Mary 66,75
    Robert 66,75
Gammon, Richard 153
Gamwell, Ann 50
Gandrud, Mrs. B. W. 23,34
Garnagan, Martha 100
    Mary 100
Garner, Elizabeth 34,50
    John 34
    John F. 50
Gibbons, Epps 163
Gibbs, Barbara 65
    Mary 88
    Nicholas 65,88
Gibson, Tiry 163
Gillenwaters, Wm. 163
Gillespie, James 44
    Mary 81
    Pollie 44
    William 46
Gilliam, Devereaux 62,75
    Polly 62
    Susannah 75
    Thomas 65
Grainger, Mary 62
Graves, Betsy 86
    Boston 86
    Sarah 86,88
Green, James I. 42
Greer, Alexander 144
Gresham, L. P. 77
Grills, Eleanor 60
    John 75
Groves, Susan 85
    William 85

Hackney, Jacob 163
Hailey, David 98
Halfley...33
Hall, Nancy 65
    Thomas 19
Hamblen, John 173
Hambright, Frederick 77
    John H. 77
    Nancy 77
    Sarah 77
Hamer, Marguerite B. 63
    Philip M. 7
Hardin, Joseph 77
    Sarah 77
Harris, Madison Monroe 87
    Simon 87
Hart, Susannah 17
    Thomas 17
Hayne...60
Hays, Nancy 65
Henderson, Archibald 4,12,
    21
    Richard 62
Henry, Elizabeth Garner
    34,50
    James 44,50
    Jean McNabb 50
    Rachel 34
    Samuel 34,44,50
Hickey, John 83
Hinshaw, William Wade 51
Hodges, Martha 117
Hogg, Amelia 21

Hogg, James 21
Holt, Emily 60
  Robert 60
Hooke, John 61
Houston, Elizabeth Mc-
  Croskey 44
  Elizabeth Paxton 40
  Ester 41,44
  Margaret 33
  Martha Lyle 40
  Matthew 40,44
  Samuel 40,44
  Samuel Rutherford 33
Huffaker, Hugh D. 79
  Michael 79
Humes, Thomas W. 61
Huse, John 36

Ingles, Eleanor 60
  Rhoda 60
  Thomas 60
Irwin, Ann 66,75
Ish, Elizabeth 52
  John 52

Jackson, Andrew 62
  Annis 81
  Peter 81
James Marquis 40
Jarnagan(Jarnigan), Mary
  104
Jarnagin, Lavinia 101
  Mary 100
Johnson, Margery 64
  Mary Lou 84
Johnston, Amelia 21
  Thomas 163
  William 21
Jones, James 144
  Jane 52
  Joanne 52
Jordan, Weymouth T. 60
Julian, Rebecca 65

Kain, Jennie 85
  Kittie 85
  Mattie 85
Kellogg, Louise Phelps 10
Kenedy, Rachel Penny 50
Kepener, Elizabeth 52
King...163

Lackey, Archibald 48
  James 46
Lambert, John, Sr. 42
Lathim, Elizabeth 119
Laughlin, Susannah 52
Lavender, John 62
  Polly 62
Lawson, Hugh 77
  Mary 62,77
Lea, Lavinia 101
  Major 98
Leeper, Gawen 68
Lincoln, Isaac 144
Long, Christian 34
  Henry 34
  Jacob 34
Low, Caleb 71
Lowery, William 42
Loy...88
Lucas, George 71
Lusk, Robert 144
Luttrell, Annis 81
  James C. 81
  James C., Jr. 81
  John 17
  John King 81
  Laura E. 66
  Mary 68
  Richard 68
  Samuel B. 81
  Susannah 17

McAdoo, William Gibbs 12
McAffrey, Patsy 62
McAffry, Martha 16,62
McAntyre, Jean 33
McBee, Abigale 79
McCallie...35
McCampbell, Solomon 71
McCarty, Benjamin 98
McCleary, Abraham 69
  Rachel 93
McClung, Calvin Morgan 77
McElroy, Mary 66,75
McGhee, Lawson 77,143
McKamie, J. 35
McKinley, Prudence 76
McMillan, Fay E. 2
McMurray, William 35
McNabb, Jean 50
McNutt, George 63,64
  Isabella 64
  Rebecca 63
McTeer, Will A. 26,35
  Wilson 35

Macklin, Sarah 113
Maclin, Elizabeth 60
Manifee, Thos. 72
Manifold, Annabel 69
  Benjamin 69
  J. B. 69
Marshall, Bartley(Bartlett)
  98
  J. W. 23
Martin, Joshua Lanier 35
Massengill, S. E. 76
Masterson, William H. 23
Matthes, Susannah 52
May, Mary McConnell 62
Mead, Marston 100
  Sally 100
  Thomas 5
Mebane, Isabelle 62
Meigs, Return J. 16
Mellen, George F. 60
Menefee, John 71
Merritt, Frank 141
Metlock, Giddian 148
  Gidian 144
Millar(Miller) Andrew 48
  David 42
  Eve 74
  Martha 48
  Mary Louisa 62
Miller...88
Mills, Isham 163
Moore, (Mrs.) John Trot-
  wood 5,102
  Keziah 67
  Phoebe 93
Morrow, Isabelle 62
Murphey, Martha 117
  Sarah 117
Murphy, Alice 59
  Dennis 59
Musgrove, John, Jr. 153
Myers, Joseph 47

Nave, Peter 148
  Robert T. 143
  Teter 144
Neil...163
Nelson, Alexander 163
Nichols, William 163
Norwood, John 47

Oliver, Douglas 2
Overton, John 62
  Mary McConnell 62
Owen, Ann 117
  Thomas McAdory 35

Parham, W. E. 48
Parks, Joseph 163

Patterson, Rhoda 82
Paxton, John 46
  Samuel 39
  W. M. 39
Payne, Rachel 93
Peters, Genevieve E. 88,
  119
Pickens, John 35
  Lettitia Hannah 35
Pickins, James 153
Pomfret, Elizabeth 89
Powell, Samuel 163
Price, Prentiss 97,149,150
Priggmore, Keziah 67
Prigmore, Joseph 62

Queener, Verton M. 38

Ramsey, Francis Alexander
  61
  James Gettys McGready
  61
  J. G. M. 10,81,150
Rawlings, Michael 45
Reed, Lambert 33
  Margaret 33
Rees, Ann 65
Ridenour, George L. 4,115
Roane, Archibald 38
  Sarah 38
Roddye, John 119
Rothrock, Mary U. 8,29,57,
  59
Roulstone, George 2,23,54,
  63,97,121,141,152,265
Rowan, Elizabeth 119
Rowland, Jane 117
Royce, Charles C. 3,26
Roysdan, Risden 20
Ruble, Peter 214
Russell, George 104,110
  Mary 104
Rutledge, Robert 153

Saffell, Samuel 47
Saunders, W. L. 265
Sawyers, John 87
Schmidt, C. D. H. 33
Scott, Edward 2,39,97
Seeber, Raymond C. 6
Sevier, John 42,52,79
Shall...60
Sharp, Margaret 39
Shelby, John, Jr. 153
Simpson...163
Slavins, William 163
Sloan, Archibald 45
  John 45
  William 45
Smith, Edward 144
  Stephen 163
Snodderly...88
Sommerville, John 110
Stubblefield, Robert Lox-
  ley 119
Summers, Lewis Preston 12,
  38,61
Swanson, Mrs. Emily 234

Taylor, Ann 117
  Mrs. Daniel 117
  Jane 117
  Nathaniel 144
Tedford, Alexander 46
  John 45
  Mary 41
  Robert 45
Thomas...33
  Jacob 34
Thwaites, Reuben Gold 10
Tillman...88
Tindall, Jeremiah 71
Tipton, Abraham 93

Tipton, Benjamin 35
    Joseph 144
    Phoebe 93
    Reuben 93
    Samuel 144
Titsworth, Thomas 153
Todd, Martha 100
Treadwell, Mae L. 84
Trimble, Letitia 63

Vernon, Abraham 173

Wallace, Esther 41
    Matthew 42,43
Walling, James 163
Walton, Jesse 188
Warren, Charles 47
Washington, George 16
Waterhouse, Richard G. 38
Watterson, Elizabeth 61
    Henry 61
Wayland, Mrs. Charles F.,
    Sr. 97
Weakley, R. 216
Webster, Reuben 117
Weir, Joseph 38
    Margaret 38
Wheeler, James 153
White, James 62,64,77
    Mary 64,77
    Mary Lawson 77
    Mary McConnell 62
    Melinda 77
    Moses 77
    Runa 23
Whitenbarger, Henry 47
Whiteside, Jenkin 110
Whitney, Henry D. 97,121,
    141
Whittle, W. O. 35
Widner, Eve 74
    Lewis 74
Wilkerson, Sally 100
    Thomas 100
Williams...35
    Eleanor 33
    Joseph 77
    Melinda 77
    Rebeckah 77
    Samuel C. 4,20,61,63,
    72,90,188
    Samuel Cole 24,141
Wilson, Samuel T. 88
    Thomas 71
Windham, Reuben 103
Witt, Abner 82
    Charles 100
    Mary 100
    Rhoda 82
Wooten, John Morgan 77
Wyley, James 42
Wysong, Elizabeth 61

Yancey, Ambrose 216
Yarnell, Daniel 71
    Joseph 71
    Michael 71